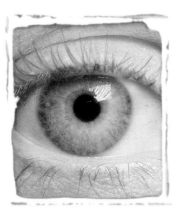

CRIMINAL PROFILING

CRIMINAL PROFILING

AN INTRODUCTION TO BEHAVIORAL EVIDENCE ANALYSIS

Brent E. Turvey, M.S.

Contributors:
Det. John J. Baeza
Eoghan Casey, M.A.
W. Jerry Chisum, B.S.
Dr Diana Tamlyn

ACADEMIC PRESS

A Harcourt Science and Technology Company

San Diego   San Francisco   New York   Boston
London   Sydney   Tokyo

Academic Press
A Harcourt Science and Technology Company
Harcourt Place, 32 Jamestown Road, London NW1 7BY, UK
http://www.academicpress.com

Academic Press
A Harcourt Science and Technology Company
525 B Street, Suite 1900, San Diego, California 92101-4495, USA
http://www.academicpress.com

ISBN 0-12-705040-X

A catalogue record for this book is available from the British Library

Cover design by Kathy Bakken
Interior design by Design/Section, Frome
Printed and bound in Great Britain by Butler & Tanner Limited, Frome and London

01 02 03 04 05 06 BT 9 8 7 6 5 4 3 2

Then I look about me at my fellow-men; and I go in fear. I see faces, keen and bright; others dull or dangerous; others, unsteady, insincere,—none that have the calm authority of a reasonable soul.

(H.G. Wells, *The Island of Dr Moreau*)

CONTENTS

A color plate section appears between pages 94 and 95

DETECTIVE JOHN J. BAEZA

John Baeza started his career in law enforcement as a New York State Correction Officer working at the Sing-Sing and Otisville correctional facilities. He has been employed by the New York City Police Department for eleven and a half years. He began his police career in Harlem's 32nd Precinct as a patrol officer. He was then assigned to the Manhattan North Tactical Narcotics Team where he performed undercover work for three years. He was promoted to Detective during his Narcotics assignment. For the last four and a half years he has been assigned to the Manhattan Special Victims Squad where he investigates sex crimes and child abuse cases. He is enrolled at SUNY Empire State College where he is pursuing a degree in Psychology. His research interests include the behavior of serial rapists.

He can be contacted at jbaeza@frontiernet.net

EOGHAN CASEY, M.A.

Eoghan Casey is currently a full partner, instructor, and educational technology developer with Knowledge Solutions LLC. In his courses, he teaches individuals to investigate crimes that involve computer networks and to use the Internet as an investigative tool. Through Knowledge Solutions, he consults on criminal cases that involve computers, networks, and the Internet.

Eoghan received his Master of Arts in Educational Communication and Technology from New York University. At NYU, he used cognitive science theories to develop an innovative approach to teaching criminal profiling and cybercrime. His approach is implemented in many of the courses offered by Knowledge Solutions. He also holds a Bachelor of Science in Mechanical Engineering from the University of California, Berkeley. During his studies at Berkeley, he focused on real-time computer control of mechanical systems. He has worked as a network administrator, satellite controller and software programmer and has extensive knowledge of the Internet and its operation.

He can be contacted through the Knowledge Solutions website at http://www.corpus-delicti.com

W. JERRY CHISUM, B.S.

William Jerry Chisum has been a criminalist since 1960. He studied under Paul Kirk at UC Berkeley where he received a Bachelor's Degree in Chemistry. He worked in San Bernardino, then set up the Kern County Laboratory in Bakersfield. After joining the California Dept. of Justice, he took a leave of absence (1971–73) to work at Stanford Research Institute. He has been involved in Laboratory management and administration for most of his career.

He has been President of the California Association of Criminalists three times. He has also served as President of the American Society of Crime Lab Directors and as President of the Stanislaus County Peace Officers Association. In October of 1998, he retired from 30 years of service with the California Department of Justice, and continues working through a private consultancy.

He can be contacted through his website at http://www.ncit.com

DR DIANA TAMLYN, M.B. B.S., M.R.C. PSYCH., FORENSIC PSYCHIATRIST

Dr Diana Tamlyn qualified in medicine in 1981, which makes her "a lady of a certain age." She has practiced psychiatry for the past 16 years, and is just beginning to get it right. She has published research on schizophrenia and has developed an interest in the mad, the bad, and the dangerous. Currently based at Rampton Special Hospital, she is also in independent medico-legal practice, does research work with West Yorkshire police, and is a member of the Parole Board. Dr Tamlyn lives in the Yorkshire Dales with her family, several sheep and a temperamental computer. She does not own a pair of walking boots.

BRENT E. TURVEY, M.S.

Brent Turvey is a forensic scientist and criminal profiler. As a full partner with Knowledge Solutions LLC, he teaches courses on the subject of criminal profiling, serial rape, and serial homicide. He also maintains a full caseload as a forensic scientist and criminal profiler working with both law enforcement and defense clients throughout the United States. He has a great deal of experience with, and specializes in, cases that involve rape and/or homicide behavior.

Brent has been studying violent and predatory criminal behavior since 1990. He holds a Bachelor of Science in History, and a Bachelor of Science in Psychology (with a great deal of independent study work in forensic psychology as it relates to serial homicide behavior). It was during his undergraduate years, while conducting research and interviews with incarcerated serial offenders, that he was inspired to combine criminal profiling theory, psychological theory, and the forensic sciences for the purposes of investigating serial crime.

Brent also holds a Master of Science in Forensic Science from the University of New Haven in West Haven, Connecticut where he concentrated in the area of Advanced Investigation.

He can be reached through the Knowledge Solutions website at http://www.corpus-delicti.com

Criminal Profiling – An Introduction to Behavioral Evidence Analysis is first and foremost a book organized and designed to instruct on the subject of its title. It was the movie *The Silence of the Lambs*, that widely popularized the role of the criminal profiler in a law-enforcement setting, and it is talk TV and radio that has now nourished its reputation and public acceptance as an integral component of the criminal-investigation process. For forensic scientists, such as myself, profiling is a curiosity of sorts. Is this just another ploy by wannabe scientists looking for acceptance and recognition, or is the profiler a legitimate adjunct to the criminal investigative process? As with any new endeavor, the answers are not clear cut. Often the power of personality and individual charisma, along with the old-boy network has determined whether profiling information will be sought in an investigation, and just who will provide the service. Nevertheless, the passage of time has had the effect of imposing discipline and order on the profiling profession.

Criminal Profiling amply demonstrates that this endeavor is emerging as a legitimate adjunct to crime-investigation services, but with the caveat often cited by the author that profiling is a discipline that demands adherence to the principles of team work between all the elements of the investigation. I find it particularly gratifying that the author places great emphasis on the necessity for the profiler to thoroughly evaluate physical evidence which has been properly analyzed in a scientific setting. Likewise, the author places strong emphasis on the requirement to evaluate information derived from a systematic reconstruction of the crime scene. While such efforts certainly are necessary adjuncts to reduce the subjectivity associated with criminal profiling, the reader is being continually reminded throughout the book that profiling is ultimately an art dependent on the experiences and expertise of the profiler.

Through the efforts of Brent Turvey and other professionals, criminal profiling is materializing into a structured discipline amenable to the confines of the classroom. Now this certainly does not mean that the reader can expect to complete this book and wear the garb of an instant expert. Years of practical investigative experience is an essential ingredient of the successful profiler. Nevertheless, the legitimization of criminal profiling as a profession demands that it has strong and acceptable academic underpinnings. *Criminal Profiling* satisfies those objectives.

Criminal Profiling is a serious and long-overdue effort at structuring a body of knowledge into a cohesive subject. Brent Turvey has provided the reader with a roadmap to comprehending the principles underlying criminal profiling. The knowledge gleaned from this book can only strengthen the foundational skills of the prospective and active criminal investigator.

Richard Saferstein, Ph.D.

Nothing is more wretched than a man who traverses everything in around,
and pries into the things beneath the earth, as the poet says, and seeks by
conjecture what is in the minds of his neighbors, without perceiving that it is
sufficient to attend to the daemon within him, and to reverence it sincerely.

(Marcus Aurelius, *Meditations, II: 13*)

Students, clients, colleagues, and new friends… each finds their own way to ask me the same question: "What made you decide to choose this work?" It is an incredibly important question to ask. It tends to surface when the conversation runs over ground that is particularly painful for them, as they begin to reflect on themselves and their relationship to those who commit violent crime.

How do people do these terrible things? How can they be stopped? Why am I drawn to understand them? Am I more alike them than not? Am I responsible for them? How could anyone do something like this to someone else? What makes the work important enough to you, that you would take on the burden of knowledge, and risk finding out things that are still difficult to speak of openly?

Before I unpack my emotional bags and give my answers, I think about who they are and what they may need. I try to measure my response out accordingly. The question that I'm trying to answer for myself before I give them both barrels is whether or not they really want to hear the response that I am about to give.

The truth is I didn't choose this work. It chose me. Or put a different way, what didn't kill me defined me.

Now, bear with me here as I am going to leave a lot of the details associated with this part of my life out. Not necessarily for my sake, but for the sake of the person involved, and for the sake of brevity. Suffice it to say that as much as I've related here, it's not even the half of it. It's much worse.

It began in March of 1987. I was almost 17 years old, and still a high-school student in Tigard, Oregon (a small, semi-affluent suburb of Portland). A friend of mine named Tom invited me to go with him to a supervised youth sleepover at the local YMCA where he volunteered his time.

At the time, I was painfully depressed over life in general, felt that I had a right to be miserable, and genuinely wanted nothing more than to be left completely alone. But my friends were pretty faithful, and we spent a lot of time talking about life, late into many nights. What happened today, what would we do tomorrow, and what did we miss about yesterday? My friends even put up with my ridiculously self-serving misery poetry, and encouraged my dangerous flirtation with marathon-length music binges consisting almost exclusively of Pink Floyd and post-Genesis Peter Gabriel.

So, back to the YMCA: I was actually staying with my best friend, Ben, because my parents and I had been arguing and we needed some distance from each other. Tom and I packed our bags for the night (it was Friday), left Ben's, and headed out for the YMCA. When we met up with the youth group, we decided to spend our social time lifting weights (an interest that Ben did not share, and that I have all but successfully disabused myself of).

While we were lifting and talking about lifting and how much more we should be lifting, two girls from the group came over to speak with us. They both knew Tom. One of them was Kelly (not her real name). Kelly was a little more than a year younger than Tom and I, attended St. Mary's Academy in Portland, volunteered some of her afternoons at the YMCA, and was very attractive (and incredibly intelligent, I would later learn and fail to fully appreciate). Naturally, I was completely disinterested in her, being the self-absorbed idiot that I'd become by that time.

Undeterred by my idiocy, she followed Tom and I around for the rest of the evening. Looking back, she was probably trying to cheer me up. But I had learned the fine art of being disconsolate, so her work was not easy.

We wound up having a conversation together that took us well past midnight. I came to the conclusion that she was very intelligent, very presumptuous, and very persistent. I don't recall the exact conversation anymore, but I'm sure that I managed to make everything we spoke about relate to my own pain and misery, and the injustice of being 16 and without my own car or something insipid like that. Regardless, she found a way to make a big impression on me by simply being herself, and by listening to me complain.

With the omission of a few slightly embarrassing, mostly innocent and only semi-important details that established her in my mind as unabashed and curious, that one-night sleepover concluded and I found myself wondering who this girl was and whether or not I would ever see her again.

By that Sunday I was back at my friend Ben's house, where I was still staying. Kelly was Tom's acquaintance, and we were waiting for Tom to come over so that he could give us her telephone number. I was thinking about calling her but hadn't really come up with a plan regarding what I would say if she were actually on the other end of the phone. While we were waiting, Kelly called asking for Ben because she was looking for *my* telephone number.

I became very nervous very quickly. The phone found its way into my hand. She did most of the talking. And to my shock, she asked me out. I had never been out on a date, let alone asked anyone out on a date, let alone been asked out on a date by anyone. I was excited and horrified.

On our first date, I picked her up from the YMCA in Portland sometime in the evening and took her home to a house near the farming community of Wilsonville. It's about an hour drive if you don't take the Interstate. We stopped at a little park in the city of Metzger, where I used to go with my sisters, when I was five or six, before my father died of cancer. We talked a lot. It seemed to go very well.

Over the next month or so, I inflicted her with my narcissistic, self-deprecating love poetry, as well as full courses of Pink Floyd and Peter Gabriel played as loud as the stereo in my mother's station wagon could manage. To her credit, she listened attentively and really seemed to care about what I had to say. Again, this was a completely new experience for me; a beautiful, intelligent, and attentive human was interested in who I was and how I felt.

I was truly devoted to my friend Ben, and felt like I was less when I wasn't with him. Before long I was able to coerce it so that Ben, Kelly, and I were doing things together. Movies, dinner, long drives. I was very close to Ben. He was the most important person in the world to me at that time and for many years after. It was important for me to include him, because he was an important part of who I was.

For a little while, a month or so, it seemed as though I had the world figured out. My problems seemed less heavy when distributed evenly between the three of us, I never had to be alone (always a huge issue with me), and Ben and Kelly really got along well (her unabashedness was the perfect antidote for his constant fear of public humiliation). We were having a lot of fun together. I forgot how miserable I was through these two people, their friendship, and Kelly's great affection.

It was sometime in May when Kelly disclosed to me. Disclosure in this instance meant that she told me about her history of sexual abuse. Of course I didn't know what it meant to be disclosed to. And I certainly didn't know that disclosure was the type of thing that happened often enough for it to have a name.

But sure enough, there we were in my 1973 Toyota Corolla (my parents paid $350 for it), listening to the end of "Mama," by Genesis. It was one of my favorites at the time. And Kelly said to me, something along the lines of, "This makes me think about someone who is going to rape someone, and hurt them. Did I ever tell you that I was sexually molested?" The words materialized that easily.

Now keep in mind that my experiences with life were very limited, and my experiences with dating and the opposite sex were very much in their infancy. Still, with a stepfather who was an attorney and a mother who was a RN, you'd think I would have been able to handle it a little better. But ultimately I didn't.

That night in the car, she detailed to me the full extent of her past abuse. As I remember it, she told me that from the time she was 9 or 10 until the time she was 12, her older brother (eight or so years older) had sexually molested her on a regular basis. As I recall, it ended when she invited a friend over to spend the night and her brother attempted to have sex with the friend. Kelly intervened on the friend's behalf, and Kelly was struck. She then went to her parents and told them what had been going on. The police were called, but ultimately the police and Kelly's parents worked to convince her that keeping her brother's behavior a secret was the best thing for everyone. So they did, and it was never spoken of.

A year or so later, her family had moved to Tampa Bay, Florida (her father was a salesman and they moved around a great deal). An older man named "Joe" soon befriended a now very depressed and emotionally ashamed Kelly. He watched her ride through the park every day on her bike. She loved to ride (or more accurately, she loved any activity that kept her out of her home). So Joe watched and waited and when he was ready, when he had learned enough, he approached her. Joe began to invite her over to his trailer after school. He was nice to her; bought her gifts, flowers, and made her feel special and important and above all, desirable. He also introduced her to alcohol and pornographic films. He would get her a little drunk, turn on his pornographic films, and have her perform sex acts on him. In time, he was also performing sex acts on her. In exchange for this, she was given gifts, treated like an adult, and made to feel needed.

I'm not sure how that relationship ended. But it did end when her family moved out of Florida to Oregon, and she began attending St. Mary's Academy in downtown Portland. Keep in mind that St. Mary's Academy is no joke. They put out some brilliant girls there. And Kelly quickly proved herself to be one of them.

About this time her ongoing self-esteem problems intensified, and she wanted to talk about her past abuse. She approached a school counselor at St. Mary's and tried to disclose the sexual abuse involving her brother. According to Kelly, the female counselor told her to "stop making up stories" and gave her a litany of consequences that she could suffer for telling such terrible lies.

So she buried it inside of herself again, telling maybe one or two friends and swearing them to secrecy.

A year or so after that, Kelly told me, she got into a relationship with a really nice college guy who attended Portland State University (only a block away from St. Mary's Academy). This guy met her at the YMCA where he was a part-time counselor. He was, by all appearances, a good Christian boy who bought her Ziggy paraphernalia and told her that she was special. The week before she met me for the first time at the YMCA, he had taken her to his grandmother's house in Lake Oswego, gotten her really drunk, and forced her to have sex with him on the kitchen floor.

It appeared to my limited senses that Kelly was very ashamed of what had happened. She seemed to feel that these were things that she had brought on herself. That she had encouraged them and that she could have prevented them from happening. Kelly appeared to believe that she was to blame for these things. And she secretly believed that perhaps she even deserved them. She had resolved to keep them a secret so that others wouldn't think she was a bad person.

But she needed to tell me. She wanted my acceptance, and needed me not to judge her. She needed a true friend.

Keep in mind that the only person I had ever loved outside of myself by that time was Ben. And he could take care of himself (6'4", 250lbs, very strong, very intimidating when he wanted to be). So it was really the first time that I'd ever felt someone I truly loved was in real pain and needed protecting. I began to feel these strong protective desires swell up and over me.

Thanks to my stepfather, I felt that I knew what to do with these feelings in general. My stepfather, the attorney, had imbued in me since the age of seven a potent and unswerving sense of justice and how it can be lawfully achieved. He also taught me that the only way to handle bad things was to tear them down to their essential truths, and throw a lot of light on them so that everyone could see just how erroneous or harmful those truths were.

Now, incest and sexual molestation can only exist for any length of time in an environment of mutually agreed upon secrecy. Both the victim and the offender have a great deal to lose if the truth comes out. Ultimately the victim cannot fully heal and move forward unless the truth is reconciled in them, and the perpetrators of the abuse are made accountable. If the victim is made to be accountable for the abuse, while the offender escapes all responsibility, the victim's shame and guilt and confusion increase dramatically.

Knowing this (a little knowledge making me incredibly dangerous), knowing that the brother, and now in my view the parents, had never been held accountable for Kelly's sexual abuse, I decided it was my duty to hold them accountable. This was arrogant presumption. Especially given her evident pain and my growing inability to deal with that pain directly.

But before I could do much more than take a few steps backward and regroup and try to figure out who I was in this completely new world, things took an unexpected turn.

Kelly's father accepted a sales position with his company in Columbus, Georgia. This was a huge deal because they were not supposed to ever move again. He had promised the family stability, and even purchased a beautiful new home with some land. It was no small decision.

Kelly became more depressed. She needed my support, and I was too busy making her pain my own to be there for her in the way that she needed. And her family did not want her discussing their past with me at all. So she found a very powerful way to let us all know just how fragile, alone, and confused she was.

What happened next changed me in a way that I'll probably never fully understand. And it taught me that most people, no matter how well intentioned, can't step outside of their own assumptions about life and others unless someone whacks them on the head with a very big sledgehammer. (Notice that I just made the whole thing about me again. You think you've made progress, grown a little, but then there it is.)

I remember that school had not yet let out, but that it was warm. So that puts it somewhere in May. The end of May, maybe. I know that it was before my seventeenth birthday. It's gross to me that I cannot remember the exact day. And telling.

Ben and I were at his place. I had long since moved back home by then but Ben and I still spent a lot of time together. He lived only a mile or so down the road into town from Kelly. Whenever I dropped her off I would go immediately to post-mortem the day with him.

That day Kelly and I had been out sailing with my family and friends from church. I was brooding and inattentive. She played with some toddlers who were along for the ride. I dropped her off that evening and headed directly for Ben's to whine – she was just not getting through to me.

Before dark the phone rang in Ben's room and it was Kelly. I immediately recognized an unusual sluggishness in her voice, like she was drunk. I asked her where she was calling from, and she said that she was calling from her bedroom. Then she said that she couldn't feel her legs, and that she wanted to go to sleep because she was very tired.

She had taken almost a full bottle of over-the-counter rubbing alcohol, which I'm told is a potentially fatal amount.

This was my fault, I kept thinking. My arrogance. If I had just listened and heard her, really heard her, then she wouldn't have needed to do this to herself. If she dies, it will be because I was not strong enough to see past my own self-interests to the hand that was reaching out to grab mine.

While I kept her on the phone, Ben ran around to the neighbors' homes begging them to let him in so that he could use their phone to call the poison control center. This took almost a full 15 minutes, because Indian

Woods, the community that Ben lived in, was particularly paranoid about giving help to strangers or those who look strange. Eventually poison control began monitoring the call, and an emergency unit was dispatched to Kelly's home. They broke down the fence that enclosed the property, they smashed through the front door, bypassing her parents, and followed my instructions right into her bedroom.

Then her father picked up the phone on the other end of the line and said, "Who the hell is this?" When I told him what was going on, he slammed the phone down while shouting, "Kelly, what in the hell have you done?"

He was very angry about the cost of the doors, the fence, and the ambulance ride. And they told her so while she was recovering that night in the hospital.

The next day, Kelly was released from the hospital and I spent the day at her house with her. I sat on this very comfortable couch and she slept with her head on my chest, leaving a big pool of drool. The smell of her perfume was on everything ("Beautiful," by Estée Lauder), and I just kept running my right hand over and over her face, and through her hair. The quiet after the storm. What a moment of pure exhaustion, and pure relief that must have been for her. For me, it was a moment of honesty. Of realization and resolution.

I think that was probably the first time that I realized that people outside of myself could be hurt, and that their pain mattered. This is something that is supposed to become evident in one's moral development by the time one is eight or nine. But I've always been a little slow.

Her mother came in once or twice to speak with me. "She kept asking for you at the hospital. Did she tell you why she did this? Do you know why she did this?" her mother asked, and I could tell that she was really concerned, even a bit confused.

But it was not a conversation that I was able to have with Kelly's mother. All that I could think of then was that Kelly could have died. And that she did not deserve to be marginalized or ignored. I knew what a suicide attempt was. She needed me to hold on, and not let go. I resolved from that point forward to hear her before I heard anything else. And it was that day that I surrendered whatever good judgement I had left.

Kelly went into weekly family therapy that consisted of her and her mother. Her father did not wish to participate, and her oldest brother, the abuser, was married and living in Florida. In therapy, she talked about her brother sexually abusing her for so many years. She also disclosed the relationship with Joe, from Tampa Bay, and the more recent rape at the hands of her Christian boyfriend. Both parents were in disbelief – but maintained stringent denial. They even told both Kelly and the therapist that they thought her brother had only tried to have sex with her the one time, that it had been an isolated incident.

Needless to say, both parents came to focus on me as the cause of their family's current pain. I had stirred embers that had been left to die down, they believed. After all, from their point of view, Kelly was the current problem and not the improprieties of their son so many years ago. That was evident from all of the things that Kelly had let happen since then. That was where the focus needed to be.

The therapist agreed.

Kelly was scheduled to move away with her family to Georgia in August. She did not want to go. First, because we had grown very close. And second, because her older brother, who lived in Florida, was really looking forward to her return, and had stated a number of times how mature she was looking lately.

When the time came she refused to get on the plane. She was taken over to juvenile hall and told that she could either get on the plane willingly or be handcuffed and thrown on the plane as a prisoner. We later learned that this would not have been legal, as she was still a legal resident of Oregon, but she didn't know it at the time and complied in fear.

Within a week of being in Georgia she ran away.

The four days that she was missing were the longest of my life. The opening lines from Dante's *The Inferno* come to mind:

> Midway in our life's journey, I went astray from the straight road and woke to find myself alone in a dark wood… Its very memory gives a shape to fear.

Every person I encountered, from my parents, to law enforcement, to counselors, told me that her chances of survival on her own were very low. She was very likely dead, they told me. I was told the horror stories of hitchhikers that had accepted rides from the wrong people, and the survival rates of runaways. I was shown pictures that fed my fears.

Looking back on that time now, I cannot believe the misguided and horribly ignorant information that law enforcement and counselors were giving me.

On the evening of the fourth day Kelly called me from Louisville, Kentucky. The relief I felt was overwhelming. She told me that she'd hitched a ride with a trucker headed cross-country and intended to go either to California, to be with friends there, or to Oregon. Either way, she was determined not to go back.

I went to the bank, emptied out my college fund, and bought her a plane ticket to Sea-Tac Airport in Washington State. I picked her up the next day and we spent the next two months hiding out, calling her parents to negotiate some sort of peaceful end, and waiting for December to roll around so that Kelly could turn 16 and declare herself an emancipated minor.

I was particularly concerned because her parents, while she was missing, had already arranged for Kelly to become a full-time resident of the Bradley Center. This is a private, secure mental hospital in Columbus, Georgia. Her parents explained how this was just what she needed, and how it would help her to forget the past. When I told Kelly about her parent's plans, it took away any doubts that she was doing the right thing.

We knew that things could not continue the way they were, however. We tried to keep our lives from being completely on hold until she turned 16. She got an apartment in Salem, Oregon. She got a job as a waitress. And she enrolled in the local community college. I commuted back and forth from Salem to Tigard almost daily, starting my senior year in high school just in time.

At the end of October, she was picked up by local law enforcement and flown back to Georgia. They immediately placed her into the Bradley Center where she stayed until she was of legal age. They held her against her will, and they medicated her against her will. They told her that I was the problem in her life, that I had caused all of her troubles, that she in turn had caused her parents great suffering, and that she owed it to them to "grow up" and "accept responsibility for her actions like an adult."

When this did not work right away, they told her that I had married an Asian woman and moved to Korea. The therapist and the family agreed that this lie was essential to breaking down her will. That and the medication.

Ultimately, they achieved their objective with her. They got her to accept responsibility for the sexual abuse, they were able to have her fixate on me as the source of all of her troubles with her parents, and she was released as an outpatient just before her seventeenth birthday. Though she was not told this, they could not have held her past her seventeenth birthday. So placing her on outpatient status and letting her believe that this was a reward for good behavior was a very clever tactic.

Needless to say, I was not allowed to see her or make contact with her, though I tried everything that I could think of. I tried harder than one could imagine. But in the end I was unsuccessful on every level.

The experience, and the events that it precipitated, left in me a very pointed understanding of how inadequate the judicial system is, how ignorant the law can be, in application, and how ignorant and unethical the mental health community can be. I also came to understand that people under an arbitrary age are really without constitutional rights. And that they are really no more than property, and can be treated as such even when the environments that they live in by all standards are criminal.

So as I proceeded into my undergraduate work I began to study sex offenders. I wanted to know why they did what they did. I wanted to understand how they chose their victims, what they wanted from them, and how they avoided the attention of law enforcement. But I didn't want to go into sex offender treatment. I was doing all of this for one single reason – to learn as much as I could so that I could help investigate sex offenders and stop them.

After a number of years doing undergraduate research with the published literature, I came to the conclusion that offender interviews were in order. It was time to confront offenders in prison and ask them the tough questions. The published works of people like Robert Hazelwood and the late Bruce Danto had inspired me, and I wanted to duplicate their efforts.

It was after my first interview with the incarcerated serial murderer Jerome H. Brudos that I realized how truly naïve my understanding of sex offenders was. I spent five hours with him, and he lied to me almost the entire time. He lied about almost everything he had ever done (or rather, he claimed, everything that he hadn't done). The only reason that I was not completely taken in by his charming personality and generous, affable nature, was the fact that I had reviewed the investigative file. Prior to the interview, I had gone to the Marion County Sheriff's Office in Salem, Oregon. I had read autopsy reports on all the victims, looked at the crime scene photos, and read the investigators' reports. I had even seen some of the photos that Jerry had taken of himself posing with his victims.

I learned an important lesson through that experience. The lesson was that offenders lie. The only way to get an objective record of the behavior that occurs in a crime scene between a victim and the offender is through the documentation and subsequent reconstruction of forensic evidence. It's a lesson that I took to heart.

I decided then and there that what I needed to complement my undergraduate study in psychology was graduate-level education in the forensic sciences. Finding back issues of the *Journal of Forensic Sciences*, I searched for graduate programs in the forensic sciences all over the country.

Ultimately I applied to and was accepted in the Graduate Forensic Science Program at the University of New Haven in West Haven, Connecticut. There I found instructors of the highest caliber, and was able to learn some of the most important lessons of my academic career. These lessons were important because they actually carried over into my professional career.

The career that I've chosen, the method of criminal profiling that I employ, and this work that you are about to read, all stem from those events that began late one night at the YMCA on Barbur Boulevard in Portland, Oregon when I met a girl named Kelly. She was a single victim with multiple offenders over time, who was pathologically ignored and ultimately re-victimized by a mental health and legal community that was and remains inadequate to the task of understanding and competently investigating crimes of a sexual nature.

With this work I am fulfilling a deeply personal promise that I made as the result of those early experiences with Kelly. It has been and remains my determination to learn as much as I can from those who are my betters, to share as much I can with those colleagues who surround me, and teach as much as I have learned to those who are following the path behind me. Education, after all, is a process and not a result.

It is my deepest honor to be working on this project with the help of so many talented and brilliant colleagues. And it is my greatest hope that readers will take things from this work that they did not understand or appreciate before, that they will share things they take from this work with their colleagues, and that they will teach the things they take from this work to their students.

Brent Turvey

THE PROFESSIONALIZATION OF CRIMINAL PROFILING

Brent E. Turvey, M.S.

*...it is a natural failing of man to be
pleased with his own inventions.*

(Sir Thomas More, *Utopia*)

Criminal profiling, as set forth in this work, is a multi-disciplinary forensic practice. It requires, at the very least, applied knowledge in criminalistics, medico-legal death investigation, and psychology. However, criminal profiling, even as it will be here defined, has not yet achieved the status of a "profession."

It has been said that any profession is defined by its ability to regularize, to criticize, to restrain vagaries, to set a standard of workmanship and to compel others to conform to it. This definition assumes uniform terms, definitions, ethics, standards, practices and methodology. Despite any belief to the contrary, such things do not exist in the community of individuals that are engaged in criminal profiling.

This likely comes as a great surprise to the general public, and even to some in the law enforcement community. What is likely to be more of a revelation is the main reason behind it. The plain truth is that a great number of profilers oppose professionalization in any way, shape, or form.

There are many factors contributing to the lack of interest in professionalization in the criminal-profiling community. One would have to be that too few practicing criminal profilers have sat down under a banner of truce, in an attempt to establish non-partisan professional mechanisms for identifying competency, cultivating it, and conferring authority upon those who possess it in accordance with agreed-upon criteria. Profilers just do not seem to agree on anything.

Furthermore, there are practical issues at work against it. First, profilers tend to keep their cases to themselves and not publish them due to information sensitivity and confidentiality issues (a problem in most of the forensic sciences, but one that can be overcome by *sanitizing* cases; stripping them of identifying information for educational use). Second, many state and federal agencies preclude information sharing with outside entities either by policy or by political intimidation. And finally, there are no non-partisan profiling professional organizations working on the development of uniform ethics, standards, and practices. The result is that profilers have few mechanisms for open professional discourse and information sharing; they are disenfranchised from each other by the nature of the work and the agencies that they work for.

Another factor that has affected professionalization is the resistance of numerous established profilers to the idea of developing standards and practices, which they perceive as a limitation on creativity. Some have argued that criminal profiling should remain more art than science, and should not be professionalized. That to do so would deprive individuals of the ability to nurture originality and kindle the fires of genius.

This is an interesting and even seductive argument. But I suspect that it is deeper than that. All of the above issues could be overcome if the desire was there.

Perhaps the largest contributor to the resistance against professionalization in the criminal-profiling community is individual *ego*. The varied practitioners of criminal profiling, as individuals or as representatives of the many agencies and confederations involved (this author included), cannot agree on the subject of what criminal profiling involves and who is qualified to do it. We wish to preserve our own role in the criminal-profiling community, and often do not wish to be compelled to change our current level of skill, training or ability. Unfortunately, the plain truth is that many of those engaged in criminal profiling (or who refer to themselves as profilers) have little or no applied case experience, inadequate levels of training, and exist almost parasitically on the ignorance of the professional communities that profilers are intended to serve.

Possibly the most disturbing part of the ego problem is the incredible arrogance of some criminal profilers, that they alone are qualified to do the work by virtue of their subjectively derived expertise (much of which tends to be unrelated to those areas of study that inform the criminal-profiling process). This paradigm disallows for the possibility that there are competent, cogent, and reasonable ideas outside of one's own experience or sphere of influence. This paradigm also encourages the ludicrous myth that profilers are born with an intuitive "gift" that is denied others, by disallowing those associated with a certain person or agency from "looking outside of the valley" for knowledge.

The nature of these ego-based disagreements in the criminal-profiling community has been at times civil, at times belligerent, and at times openly vicious. They have caused hurt feelings along individual and agency lines, as well as between the academic, mental health, and law-enforcement communities. The unending byproduct has been a pathological failure of practicing criminal profilers to resolve interprofessional, interpersonal and/or interagency differences and communicate effectively with each other. The competent minds involved in the work are often unable to appreciate each other due to the egos of their supervisors, or their own personal pride. The incompetent are deeply concerned about the very real fear of being exposed as a fraud and protect themselves by hiding their methods and being obscure or intellectual.

As a result of everything working together against professionalization, the following unresolved issues remain major points of contention in the criminal-profiling community:

- educational requirements for criminal profilers;
- the appropriate use of profiling terms and definitions;
- agreement regarding basic information that a profile should account for or contain to be considered a "profile";
- competent descriptions of applied, duplicable methodology;
- agreement regarding the appropriate uses of profiling in an investigation, and at trial;
- agreement regarding standards of competency;
- agreement regarding ethical and unethical conduct;
- agreement upon whether or not the profiling process should be peer reviewed.

The failure to address these basic considerations has caused great confusion not only in the profiling community but, as suggested, in public perception as well. The myths and misinformation regarding criminal-profiling techniques and practices are furthermore rampant in the popular media. These include misconceptions laid in the minds of police officers on the street, detectives at the crime scene, criminalists in the lab, lawyers at trial, and judges on the bench. It has also left the door open for the proliferation of many dangerously unqualified, unscrupulous individuals into the practice of creating criminal profiles.

So that brings us to my own motivation for bringing together all of these competent professional minds and writing this book. I, for one, am a firm believer in the reality that criminal profiling must begin to professionalize, and become more scientific and multidisciplinary in its approach. As criminal profiling becomes more accepted as a forensic discipline, and as it becomes more an accepted part of the investigative and judicial process, those involved have a duty to develop competent standards and practices, and robust methods. We also have a duty to move beyond reliance upon vague references and subjective expertise, and agree to demonstrate accountability for our methods.

This duty exists because in the forensic disciplines our opinions and interpretations are allowed to impact whether people are deprived of their liberties, and potentially whether they live or die. It becomes that simple. The courts have taken a great deal from criminal profilers on trust up until now (inconsistently bothering to question them at all, especially when they are affiliated with law enforcement). But we have been abusing it with our lack of competency and our lack of professionalism. Though profiling has been around in various forms for a hundred years (and more), we have not developed more reliable methods, we have not performed competent scientific research, and we have not always been fully honest about the limitations of our interpretations.

This work, then, is a first attempt to create a reference text of applied knowledge regarding the deductive method of criminal profiling. It has the presumptuous goal of laying out that method in a clear fashion, while establishing and exploring specific details surrounding terminology and core profiling concepts. The other goal of this work is to help firmly establish the basis for the relationship between physical evidence (the forensic sciences), behavioral evidence, and criminal profiling. Along the way, it is also hoped that some of the many popular misconceptions about criminal profiling that have been encouraged in the fictional and non-fictional media can be effectively relegated to submission.

This work was undertaken with two concepts in mind. First, that a criminal profiler should do no harm, proceeding with the requisite care and uncertainty. And second, that a criminal profiler's first onus is to the competent investigation of fact, and not to any particular agency or group.

The time for isolationism and for sectionalism is over. The time for politics is also over. The criminal-profiling community cannot continue to play to the images portrayed in the popular media and expect to achieve professional credibility, or maintain professional integrity. The criminal profiling community must begin to communicate and agree upon standards, practices, terminology and methods. It must move away from reliance upon subjective expertise and move towards a more professional, more scientific approach if it wishes to carry through into the next century.

The human price for not meeting this challenge is simply too high.

The author would like to extend his deep personal and professional appreciation to the following friends and colleagues for their support, encouragement, and guidance:

Det. John J. Baeza, Sex Crimes. A close friend and a valuable colleague. For his analytical mind, for his patience, for his unwavering integrity, for his dedication to victims, and for putting up with our edits (he would still be writing right now, but we had to cut him off somewhere!). *Personal quote:* "I know you're busy. Sorry to bother you."

Kathy Bakken, Graphic Designer. Our brilliant graphic designer. For her creative skills, her commitment to the project and most importantly her friendship. We are so undeserving of the effort and the time that she put into the cover for this work that it is almost embarrassing.

Eoghan Casey, MA. A close personal friend, a partner, and brilliant mind. Without his patience and his dedication and his clarity of purpose (which changes at least once a day), I would not be the person that I am. The room that John Baeza's appendix did not occupy was taken up by Eoghan's contribution. *Personal quote:* "Let's poke it with a stick and see what happens."

W. Jerry Chisum, Criminalist. For his love of the work, his friendship, his exacting nature, his example of professionalism and integrity, and for getting his contribution in on time.

Nick Fallon, Editor. Our fearless Editor at Academic Press. For his encouragement, for his eager responsiveness, for the latitude to be innovative, and for his efforts on behalf of the project, without whom this work would not have been given the same attention in the publishing phase. (In other words, we'd all just like to apologize in advance.) *Personal quote:* "You're such a well-behaved author."

Dr Robert E. Gaensslen, Criminalist. Under whom I studied at the University of New Haven. He once said something that I'll never forget: "You don't have to make the mistake to learn the lesson." Those are words that I live by.

Dr Henry Lee, Criminalist. Under whom I studied at the University of New Haven. For his enthusiasm, for his tirelessness, and for teaching me to read the language of crime scenes. *Personal quote*: "Brent... why don't you eat your pizza crust?"

Grove Pashley, Photographer. Kathy Bakken's partner in crime, and our photographer. For his friendship most importantly. And to no small extent for taking the time and the care to make our cover photos look good, and make my head look so much less misshapen than it is in real life. Truly a miracle worker. *Personal quote*: "Maybe I'm just being too naïve, but..."

Dr Stephen Pittel, Forensic Psychologist. For being an invaluable professional sounding board, for showing me all of the best places to eat in Berkeley, and for entrusting me with all of his Jurgen Thorwald books as I prepared for this project. And for putting up with the fact that I was raised culturally bereft.

Det. Rick Ragsdale, Robbery-Homicide. For his friendship, for his integrity, and for his insight into cold cases. And most importantly, for putting up with my incessant questions and for being a solid sounding board for ideas in general. His dedication to truth and his commitment to precision are examples that I aspire to. *Personal quote*: "I thought I was wrong once, but I was mistaken."

Dr Richard Saferstein, Criminalist. A special word of appreciation for Rich. But for his advice and personal encouragement this project would have seen many more years in the procrastination phase. My deep personal gratitude for that generosity, and for taking time to provide our readers with his insights.

Daniel J. Stidham, Attorney. For his tireless efforts in the search for the truth. Truth may yet have its day in court in Arkansas.

Dr Diana Tamlyn, Forensic Psychiatrist. For her good humor, her collaborative nature, and for her very pragmatic disposition. There is nothing more valuable than someone who is willing to tell it like it is (even if they do wait until the last possible second to say it).

SA Howard Teten (ret.), Criminal Profiler. A great deal of appreciation needs to be extended to Howard for the advice he has given me, as I have needed it from time to time. His inspiration as a father of criminal profiling, and his vision for combining psychology and the forensic sciences in profiling work, has in no small way shaped my own thinking. I can only hope this work lives up to the high standard that his example has set for the field.

SA Max Thiel (ret.), Criminal Profiler. Under whom I studied at the University of New Haven. For his encouragement, for his lessons, and for his willingness to take extra time when he had it to give. His insights into profiling and auto-erotic death were a good stone to break my ideas on, and I am richer for it.

Dr John Thornton, Criminalist. For his friendship, his professional advises, for taking the time to explain things slowly, and for being a valuable sounding board. Though not the reason I became a forensic scientist, one of the reasons I remain one.

Barbara J. Troyer-Turvey, Director of Forensic Services. My wife, my partner, my conscience. Without her emotional and technical support, her insight, and her dedication to detail, this work would not have been possible.

Students who went the extra mile:
I would like to extend my gratitude for the research efforts and work done on behalf of this project by the following students. We were that much better for their involvement:

- **Paul Catalano**, of Herdsman, Western Australia.
- **Leisa Crompton**, Research Assistant for Knowledge Solutions LLC.
- **Billie J. Workman-Gray**, Criminal Justice student from Grafton, West Virginia.

I would also like to extend my professional gratitude for the excellent quality of the published works by:

- **Vernon Geberth**.
- **Dr A. Nicholas Groth**.
- **Dr Robert Hare**.
- **SA Robert Hazelwood (ret.)**.

CHAPTER 1

AN OVERVIEW OF CRIMINAL PROFILING

Brent E. Turvey, M.S.

History is nothing but a pack of tricks that we play upon the dead.

(*Voltaire,* quoted in *Peter's Quotations* 1989)

The process of inferring distinctive personality characteristics of individuals responsible for committing criminal acts has commonly been referred to as criminal profiling. It has also been referred to, among other less common terms, as behavioral profiling, crime-scene profiling, criminal-personality profiling, offender profiling, and psychological profiling. There is currently a general lack of uniformity or agreement in the application of the above terms to any one profiling method. As a result of this, and as a result of the varied professions involved in the profiling process, these terms are used inconsistently, and interchangeably. For our purposes, we will use the term 'criminal profiling' throughout this text.

Criminal profiling is a subcategory of criminal investigative analysis; a term that accounts for several of the services that may be performed by forensic behavioral specialists. These services are said to include (Burgess and Hazelwood 1995):

- indirect personality assessment;
- equivocal death analysis;
- trial strategy;
- criminal profiling.

The scope of this text is such that it will cover these other forms of criminal investigative analysis in as much as they relate directly to the criminal profiling process.

Before we can appreciate the specific criminal-profiling methodology and concepts in this text, however, we must first understand what has come before us, and by extension how we have come to the place that we are now. That is the role of history. Someone once said that history is mostly guessing; the rest is prejudice (Novick 1988). Ironically, many have said the same thing about criminal profiling, and with good reason, as we will explore later.

It has also been argued that a competent, accurate history can only be written generations after an event or series of events. This supposedly provides the requisite clarity and objectivity on the part of the historian, and presumably keeps them from feeling the pressure to paint facts in a light more favorable to their confederates. The reality is that true objectivity can never be attained in even the most informed recounting of history, because despite any other valiant efforts one cannot hope to separate the message from the messenger. This is something to keep in mind when reading this or any of the available histories of profiling (which are very few), or histories of anything else for that matter. The historical view here will, despite all attempts at objectivity, be presented through the eyes of the author, in the author's language.

When researching the history presented herein, I found that other authors have most commonly associated criminal profiling with the psychiatric profession, and then with the work done by the Federal Bureau of Investigation (FBI) (Burgess *et al.* 1997 and 1988; Geberth 1996; Holmes and Holmes 1996). As such, the varied and curiously brief histories of criminal profiling that have been presented in published works to date tend to focus only on the twentieth century. Furthermore, they all seem to repeat the same things without much interest in going beneath the surface origins of criminal profiling efforts in a few well-publicized crimes.

This work is interested in theories, methods and techniques developed well before the conceptualization of formal psychoanalytic models of thinking. Subsequently the historical view presented here takes a bit more into account, and examines the nature of the roles and contributions of multiple disciplines. While incomplete, it does lay the groundwork for a basic understanding of those contributing perspectives. Readers are encouraged to use this historical rendering as a first blush only, and to look beyond it for their own more complete understanding of the history and origins of criminal profiling.

A MULTI-DISCIPLINARY HISTORICAL PERSPECTIVE

Modern criminal profiling is owing to a diverse history grounded in the study of criminal behavior (criminology), the study of mental illness (psychology and psychiatry), and the examination of physical evidence (the forensic sciences). In its many forms, it has always involved the inference of criminal characteristics for investigative and judicial purposes. The reasoning behind those inferences, however, has not always been consistent. Ranging from a basis in statistical argumentation, to recognizing patterns of criminal behavior, to intuitive opinions based on one's experience.

THE SEARCH FOR ORIGINS: THE CRIMINOLOGISTS

Integral to criminal profiling has been both understanding origins for criminal behavior and classifying criminal behavior. This pursuit falls under the banner of criminology. Criminology is the study of crime, criminals, and criminal behavior. It involves the documentation of factual information about criminality and the development of theories to help explain those facts.

The renowned Italian physician, Cesare Lombroso (1835–1909), is generally thought to have been one of the first criminologists to attempt to formally classify criminals for statistical comparison. In 1876 Lombroso published his book *The Criminal Man*. By comparing information about similar offenders like race, age, sex, physical characteristics, education, and geographic region, Lombroso reasoned that the origins and motivations of criminal behavior could be better understood and subsequently predicted.

Lombroso studied 383 Italian prisoners. His evolutionary and anthropological theories about the origins of criminal behavior suggested that, based on his research, there were three major types of criminals (Bernard and Vold 1986):

Born criminals: These were degenerate, primitive offenders who were lower evolutionary reversions in terms of their physical characteristics.

Insane criminals: These were offenders that suffered from mental and/or physical illnesses and deficiencies.

Criminaloids: These were a large general class of offenders without specific characteristics. They were not afflicted by recognizable mental defects, but their mental and emotional make-up predisposed them to criminal behavior under certain circumstances. This classification has been compared to the diagnosis of psychopathic personality disorder that came later from the psychiatric community.

According to Lombroso's theory of criminal anthropology, there are 18 physical characteristics indicative of a born criminal, providing at least five or more are present. Some of the physical characteristics Lombroso thought indicated a born criminal included the following:

1 Deviation in head size and shape from the type common to the race and region from which the criminal came.

2 Asymmetry of the face.

3 Excessive dimensions of the jaw and cheekbones.

4 Eye defects and peculiarities.

5 Ears of unusual size, or occasionally very small, or standing out from the head as do those of the chimpanzee.

6 Nose twisted, upturned, or flattened in thieves, or aquiline or beak-like in murderers, or with a tip rising like a peak from swollen nostrils.

7 Lips fleshy, swollen, and protruding.

8 Pouches in the cheek like those of some animals.

9 Peculiarities of the palate, such as a large, central ridge, a series of cavities and protuberances such as are found in some reptiles, and cleft palate.

10 Abnormal dentition.

11 Chin receding, or excessively long, or short and flat, as in apes.

12 Abundance, variety, and precocity of wrinkles.

13 Anomalies of the hair, marked by characteristics of the hair of the opposite sex.

14 Defects of the thorax, such as too many or too few ribs, or supernumerary nipples.

15 Inversion of sex characters in the pelvic organs.

16 Excessive length of arms.

17 Supernumerary fingers and toes.

18 Imbalance of the hemispheres of the brain (asymmetry of the cranium).

His theory of criminal origins was evolutionary in nature, suggesting that they represented a reversion to a more atavistic human state. Non-criminals, of course, were thought to be more evolved, and therefore less ape-like. Lombroso felt that based on his research, he could recognize those physical features that he had correlated with criminality. This notion was something akin to a 'mark of Cain,' by which all evil could be biblically identified and classified, to be subsequently cast from Eden.

Many similar attempts have been made by criminologists since then to classify and label criminals and potential criminals based upon intelligence, race, heredity, poverty and other biological and/or environmental factors.

These would include body type theorists. The German criminologist Ernst Kretschmer, for example, argued that there is a high degree of correlation between body type, personality type, and criminal potential. In 1955, Kretschmer proposed that there were four main body types, based upon an unconfirmed study of 4,414 cases. These types were as follows:

- Leptosome or asthenic: Those who are tall and thin. Associated with petty thievery and fraud.

- Athletic: Those with well-developed muscles. Associated with crimes of violence.

- Pyknic: Those who are short and fat. Associated most commonly with crimes of deception and fraud, but sometimes correlated with crimes of violence.

- Dysplastic or mixed: Those who fit into more than one body type. Associated with crimes against decency and morality, as well as crimes of violence.

Kretschmer's theories, however, were viewed as extremely dubious because he never disclosed his research, his inferences and descriptions were always incredibly vague, and no specific comparisons were performed with non-criminal populations. In short, he would not submit his findings for any form of peer review, and his approach was clearly non-scientific. As a result, many argued that his theories regarding his findings were nothing more than unfounded inference and correlation masquerading as science.

The assumption beneath many of the criminological studies into biological and environmental criminal origins has been, and continues to be, that if the right combination of shared characteristics can be decoded, then criminal behavior can be predicted, and criminal potential can be inferred and manipulated. The danger, of course, being that sharing arbitrary characteristics with any one criminal type does not make one a criminal, and the term 'criminal' should be applied to reflect a legal reality as opposed to being the basis for an inductive probability.

Furthermore, while Lombroso and Kretschmer's specific theories may seem absurd to some in light of modern wisdom, the scientific community has yet to abandon the spirit of Lombroso's three essential criminal classifications. Both modern criminologists and the modern scientific community of forensic neurologists, psychiatrists, and psychologists continue to look for the 'mark of Cain.' Today's tools include CAT scans, cutter enzymes, and heuristic personality inventories. Modern methods of correlating brain abnormalities, genes or personality types with criminal potential could be criticized in the same fashion as the theories of Lombroso: as an unconscious intention of the scientific community to stamp a preconceived idea about the origins of criminal behavior with the approval of science.

WHITECHAPEL: THE FORENSIC PATHOLOGISTS

Forensic pathology is the branch of medicine that applies the principles and knowledge of the medical sciences to problems in the field of law (DiMaio and DiMaio 1993). It is the charge of the forensic pathologist to document and understand the nature of the interaction between the victim and their environment in such a manner as it caused their death. In medico-legal death investigations, the forensic pathologist is in charge of the body of the deceased and all of the forensic evidence that is related to that body (i.e. wound patterns, diseases, environmental conditions, victim history, etc.).

During the Whitechapel murders in Great Britain in 1888, Dr George B. Phillips, the divisional police surgeon (the equivalent of a forensic pathologist), engaged in a more direct method of inferring criminal characteristics. Not by comparing the characteristics of statistically averaged offenders. Rather, he relied upon a careful examination of the wounds of a particular offender's victims. That is to say, he inferred a particular criminal's personality by examining the behavior of that particular criminal with their victim.

In this paradigm, offender behavior is manifested in the physical evidence as interpreted by an expert in the field of wound pattern analysis.

Figure 1.1

Front page of the Police News, *September 22, 1888 depicting illustrations of the fate of Annie Chapman.*

For example, Dr Phillips noted that injuries to one of the Whitechapel victims, Annie Chapman, indicated what he felt was evidence of professional skill and knowledge in their execution. In particular, he was referring to the post-mortem removal of some of Annie Chapman's organs, and what he felt was the cleanliness and preciseness of the incisions involved. As discussed in *Appendix 1* of this work, the premises of this and other conclusions about the unknown offender's characteristics deserve a more critical eye.

Whatever the basis of inferences regarding the unknown offender's level of skill, and despite its dubious accuracy given modern understanding of wound patterns in the case, the implication of this type of interpretation is very straightforward. As Dr Wynne E. Baxter, Coroner for the South Eastern District of Middlesex stated to Dr Phillips during a coroner's inquest into the death of Annie Chapman, "The object of the inquiry is not only to ascertain the cause of death, but the means by which it occurred. Any mutilation which took place afterwards may suggest the character of the man who did it." Behavior, they understood, was evidence suggestive of personality characteristics (Sugden 1995).

At the time of the Whitechapel, or Jack the Ripper, murders, coroners were required to inquire into the nature, character, and size of all wounds and document them thoroughly (though not necessarily by photograph). This practice speaks to the value placed, even then, on what today may be referred to as wound pattern analysis.

It is extremely unlikely that the Whitechapel murders were the first crimes where those involved engaged in wound pattern analysis. However, the investigation does offer some of the earliest written documentation of the types of inferences drawn from violent, aberrant, predatory criminal behavior by those involved in criminal investigations.

Understanding the nature and extent of victim and offender injuries is considered an important aspect in criminal profiling to this day. Knowing what happened to a victim, through their specific injuries (or lack thereof) and other forensic evidence is crucial to the goal of understanding the characteristics of the offender responsible. Modern criminal profilers have therefore come to understand that a deep appreciation of forensic pathology, as well as the many other forensic sciences, can provide them with that type of information.

PROFILING IN THE 1900S: THE PSYCHIATRISTS

Psychiatry is the branch of medicine that deals with the diagnosis and treatment of mental disorders. A forensic psychiatrist, or alienist, is a psychiatrist that specializes in the legal aspects of mental illness. The psychiatrist is trained to elicit information specific to mental disorders through face-to-face clinical interviews, a thorough examination of individual history, and the use of tested and validated personality measures. It has been historically uncommon for a psychiatrist to apply their expertise to investigative matters.

In this century, however, the work of the American psychiatrist Dr James A. Brussel of Greenwich Village, New York is considered by many to have advanced the investigative thinking behind the criminal profiling process significantly. As a clinician, his approach to profiling was diagnostic. Dr Brussel's method included the diagnosis of an unknown offender's mental disorders from behaviors evident in their crime-scenes. He would infer the characteristics of an unknown offender, in part, by comparing their criminal behavior to his own experiences with the behavior of patients who shared similar disorders.

Dr Brussel also subscribed to the opinion that certain mental illnesses were associated with certain physical builds, not unlike the theories of criminologists a century before. As a result, an unknown offender's likely physical character-istics were included in Dr Brussel's profiles of unsolved cases.

During the 1940s and 1950s, the 'Mad Bomber' terrorized the city of New York. He set off at least 37 bombs in train stations and theaters all over the city. Dr Brussel made an analysis of the case. He determined that the man responsible for the crimes was paranoid, hated his father, was obsessively loved by his mother, lived in the state of Connecticut, was of average build, middle-aged, foreign born, Roman Catholic, single, lived with his mother or sister, and wore a buttoned, double breasted suit. When the police arrested George Metesky for the bombings in 1957, Brussel's profile was determined to be very accurate, right down to the suit (Geberth 1996).

Between June of 1962 and January of 1964, 13 sexual strangulation homicides were committed in the city of Boston, Massachusetts that law enforcement felt were related. Traditional investigative efforts by law enforce-ment to develop viable suspects and identify the 'Boston Strangler' were unsuccessful. A profiling committee composed of a psychiatrist, a gynecologist, an anthropologist, and other professionals was brought together to create what was referred to as a "psychiatric profile" of the type of person responsible for the killings.

The profiling committee came to the opinion that the homicides were the work of two separate offenders. They based this opinion on the fact that one group of victims was older women, and that one group of victims was younger women. The profiling committee also felt that the psychosexual behavior

Figure 1.2
George Metesky, New York's 'Mad Bomber', 1957.

differed between the victim groups. They felt that the older victims were being strangled and murdered by a man who was raised by a domineering and seductive mother, that he was unable to express hatred towards his mother and as result directed it towards older women. They felt that he lived alone, and that if he was able to conquer his domineering mother that he could express love like normal people. They were further of the opinion that a homosexual male, likely an acquaintance, had killed the younger group of victims.

But not everyone agreed with the profiling committee. Law enforcement invited Dr Brussel into the investigation in April of 1964, in hopes that he would provide them with the same types of insights that helped solve the Mad Bomber case in New York. Dr Brussel disagreed with the profiling committee. He was of the opinion that the homicides were the work of a single offender. But by then the killings had stopped and the profiling committee was disbanded.

In November of 1964, Albert DeSalvo was arrested for the 'Green Man' sex crimes. He subsequently confessed to his psychiatrist that he was the Boston Strangler. Since he so closely "fit" the profile that Dr Brussel had provided law enforcement, they identified him as their offender and closed the case without filing charges. In 1973, while serving a sentence for the Green Man crimes, a fellow inmate stabbed DeSalvo to death in his cell. DeSalvo was never tried for, or convicted of, the crimes committed by the Boston Strangler, and therefore neither profile has ever been validated.

Brussel's method of inference relied largely upon his subjective psychiatric expertise, and the theories of criminology that related back to those of Lombroso. It also relied heavily on his personal knowledge of the often homogenous population demographics in the areas concerned, which are ever changing and no longer homogenous. The result was a synthesis of generalizations, any one of which could have easily been incorrect, and would have subsequently been explained away by a lack of information here or there.

It should be noted that only one of Brussel's profiles was ever validated (though it was not formally written, so one can never be certain). The other is merely presumed to be valid without any sort of forensic corroboration. The concern here being that reliance upon a profile alone, any profile, for the ultimate closure of a case leaves open the possibility that justice may not be fully served.

Figure 1.3

Albert DeSalvo, arrested for the 'Green Man' crimes in November of 1964. He was never tried for the crimes committed by 'The Boston Strangler'.

THE FBI: A MULTI-DISCIPLINARY APPROACH

It was also during the 1960s that the American law enforcement officer Howard Teten began to develop his approach to criminal profiling while still at the San Leandro Police Department in California. Teten studied under and was inspired by Dr Paul Kirk, the internationally renowned criminalist, Dr Breyfocal, the then San Francisco Medical Examiner, and Dr Douglas Kelly, a psychiatrist noted for his work in the Neurenburg War Trials. They had been his instructors at the School of Criminology, at the University of California, Berkeley during the late 1950s. His inspiration for the work also included the work of Dr Hans Gross, an Austrian magistrate. A multidisciplinary understanding of forensic science, medico-legal death investigation, and psychiatric knowledge became the cornerstone of Teten's investigative skills early on, and shaped his approach to criminal profiling.

As a special agent for the Federal Bureau of Investigation, Howard Teten initiated his criminal-profiling program in 1970. He taught criminal-profiling techniques as an investigative aid, to be used in conjunction with other investigative tools. Teten taught his first profiling course, called Applied Criminology, to the FBI National Academy in 1970. Later that same year, Teten rendered his first actual profile as a FBI agent in Amarillo, Texas.

In 1970, Teten also teamed with Pat Mullany, then assigned to the New York Division of the FBI, to teach the abnormal psychological aspects of criminal profiling. Mullany and Teten team-taught at several other schools around the country during the next year while Mullany was stationed in New York. They would dissect a crime, Mullany would talk about a range of abnormal behavior, and Teten would discuss how that behavior could be determined from the evidence found at the scene.

In 1972, the federal government of the United States opened the new FBI Academy and Teten requested that Mullany be transferred there. Shortly after coming to the new FBI Academy, Teten and Mullany applied their concepts to the first FBI hostage negotiation guidelines. In 1974 and 1975, Mullany negotiated several major hostage situations successfully with these new techniques. These adaptations, based upon criminal-profiling techniques, were the first to be taught to all FBI negotiators. They were later modified and expanded by FBI Special Agents Con Hassel and Tom Strenz.

1972 was also the year that a FBI Agent named Jack Kirsch started the FBI's Behavioral Science Unit (BSU). He was a major contributor to criminal profiling in that he was farsighted enough to give both Mullany and Teten the freedom to do research and construct profiles in addition to their regular duties. After they had solved a number of cases, the word spread. Soon police departments were making daily requests for profiles. Special Agents Con Hassel and Tom Strenz were subsequently trained to handle half of the teaching of the Applied Criminology course.

Pat Mullany left the FBI in 1975 and for a few years Howard Teten's partner became Special Agent Dick Ault. Then in 1978, it was Special Agent Jim Reese. That same year Howard Teten retired from the FBI. Heading the BSU, after

Jack Kirsch, were Special Agent John Phaff, and then Special Agent Roger DePue in 1978. Special Agent John Douglas took over the BSU when DePue retired. Neither Pat Mullany nor Howard Teten, the formative minds behind the development of early criminal-profiling techniques at the FBI, ever headed the unit (Teten 1997).

The BSU has undergone restructuring in the 1990s, and the FBI's profiling unit no longer goes by that name. Currently, the FBI's profiling unit operates under the National Center for the Analysis of Violent Crime (NCAVC) at the FBI Academy in Quantico, Virginia. Originally, this was the research branch of the FBI's profiling initiative. But as the FBI has done little published, peer-reviewed research in the area of criminal profiling since the days of John Douglas and Robert Ressler, the function of that branch has not seen its fullest potential. Even the *Crime Classification Manual*, the NCAVC's major publication, has remained a book of theories only.

The FBI is no longer alone in the development of formal profiling units, or research into the area of criminal-profiling theory and methodology. Many law enforcement agencies in the United States have their own dedicated profiling units, and their number has grown internationally as well. In the United States, profiling units can be found in a number of federal agencies, as well as numerous state law enforcement agencies. Internationally, law enforcement agencies with dedicated profiling units can be found in countries such as Australia, Canada, England, and the Netherlands.

Furthermore, there are quite a few private companies and organizations involved in criminal profiling casework and research around the world. Some of the first precedent for this was set in the mid-1980s, by former FBI profilers who retired to consult on their own or through the Academy Group, Inc. based in the state of Virginia. Though some former FBI profilers will publicly admit that their techniques and methods have not changed in years, they have been learned by others. Those others have adapted, built upon, and ultimately reshaped profiling methodology in both law enforcement and the private sector alike.

CRIMINAL PROFILING: THE MODERN PROFILING COMMUNITY

The profiling community is made up of professionals and non-professionals from a variety of related and unrelated backgrounds. Chapter 19 of this book will get into the specifics of what type of profiling work is being done and by what groups of individuals. Suffice it to say at this point that the unwillingness of the profiling community to set standards and validate methodology, combined with the resulting confusion of end users (law enforcement, attorneys, private companies, etc.), has flung the door wide open to both the best and the worst of characters.

Regardless of who is involved, and regardless of the professional outlook, criminal profiling still is not generally a career by itself. Rather it is a multi-disciplinary skill that is nurtured and developed once one has become proficient in other requisite disciplines. Hence, there are very few full-time criminal profilers. This is changing, however, as awareness about what profiling involves increases, as more competent training becomes available, as the literature increases, and as those in the profiling community begin to communicate.

REFERENCES

Bernard, T. and Vold, G. (1986) *Theoretical Criminology,* 3rd edn, New York: Oxford University Press.

Burgess, A., Burgess, A., Douglas, J. and Ressler, R. (1997) *Crime Classification Manual,* San Francisco: Jossey-Bass, Inc.

Burgess, A., Douglas, J. and Ressler, R. (1988) *Sexual Homicide: Patterns and Motives,* New York: Lexington Books.

Burgess, A. and Hazelwood, R. (eds) (1995) *Practical Aspects of Rape Investigation: A Multidisciplinary Approach,* 2nd edn, New York: CRC Press.

DiMaio, D. and DiMaio, V. (1993) *Forensic Pathology,* New York: CRC Press.

Geberth, V. (1996) *Practical Homicide Investigation,* 3rd edn, New York: CRC Press.

Holmes, R. and Holmes, S. (1996) *Profiling Violent Crimes: An Investigative Tool,* 2nd edn, Thousand Oaks: Sage Publications.

Novick, P. (1988) *That Noble Dream: The "Objectivity Question" and the American Historical Profession,* New York: Cambridge University Press.

Sugden, P. (1995) *The Complete History of Jack the Ripper,* New York: Caroll & Graff Publishers, Inc.

Teten, H. (1997) *Personal communication to the author,* May 5.

CHAPTER 2

INDUCTIVE CRIMINAL PROFILING

Brent E. Turvey, M.S.

Do not fall a hasty prey to first impressions.

(Marcus Aurelius, *Meditations, V:36*)

…do not guess, try to count, and if you cannot count, admit that you are guessing.

(G. Kitson Clark, the English historian regarding generalizations)

The profiling community is awash with an abundance of subjective, inductive criminal profiling techniques and ideas that we will not detail here, as it would be an onerous task. This chapter, rather, will focus on explaining inductive reasoning. It will discuss how it is generally manifested in criminal-profiling techniques, and the shortcomings that are inherent. Readers should consider this chapter an overview of inductive thought and argumentation in criminal profiling, and not a final analysis by any means. Another purpose of this chapter being to help demonstrate to the reader what the deductive method of criminal profiling is *not*.

ENDORSING THE SUPERNATURAL

In 1981, the American author Thomas Harris wrote a book called *Red Dragon*. With the assistance of research provided by the FBI's then Behavioral Science Unit, Harris was able to construct a fairly competent, yet fictional, account of a criminal profiler, named Will Graham, who used both physical evidence and investigative intuition to "get inside the mind" of serial murderers. The story very effectively presented criminal profiling as a blend of forensic science, investigative ability, and intuitive but ultimately self-destructive empathy. The 1984 film *Manhunter*, based on the book, stayed fairly true to the original story line, and could easily be described as one of the most competent blends of cutting-edge forensic science and criminal profiling at the time.

As a result of that work, and its far less technically accurate sequel, *The Silence of the Lambs*, the mystique and the dark, brooding romance of the life of a criminal profiler captured the excitement of the general public.

Today there are an abundance of fictionalized accounts of criminal profilers. And they are frequently depicted as supernatural individuals, reliant upon phenomenological abilities and insights. They tend to further rely upon generalizations that have to do with subjective moral judgements like good and evil, and less upon objective things like forensic evidence and critical thinking skills. This is par for the course for people who write works of fiction, where writing devices allow for better drama and more interesting characters and the like. However, this is not an accurate representation of criminal profiling in real life.

The profiling community, while not officially embracing the view that profilers are somehow psychic, does very little to directly discourage it. In fact, the technical advisers on the American television programs *Millennium* and *Profiler* include individuals of the highest caliber. Neither, to my knowledge, endorses the idea of profilers having sight beyond sight. However, their presence as advisers, which is nothing short of an endorsement, has left many in the general public with the impression that it may be so.

To add to the confusion, very prominent criminal profilers have made public statements suggesting that the ability to profile is innate. That is to say, one is either born with it (the ability to profile), or one is not. Which sort of begs the question as to why there should be a need for training of any kind.

Contrary to popular belief, however, and contrary to the ridiculous suggestion that criminal profilers are "born with it", there is nothing innate, mystical or magical about the criminal-profiling process. It does not involve psychic ability, and does not rely upon the supernatural in any way. Many, however, would prefer that this perception remain to preserve their own role in the criminal profiling community, and not have to be accountable for a method or for the consequences of their conclusions.

So what does criminal profiling involve, and what does current criminal-profiling methodology rely upon? A lot of it has been, sadly, a matter of unquestioned, unqualified expertise. The use of subjectively informed experience and expertise as the sole basis for opinions in criminal profiling is one of the numerous types of inductive argumentation and reasoning.

ARGUMENTATION AND REASONING

There are essentially two general categories of reasoning behind the criminal-profiling process, as with most forms of logic and thinking. One can be described as *inductive*, referring to a comparative, correlational and/or statistical process reliant upon subjective expertise that is most like the development of psychological syndromes. The other has been described by the author as *deductive*, and refers to a forensic-evidence-based, process-oriented, method of investigative reasoning about the behavior patterns of a particular offender.

INDUCTIVE REASONING: WHAT IS IT?

It is important to understand that inductive and deductive reasoning are poorly understood concepts even among those with a formal education (who are really supposed to know better). Not only is one often confused for the other, but also inductive arguments can be presented deductively. Then there is the notion of reasoning from the general to the specific and the specific to the general that just confuses everyone into a corner, eventually, depending upon how the definitions are applied. It soon becomes clear that without the religious employment of critical thinking skills, and without a full understanding of logic and argumentation, we proceed at our own peril when we presume to reason at all.

The following is a good example of an inductive argument being presented deductively (as though both the premises and the conclusions must be correct):

Inductive reasoning with the appropriate qualification:

- Premise: Most known serial murderers are Caucasian.
- Premise: Most known serial murderers are male.
- Premise: Most known serial murderers operate within a comfort zone.
- Conclusion: It is likely that any given serial murderer will be a male Caucasian operating within a comfort zone.

The same example of inductive reasoning, presented with too much certainty (deductively):

- Premise: Most known serial murderers are Caucasian.
- Premise: Most known serial murderers are male.
- Premise: Most known serial murderers operate within a comfort zone.
- Conclusion: The given serial murderer will be a male Caucasian operating within a comfort zone.

This kind of overstatement is common in criminal profiles.

Readers are, therefore, encouraged to seek out texts on logic, reasoning, critical thinking, and argumentation, in addition to the material presented here, in order to advance their level of understanding in these areas outside of their relationship to criminal profiling. We just cannot know enough about critical thinking and checking assumptions. As it will be stated in this work many times, until the reader is sick of hearing it, learning is a process and not a result.

So what is inductive reasoning?

Let us begin by remembering that propositions are the basic building blocks of any form of argumentational reasoning. A proposition includes a conclusion that is argued for on the basis of one or more premises. Premises are either true or false (Walton 1989). This is not unlike a criminal profile. A criminal profile is a set of offender characteristics, or conclusions, based upon premises that should be articulated in the body of the profile itself.

As already suggested, *deductive reasoning* involves conclusions that flow logically from the premises stated. It is such that if the premises are true, then the subsequent conclusion must also be true. *Inductive reasoning* involves broad generalizations or statistical reasoning, where it is possible for the premises to be true while the subsequent conclusion is false. For the purposes of criminal profiling, this author further extends the definition to include arguments where the arguer assumes the validity of the premises, but does not bother to actually validate them.

INDUCTIVE CRIMINAL PROFILING

Most inductively rendered profiles are justly equated with psychological *syndromes.* It is important to understand that a psychological syndrome is merely a cluster of related symptoms. Another way to describe it is as a group of signs and symptoms that collectively suggest or characterize a grouping of individuals. The clinical diagnosis of any syndrome involves comparing an individual's behavior and symptoms with the behaviors and symptoms of others in similar circumstances that have been studied in the past. The mental-health community christened the first psychological syndrome in 1980, when Post-Traumatic Stress Disorder (PTSD) was officially recognized by inclusion in the *Diagnostic and Statistical Manual of Mental Disorders* (DSM-III). Since that time, the investigative term "profile" has slowly become synonymous with the psychological term "syndrome" in the eyes of the legal community. This has occurred because of the similarities in the way that inductive criminal profiles and psychological syndromes have been constructed and used to support argumentation in court.

An inductive criminal profile is a set of offender characteristics that are reasoned, by correlational, experiential, and/or statistical inference, to be shared by offenders who commit the same type of crime. An inductive profile is best understood as an average. It is the product of statistical or comparative analysis and results in educated generalizations, hence the use of the term 'inductive'. It is indeed very much like a syndrome in its construct.

Inductively rendered criminal profiles include those based upon formal and informal studies of known, incarcerated criminal populations. They also include criminal profiles based solely upon a person's practical experience, where anecdotal data is recalled by an individual and used to form the basis for reasoning regarding specific offender characteristics. The result of inductive profiling is often a boilerplate, an average profile consisting of generalizations about the characteristics of a certain type of criminal that those who use inductive profiling techniques believe can be accurately inferred to unknown offenders.

Furthermore, as already suggested, the experience of this author is that most inductive profiles involve arguments where the premises themselves have been assumed. That is to say, most inductive profilers do not bother to check the validity of their premises, or simply assume a premise for the sake of arguing a conclusion. This happens far more often than most profilers care to admit, largely due to the fact that they do not possess the knowledge or ability to check the veracity of their premises. The result is a lot of unqualified, poorly constructed argumentation that goes unchecked because of the experience of those making the arguments.

Inductive arguments come in many forms. There are two types of inductive arguments, however, that seem to be more prevalent in criminal profiles than others. The first is the *inductive generalization*, which argues from the specific to the general (many of those the author has encountered believe that this is the only defining characteristic of inductive reasoning, having gone as far as their dictionary to research the matter). In this instance, conclusions are formed about characteristics from observations of a single event or individual, or a small number of events or individuals (Walton 1989). Then a hasty generalization is made suggesting that similar events, or individuals, encountered in the future will share these initially observed, or sampled, characteristics.

Example of an inductive generalization
A 24-year-old white female is raped in her apartment on the first floor. A detective working on the case goes to the press and states that there is a sexual predator on the loose who only attacks white females who live on first-floor apartments.

Such a statement would be totally uniformed, and as such investigatively irresponsible regardless of whether or not it were true. Not only is it possible for the same rapist to attack victims in other locations based on opportunity, but an offender could read this statement in the news and make it a point not to attack victims in first-floor apartments ever again.

The second type of inductive argument common to criminal profiling is the *statistical argument*. The truthfulness of statistical arguments is a matter of probability, a matter of likelihood (*ibid.*). They may sound good, even convincing, and tend to play to our "common sense" stereotypes. This is one of the reasons they are so seductive. But they are inherently unreliable and problematic.

> **Example of a statistical argument**
> A 24-year-old white female is raped in her apartment on the first floor. Published research indicates that serial rapists tend to attack within their own age range and do not normally attack outside of their own race. Therefore it can be inferred that the offender responsible for the unsolved rape is most likely a white male and approximately 24 years old.

The above argument is inductive because its premises may not be true, it refers to the behaviors of average rapists, and includes the non-numerical statistical term "most likely." If the profiler did not include that term, the conclusion could still be false which is what really makes this argument inductive.

Inductive arguments should always, therefore, contain the requisite qualifiers such as 'normally,' 'likely,' 'often,' 'many,' 'rarely,' 'most,' 'some,' 'probably,' 'usually,' 'always,' 'never' and so on. The trouble is that many criminal profilers have stopped using such qualifiers in their language to bolster their reasoning and conclusions without telling the end users of the profiling process. This is because they know that inductive reasoning is far weaker, and far less accurate, than deductive reasoning. Other major reasons for the failure to qualify conclusions, and premises alike, include ego and ignorance; many profilers do not really wish to share the weakness of their arguments with end users, or open themselves to the questions and criticisms that would follow.

It is also important to keep in mind that an inductive argument can contain both inductive generalizations and statistical arguments; they are not mutually exclusive.

The datasets currently used to compile and statistically generalize inductive criminal profiles are collected largely from three sources: *formal and informal studies* of known, incarcerated criminal populations, and the inherent clinical and non-clinical interviews upon which those studies are based; *practical experience*, from which isolated anecdotal (memory and experience) data is recalled by the profiler; and *public data sources*, including the popular media (for example, the FBI admits that newspaper articles are collected by its personnel and used to fill out its computerized database of violent criminal offender activity in the United States).

The advantages of inductive criminal profiling models are readily apparent. Foremost is that inductive profiling methods are very easy tools to use, for which no specialized forensic knowledge, education, or training in the study of criminal behavior or criminal investigation is required. This means that those using these methods need not spend time or effort getting training.

Additionally, general profiles can be assembled in a relatively short period of time without any great effort. Inductive profiles are a great time saver. They offer a quick cut sheet of potential characteristics. These generalizations may then be used in an attempt to predict some of the potential elements of individual criminal behavior, but not with a great deal of consistency or reliability.

The major disadvantages of the inductive criminal profiling model are equally apparent to the critical thinker.

First, the information itself is often generalized from limited population samples, and not specifically related to any one case, therefore it is not by its nature intended for constructing a "profile" of an individual person. It is a generalized set of representations, averaged from a small group of individuals who may or may not have been appropriately sampled, depending on the knowledge and ability of the person collecting and assembling the data.

Second, and perhaps most commonly noted, is that *inductive* profiles are generalized and averaged from the limited data collected only from known, apprehended offenders. An inductive criminal profile cannot fully or accurately take into account current offenders who are at large, therefore it is by its very nature missing datasets from the most intelligent or skillful criminal populations; the criminals who are successful in continually avoiding detection by law enforcement.

A third major disadvantage is that, as with any generalization, an inductive criminal profile is going to contain inaccuracies that can and have been used to implicate innocent individuals. This occurs when an inductive criminal profile is used as some sort of infallible predictive measure by an unprofessional, trigger-happy profiler.

And finally, perhaps the most important disadvantage from an investigative point of view is that inductive profiles tend to be unqualified and non-specific.

Examples of these disadvantages are elucidated in evaluations of two separate inductive criminal profiles detailed in Appendix II of this book.

False premises of the inductive criminal-profiling model, when applied to a specific criminal investigation, include the following:

- A profiler can perform an interpretation of physical evidence suggestive of behavior without knowledge of, or experience in, crime-scene reconstruction, and without actually having to visit the crime-scene itself.

- Small groups of known offenders, who commit the same types of crimes as unknown offenders, have commonly shared individual characteristics that can be accurately generalized back to initially similar individual unknown offenders.

- Offenders who have committed crimes in the past are culturally similar to current offenders, being influenced by at least similar environmental conditions and existing with the same general and sometimes specific motivations.

- Individual human behavior and characteristics can be generalized and even predicted from the initial statistical analysis of characteristics and behavior in very small samples.

■ Behavior and motivation do not change within an individual over time, being static, predictable characteristics.

STATISTICS AND SCIENCE

Poorly rendered statistical studies have been getting a free ride at trial for too long.

The use of statistical methods, or complex instrumentation, does not automatically make any discipline, process, or finding scientific and subsequently valid. Data by itself is only data. It is the employment of the scientific method, or hypothesis testing, in the interpretation phase that gives the data meaning and validity.

This reality becomes important when we examine the inductive data that has been generated in the area of criminal profiling. Not only do the normal inductive fallacies of logic apply to this type of research, but also the standards for publishing such research appear almost non-existent. For some reason, that has not kept such studies out of court, referenced as the basis for expert opinion.

For example, an article was published by Dietz *et al.* (1996) in the *Journal of Forensic Sciences* on the subject of sexually sadistic serial murderers.

Now before we analyze this study, it must first be recognized that Dietz *et al.* have done some very interesting and insightful work in the area of criminal profiling, much of which this author has benefited from. That they put their studies in print for all to see is in itself highly commendable and not at all common. So, no matter what shortcomings may be evident in the work itself, at least they put their name on it, put it out there, and participate in the ongoing conversation that is academic research.

Having said that, this author offers the following analysis for the benefit of the readers: This article presents the individual characteristics, *modus operandi*, and victim characteristics of 20 sexually sadistic serial murderers. It lays out the data in such a way that it could be looked to as an inductive profile of the average sexually sadistic serial murderer. As an inductive criminal profile, based on only 20 known offenders, it is already inherently flawed for investigative and courtroom use. It is an argument that is open to abuse as an inductive generalization. This is a problem because investigators and profilers have used the unvalidated results of this study to bolster investigative and courtroom opinions. But let us set that aside for the moment.

It is published in arguably the most prestigious peer-reviewed journal in the forensic sciences. Furthermore, each of the authors has many years of experience, with distinguished professional reputations for excellence (Dietz *et al.* 1996). Unfortunately, the study is rife with the kind of basic errors in methodology that have pervaded this type of research since Lombroso. Let me explain:

LOW n

The sample in this study is low (n=20). Arguably this is too low for any meaningful conclusions to be drawn at all. Such a small sample can hardly be considered representative of the many known individuals who could easily fall into the broad parameters of this study, let alone provide any insight into unknown offenders.

NO CONTROL GROUP

The data collected was not compared to any manner or form of baseline group of non-sadistic serial murderers. The data collected was furthermore not compared to non-criminal forensic populations. The data collected was furthermore not compared to non-criminal populations made up of individuals from the same geographic and demographics (the geographic region of the sample is not discussed at all). Without these sorts of comparisons, the meaning of data cannot really be interpreted. It has no context. It is what is referred to as a 'dangling comparison.'

QUESTIONABLE DATA SOURCE

This research was done with the data collected by the NCAVC. It is said that a variety of materials were used to determine whether or not those studied fit the criteria of being sadistic and having killed three victims or more separated by time and place, or both. Both can be incredibly subjective criteria, the interpretation being potentially subtle and a matter of expertise. But we also know that the NCAVC uses newspaper articles to fill out its databases, and could contain untold inaccuracies (as do any and all newspaper accounts by virtue of law enforcement agendas when releasing information to the public). We simply have no way of knowing the veracity of the data. These potential inaccuracies in interpretations and available data could easily affect the outcome of any study.

AMBIGUOUS OR POORLY RENDERED CONCLUSIONS

The conclusion of the study is that the "…research suggests that the sexually sadistic killer represents one distinctive type of serial murderer whose expertise and thoroughness makes him a particularly dangerous threat to society." First, that the sample represents one distinctive type of killer should be inherent in the fact that they were able to meet the study's sample criteria (thus distinguishing them). This is stating the painfully obvious. Second, there are numerous sexually sadistic serial murderers (by the author's definition) that lack thoroughness and criminal expertise. Third, there are documented cases of sadistic female serial murderers. And fourth, there is no explanation as to how sadistic serial murderers are any more threatening to society than other types of serial murderers, as the special ability to avoid detection from law enforcement has not been correlated with sexually sadistic serial murderers. Law enforcement has a hard time catching many kinds of violent serial criminals, and they all represent a particularly dangerous threat to society.

The bottom line here is that, while pruriently interesting, this study is the equivalent of noise without a message. Unfortunately, legitimate students and researchers must wade through it in order to find actual information.

Readers are therefore faced with the challenge to think critically at all times when reading research and conclusions of any kind. Just as much as it is the duty of the researcher to present their findings accurately and without bias (admit when they are uncertain or are guessing), it is the duty of those who read what is published to avoid falling prey to poorly rendered generalizations and bad science.

THE USE OF INDUCTIVE METHODS

The purpose of this chapter is not to advocate for a total abandonment of inductive methods and argumentation. For example, an appropriate use could be for the purposes of diagnosis and treatment, as in the case of psychological syndromes. Another appropriate use could be for statistical research and analysis. These are things that can be helped and facilitated by inductive methods.

The author would argue, however, given the many fallacies, shortcomings, and sheer weaknesses inherent in current inductive criminal profiling practices, that they are inappropriate for use in creating criminal profiles either for investigative work or for addressing guilt issues at trial. As will be further elucidated in Chapter 5 of this work, the first onus of the criminal profiler in any investigative or legal proceeding is the responsibility to do no harm by virtue of misleading the investigation of fact, or by virtue of implicating the innocent. Inductive criminal-profiling practices have a very strong potential to do both.

REFERENCES

Burgess, A., Burgess, A., Douglas, J. and Ressler, R. (1997) *Crime Classification Manual*, San Francisco: Jossey-Bass, Inc.

Burgess, A. and Hazelwood, R. (eds) (1995) *Practical Aspects of Rape Investigation: A Multidisciplinary Approach*, 2nd edn, New York: CRC Press.

Dell'Erba, A., Di Paolo, M., Fineschi, V. and Procaccianti, P. (1998) "Typical Homicide Ritual of the Italian Mafia (Incaprettamento)," *The American Journal of Forensic Medicine and Pathology*, 19 (1): 87–92.

Dietz, P., Hazelwood, R. and Warren, J. (1996) "The Sexually Sadistic Serial Killer," *Journal of Forensic Sciences*, 41 (6): 970–974.

Lindberg, L. and Lindquist, O. (1998) "Violent Mass Shootings in Sweden from 1960 to 1995: Profiles, Patterns, and Motives," *The American Journal of Forensic Medicine and Pathology*, 19 (1): 34–35.

Walton, D. (1989) *Informal Logic: A Handbook for Critical Argumentation*, New York: Cambridge University Press.

CHAPTER 3

THE DEDUCTIVE METHOD OF CRIMINAL PROFILING

Brent E. Turvey, M.S.

...the value of an interpretation is judged by how well it accounts for the facts; if contradicted by the facts, it must be abandoned.

(Peter Novick, *That Noble Dream*)

After all of the issues discussed in the previous chapter, one might conclude that this chapter would likely undertake to explain how vastly superior the deductive method of criminal profiling is to inductive methods. One might further conclude that this chapter would likely exalt the scientific validity and infallibility of that same method. But even ego must give way to reason.

Not only will this chapter refrain from presenting the deductive method of criminal profiling as purely scientific or infallible, but it will also refrain from presenting it as purely deductive[1].

This chapter will review critical thinking, the scientific method, and how they both come to bear on the deductive-profiling method. Hopefully, readers will begin to understand that the deductive method of criminal profiling is process oriented. That is to say that the value is in the pervasive thoroughness of the process, as it forces the tenor of any investigation to view forensic evidence, victim behavior, and criminal behavior in a holistic, integral fashion. The thoroughness inherent in the steps leading up to the actual inference of offender characteristics, in terms of its contribution to any investigation into fact, has a value of its own. This makes the deductive method of criminal profiling more part of a philosophy of criminal investigation, and less a black box into which things are placed in search of a fixed, predictable result.

This also means that it requires more work, and not less, but returns more precisely measured long-term investigative gain as opposed to unwieldy quick fixes.

CRITICAL THINKING

There are many definitions for the term 'critical thinking'. Their unifying concept is that critical thinking tends to involve questioning assumptions in

[1] *Every so often I write something that is certain to be read back to me in classrooms and courtrooms for years to come. When I wrote this passage, I could almost hear lawyers and students alike scribbling dutifully in their notepads. I encourage this, make no mistake, but I also advise readers not to make any hasty generalizations on the basis of that statement alone. In other words, read on, then reason it through.*

arguments that we encounter in any context. This means rigorously questioning the assumptions beneath the reasoning and opinions of others, as well as our *own*.

According to Michael Scriven and Richard Paul (1996):

> Critical thinking is the intellectually disciplined process of actively and skillfully conceptualizing, applying, analyzing, synthesizing, and/or evaluating information gathered from, or generated by, observation, experience, reflection, reasoning, or communication, as a guide to belief and action.
>
> Critical thinking can be seen as having two components:
>
> 1 a set of skills to process and generate information and beliefs; and
>
> 2 the habit, based on intellectual commitment, of using those skills to guide behavior.
>
> It is thus to be contrasted with:
>
> 1 the mere acquisition and retention of information alone (because it involves a particular way in which information is sought and treated);
>
> 2 the mere possession of a set of skills (because it involves the continual use of them); and
>
> 3 the mere use of those skills ("as an exercise") without acceptance of their results.
>
> Critical thinking varies according to the motivation underlying it. When grounded in selfish motives, it is often manifested in the skillful manipulation of ideas in service to one's own, or one's groups', vested interest. As such, it is typically intellectually flawed, however pragmatically successful it might be. When grounded in fair-mindedness and intellectual integrity, it is typically of a higher order intellectually, though subject to the charge of "idealism" by those habituated to its selfish use."

Sadly, most of the students encountered by this author have no idea what critical thinking is, what it involves, or how it can be useful in problem solving. In fact, it is extremely unlikely that a student reading this text will have formally encountered the concept of critical thinking at all, even in undergraduate or master's level courses. This is very likely because critical thinking concerns itself with a single question that increasing numbers of university professors appear to be either annoyed with or ill-equipped to respond to: *why?*

Students of criminology, sociology, psychology, and forensic science alike are often stacked, packed, sorted, and assigned into university curriculum, taught by unqualified individuals with little or no applied knowledge who have left no room in the syllabus for discussions about *why*[2]. Students are often expected to cram into overly full classrooms, and remain perfectly quiet under the intimidation of an intellectually reassurance-oriented professor, who fears any challenge to their authority. They are expected to remain silent, while alleged pearls of wisdom are spooned out, and to never question their veracity. Even under the best circumstances, students are often sanctioned in a variety of direct and indirect political ways for asking even basic questions. These questions can include suggesting openly that there is more than one way to

[2] *This sentence alone is guaranteed to get me some heated emails from retired law enforcement who went and earned their PhDs after retiring from six years of working patrol with no actual experience in anything like homicides or sex crimes. It is also likely to get me similar emails from those who make a living teaching outside of their expertise or scope of applied knowledge, such as criminologists who teach forensic science courses without any actual training in it themselves.*

solve a problem, that the opinions of the instructor are uninformed by applied knowledge, or that the assigned textbook is complete and utter puffery.

No matter what the issue or concern, students have been and continue to be conditioned not to question, not to critically think, and to accept information as fact by virtue of the alleged expertise of their instructors. This reality is a dangerous, ego-driven farce. It is dangerous because questioning assumptions is a basic tenet of any forensic discipline. The reason it is dangerous will become apparent as we continue through this chapter.

That students have been conditioned away from the virtues of critical thinking in any university setting is also ironic. The irony being that the greatest gift given to a student by a liberal arts education used to be strong critical-thinking skills. That was the theory, at any rate.

For our purposes, the tragedy is compounded further because good critical thinking skills are at the very heart of what makes a competent criminal profiler. Therefore, before we continue with this chapter, or with the rest of this text for that matter, we need to do something. We need to give ourselves permission to think outside of the confines that our colleagues, friends, parents, instructors, and experiences have placed around our minds. We need to give ourselves permission to question any and all assumptions, premises, or arguments given to us and demand corroboration no matter what the source. We need to free ourselves from those old habits of simply listening, taking notes, and accepting, and get into the habit of asking those who would purport to know things: *why*?

DEDUCTIVE REASONING

Deductive reasoning, strictly speaking, involves arguments made where if the premises are true, then the conclusions must also be true. In a deductive argument the conclusions flow directly from the premises given (Walton 1989).

It is also said that deductive arguments reason from the general to the specific. In terms of criminal profiling, the author interprets this to be recognizing an offender's general patterns of behavior, as they tend to be suggestive of specific offender characteristics – but this is as semantic as the idea of truth itself.

Example of deductive reasoning:

- Premise: The offender disposed of his victim's body in a remote area of the mountains.
- Premise: Tire tracks were found at the disposal site.
- Conclusion: If the tire tracks belong to the offender, then the offender has access to a vehicle and is able to be mobile.

Notice how both premises work together to create a convergence of physical (tire tracks) and behavioral (remote area for disposal) evidence that suggest a specific conclusion. Also take note of how that conclusion might be used for suggesting investigative strategy in unsolved cases (i.e. increasing the area in which the offender may have potentially committed other offenses).

THE SCIENTIFIC METHOD

A *science* is a body of specific knowledge pertaining to the observable (natural or physical) world; a collection of facts established by the *scientific method*. The scientific method is a way of obtaining knowledge through a dynamic process of gathering information and testing it, called *experimentation*. Experimentation involves both inductive and deductive reasoning. Inductively speaking, isolated facts are gathered and combined to form a general idea or hypothesis. Deductively speaking, generally accepted rules are used to form specific conclusions within the process. So in a science, induction is the beginning of reasoning, a place to begin, and the formation of a deductively valid argument is the desired conclusion.

The first formal documentation of the scientific method is attributed to Hippocrates, a Greek physician who lived around the fifth century BC. He was known as the father of medicine, and is credited with having dismissed the idea that illnesses were caused by magic, demons, or evil spirits. He believed that observation and rational thinking were a physician's best tools for determining the causes of disease.

These basic tenets of the scientific method are fairly straightforward, and bear mentioning if not for the simple fact that many students of even scientific disciplines, again, go their entire academic careers without ever being formally exposed to them.

THE DEDUCTIVE METHOD OF CRIMINAL PROFILING

A *deductive criminal profile* is a set of offender characteristics that are reasoned from the convergence of physical and behavioral-evidence patterns within a crime or a series of related crimes. Pertinent physical evidence suggestive of behavior, victimology, and crime-scene characteristics are included in the structure of a written profile to support any arguments regarding offender characteristics. This author refers to this as a deductive process because it involves reasoning in which conclusions about offender characteristics follow directly from the premises presented, and where the profile itself is concerned with a specific pattern of behavior as opposed to reasoning from the characteristics of an average offender type.

The information used to argue a deductive criminal profile includes the following:

FORENSIC AND BEHAVIORAL EVIDENCE (EQUIVOCAL FORENSIC ANALYSIS)

A full forensic analysis must be performed on all available physical evidence before this type of profiling can begin. This ensures the integrity of the behavior and the crime-scene characteristics that are going to be analyzed by the profiler. The behavior between the victim and the offender that is to be used in the profile must be established. It cannot simply be assumed by the profiler or inferred by an untrained profiler. It should be done using accepted reconstructive techniques, i.e. wound pattern analysis, bloodstain pattern analysis, bullet trajectory analysis, or the results of any other accepted form of forensic analysis that can be performed which has a bearing on victim or offender behavior. It should also include the use of victim statements, witness statements, and any crime scene documentation such as photographs, sketches, and reports.

VICTIMOLOGY

Victimology is the thorough study and analysis of victim characteristics. The characteristics of an individual offender's victims can lend themselves to inferences about offender motive, modus operandi, and the determination of offender signature behaviors. Part of victimology is risk assessment. Not only is the profiler interested in the amount of risk a victim's lifestyle places them in as a matter of routine, but the amount they were in at the time of the attack, and the amount of risk the offender was willing to take to acquire them. In the deductive method of criminal profiling, almost as much time is spent profiling each individual victim as rendering characteristics about the offender responsible for the crime.

CRIME-SCENE CHARACTERISTICS

Potential crime-scene characteristics include, among many others, method of approach, method of attack, method of control, location type, nature and sequence of sexual acts, materials used, verbal activity, and precautionary acts. Crime-scene characteristics are determined from the forensic evidence and the victimology. As they are dependent upon evidence, and evidence may not always be available, all crime-scene characteristics will not be established all the time. In cases involving a related series of offenses, such as in serial rape, or serial homicide, crime-scene characteristics are determined individually and analyzed as they evolve, or fail to evolve, over time. An offender's crime-scene characteristics help the profiler discriminate between *modus operandi* behaviors and signature behaviors, as well as lending themselves to inferences about offender state of mind, planning, fantasy and motivation.

Assumptions of the deductive criminal-profiling method include:

- No offender acts without motivation (though sometimes only the offender knows the precise motivation).

- Every single offense should be investigated as its own unique behavioral and motivational existent.

- Different offenders exhibit the same or similar behaviors for completely different reasons.

- Given the nature of human behavior, human interaction, and environmental influences, no two cases are completely alike.

- Human behavior develops uniquely, over time, in response to environmental and biological factors.

- Criminal MO behavior can evolve over time and over the commission of multiple offenses.

- A single offender is capable of multiple motives over the commission of multiple offenses, or even during the commission of a single offense.

- Statistical generalizations and experiential theorizing, while sometimes initially helpful, are incomplete and can ultimately mislead an investigation, and encourage investigative laziness – when we think that we have all of the answers in a case, not only might we only collect evidence that fits those answers, we might think that a thorough investigation is no longer requisite at all.

THE SCIENTIFIC METHOD AND THE DEDUCTIVE METHOD OF CRIMINAL PROFILING

The use of the scientific method makes serious headway in liberating the profiler from many personal biases such as race or gender prejudices, stereotypes, and personal experience/anecdotal generalizations. It also marshals the profiler from using unrelated yet similar cases as a basis for interpretations and conclusions regarding the motivations of a particular offender. Only the behavior patterns recognizable in the behavioral evidence in the case(s) at hand should be allowed to influence the final profile.

This is in keeping with one of the major tenets of deductive profiling, which is that *no two criminals, or people, are exactly alike*. Each is the product of a unique set of sequential, developmental experiences and emotional/ psychological associations at varying continuums of intensity. Therefore each criminal has the potential to create crime scenes in their own way, to satisfy their own psychological and emotional needs. There may be general similarities across criminals, but the deductive method of criminal profiling can be used to help illuminate the differences in the meaning of convergent behaviors to individual offenders.

Do not get the impression that this author is attempting to pass the deductive method of criminal profiling off as a science. That kind of overstatement would not be appropriate[3]. This is due to the reality that the motives and origins of human behavior are far too multi-determined for that kind of predictable certainty (see Chapter 14). The first three general steps of the deductive profiling process (forensic analysis, victimology, and crime-scene characteristics) are for the most part based on the scientific tenets of crime scene reconstruction, and the established forensic sciences. These three steps are best viewed as a language for crime-scene reconstruction, as an expression of what occurred and how. However the fourth step, the deduction of offender characteristics from *a convergence of physical and behavioral evidence*, is still considerably artful, and therefore a matter of expertise and not science. All four steps comprise the final, fully rendered criminal profile. The process of analyzing and recognizing behavior patterns in that physical and behavioral evidence, and deducing or inferring offender characteristics, is referred to by the author as 'behavioral evidence analysis'.

The scientific method may be described as containing the following basic steps: observation, the collection of data, conjecture, hypothesis testing, and the development of theory (Lee *et al.* 1983). The following is one way that the scientific method can be applied in the deductive method of criminal profiling:

1   *Define a problem (observation).* For a particular case, assess the known forensic and behavioral evidence, the known victimology, and determine the known crime-scene characteristics.

2   *Gather pertinent information (collect data).* Determine, based on 1, what further evidence and/or information needs to be collected, analyzed or examined to competently inform the forensic and behavioral evidence, the victimology, and the crime-scene characteristics.

3   *Form a working hypothesis or explanation (conjecture).* Construct a written Threshold Assessment (see Chapter 5). This should contain information regarding known physical evidence, known victimology, known patterns of behavior (i.e. MO and signature aspects), potential motivations, and personality characteristics. Use this as an investigative tool to help demonstrate what further information is required for the final profile.

4   *Do experiments to test the hypothesis (hypothesis testing).* Re-assess offender characteristics in light of the full analysis and interpretation of available physical and behavioral evidence, and re-evaluate the offender characteristics as any newly linked case evidence and subsequent case analysis are made available. Seek out the insights and opinions of appropriate forensic scientists to interpret any questioned areas.

5   *Interpret the results.* Interpret the validity of offender characteristics in light of burgeoning case evidence. Discard any offender characteristics that are unsupported by the physical and behavioral evidence and retain those that are.

6   *Draw a conclusion and modify the hypothesis as needed (develop theories).* Look for behavior patterns suggestive of offender characteristics. Construct a written profile of the offender who committed the offense(s) in question, containing psychological, emotional, personality, and relationship information, as deduced from a convergence

[3] *Profiling is a matter of expertise. But don't let that throw you. Keep in mind that psychology is not a science in a courtroom either. It might even be interesting to see a Daubert hearing on the general acceptability of psychological methodologies by that professional community. As for the deductive method of criminal profiling, I would say that it is best described as a skill, rather than simply forcing it into the category of art or science. It is a difficult skill with some heuristics, but a skill just the same.*

of observed patterns in the physical and behavioral evidence, the victimology, and the crime-scene characteristics. Any elements in the profile should be based on a demonstrable convergence of the behavioral evidence.

This does not by any stretch of the imagination suggest that the deductive method of criminal profiling is wholly scientific. Any discipline that involves interpreting the multi-determined nature of human behavior cannot be referred to as a hard science with a straight face. However, it does demonstrate that the deductive method of criminal profiling can be informed by the same thinking strategies.

REFERENCES

Lee, H., DeForest, P. and Gaensslen, R. (1983) *Forensic Science: An Introduction to Criminalistics*, New York: McGraw-Hill, Inc.

Paul, R. and Scriven, M. (1996) "Defining Critical Thinking," Draft statement for the National Council for Excellence in Critical Thinking, Center for Critical Thinking.

Walton, D. (1989) *Informal Logic: A Handbook for Critical Argumentation*, New York: Cambridge University Press.

CHAPTER 4

GOALS OF THE DEDUCTIVE METHOD
OF CRIMINAL PROFILING

Brent E. Turvey, M.S.

Look beneath the surface: never let a thing's
intrinsic quality or worth escape you.

(Marcus Aurelius, *Meditations VI:3*)

Perhaps the most common misconception about criminal profiling is that its main purpose is to achieve a static, inflexible result, not unlike a clinical diagnosis. These diagnoses are then presumably applied to a crime or series of crimes, and can then be used to suggest *whodunit*. This is evidenced by a persistent but ultimately misinformed belief that there is an average psychological or behavioral profile of a typical serial murderer, a typical rapist, or even a typical crime-scene. Criminology theory texts such as the *Crime Classification Manual* (Burgess *et al.* 1997) and *Serial Killers* (Norris 1988), which have inappropriately set out to turn penal classifications into clinical diagnosis, have fed this unfortunate misperception[1].

This is a clinical view of profiling that regards clusters of offender behavior, and subsequent penal classifications, as potential clinical disorders that can be diagnosed for the purposes of recommending treatment. That is a highly commendable position to take if one is a forensic psychologist or a forensic psychiatrist. However, the goals of offender treatment are unrelated to the goals of criminal profiling. As criminal profilers are rarely clinicians, and do not even have the same educational goals, or training, it should follow that not every clinical paradigm will be appropriate for use by the criminal profiler. The concept of a fixed diagnosis for criminal behavior based on penal classifications, which assumes shared characteristics from a shared origin, and a potentially treatable mental defect on the part of the offender, is one such inappropriate tool.

[1] *A great deal of the published literature concerning offender classification systems has been built on interesting but incomplete case studies, as well as untested and unvalidated hypotheses. Ultimately, the basis for such classifications may be found in subjective penal descriptors, diagnostic terminology, and morally derived judgments.*

DEDUCTIVE PROFILING AS A PROCESS, NOT AS A RESULT

Humans learn, change, and grow. Humans are also affected by time, place, and other humans. Therefore a deductively rendered criminal profile where the suspect is a human cannot be viewed as a static, fixed result that will hold true for all time. It can evolve and can become more refined as it is checked against new evidence and related cases over time. That is to say that each time a new offense is committed, each time a new attack occurs or a new body is located, and each time new evidence is collected and analyzed, the integrity of the criminal profile should be reassessed. A deductively rendered profile learns. New information is not used to support the old profile, or to pigeonhole the offender, or to rationalize investigative assumptions. It is used to make a more complete and more accurate profile of the offender responsible for the crimes at hand. Deductive profiling and behavior-evidence analysis, therefore, should be viewed not as a process after a fixed result, but as an ongoing, dynamic, critical, analytical process that examines offender behavior as it evolves over time.

THE GENERAL PURPOSE OF DEDUCTIVE PROFILING

The first onus of the criminal profiler, as opposed to the treatment orientation of the clinician, is to fact finding in a criminal investigation for the purpose of servicing justice. The profiler's first duty is to public safety. The clinician's first duty is to the treatment of the client. This is an important difference in terms of ethical obligations when considering the potential goals and purposes of the deductive method of criminal profiling (see Chapters 18 and 19).

A criminal investigation of any kind should start with the assumption that every human on the planet is a suspect. That is to say, the suspect set is universal. The general purpose of the deductive method of criminal profiling is to use behavioral-evidence analysis to assist an investigation, at any phase, in moving from that universal set of suspect characteristics to a more discrete set of suspect characteristics. It cannot typically point to a specific person, or individuate one suspect from all others. It can, however, give insight into the *general* personality and characteristics of the person responsible[2]. This type of insight can be used to educate an investigative effort, as well as attorneys, judges, and juries in court.

PHASES OF PROFILING

The deductive criminal profiling process has two separate but equal phases, divided not by the method that is employed to arrive at conclusions, but rather by their divergent goals and priorities. Goals and priorities are dictated by a necessity that is dependent upon when, in a given case, a profiler's services are requested. These are the *investigative phase* and the *trial phase*, before a suspect has been arrested and after.

[2] I am often asked by clients to give a quick, cursory answer to their immediate questions regarding a case in the absence of having performed a complete investigation and analysis. However, it's not that simple. Criminal profiling requires not less, but more work on the part of supporting personnel. In unsolved investigations this time investment pays off in terms of avoiding future mistakes, delays, and keeping the investigation on track (as well as providing for a competent prosecution). I have never had a client regret that a thorough analysis of their case materials was made, though it's bound to happen.

The investigative phase gets all of the media attention, and is the focus of all of the popular fiction on the subject of criminal profiling. When we think of a criminal profiler, we have been conditioned to think of unsolved serial murder cases, and of remote locations where teams of forensic scientists work to recover decaying human remains. The profiler is often characterized as a socially alienated protagonist, deeply troubled by their own selfless insights into the minds of the unknown offenders that they are themselves hunting. This view presented by fiction and the media is not only completely skewed, but it is only the first half of the equation.

The trial phase is the second half of the equation, and has received much less explicit attention in not only the media, but in the published literature as well. Though equally important, it does lack the romance and recognition associated with high-profile serial cases, making it less marketable.

INVESTIGATIVE PHASE

The investigative phase of criminal profiling generally involves behavioral-evidence analysis of the patterns of unknown offenders for known crimes. Criminal profilers tend to be called in to extremely violent, sexual and/or predatory cases when witness testimony, confessions, and/or physical evidence has not been enough to move the investigation forward. The decision to call a profiler into an investigation is typically reactive, with agencies waiting months or even years (if at all) due to a lack of access to a competent profiler, or a lack of understanding about what criminal profiling is and how it can aid an investigation. This is going to change, however, given the increasing number of profiling units in law enforcement, and the burgeoning proliferation of profilers as experts into the courts.

In the investigative phase, criminal profilers are admonished to remain objective regarding suspect information whenever possible. Suspect information might consciously or subconsciously influence the final profile, causing it to be tailored (Burgess *et al.* 1988).

PRIMARY GOALS

- To reduce the viable suspect pool in a criminal investigation, and to prioritize the investigation into those suspects.
- To assist in the linkage of potentially related crimes by identifying unique crime-scene indicators and behavior patterns (i.e. signature aspects).
- To assist in assessing the potential for escalation of nuisance criminal behavior to more serious or more violent crimes (i.e. harassment, stalking, voyeurism).
- To provide investigators with investigatively relevant leads and strategies.
- To help keep the overall investigation on track and undistracted.

TRIAL PHASE

The trial phase of criminal profiling involves behavioral evidence analysis of known crimes for which there is a suspect or a defendant (sometimes a convicted defendant). This takes place in the preparation for both hearings and trials (criminal, penalty, and/or appeal phases of the trial are all appropriate times to use profiling techniques)[3].

[3] In both investigative and trial phases, the deductive method of criminal profiling is employed in exactly the same way. Only the conditions and potential inputs are different; the crime scenes are often fresher in the investigative phase, for example.

PRIMARY GOALS

- To assist in the process of evaluating the nature and value of forensic evidence to a particular crime.
- To assist in the process of developing interview or interrogative strategy.
- To help develop and gain insight into offender fantasy and motivations.
- To help gain insight into offender state of mind before, during, and after the commission of a crime (i.e. levels of planning, evidence of remorse, precautionary acts, etc.).
- To help suggest crime-scene linkage by virtue of MO and signature behavior.

THINKING STRATEGIES

To best achieve any of the goals of the criminal profiling process, a profiler must first and foremost be a critical, analytical thinker. As discussed in Chapter 2, a profiler must have strong, well-honed critical thinking skills, and approach their cases both objectively and methodically. They must be willing to question all assumptions, and trained to ask all of the right questions.

In addition to this, profilers must also know themselves. They must know who they are, and have a firm grasp of their own personality. They must be able to distinguish their own needs, tastes, desires, and morality so that they may more clearly perceive the needs, tastes, desires, and morality of a given offender. That means a profiler must know who they are with an extremely irregular level of personal comfort. This is not a simple or by any means trivial point.

In the absence of self-knowledge and critical-thinking skills, the profiler risks transference of their own issues, needs and morality into a profile, rendering it no more than a projection. It is not uncommon for untrained and undisciplined profilers to create profiles that tell more about their own needs than the patterns of behavior being profiled. To avoid this pitfall, and to keep the profiling process a critical, analytical, and objective endeavor, profilers are admonished to follow these general guidelines regarding thinking strategies (topics inspired by Burgess and Hazelwood 1995).

OPEN-MINDEDNESS

The idea of having an open mind is not in conflict with the idea of critical thinking. It means not being influenced by biases, prejudices, or a-priori theories. It means being open to all possibilities and assuming nothing. A part of that open-mindedness includes accepting two very important realities. First, that any behavior, no matter how repulsive or disgusting or unthinkable to us, can be eroticized. Second, that there are those who practice what can be referred to as alternative morality, where their value systems and pleasurable associations include ideas completely foreign to our own. An example of one such idea or association is that hurting others is pleasurable, and feels good.

The point of having an open mind is not to simply allow all ideas and theories the same weight and priority at any cost, but rather to keep our own associations, biases and prejudices from clouding the possibilities. Once something solid and reasonable has been located in an open mind, the critical thinking must begin.

THINKING LIKE A CRIMINAL

No two criminals think completely alike. Different specific needs, experiences, and associations motivate each one. It is therefore impossible to think like a criminal, in general. A better thinking strategy is to try and understand the level of knowledge and skill of the offender at hand. Examine all behavior through the perceptions evidenced by that offender, and try to understand the needs being satisfied by each behavior in the context of other behavior and interactions. A single offender behavior, out of context, will rarely have any useful, inferable meaning. It is only the patterns and convergence of specific offender behaviors that can evidence any inferable meaning. Those behavioral convergences may then be used to suggest the motivations for specific behaviors[4].

AVOID MORAL JUDGEMENTS

Never use terminology in a profile that describes an offender as sick, crazy, nuts, a scumbag, worthless, immoral, etc. This terminology represents a moral judgement based on a profiler's personal feelings. Personal feelings have no place in a criminal profile. A good way to achieve this is by not using adjectives, or using as few as possible, when describing an offender's personality characteristics.

LIFE EXPERIENCE

It is often suggested that age will beget experience, which will beget wisdom. This is not the case at all. There are quite a number of people in the world who fail to learn from their mistakes, or their successes, and who are

[4] Consider a rapist who attacks a victim in a park. He pulls the victim's shirt up over the victim's face and leaves it there for the duration of the attack. This behavior has a number of results:

- covers the victim's eyes;
- cover's the victim's face;
- traps the victim's arms;
- exposes the victim's breasts

So which one is the intended result? The answer is that unless we know what other behaviors were engaged in, and have more insight into the context of the behavior, we cannot really make a valid argument.

Now let's say that the offender pulls the victim's shirt up and covers her face some ten minutes into the attack, just before vaginal penetration, and calls her someone else's name during all subsequent sex acts. A pretty good argument for a displaced fantasy begins to emerge.

But don't be too inflexible here. A single behavior can easily be a part of satisfying more than one need or desire at a time.

ultimately denied wisdom, or applied knowledge, of any kind. Life experience does not necessarily equal special knowledge or insight. Furthermore, all investigative or law enforcement experience is not equal. Note the differences below, just as a comparative example:

- 15 years in law enforcement;
- 15 years as a homicide detective;
- 15 years as a homicide detective in a rural county;
- 15 years as a sex crimes detective;
- 15 years as a sex crimes detective in a major metropolitan police department;
- 7 years in vice; 8 years on patrol;
- 3 years on patrol; 12 years as a guard at the jail.

While each example represents 15 years in what can be generally referred to as law enforcement experience, the specific nature and quality of that experience is quite varied. The point is that before we go around applying investigative or law enforcement experience, or accepting the experiences of another, as the basis for our reasoning, we must have an understanding of the precise nature of that experience. Subsequently, the applied knowledge gained from that experience must be measured, weighed, and applied appropriately rather than indiscriminately.

INTUITION

Invariably, an accumulation of any amount of life experience leads to intuition. That is, knowing or believing without the use of reason, or rational, articulable processes. If we have a belief, or something that we "just know," and are unable to articulate the reasoning behind it, it is likely that intuition or gut instinct is the culprit. Seductive as they are, intuition and gut instincts can be extensions of bias, prejudice, stereotyping, and accumulated ignorance. They can be extremely damaging to investigative efforts, and should be left out of investigative strategy, suggestions, or final profiles unless reasonable, articulable arguments for their inclusion exist.

COMMON SENSE

Common sense is best defined as native good judgement. Put another way, it refers to knowledge accumulated by an individual that is useful for, but specific to, making decisions in the locations that they frequent. Common sense, then, is not common. What is socially acceptable, reasonable, and expected does not always transfer from country to country, state to state, city to city, neighborhood to neighborhood, or even person to person. Therefore, using our own common sense, our own eyes and beliefs, to gain insight into the behavior of another can be an expedition into the absurd. It assumes, incorrectly, that the offender and the profiler share a perception of what is common sense, as though they are creatures that inhabit the same cultures[5].

REFERENCES

Burgess, A., Burgess, A., Douglas, J. and Ressler, R. (1997) *Crime Classification Manual*, San Francisco: Jossey-Bass, Inc.

Burgess, A., Douglas, J. and Ressler, R. (1988) *Sexual Homicide: Patterns and Motives*, New York: Lexington Books.

Burgess, A. and Hazelwood, R. (eds) (1995) *Practical Aspects of Rape Investigation: A Multidisciplinary Approach*, 2nd edn, New York: CRC Press.

Norris, J. (1988) *Serial Killers*, New York: Anchor Books.

[5] *The meaning of behavior is different from region to region and culture to culture. For this reason I always get someone to act as my local cultural guide when I profile criminal behavior outside of places that I am familiar with. Usually the detectives or investigators involved with the case will suffice.*

For the record, I need a cultural guide not only when I profile 3,300 miles away in Manhattan, but also when I go across the Bay into San Francisco, or when I drive 45 minutes east to San Joaquin County, CA.

CHAPTER 5

CASE ASSESSMENT

Brent E. Turvey, M.S.

It is a capital mistake to theorize before one has the data.
Insensibly one begins to twist facts to suit theories,
instead of theories to suit facts.

(Sir Arthur Conan Doyle, quoted in
Peter's Quotations 1989)

Convictions are more dangerous enemies of truth than lies.

(Friedrich Nietzsche, quoted in
Peter's Quotations 1989)

When dealing with any type of case, the amount of documentation and information can become overwhelming. It is therefore important to have consistent, organized methods of sorting through that documentation in order to understand the nature and extent of what is there. The purpose of *case assessment* is to accomplish just that, and inform how those involved in a case may or may not be able to proceed. Case assessment is all about developing strategy; a game plan. Properly integrated into the overall investigative process, along with the informed judgement of investigators and forensic scientists, good case assessment tools can effectively educate the investigative decision-making process and subsequent investigative priorities.

In this chapter readers will be presented with two case assessment tools. The first is the *threshold assessment*, which is a preliminary analysis tool, for use by criminal profilers as a first step towards creating a criminal profile. The second is a *case assessment form*, which is designed for use by any investigator or detective as a face sheet summary for cold-case investigations.

THE THRESHOLD ASSESSMENT

A criminal profile is a court-worthy document that accounts for the physical and behavioral evidence relating to the victimology and crime-scene characteristics of a particular case, or a series of related cases, in order to infer or conclude investigatively relevant characteristics of the offender responsible. These inferences and conclusions are demonstrated in the profile by a convergence of behavioral evidence, suggestive of offender behavior patterns from which the profiler draws meaning. A criminal profile makes no assumptions about offender or victim behavior, and is firmly grounded in the analysis and interpretations of physical evidence by forensic scientists including reconstruction criminalists, forensic pathologists, and forensic toxicologists to name but a few.

A *threshold assessment* (TA) is an investigative document that reviews the *initial* physical evidence of behavior, victimology, and crime-scene characteristics for a particular case, or a series of related cases, in order to provide immediate direction. It is not informed by complete access to all crime-scene documentation, victim information, or the full analysis and interpretation of physical evidence by the necessary forensic scientists. It makes assessments of what is *currently understood* to be fact. It can include suggestions regarding potential evidentiary connections and analysis, insight into interview strategy, and any investigatively relevant first impressions that the profiler has regarding investigative priority and direction.

A TA should not include firm conclusions or opinions. That is the place of a full criminal profile. A TA is meant to be an investigative compass, or to-do list, compiled in any phase of a case that outlines what is known and what needs to be investigated further[1]. It provides initial observations, concerns, and priorities. It should be made up of investigatively relevant questions, investigatively relevant suggestions, and first impressions where appropriate.

Though it can have the same written structure as a criminal profile, a TA is rendered under different circumstances for different purposes. It should not be presented as, or used for the same purposes as, a full criminal profile. It is important to keep the different circumstances and purposes of criminal profiles and TAs in mind when we write our own reports, or when reading any reports generated by another profiler who may not know the difference. (At the end of Chapter 16, we will discuss why profiles should be written, as opposed to verbal, when so few criminal profilers care to write anything down.)

WHY A THRESHOLD ASSESSMENT?

There are two main reasons for a making a threshold assessment of a case, as opposed to simply waiting out information and rendering only the full criminal profile.

First, as we have already discussed, it provides investigative direction. A TA compiles and presents information and suggestions in a way that is concise and effective[2]. It serves the general profiling goal of keeping an investigation on track. It also directs investigators to gather the type of information that will assist in creating the full criminal profile, and that will provide additional grist

[1] Articulable premises should still support any first impressions included in a TA, even if those premises are assumptions and not fact.

Also, a good way to tell whether you are reading a threshold assessment or a criminal profile (it should be clearly marked on the document) is to look at how many pages it is. A TA is likely to be much, much shorter because there is less going into it.

[2] For these reasons, a TA is just as effective a tool in the trial phase of a case as the investigative phase. The equivocal forensic analysis section of a TA is something that has benefited my attorney clients more than a full criminal profile. This is because it often points them towards forensic evidence that they did not even know they had.

for leads, theories, and opinions apart from the profiling effort. This is because the type of suggestions for information gathering in the TA (designed to inform a criminal profile) will help everyone involved in an investigation, not just the criminal profiler.

Second, and most often in the investigative phase, is the issue of public safety. In some cases, especially those where future offenses may be imminent, we may not have the luxury of waiting for investigative guidance from a criminal profile. We may decide that it is in the best interest of the affected community to draw up some insights based on initial and subsequently incomplete information. Investigators may only have time to get a profiler's first blush response from available case materials in order to organize investigative efforts within a given time constraint.

The decision to construct a threshold assessment should be made only after a cost–benefit analysis of doing so has been made. The cost of writing down seductive, and potentially misleading ideas and insights that may be extremely difficult to dislodge later on, should be weighed against the benefits of being able to organize effective investigative strategy in a timely manner. In the experience of this author, the troubles with using a TA come about when it is presented as, or used in replacement of, a criminal profile. If the members of a case effort are aware, up front, of the nature and purposes of a given threshold assessment, then the miscommunications and overstatements of opinions that are the hallmark of investigative disaster can be more easily avoided. This requires not only truth in advertising on the part of the criminal profiler (not overstating or misrepresenting information in the TA), but also a responsibility on the part of other members of the case effort to use the information in the TA appropriately.

This outlook and designation also has implications for courtroom use, as the TA cannot be confused with a criminal profiler's firm opinions as to the characteristics of a given offender. First, because it has very few conclusions in that regard and only seeks to provide preliminary investigative direction. Second, because it is not a criminal profile.

EXAMPLE

Every once in a while, the author will be asked by a news agency to opine on a particular crime or related series of crimes that has caught the public attention. It is the author's practice in such instances to provide information on general profiling tactics and basic threshold insights on the specific case, and to qualify them appropriately. The cost–benefit issues mentioned in the previous section are also weighed out heavily, as well as specific concerns about information published in the media that are addressed in Chapters 20 and 24, and Appendix IV.

In the example TA provided, the author was asked by a news agency to do a threshold assessment of the behavior of a serial rapist operating in Las Vegas, Nevada.

As this has been made completely public, full use in this textbook is not prohibited by a confidentiality agreement of any kind.

Please keep in mind that this offender is a *serial rapist* until he accidentally or intentionally kills someone. This can happen with non-homicidal rapists who use potentially lethal methods of control (brutal force, ligature, gun, knife, etc.) or who use brutal force to satisfy psychological or emotional needs as an extension of the sexual attack[3].

The author was sent all of the information that the police provided the news agency (which was very little), and constructed it in about a week or so. It is a good example of what a threshold assessment can contain, in terms of it being used for investigative purposes. It asks specific questions and gives specific insights and specific direction. It does not form absolute conclusions or give firm opinions.

Keep in mind that this is not a boilerplate. The information contained in each deductive threshold assessment, or criminal profile for that matter, will be unique to the available physical evidence, victimology, crime-scene characteristics, and offender behavior for each case or series of related cases.

[3] The circumstances relayed here are independent of the offender's intent. Not all rapists or serial rapists are equally capable of homicidal behavior, accidental or otherwise. Each case must be evaluated separately, in its own unique context.

THRESHOLD ASSESSMENT:
Series of Unsolved Rapes, Las Vegas, NV
Investigated by Las Vegas Police Department
Earliest known offense: December 25th, 1996

THRESHOLD ASSESSMENT BY:
Brent E. Turvey, MS
Forensic Scientist & Criminal Profiler
Knowledge Solutions, LLC
1271 Washington Ave. #274
San Leandro, CA 94577
(510) 483-6739; bturvey@corpus-delicti.com

FOR:
Las Vegas Review-Journal
1111 W. Bonanza Rd.
Las Vegas, NV 89125-0070
Contact: Glenn Puit; (702) 383-0281

EXAMINATIONS PERFORMED:
This examiner made this threshold assessment of the above mentioned series of rapes based upon information provided to the Las Vegas Review-Journal by Sgt. Clint Robison of the Las Vegas Police Department. This assessment is not intended to be, nor should it be confused with or presented as, a full criminal profile.

This examiner did not personally visit the crime scenes, nor did this examiner have access to crime-scene photos and victim statements.

THRESHOLD ASSESSMENT
Equivocal Forensic Analysis

The purpose of the Equivocal Forensic Analysis is to maximize the exploitation of physical evidence to accurately inform the reconstruction of specific crime-scene behaviors.

Semen was recovered from several of the crime scenes, but the location(s) that it was recovered from is also highly significant. This should be evaluated.

The point of entry and exit in all crime scenes is said to be either windows or balcony doors. This statement must be checked for validity. It places an assumption in the investigation which rules out other possibilities in terms of offender access to the crime scenes. If this is a fact observed by witnesses (entry and exit), then that has greater validity than if the offender was only seen leaving through windows or balcony doors.

If there has been any foreplay attempts with any the victims, or if the offender removed the victims' clothing himself, this must be assessed for evidentiary value. Potential evidence would include things like saliva to be collected from the victims' inner thighs, buttocks, and breasts, as well as potential fingerprints from the fabric of the victims' clothing. While the offender did wear gloves, it has not been established whether or not the offender took them off for any period of time during the attack on the victim.

It has not been established whether or not any restraints were used in these attacks. If they were, then it needs to be established whether or not the offender made use of available materials, or brought such materials with him to the scene. Either will be very useful behavioral information in terms of offender skill, planning, and potential fantasy aspects.

The exact nature and sequence of the sexual acts in this case must be determined for an informed rendering of offender characteristics. This can be done with a thorough forensic analysis, as well as administering the Behaviorally Oriented 14 Question Interview to all of the victims.

Victimology

Victimology is best described as a thorough study of all available victim information. This includes items such as sex, age, height, weight, family, friends, acquaintances, education, employment, residence, and neighborhood. This also includes back-ground information on the lifestyle of the victim such as personal habits, hobbies, and medical histories.

The purpose of conducting a thorough victimological assessment is two-fold. First, to establish potential links between victims of any kind. And second, to gain insight into how the offender is selecting his victims and inform a subsequent assessment regarding how much risk the offender is willing to take when acquiring a particular victim.

As part of the victimology, a 24-hour timeline should be made of the victim's activities leading up to the attack.

A competent victimology will include the Behaviorally Oriented 14 Question Interview. The Behaviorally Oriented Interview is designed to elicit specific infor-mation from the victim regarding the offender's behavior, and their responses, to inform estimations regarding Modus Operandi (MO) behaviors to potential Signature behaviors. All of which give can insight into the offender's motive, and can assist in case linkage when physical evidence is not available.

The victims in this series of related cases are known to share the following traits:

Race: Caucasian
Sex: Female
Age: 22–35
Residence type: Apartment Complex
Residence Location: Las Vegas Valley, NV
Roommates: None or female roommate
Other: Each victim is adamant that their doors and windows were locked

There are many other traits, as suggested above, that require further investigation before dependable inferences can be made regarding the victimology in this case. Special attention should be paid to similarities between services utilized by, and activities engaged in by, the victims. This includes such things as reviewing any and all personnel currently or formerly employed with services provided to the apartment complexes themselves (i.e. pool cleaning services, locksmiths, security services, delivery services, and cleaning/grounds-keeping services). A list should be compiled of all shared services so that potential suspects from within their current and former personnel can be quickly eliminated, and the investigation can be kept free from distraction.

The available information in this series suggests that the offender has taken very few risks to acquire his victims:

- He selects victims who live alone or with female roommates;

- He selects locations that are easily accessible and easy to retreat from (ground floor/second floor);

- He selects a time of day that is dark, which helps to conceal his activities, that promises a victim who will be susceptible to a surprise Method of Approach/Attack; and that occurs when fewer people will be up and around to take notice of his activities;

- He engages in multiple precautionary acts (see discussion below) to conceal his identity.

Crime Scene Characteristics

The **Method of Approach/Attack** in this series has consistently been surprise. A surprise attack is characterized by laying in wait for the victim in some fashion, or, as in this case, approaching victims that are presumed to be asleep. This approach minimizes the amount of force necessary to control the victim, and by itself suggests an offender who has done at least some level of planning regarding the attack in advance.

The **Method of Control** in this series is known to include verbal threats to the victim, including the threat of a weapon, as well as physical intimidation. It is not known whether or not other methods of control are used to achieve victim compliance (i.e. ligatures and/or corrective force when the victim does not immediately comply to an offender command). Dependable inferences regarding the Method of Control cannot be reliably made without this information.

The **Amount of Force** used by the offender in this series is apparently minimal. That is to say, the offender used only that force he deemed necessary to commit the rapes and nothing more. This begins to suggest, but does not fully confirm, an offender who is not motivated by a sadistic need (achieves sexual gratification from victim suffering) and who is not motivated by a retaliatory need (acting out of anger and/or seeking "payback" for real or imagined injustices).

The **Victim Resistance** and the Offender Reactions to Victim Resistance have not been established.

The **Verbal Activity** of the offender in this series is known to include speaking in a soft or low voice, verbal threats to the victims' lives, including references to a weapon that has not yet been displayed during the attacks. Specific verbal activity regarding sexual activity has not been established, and specific verbal activity regarding things that the victim may or may not have been forced to say have also not been established. Without further specific information regarding both victim and offender Verbal Activity, dependable inferences cannot be reliably made.

Precautionary Acts are behaviors committed by the offender that are consciously intended to defeat specific investigative and/or identification efforts. The Precautionary Acts demonstrated by the offender in this series include:

- Time of day—Promises fewer people will be up to witness his activities as well as occurring during hours of darkness to help conceal his activities

- Use of black-colored outfit—helps to camouflage his presence during hours of darkness

- Use of masks to cover his face—conceals his facial features to prevent both victims and potential witnesses from recognizing him during the commission of his criminal behavior, and from identifying him later

- Use of gloves—prevents the transfer of fingerprint evidence during the commission of his crimes

- Potential voice alteration—prevents both victims and potential witnesses from recognizing him during the commission of his criminal behavior, and from identifying him later

Offender Characteristics

The offender characteristics discussed below are intended to be entirely preliminary, based solely on available information. They are not intended to be, nor should they be confused with or presented as, a fully rendered criminal profile.

The available information suggests that the offender is a male of good health, and at least somewhat agile.

The available information also suggests that the offender's skill level is high; he is competent and demonstrates planning in his behavior by virtue of the nature of precautionary acts in evidence.

It is important to note that the available information suggests that this offender is not primarily a sex offender, but rather a burglar. It is possible that he has been arrested for and charged with burglary and related property crimes in the past, if not actually convicted. This is strongly suggested by the offender's MO (victim selection, location selection, time of day, items taken, use of gloves, etc.).

The motivation for the rape behavior in this series cannot be accurately assessed with the information provided, but the offender more than likely has achieved his current level of skill by virtue of his profit (burglary) motivation. This offender likely started out as a burglar. Somehow, either by opportunity, or by design born out of fantasy (or both – more information is needed), the desire to rape has become part of the equation in some of his offenses.

The available information also suggests that the offender does reside in the same general vicinity of his attacks. This is suggested by the nature of his precautionary acts in context (altering his voice & covering his face), as well as the tight grouping of the attacks and the suggestion of preplanning. There is also the potential that this offender has not originally entered some of the victims' residences through the windows and balcony doors (all of the victims claim that these were securely locked), but rather through their front doors. This could be accomplished using commercially available lock-picks, or, an especially skilled offender with a professional level of access to the areas in question, either currently or previously, could have a set of keys. This possibility should be investigated as it further suggests a resident with local familiarity of the complexes involved.

Investigative Strategy

The following is a list of preliminary suggestion for law enforcement investigating the case:

Current and former employees of managerial and service agencies associated with the apartment complexes involved should be reviewed and eliminated as suspects as soon as possible.

A task force should be formed which at the very least comprises of detectives from both the sex crimes unit and the burglary unit so that information can be shared easily between the two, as well as tasks assigned and investigative direction maintained.

Victims should all be re-interviewed with the Behaviorally Oriented Interview, but not by a new person or professional. It is important that all victims are kept involved in the investigative process and not re-victimized by virtue of being shuffled through multiple interviewers who likely will not share information.

The task force should look at robberies with similar MOs, as well as consult with other law enforcement agencies in the state. The offender lives in Las Vegas now, but he may have moved there from somewhere else where he may have been involved in burglaries or sex crimes.

Keep in mind that some offenses may not have been reported, so work with the press and the public to create an environment where other victims can be empowered, and feel compelled to come forward and share information that may be helpful to the case.

Case Linkage: Conduct a thorough, rigorous profile of the offender, including signature aspects and potential signature behaviors. For example – the 20-year-old victim who was pistol-whipped was clearly not attacked by the same offender as those in this series. However, the 13-year-old and the 16-year-old may have been (more information is needed). Age is not necessarily a factor for this offender. His exact preferences and the motivations for his sexual behavior need to be established before competent linkages can be assessed in these instances.

COLD CASE ASSESSMENT

An open, unsolved case that has seen a period of relative inactivity may be referred to as a *cold case*[4]. This inactivity can be the result of a number of influences and/or circumstances. These tend to include one or more of the following:

[4] The word "cold" almost makes an assumption about the solvability of a case that may or may not be true dependant upon the skills, training, experience, and dedication of the investigator assigned to the case.

- lack of cooperation between victim/detective;
- there appears to be a lack of witnesses;
- there appears to be a lack of physical evidence;
- all leads appear to have been exhausted;
- there is a lack of political support for the investigators or department charged with the case;
- given a low priority due to the victim type (prostitute, gang/drug related, runaway, etc.);
- heavy case load of investigator assigned.

RESOLUTIONS

Cold cases generally achieve resolution in much the same way that any other case will. The difference, however, is time. With the passage of time, some cases just plain get better. They get better in terms of potential confessions, potential witnesses, and potential physical evidence. Investigators and profilers alike need to be attenuated to these potentials, and develop strategies for maximizing their use.

GUILT

Over time, the individuals involved with, or directly responsible for, the commission of a crime may become more susceptible to their feelings of accumulating guilt. They may be more willing to talk after a year, ten years, or more, living with what they have seen, done, or failed to do. This can manifest itself in the form of a confession regarding involvement, or statement from a witness who failed to come forward at the time of the original offense.

RELATIONSHIPS

Over time, relationships between people dissolve, disrupt, change, or simply end. When that happens, past allegiances in regards to confidences may also change or end. Subsequently, co-conspirators or witnesses may be more willing to talk, and more forthcoming than in interviews given at the time of the offense. This includes, but is not limited to, relationship partners, friends, and relatives who were either participants, witnesses, or who just have some small pieces of information picked up through casual conversations over the years.

FEAR

At the time of an offense, those with information may be too afraid to come forward to authorities for fear of their own safety or the safety of others. Over time, this fear may subside (geographic relocation away from the threat), the threat that they perceive may dissipate (death of the offender), or they may overcome their fear by borrowing the will of another (fear for the life, health, and future of their children or relatives). If any of these occur, then they might be more willing to speak with authorities and provide information not originally provided when interviewed at the time of the offense (if they were interviewed at all). Prime candidates tend to include, relative to the offender, ex-relationship partners, family members, and children.

NEW TECHNOLOGY

At the time of an offense, low-yield evidence may have been collected which can be now analyzed, or re-analyzed, using newly developed forensic analytical methods and technologies.

> Example
> Blood collected at the time of an offense, which was tested only for blood-group characteristics, may now be of sufficient sample and quality to undergo forensic DNA analysis, either PCR, STR, or RFLP. This can then be compared to suspect and victim DNA. In the absence of a suspect, samples can be entered into DNA databases comprising samples from convicted sex offenders and other criminals. At least 40 states have laws in place that mandate the establishment of criminal DNA databases. The FBI has already developed a national system, the Combined DNA Index System (CODIS), and states like California and Virginia are online with local offender databases.

> Example
> Hair collected at the time of an offense, which was possibly compared to witness and suspect hair based on class characteristics alone, may also be able to undergo forensic DNA analysis. Pulled hair, which has living tissue can undergo PCR and STR testing. Cut hair, or hair with no tissue, will soon be able to undergo Mitochondrial DNA analysis (mDNA) as those techniques become more refined and cases are adjudicated through the legal system.

New technologies, and potential evidence yield, can be an effective tool when interviewing witnesses or suspects. The possibility of new technology examining old evidence can assist those who have remained silent due to feelings of guilt, fear, or allegiance to be more forthcoming with authorities.

NEW EVIDENCE

At the time of an offense, potential evidence may have been overlooked by investigators, crime-scene personnel, and even forensic pathologists due to lack of experience, lack of training, lack of expertise, investigative bias, or any number of influences on judgement and perception.

Example
Photos taken of a body at the time of autopsy may contain uninvestigated wound patterns. These wound patterns can include bitemarks or other individuating pattern injuries that can easily be missed by those unfamiliar with this type of evidence.

Example
A new crime scene may be found in relationship to an old case that can be examined for potential physical evidence.

The potential examination of new evidence can be an effective tool when interviewing witnesses or suspects. The potential existence of new evidence can, again, assist those who have remained silent due to feelings of guilt, fear, or allegiance to be more forthcoming with authorities.

CASE ASSESSMENT FORM

Included in this chapter is a *case assessment form*. It was designed for use in cold case assessment, but it can actually be used to assess any case that has a lot of related documentation that needs to be reviewed. The purpose of the assessment form is to assist investigators in their methodical analysis of case materials. It is designed to help them to determine what has been done, what has not been done, and how both relate to the solvability of the case given the resource constraints of their particular department and given the skills of the detectives involved[5]. It is also useful as a face sheet for any case file, containing information that allows anyone to take the general pulse of an investigation in a few moments.

The form is best viewed as a series of questions that need to be answered by detectives in order to inform their assessment regarding solvability and potential case strategy. The process of filling out the form is not instantaneous, and may take significant time investment up front. However the reward is a competent working knowledge of the state of the case, a good summary of the case for others, and a definite idea regarding the types of things that can be done to increase the case's solvability. It is also numbered to lend itself more easily to entry into database software.

The case assessment form is not a substitute for bad investigative skills. It cannot impart the need for thoroughness, though it requires it. And it cannot teach the value of teamwork, though it demands it. It is designed to benefit from a healthy working relationship between the professionals involved in a case, and allow each to give their own comments and opinions as to direction.

[5] *The resources of every department are different, and the skills of every detective are different. Therefore, any assessment must be done with those variables in mind. This negates the possibility of creating a single form for all cases, detectives, and departments, with a general solvability rating. What is solvable in the jurisdiction of one agency, with a given set of resources, is not necessarily solvable in another.*

Detectives and others must use the information that they have to make their own decisions.

Figure 5.1

Case Assessment
form

CASE ASSESSMENT FORM

1) Victim Name: _____ 2) DOB:_____

3) Residence: _____ 4) Emplymt: _____

5) MM/DD/YY Offense: _____ 6) Day of Wk: ____

7) MM/DD/YY Assessment: _____

8) Offense Type
☐ Robbery ☐ Abduct./ Kidnapping ☐ Rape/ Sexual Assault
☐ Homicide ☐ Arson ☐ Drug/ Gang ☐ Other: _____

CRIME SCENE
9) Primary Scene:
☐ Indoors ☐ Outdoors ☐ Vehicle / ☐ Rural ☐ Suburban
☐ Urban ☐ Other: _____ / _____

10) Address(es):
_____
_____

11) Secondary Scene(s) / Disposal Site:
☐ Indoors ☐ Outdoors ☐ Vehicle / ☐ Rural ☐ Suburban
☐ Urban ☐ Other: _____ / _____

12) Address(es):
_____
_____

13) Documentation / Reports:
☐ Investigators' notes/ rep. ☐ Crime Scene Video
☐ Crime Scene Sketch ☐ Crime Scene Photos
☐ Recorded Interview (V/S/SP/W)

14) PHYSICAL EVIDENCE
☐ Blood ☐ Fingerprints ☐ Firearms ☐ GSR ☐ Hair/Fiber
☐ Impressions / Patterns ☐Semen / Sperm ☐ Skin ☐ Soil
☐ Toolmarks ☐ Vegetation ☐ Other: _____

Type	Source/Item #	Analysis	By
a.			
b.			
c.			
d.			
e.			
f.			

M.E. / CORONER / SANE/ PSYCH.
15) Documentation / Reports:
☐ Autopsy Photos ☐ Autopsy Rep. ☐ Sex. Assault Kit ☐ Hospital Rep.
(MD/RN) ☐ Tox. Rep. ☐ Psych. Rep.

16) Case No.: _____ **17) Cause of Death:** _____
_____ **18) Injuries:** _____
_____

19) Investigating Agency: _____
_____

20) Case No.: _____

21) Investigator (s) Previously Assigned:
_____

22) Investigator(s) Currently Assigned:
_____

23) PARTIES INVOLVED

Name	DOB	Relationship to case*	Interview / Date
a.			
b.			
c.			
d.			
e.			
f.			
g.			
h.			

*Victim's Family, Spouse, Son, Daughter; Suspect, Witness, etc.

WARRANTS SERVED
Location   Date
24) Search: _____ _____
_____ _____

25) Arrest: _____ _____
_____ _____

INVESTIGATIVE ACTION:
☐ **Internal case linkage** **Date:** _____.
 Solved / Missing Persons
☐ **Teletype broadcast** **Date:** _____
 Local / States / National
☐ **Database case linkage** **Date:** _____
 ViCAP / ViCLAS / HEAT / HITS / other: _____
☐ **Evidence database linkage** **Date:** _____
 CODIS / AFIS / Drugfire / other: _____

REVIEWED BY:
(*Indicates comments/ notes attached)
Lead Investigator: _____

Previous Investigator: _____

Criminalist: _____

ME/ Coroner/ SANE / Psych: _____

District Attorney's Office: _____

The lead investigator may then use those suggestions and opinions to set priorities and give investigative direction. Good detectives and investigators will use what is useful regarding the form, and modify it to address the peculiarities of their own agencies and caseload (see Figure 5.1).

CASE ASSESSMENT FORM INSTRUCTIONS

1 Enter victim's name.

2 Enter victim's date of birth.

3 Enter victim's place of residence.

4 Enter victim's type of employment.

5 Enter the date of the offense.

6 Enter the day of the week that the offense occurred on (M, T, W, Th, F, S, Su).

7 Enter the date that the assessment form was filled out.

8 Check the type of offense involved. Check more than one when appropriate.

9 Check the type of primary crime-scene involved (find this out for yourself; do not fall prey to the assumptions of others). Check the geographic/demographic location type.

10 Enter the address of the primary crime-scene (latitude and longitude in rural areas).

11 Check the type of secondary crime-scene(s) involved (find this out for yourself; do not fall prey to the assumptions of others). Check the geographic/demographic location type(s).

12 Enter the address of the secondary crime-scene(s) (latitude and longitude in rural areas).

13 Check the type of crime-scene documentation that you have available. If you don't have something, find out why. Check more than one when appropriate.

14 Check the type of physical evidence that was originally collected. Double-check documentation for potentially missed evidence. Check more than one when appropriate. 14a–f and so on should contain individual item detail. Continue on the back of form or attached paper when necessary.

15 Check the type of Medical Examiner, Coroner, Sexual Assault Nurse Examiner, or Psychiatric/mental health documentation that you have available. If you do not have a certain type of documentation that you believe you should have, find out why.

16 Enter the case number of the report(s) involved.

17 Enter the cause of death (not the manner or mode), when appropriate.

18 Enter a brief description of the types of injuries suffered by the victim.

19 Enter the name of the investigating agency (your agency).

20 Enter the case number assigned by your agency.

21 Enter the name of the investigator and the agency originally assigned to the case, when appropriate.

22 Enter the name of the investigator and the agency currently assigned to the case (your name, unless filling it out for someone else).

23 Enter the names of all the people involved in the case from suspects to witnesses to victim relations, etc. Give their date of birth, and give an indication as to when they were interviewed (if at all) and the date. Write one date for each subsequent interview.

24 Enter the addresses and dates of any search warrants served relating to this case.

25 Enter the addresses and dates of any arrest warrants served relating to this case.

26 Circle and date any investigative action taken.

27 Once completed, send the form around to the individuals suggested on the form. Have them attach their own comments to the form on separate sheets, and date and initial the form to evidence that they have done so.

THE NEED FOR TRAINING

Many police agencies recognize the need for action when they have enormous backlogs of unsolved cases which, for any combination of the reasons already mentioned, have fallen into the "cold" category. One solution has been to develop cold-case units, or to assign just one or two detectives exclusively to investigate these cold cases. To a lesser extent, cold-case task forces have also been formed as a solution. These initiatives tend to be only marginally successful or outright failures.

The first reason for this is attitude. One must not approach a cold case with the mindset that it is going to be difficult or unsolvable. The most constructive and solution-oriented way to approach a cold case is by not treating it as though it is cold. Cold-case investigations should be proceeded upon no differently than if the offense had occurred that day. This attenuates the detectives to a more constructive mindset, and most importantly reduces the amount of bias influencing preconceived ideas about a case's solvability.

The second reasoning is inadequate training. It is true that a few cases merely require investigative attention and they will begin to solve themselves. But others, evidenced by the fact that they have not yet been solved, obviously require more.

According to one aggregated study (Horvath and Meesig 1996):

- Only 5–25 percent of criminal cases in the United States involve the use of physical evidence at trial.

- Detectives/attorneys are infrequently trained to understand or use physical evidence at trial.

- Physical evidence is most often used at trial when it can help get confessions or corroborate witnesses.

What this study suggests is that while detectives are very skilled at interviewing suspects and witnesses, they often have no idea how to use physical evidence.

If a cold-case unit utilizes detectives with the same type of training given other detectives in the past, then the results achieved by that unit should not be expected to be much different than the results already achieved.

Cold cases are not just about overtaxed resources and case backlogs. They are a red flag for a training need. This means that giving detectives time and resources to work on cold cases is not enough. They must also have additional training. This additional training, as suggested by the Resolutions section, above, should include at least basic, but ideally intermediate and advanced, courses in the various forensic sciences (i.e. criminalistics, medico-legal death investigation, forensic pathology, forensic odontology, bloodstain pattern analysis, forensic DNA analysis, etc.).

In the absence of getting such training it is absolutely imperative that detectives who work on cold cases have access to, and work closely with, those who possess it.

REFERENCE

Horvath, F. and Meesig, R. (1996) "The Criminal Investigation Process and the Role of Forensic Evidence: A Review of Empirical Findings," *Journal of Forensic Sciences*, November, 41 (6): 963–9

CHAPTER 6

EQUIVOCAL FORENSIC ANALYSIS

Brent E. Turvey, M.S.

...the use of physical evidence and application of the forensic sciences, in spite of the popular perception to the contrary, are not prominent in reality; systematic sleuthing and scientific successes do not characterize the criminal investigative process or what might be called, in other words, detective work.

(Horvath and Meesig 1996)

The criminal personality profile is based on a good crime-scene examination and adequate information supplied to the profiler.

(Geberth 1996)

The word *equivocal* refers to anything that can be interpreted in more than one way or anything where the interpretation is questioned. An *equivocal forensic analysis* refers to a review of the entire body of physical evidence in a given case that questions all related assumptions and conclusions. Criminal profilers are admonished to make this the first step of any case they are asked to analyze.

One cannot render a thorough criminal profile until the physical evidence has been analyzed and interpreted. The criminal profiler establishes behavioral evidence (victim and offender behavior) using a reconstruction of the physical evidence. The analysis of that behavioral evidence is how a criminal profile is generated. A competent criminal profiler must be able to establish the veracity and meaning of physical evidence, with their own knowledge of forensic science and that of fellow forensic scientists and colleagues. If the physical evidence, and any subsequent reconstruction, lacks veracity or merit, then so does any criminal profile upon which it is based.

PURPOSE

An equivocal forensic analysis is of paramount importance because it helps to preserve the criminal profiler's objectivity by protecting them from investigative assumptions. Many profilers assume that the cases they are asked to review have been thoroughly and competently investigated. They assume that law enforcement and crime lab personnel have worked together to form cohesive, informed theories about victim–offender behavior and basic crime-scene characteristics (i.e. whether or not a scene is primary, secondary, or a disposal site; whether or not victims in a particular series knew each other, etc.). Many profilers do not see the need to question the assumptions of law enforcement or the conclusions of forensic personnel. They view it as bad form, or perhaps even as impolite. Nothing could be further from the truth.

The reason behind the equivocal forensic analysis is very straightforward. It assists the profiler from falling into the trap of *a priori investigative bias*. A-priori investigative bias is a phenomenon that occurs when investigators, detectives, crime-scene personnel, or others somehow involved with an investigation come up with theories uninformed by the facts. These theories, which are most often based on subjective life experience, cultural bias, and prejudice, can influence whether or not investigators recognize and collect certain kinds of physical evidence at the scene. A-priori investigative bias can also influence whether or not certain theories about a case are ever considered.

Because of the prevalence of a-priori investigative bias, we must admit that the recognition, documentation, collection, and examination of physical evidence prior to the profiler's involvement is potentially incomplete, uninformed, biased, incompetent, and even criminally affected. Though it may seem otherwise, this is not an anti-law-enforcement view. In fact, the best detectives on the job commonly express the same concerns and welcome this type of expertise and review. If not, they must understand that, as the profiler may base court-worthy conclusions on this information, it is their responsibility to establish its veracity for themselves and not take anything on faith.

If an investigator, detective or an attorney asks a profiler to review a rape homicide, the first thing that profiler should ask is how they established that it was a rape and how they established that it was a homicide. Question all assumptions.

The next question is "How could this be? Don't all detectives and investigators in law enforcement have at least basic training in the forensic sciences? Aren't they required to work closely with crime lab personnel when developing theories about what occurred in a case and how they will proceed with their investigation of potential suspects? Don't they check their investigative assumptions?" The answer, too often, is no (see Figures 6.1 and 6.2).

Figures 6.1/6.2

Trash found in a fire pit at an outdoor crime scene, less than 10 yards from the bodies of three teenagers who had been shot to death. This trash was not present in early crime-scene photos taken of the scene, and it was later determined that it belonged to investigators. The trash could have been collected as evidence and sent to the lab for analysis, resulting in wasted time and resources (not to mention the fact that the disposal of the trash at the scene may have destroyed or contaminated other potential physical evidence).

As we discussed in the previous chapter, the level of forensic science knowledge and training within the law enforcement and prosecutorial (let alone defense) communities is very low (National Institute of Justice 1997). In many cases it is even non-existent.

It has been suggested (Horvath and Meesig 1996), and this author agrees, that physical evidence is rarely used in criminal investigations at all. This is not because of a lack of evidence availability, according to the study. Rather, physical evidence and forensic analysis are often ignored, even when available, due to the attitudes and mindsets of individual investigators and prosecutors who only see the value of physical evidence in light of their own limited knowledge and experiences[1].

Cases where physical evidence is exploited to its fullest value in a criminal investigation and subsequent prosecution, are the exception rather than the rule. The data show that in many cases physical evidence is not even collected. The data also show that when physical evidence is collected, it is rarely analyzed but rather sits on an evidence shelf for undetermined periods of time. And when it has been collected properly, and analyzed, the results of that analysis are infrequently used for anything in court other than to promote prosecutorial theory (*ibid.*). It is also the experience of this author that when it is believed that the physical evidence may not match up with prosecutorial theories, it may remain on the shelf, untested and unanalyzed.

All of these possibilities being the case, potentially influencing the nature and quality of the information and interpretations that a criminal profiler gets up front, the need for the equivocal forensic analysis becomes apparent. With so much room for error, the criminal profiler must be capable of competently discriminating the meaning of physical evidence, and must not be afraid to question any investigative assumptions or conclusions. This does not mean that the profiler assumes that the information they are getting is incorrect, but rather that they have a responsibility to establish what is known and knowable about victim–offender behavior for themselves before they undertake to profile.

[1] More than once this author has encountered incredulous prosecutors who do not ask the state crime lab personnel to reconstruct even the most complex multiple homicides. They will argue that the case does not require "complicated, scientific forensics" to understand what happened, just common sense. And if you've read Chapter 4, you already know what I think about "common sense."

INPUTS

Nobody creates a criminal profile on their own. Behind each criminal profile is a mountain of information collected by a hundred people. Their subsequent role in the creation of a profile is at least as important as the role of the profile in the investigation. Those who would not admit the role of others in their own profiling process are either being dishonest or are creating uninformed profiles.

It is really a very basic concept; good crime-scene examination begets more competent physical evidence begets a more competent reconstruction

[2] *One of the issues that comes up a lot is whether or not profilers need to actually visit the crime scene.*

Many profilers do not believe that it is necessary at all, and will even give profiles verbally, over the phone, without having reviewed any of the documentation firsthand.

My practice is to visit the scene when possible (the crime scene may have been destroyed or may be unreachable for some reason). Not going, when reasonable, always makes for a less competent profile. Why? Because it gives the profiler an applied context and perspective for what could have occurred at that crime scene and how. For example:

Spatial sense is just not complete from two-dimensional photos or a description alone. You might have a hard time understanding this until the first time you visit a crime scene and realize that the slope in the photo that you have to walk down to get to the crime scene is actually a nearly 90 degree drop-off.

Visiting an outdoor crime scene gives you a chance to experience transfer evidence firsthand. Those thistles sticking all over your clothes would probably stick to anything or anybody else that was in the same location.

begets a more competent criminal profile. That means everyone needs to cooperate, and nobody should render a criminal profile in a vacuum. Everyone works together, and everyone does the best job that they can, or the result will reflect it.

While every case is different, and has its own unique peculiarities in terms of what occurred and how it was documented, there are basic items of forensic information, or *inputs*, that should be reviewed and considered before a competent criminal profile can be rendered.

A brief summary of inputs are given below, but readers are urged to avail themselves to the following references for a better understanding of the forensic sciences, and the nature of the documentation that can and should be available to them when performing an equivocal forensic analysis:

- DeHaan, J. (1997) *Kirk's Fire Investigation*, 4th edn, Upper Saddle River: Prentice-Hall.
- DeForest, P., Gaensslen, R. and Lee, H. (1983) *Forensic Science: An Introduction to Criminalistics*, New York: McGraw Hill.
- DiMaio, D. and DiMaio, V. (1993) *Forensic Pathology*, New York: CRC Press.
- Geberth, V. (1996) *Practical Homicide Investigation*, 3rd edn, New York: CRC Press.
- Inman, K. and Rudin, N. (1997) *An Introduction to Forensic DNA Analysis*, New York: CRC Press.
- National Institute of Justice (1997) "National Guidelines for Death Investigation," Research Report 167568, Washington DC: NIJ.
- Rynearson, J. and Chisum, W. J. (1997) *Evidence and Crime Scene Reconstruction*, 5th edn, National Crime Investigation and Training.
- Saferstein, S. (1998) *Criminalistics: An Introduction to Forensic Science*, 6th edn, Upper Saddle River: Prentice-Hall.

DOCUMENTATION

The exact nature of any documentation and reports generated in relation to a particular case will vary based on the availability of evidence at the scene, the skill of forensic personnel involved, and the skill of investigators involved. The rule of thumb for investigators and crime-scene personnel alike is that it is better to over-document a crime scene than to under-document it. One can never burn too much film or take too many notes at a crime scene[2].

CRIME-SCENE VIDEO

The very first documentation of any crime scene in its pristine, undisturbed state should be in the form of crime-scene video. It is low-cost, relatively easy to do, and can provide an uninterrupted, context-rich record of the crime scene.

In the absence of being able to visit the scene, this in combination with still photos is the best way to appreciate the nature and extent of the crime-scene as it relates to the events that took place in it.

CRIME-SCENE PHOTOS

Crime-scene photos provide, in concert with video, the best chance to see physical evidence from the crime-scene in context and up close. Depending upon the nature of the scene, they also provide the opportunity to look for environmental items that have psychological value (i.e. literature, sexual paraphernalia, etc.) and the potential sources of unexplained wound patterns on the body of the victim, either of which may have been otherwise undocumented.

They also provide the opportunity to find new physical evidence that may have been missed all together.

INVESTIGATORS' REPORTS

Every person who goes into a crime scene, whose name is on the security log, may be required to write a report of their activities and observations. This is by no means universal, as standard operating procedure for report writing varies from agency to agency. The importance of these reports is that they can be used to help establish who saw what, who collected what, and whether that record is consistent with other reports and any reconstructed physical evidence. Profilers should pay close attention to these reports as they often offer important insights into crime-scene detail that may not otherwise get mentioned.

In this author's experience, younger patrol officers tend to write the most detailed and subsequently most useful reports. They do not have the training or experience to know what is trivial, so they are more likely to include everything that occurred. Seasoned officers with more experience tend to leave out a great deal, and recount only what they believe is important. In any case, these reports reflect the personality and experience of the person writing them, so no two are precisely alike. Profilers should therefore read all that are available to get the most complete picture of crime-scene activity and observations.

CRIME-SCENE SKETCHES

Before any crime scene is released, a *rough* crime-scene sketch should be made (hand-drawn and not to scale, but with measurements). The purpose of the sketch is to show the relationship of the physical evidence that was collected to the physical environment. This can be compared to the evidence logs, the investigator's reports, and the final crime-scene sketch (court-worthy, done to scale under controlled conditions, in a neat, legible fashion).

The crime-scene sketch is also useful for its evidentiary value in determining what might not have been collected.

CRIME-SCENE EVIDENCE LOGS AND EVIDENCE SUBMISSION FORMS

Every item of evidence that has been recognized, documented, and collected at the crime scene (including things like rolls of film and videotape) should be on the evidence logs. This provides the profiler with a record of what was found. This record can be compared with items in the documentation (scene photos and videos) that may not have been collected, that may have been lost, or that may still require analysis by the crime lab. Not everything that gets collected makes it to the lab for analysis. The evidence submission forms should be compared to the crime-scene evidence logs to determine what was sent where, and for what tests. Not everything that is submitted to a crime lab for analysis gets the appropriate attention, because in some cases the investigators in charge are the ones who decide what tests get done, as opposed to the forensic scientists who receive the evidence[3]. Following up on these items, and knowing what type of information they can give to the investigation, in terms of potential behavior, is very important.

[3] It is not common for a criminalist in a crime lab to know the nature of the relationship between a piece of evidence and the crime scene. They often just get an evidence bag with an item marked with a number and a request for a test. Unless the detective makes an effort to inform them of the context of the case, the criminalist simply does what is requested of them without being able to give any applied insight.

This is a great irony as the person with the most insight into how to exploit that evidence for information would be the criminalist, while often the person requesting the test may know basically nothing about forensic science. Again, this is a policy/teamwork issue.

RESULTS OF FORENSIC ANALYSIS

Reports detailing the results of forensic analysis are prepared by the criminalists from a crime lab who have performed tests on evidence submitted to them by detectives. There are many different types of physical evidence and subsequent analysis that can be performed on them. As stated at the beginning of this section, readers are encouraged to avail themselves of the references that are provided and familiarize themselves with the great breadth of possibilities. This is by no means a small task, and even the most learned professionals require constant retraining.

MEDICAL EXAMINER'S AND CORONER'S REPORTS

Depending upon the laws regulating the area where the crime was committed, and the nature of any death, an autopsy may have been performed and an autopsy report may have been generated. The person performing the autopsy may be a coroner or a medical examiner. Both may be referred to as a forensic pathologist.

The Centers for Disease Control (CDC) estimates that medical examiners and coroners investigate 20 percent of the approximately two million deaths that occur in the US each year. Investigation practices and requirements vary widely between and even within jurisdictions. At the present time, 22 states in the US use a medical examiner system, 11 use a coroner system, and 17 use a combination.

Medical examiners may have state, district, or county jurisdiction and are appointed. They must be licensed physicians and may even be Board Certified as Forensic Pathologists (there are less than 1000 BCFPs in the United Sates). *Coroners*, however, are most often elected or appointed officials, and are generally not required to be licensed physicians. In some cases, they need only meet an age requirement and reside in the district. This can have an enormous impact on the nature and quality of the medico-legal death investigation performed in a given case, and can make the necessity of an equivocal forensic analysis even more crucial to a competent profile.

At worst, the ME/Coroner's report is a misleading document full of errors and misinterpretations by a grossly unqualified individual. At best, it is a highly competent document that gives the nature and extent of victim injury, and opines as to the causes and manner of death. A profiler should review such reports with autopsy photos nearby, and compare the descriptions of injuries to the corresponding photos and diagrams. An autopsy report without the photos is not nearly as informative or useful in helping the profiler understand the nature of the interaction between the victim and their environment in such a way as it caused or led to their death. Look for injuries that are not documented, or explained, and account for all injuries that are the result of Emergency Medical Service (EMS) activity. Pay particular attention to opinions regarding whether injuries are ante-mortem, peri-mortem, or post-mortem, as these considerations are important when interpreting the meaning of offender behavior later on.

AUTOPSY VIDEOS

It is very uncommon for medical examiners or coroners to videotape their autopsies, though many are equipped with the facility to do so. In the absence of being present during an actual autopsy, this would be the next best thing, and provide the profiler with knowledge of the victim's injuries in context, otherwise unavailable to them except through two-dimensional photos.

AUTOPSY PHOTOS

These can be some of the most important documentation in a death investigation. They should provide close-up and contextual shots of all internal and external injuries, both before and after the victim has been cleaned up for autopsy. They also provide an excellent opportunity for finding overlooked or misinterpreted wound patterns. They should be reviewed in the context of the autopsy report, and should be compared to statements made by representatives of the ME or Coroner's office who were at the scene (and likely filed their own, separate investigative reports)[4].

[4] *Here's the big secret (to some): many investigators and forensic pathologists take handwritten or audio notes of observations that they don't include in their final reports. So it's important to know that these notes not only exist, but they are therefore discoverable by opposing counsel.*

I worked a case where, after digging through the autopsy notes for a few hours, I found a list of conclusions made by the ME that never saw its way into the autopsy report or courtroom testimony. On this list was the conclusion that the victim was pregnant, which, in a case of a brutal rape homicide where a young teenager is beaten to death, I would look at as at least a potential motive.

SEXUAL ASSAULT PROTOCOL

Often, investigators or detectives will suggest that, as the victim of a rape or sexual assault was attacked on a busy street, or in an unknown location, or in an assailant's car, that no practical crime scene can be barricaded off. Subsequently, it will be argued that no physical evidence can be collected because there is no crime scene.

This is not the case. Even when a physical, barricadable location is denied the investigators, either by a fluke of circumstances, or by the design of a precautionary offender, there is still potential transfer evidence that can be collected on the victim. In any case where a sexual assault is suspected or alleged, a sexual-assault protocol may be performed on the victim. Physical evidence transfers (from the offender and from the locations involved in an attack) onto the victim's clothing and the victim's person in a variety of recognizable and collectable forms. The victim, when available, is an extension of the crime scene.

In some cases, the sexual-assault protocol may be handled by a forensic nurse or sexual assault nurse examiner (SANE) through either a medical facility, such as a hospital or clinic emergency room, or through the local ME/Coroner's office in cases involving the death of the victim. In some cases, the sexual-assault protocol may be handled by someone with absolutely no training or experience in the recognition or documentation of forensic evidence. In any case, the professionals who perform these protocols write their own reports and opinions, document injuries on diagrams and with photos, and collect evidence for submission to the crime lab. The profiler, investigators, and criminalists in the process of informing a reconstruction of the crime should review all of this documentation. This evidence, including any wound patterns, should be compared with the victim's statements, when available, for consistency. Any inconsistencies need to be explained.

WRITTEN AND TAPED STATEMENTS FROM WITNESSES AND VICTIMS

When possible, get any audiotape associated with transcribed interviews from witnesses and victims. The flavor of what was said, as much as the content, is important in the review of this documentation for facts and inconsistencies. It is almost impossible to get a clear understanding of the nature of a conversation from a written transcript alone.

VICTIMOLOGY

This section is an edited out-take from: "National Guidelines for Death Investigation," Research Report 167568 (National Institute of Justice 1997).

The panel responsible for this document has done an excellent job of compiling and arguing for the inclusion of victim profile information in the medico-legal death investigation process. This author not only agrees with and applauds their effort, but would argue that these are appropriate guidelines for investigating victim inputs to cases that are to be profiled as well (it can be adapted for use in non-homicides).

See Chapters 9 and 10 for more information regarding the use of victimological inputs in the criminal profiling process.

NIJ: NATIONAL GUIDELINES FOR DEATH INVESTIGATION
Section E (abbreviated): Establishing and Recording Decedent Profile Information

1. DOCUMENT THE DISCOVERY HISTORY

Establishing a decedent profile includes documenting a discovery history and circumstances surrounding the discovery. The basic profile will dictate subsequent levels of investigation, jurisdiction, and authority. The focus (breadth/depth) of further investigation is dependent on this information.

For an investigator to correctly document the discovery history, he/she should:

A Establish and record person(s) who discovered the body and when.

B Document the circumstances surrounding the discovery (who, what, where, when, how).

The investigator must produce clear, concise, documented information concerning who discovered the body, what are the circumstances of discovery, where the discovery occurred, when the discovery was made, and how the discovery was made.

2. DETERMINE TERMINAL EPISODE HISTORY

Pre-terminal circumstances play a significant role in determining cause and manner of death. Documentation of medical intervention and/or procurement of ante-mortem specimens help to establish the decedent's condition prior to death.

In order for the investigator to determine terminal episode history, he/she should:

A Document when, where, how, and by whom decedent was last known to be alive.

B Document the incidents prior to the death.

C Document complaints/symptoms prior to the death.

D Document and review complete EMS records (including the initial electrocardiogram).

E Obtain relevant medical records (copies).

F Obtain relevant ante-mortem specimens.

Obtaining records of pre-terminal circumstances and medical history distinguishes medical treatment from trauma. This history and relevant ante-mortem specimens assist the medical examiner/coroner in determining cause and manner of death.

3. DOCUMENT DECEDENT MEDICAL HISTORY

The majority of deaths referred to the medical examiner/coroner are natural deaths. Establishing the decedent's medical history helps to focus the investigation. Documenting the decedent's medical signs or symptoms prior to death determines the need for subsequent examinations.

The relationship between disease and injury may play a role in the cause, manner, and circumstances of death.

Through interviews and review of the written records, the investigator should:

A Document medical history, including medications taken, alcohol and drug use, and family medical history from family members and witnesses.

B Document information from treating physicians and/or hospitals to confirm history and treatment.

C Document physical characteristics and traits (e.g. left-/right-handedness, missing appendages, tattoos, etc.).

Obtaining a thorough medical history focuses the investigation, aids in disposition of the case, and helps determine the need for a post-mortem examination or other laboratory tests or studies.

4. DOCUMENT DECEDENT MENTAL HEALTH HISTORY

The decedent's mental health history can provide insight into the behavior/state of mind of the individual. That insight may produce clues that will aid in establishing the cause, manner, and circumstances of the death.

The investigator should:

A Document the decedent's mental health history, including hospitalizations and medications.

B Document the history of suicidal ideations, gestures, and/or attempts.

C Document mental health professionals (e.g. psychiatrists, psychologists, counselors, etc.) who treated the decedent.

D Document family mental health history.

Knowledge of the mental health history allows the investigator to evaluate properly the decedent's state of mind and contributes to the determination of cause, manner, and circumstances of death.

5. DOCUMENT SOCIAL HISTORY

Social history includes marital, family, sexual, educational, employment, and financial information. Daily routines, habits and activities, and friends and associates of the decedent help in developing the decedent's profile. This information will aid in establishing the cause, manner, and circumstances of death.

When collecting relevant social history information, the investigator should:

A Document marital/domestic history.

B Document family history (similar deaths, significant dates).

C Document sexual history.

D Document employment history.

E Document financial history.

F Document daily routines, habits, and activities.

G Document relationships, friends, and associates.

H Document religious, ethnic, or other pertinent information (e.g. religious objection to autopsy).

I Document educational background.

J Document criminal history.

Information from sources familiar with the decedent pertaining to the decedent's social history assists in determining cause, manner, and circumstances of death.

RESULTS

An equivocal forensic analysis provides information regarding the strengths and weaknesses of the physical evidence that may or may not establish the following types of evidence relationships to a criminal investigation. The profiler must therefore be trained as a forensic scientist. But they must also learn to work closely with reconstruction criminalists, forensic pathologists, and other forensic scientists as one person cannot possibly interpret all of the evidence in a case for themselves.

The following list is adapted liberally from *Forensic Science: An Introduction to Criminalistics* by Lee, Gaensslen, and DeForest (1983), as well as concepts taken from Saferstein's (1998) *Criminalistics*. They agree that the aim of forensic science in every investigation is to provide useful information that helps make the facts of the case clear. In general, these are the types of evidence to behavior relationships that can be established with competently recognized, documented, collected, analyzed, and reconstructed physical evidence.

CORPUS DELICTI

The *corpus delicti*, literally translated as the "body of the crime," refers to those essential facts that show a crime has taken place.

To establish the crime of burglary, for instance, a forensic analysis of the crime scene for physical evidence could include searching for items of evidence such as, but not limited to:

- toolmarks and fingerprints at the point of entry;
- broken doors or windows;
- glass in the burglar's shoes and pants from broken glass at the scene;
- ransacked rooms;
- missing valuables;
- footwear impressions on the ground outside of the residence at the point of entry.

To establish a rape or sexual assault, however, a forensic analysis of the crime scene for physical evidence could include searching for items of evidence such as, but not limited to:

- the victim's blood at the crime scene;
- the rapist's semen/sperm in the victim's orifices;
- a weapon with transfer evidence of some kind;
- wound patterns on the victim;
- torn pieces of victim clothing;
- fibers from ligatures used by the rapist to bind the victim;
- hair/fibers from the victim in the rapist's vehicle;
- the rapist's pubic hair on the victim.

MODUS OPERANDI

All criminals have a *modus operandi* (or MO; Method of Operation) that consists of actions and behaviors committed that were necessary to complete the crime. Sometimes this MO is somewhat consistent, but often it grows and changes over time as the offender becomes more skillful, including what has been successful, excluding what has been unsuccessful (see Chapter 13) (Geberth 1996). Physical evidence can help establish that MO.

To establish the MO in the crime of burglary, for instance, a forensic analysis of the crime scene for physical evidence could include searching for items of evidence such as, but not limited to:

- tools used to gain entry (screwdriver, hacksaw, keys to the front door, etc.);
- types of items taken (valuables vs. impulse items, cash, jewelry, credit cards, sport memorabilia, clothing, etc.);
- lack of fingerprints at the point of entry, suggesting a gloved offender. [5]

[5] A very important but often overlooked concept in the documentation of physical evidence is Negative Documentation. This means simply making a record of what was not present. For example, documenting the lack of injury to a victim who has been raped, or documenting the lack of items stolen when a home has been broken into.

A profiler must learn to appreciate and examine the reasons behind those behaviors that occurred, as well as those behaviors that did not.

Figure 6.3

Female victim's clothing. Victim was made to completely undress at a remote, outdoor location (including her boots and socks), most likely to prevent her escape. The victim was raped, with semen found in her anus, vagina, and mouth. She was found shot to death nearby.

To establish the MO in the crime of rape, for instance, a forensic analysis of the crime scene for physical evidence could include searching for items of evidence such as, but not limited to (see Figures 6.3 and 6.4):

- the type of restraints used on the victim, from fiber and wound pattern evidence, if any;
- tire marks nearby suggesting the type of vehicle used, if any;
- wound patterns on the victim indicating a type of weapon used (i.e. incision marks from a knife or bitemarks on the victim's back);
- tape found on the victim's person used to cover the eyes or the mouth.

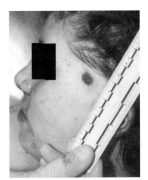

Figure 6.4

Female victim from previous case. Close-up of gunshot entrance wound to victim's face, just below the left temple. Victim was shot with a .357 handgun.

SIGNATURE ASPECTS

Some criminals demonstrate crime scene behaviors that can be called *signature behaviors*. They consist of actions committed that were not necessary to commit the crime (Geberth 1996) (see Figure 6.5). This is a more static presentation of behaviors by the offender, as they establish the theme of the crime and are committed to satisfy the rapist's psychological and emotional needs (see Chapter 14). Physical evidence can help establish those signature behaviors.

To establish signature behaviors in the crime of burglary, for instance, a forensic analysis of the crime scene for physical evidence could include searching for items of evidence such as, but not limited to:

- slashing the clothing in the closets;
- ejaculation, urination and/or defecation in specific locations;
- stealing female undergarments;
- furniture destruction;
- vandalization of vehicles in the garage.

To establish the signature behaviors in the crime of rape, for instance, a forensic analysis of the crime scene for physical evidence could include searching for items of evidence such as, but not limited to:

- type of ligature used;
- specific sequences of sexual acts;
- level of injury to the victim (from minimal to brutal);
- specific type of weapon used;
- personal items taken from the victim not related to theft, such as identification, clothing or inexpensive jewelry.

Figure 6.5

Picture of a victim's coat laying on a gravel road, a few yards from the victim's vehicle. The offender placed the coat on the ground, forced her to lay down on it, and then proceeded to rape her. This act provided some physical comfort for the victim's backside, as the offender had forced her to get undressed after forcing her from her vehicle. This was something that the offender did not have to do, and in the context of the attack was part of a reassurance-oriented aspect.

LINKING THE SUSPECT TO THE VICTIM

Blood, tissue, hair, fibers, and cosmetics may be transferred from a victim to an offender. Furthermore, items found in the possession of the suspect can be linked back to the victim. Examples include:

- the victim's vaginal epithelial cells dried onto an offender's penis or clothing;
- the victim's skin cells and hairs on a piece of rope in an offender's vehicle;
- the victim's blood on an offender's knife;
- the victim's artificial nails broken off during a struggle and left in an offender's vehicle.

It is also possible that trace evidence can be transferred from a perpetrator onto a victim. Suspect's belongings and clothing should be examined thoroughly for this type of trace evidence. Victims and their belongings, of course, should be similarly examined.

LINKING A PERSON TO A CRIME SCENE

This linkage is a common and significant one provided by physical evidence analysis. Fingerprints and glove prints, blood, semen, hairs, fibers, soil, bullets, cartridge cases, toolmarks, footprints or shoe prints, tire tracks, and objects that belonged to the criminal are examples of deposited evidence (Lee 1994).

Depending on the type of crime, various kinds of evidence from the scene may be carried away. Stolen property is the most obvious example, but two-way transfers of trace evidence can be used to link a suspect, a victim, or even a witness, to a crime scene.

DISPROVING OR SUPPORTING A WITNESS' TESTIMONY

Physical evidence analysis can indicate conclusively whether a person's version of a set of events is credible or whether the person is being deceptive. A simple example would be a driver whose car matches the description of a hit-and-run vehicle. An examination of the car may reveal blood and other tissue on the underside of the bumper. The driver may explain the findings by claiming to have hit a dog. A simple species test on the blood could reveal whether the blood was from a dog or from a human.

IDENTIFICATION OF A SUSPECT

The most conclusive evidence for individuating and identifying a suspect includes fingerprints, bitemark evidence and some kinds of DNA.

A fingerprint found at a scene, or on a victim's skin or possessions, and later identified as belonging to a particular person, results in an unequivocal identification of that person. The term identification as used here really means "individualization." [6]

[6] The identification of a suspect's DNA, or fingerprints in a scene does not by itself suggest guilt. It puts them in the scene. A bloody fingerprint, with the victim's blood, puts them there while the victim was bleeding; DNA from sperm in a vagina evidences sexual contact but not necessarily rape.

The point is that the meaning of evidence and behaviors must be assessed in the context of other evidence of other behaviors. Out of context, evidence is not as meaningful and the intent of behavior is not knowable.

This is why bitemarks are my favorite type of evidence: they can place a specific person, committing a specific behavior on a specific victim.

In rape/sexual assault cases, DNA from the rapist can be used to make an identification from the following sources (not by any means an exclusive list):

- sperm left behind at the scene or on the victim;
- blood left behind at the scene from injuries inflicted by the victim;
- tissue collected beneath the victim's fingernails, during defensive activity.

In rape/sexual assault cases, bitemark evidence from the rapist can be used to make an identification from the following sources (not by any means an exclusive list):

- bitemarks inflicted on the victim's back during the victim's struggle, to make them compliant;
- bitemarks made to victim's genital areas as part of the sexual attack;
- bitemarks made to the victim's face and extremities as a part of a punishment (child abuse).

PROVIDING INVESTIGATIVE LEADS

Physical evidence analysis can be helpful in directing an investigation along a productive path. In a hit-and-run case, for example, a chip of paint from the vehicle can be used to narrow down the number and kinds of different cars that may have been involved.

In a rape/sexual assault case, DNA evidence can be used to quickly exclude suspects as they are generated. And bitemark evidence can be used to generate suspects if submitted to local area dental organizations (when feasible).

REFERENCES

DeForest, P., Gaensslen, R. and Lee, H. (1983) *Forensic Science: An Introduction to Criminalistics*, New York: McGraw-Hill, Inc.

Geberth, V. (1996) *Practical Homicide Investigation*, 3rd edn, New York: CRC Press.

Horvath F. and Meesig, R. (1996) "The Criminal Investigation Process and the Role of Forensic Evidence: A Review of Empirical Findings," *Journal of Forensic Sciences* 41 (6): 963–9.

Lee, H. (1994) *Crime Scene Investigation*, Taiwan: Central Police University.

National Institute of Justice (1997) *National Guidelines for Death Investigation*, Research Report 167568, Washington DC:NIJ.

Saferstein, R. (1998) *Criminalistics: An Introduction to Forensic Science*, 6th edn, Upper Saddle River: Prentice Hall.

CHAPTER 7

AN INTRODUCTION TO CRIME RECONSTRUCTION

W. Jerry Chisum, B.S.

Shallow men believe in luck...

Strong men believe in cause and effect.

(Emerson, *Representative Men* 1850)

WHAT IS CRIME RECONSTRUCTION?

Reconstruction is the determination of the actions surrounding the commission of a crime. This may be done by using the statements of witnesses, the confession of the suspect, the statement of the living victim, or by the examination and interpretation of the physical evidence. Physical evidence is the material that is left, disturbed, or taken from the scene by any of the participants. Some refer to this process as crime-scene reconstruction, however the scene is not being put back together in a rebuilding process, it is only the actions that are being reconstructed.

To use a simple example, imagine a ball of clay. It is perfectly spherical except for a flattened area on one side. We theorize that the ball was dropped onto a flat surface causing it to become flattened. To test this theory we take several clay balls of the same diameter and weight and drop them from various heights. We then examine the flattened area on each. When we find one with a flattened area equal to that on the original, we postulate they were both dropped from approximately the same height.

Are there alternative solutions? Of course, the ball may have been molded that way in the first place. Could it have been pressed with a flat object? No, it would cause two flat sides – we can try this experiment to show this result. Could the area have been cut off? We can examine the surface of the clay to determine whether or not there has been a surface change. We can imagine several different ways of cutting – razor blade, laser, etc. However, each will change the surface characteristics.

To eliminate alternatives, we need to do experiments. If experiments about one part of the evidence cannot determine which alternative is correct, then we must expand our experiments to other parts of the evidence or we need to research the background of the subject. In the above simplified example, we have two alternative solutions. One, the ball was made the way we found it; the other that it fell from a determined distance. To eliminate one of the alternatives we could examine the flat surface where the ball was found. We could place pre-flattened balls on the surface and we could drop spherical balls from the predetermined height to the surface. We then determine if we can see a difference in the amount or type of residue remaining when the balls are removed. We may even leave the balls on the surface to determine if the time in contact makes a difference. We then look back at the original surface to see which of our experiments reproduces the characteristics we find.

When we are left with only one alternative then we conclude our hypothesis must be true. Or, as stated by Sherlock Holmes, "Eliminate all other factors, and the one which remains must be the truth" (Sherlock Holmes explaining his methods to Dr Watson in *The Sign of Four*, A. Conan Doyle, 1888).

The method described above is called the scientific method. We make an observation; we theorize or state a hypothesis; we conduct experiments, which support or negate our hypothesis; we conclude our hypothesis is true when the experiments support it. The problem is designing the correct experiments; we must be able to identify alternative solutions and design the experiments to distinguish between the various hypotheses without letting our personal biases and prejudices favor one or the other. While we try to be objective, we must recognize that there are factors that we do not realize are present, which influence our decisions. As stated by Thomas S. Kuhn (1997) "Subjective criteria, such as 'individual biography and personality,' play an overwhelming role in scientific decision-making". We are not able to completely eliminate these "subjective criteria" from our thought processes, but we must be aware that they are present.

Hans Gross (1924) stated that we need to observe everything and determine the reasons for what happened as a consequence. He felt that all of our life experiences gave us an opportunity to gain knowledge about cause and effect. A reconstruction analyst must observe the effects and extrapolate the causes. The problem is that, when expanded, an incident of human behavior becomes a challenging puzzle. As stated by archeologists Scott and Conner (1997):

> Reconstructing human behavior from physical evidence is a multidimensional jigsaw puzzle. Pieces of the puzzle are missing, damaged, and some are even camouflaged. The puzzle pieces come in seemingly incompatible data types – some are visual, some are in such microscopic form that it takes days of specialized analysis to show their existence and in some cases the evidence is intangible, such as oral testimony. But practitioners of these two disciplines, each for totally different reasons, sit at their desks and doggedly persist in completing these puzzles – archeologists and forensic scientists.

In detective novels, the homicide detective reconstructs the crime and deduces the guilty person. However, in actuality, the homicide detective seldom has the scientific background necessary to build the reconstruction. For the majority of detectives, the use of physical evidence is secondary to the interview and interrogation of the witnesses and suspects. The understanding of the meaning of the laboratory analyses in light of the behaviors of the participants requires a basic knowledge of the sciences involved.

Most laboratory forensic scientists have become too specialized to tie the observations together. They lack the multi-disciplinary overview of a criminalist to be able to see the links between several different observations. The emphasis in forensic science is towards the specialist; the crime lab that does not routinely send criminalists to the crime scene will not develop the necessary skills to do reconstruction analysis. The value of the evidence for reconstructive purposes lies in its location. The pattern of a bloodstain tells more about what happened than can possibly be gained by analyzing the DNA. Additionally, crime-lab administrators do not encourage the development of understanding human behavior by sending criminalists to classes on investigation, interview techniques, or other classes outside of their primary specialties. Without at least a basic understanding of human behavior, the scientist will not be able to reconstruct.

Identification technicians, the persons assigned to fingerprinting, photographing, and collecting evidence, are seldom asked their opinions about a crime. They are expected to only do their assignments. Joe Peterson found, in 1973, that interest in a case was not an acceptable behavior. Interviews with students working as ID technicians show that this is still the attitude they encounter. They are not encouraged to develop the skills necessary for reconstruction. The ID tech in a large department goes to more crime scenes than anyone else in the department. They cannot recognize evidence without making keen observations. As such, they are a potential source of information. However, since they are ignored at the scene and pressured to go from one scene to the next, they seldom develop investigative skills outside the technical aspects of their jobs.

District attorneys (DAs) have their own agendas. They want to convince the jury of the guilt of the defendant. However, the interpretation of the evidence does not always favor the prosecution. District attorneys, in preparation for prosecuting a case, put together a theory of the crime. They want to convince the jury of their theory, using whatever information is available. The less reconstruction done by the investigators, the more this role falls to the DA. Without the proper tools, this can have disastrous results.

Criminal profilers have realized they need to reconstruct the crime. To explain the behavior of the criminal they need to know what was done at the scene. The study of the crime scene holds many answers to the motives of the suspect, but only if the crime is understood. A few profilers have developed some degree of skill in this field even though they lack some of the science.

The talents of all the above are needed for a successful crime reconstruction. The people skills of the detectives, the scientific skills of a general criminalist, and the behavioral understanding of the profiler should be utilized in a team approach to the crime scene. The input of identification technicians and patrol officers responding to the scene fills in the gaps. The detective, criminalist, ID tech, and profiler must realize they have different skills and these skills are complementary. There should not be "turf" battles regarding criminal investigation. Attorneys brought in after a competent investigation and reconstruction will find their jobs easier.

WHEN SHOULD A CRIME BE RECONSTRUCTED?

A reconstruction should be undertaken when the actions and behaviors of the criminal give useful information to the investigation or to the adjudication process. Cases which do not seem to be going anywhere, "old and cold" cases, questionable death cases; all should have a reconstruction analyst examine the photos, sketches, and reports to determine if there is information that could be of value.

Example
An investigator asked for the assistance of a reconstruction analyst on a six-year-old double homicide of a man and his wife. The man was known to have dealt in cocaine and the crime was carried as a possible assassination by a dissatisfied client. No leads were ever developed in the case.

In examining the photos, the analyst noted that the wife was shot twice – once through the forearm into the chin, and once in the temple. One of the shots was with the gun in contact with the bed sheet. The blanket was pulled over the arm and the blood on the chest from the arm. The husband had been kneeling against the bed as determined by his position and the fact that his shirt and the bed-sheet were pulled, indicating he had fallen to his left after the shot in his right temple. The scene looked more like a murder-suicide by the husband. However, there was no gun present.

Careful examination of the photos showed a lamp cord looped around the husband's right wrist. It could not have been in this position with the man falling to his left without upsetting the lamp. The analyst suggested the gun had been removed by someone who did not want to touch the body.

With that information, the detective changed the direction of the investigation – he discovered that the son and a friend had found the bodies. The son went outside to await the police; the friend stayed inside to throw the cocaine and cutting supplies out the back window. Interviews of friends of the "friend" revealed that he had bragged about getting a gun from a "dead guy" about the time of the deaths. The case was closed; several weeks of investigation were wasted because careful observations and a simple reconstruction were not undertaken at the scene (see Figures 7.1 and 7.2).

Figures 7.1 and 7.2

Reconstruction should start before the first investigator walks into the crime. The investigator should gather information about anyone's theory about the case; whether it is a natural, accidental, suicidal, or homicidal death (NASH). This first theory starts the investigation. The next job is to determine what has been changed at the crime scene since the event. The first officer and the paramedics should be interviewed to determine what they did at the scene. Their duty is to public safety and the preservation of life – they cannot do their jobs correctly if they must take time to worry about details of physical evidence and crime scene preservation. The investigator must establish these changes to prevent misleading information at the scene.

In the following case example, criminalists and identification personnel were called to assist in the investigation of a stabbing.

Example
Upon arrival, they noted there were acceleration marks leading away from the entryway to the second story apartment. There were drops of blood and bloody shoe prints coming down the stairs – the bloodstains stopped near the acceleration marks. They carefully ascended the stairs, avoiding the bloodstains. The blood trail split

inside the door; to the right it led to a sink with blood on the faucet handle, to the left it led into the living room. They noted the disarray of the living room – there were food and beer cans spilled into the area in front of the TV. The coffee table was overturned, the lamp next to the TV was broken. There was a pool of blood between the overturned coffee table and the couch, and another bloodstain on the couch. There was a bloodstained knife on the bookcase near the front window.

Based on the signs of violence present at the scene, the detective had called the lab. They estimated six to eight hours of work to properly document and collect the evidence at this scene. However, the lead criminalist asked what the first officer saw. The first officer said he saw a man on the couch with a knife in his abdomen. He then proceeded to check the house for the suspect – when he returned, the paramedics were working on him so he went out to await the detectives.

The paramedics were called and asked what they had done. They said when they arrived they saw the man on the couch with a knife in his abdomen. They could not work on a soft surface so they had to move him to the floor. They could not put him on the floor as the coffee table was in the way. To move the coffee table they had to move the hassock, and the hassock knocked over the lamp. They pushed the coffee table; it turned over spilling the food and beer. They then picked up the patient and placed him on the floor. When they did, the knife came out of the man's stomach. Afraid they might put a knee on the knife, they put it on the bookcase. As they started to work on the patient, blood spurted out of the injury onto the arm of one of them, above his glove. He ran to the faucet and washed it off. As they carried the bleeding man down the stairs, the blood ran off the front of the stretcher onto the stairs. The paramedic at the rear stepped into the blood and caused the footprints. They put the man into the ambulance and rushed to the hospital – and they left acceleration skids.

This scenario illustrates that the scene is not always going to be as it was when the incident occurred. The reconstruction of violence at this scene was completely erroneous.

The investigator must determine what changes have occurred; making accurate notes so the original positions of items can be established. This information must be communicated to the reconstruction analyst. Some of these changes are predictable – these are used for reconstruction. Such changes are drying of blood, lividity, things that change according to natural laws (physics, chemistry, biology, etc.). Other changes are not predictable – such as the things done in the case above, or the damages caused by insects or animals.

WHEN SHOULD RECONSTRUCTION BE UNDERTAKEN?

Crime-scene reconstruction is of value when reconstruction is started at the scene during the initial phases of the investigation, during the investigation, and during the adjudication process. The reconstruction analyst may determine, while the interviews are being conducted, if the stories being told by the victims, witnesses, and/or suspects are true. By knowing the events as reconstructed, the detectives conducting the interviews may be able to detect deception or inconsistencies. The use of this knowledge can be a powerful tool in the hands of an experienced investigator.

The crime-scene reconstruction can also lead to further clues and evidence. For example, a bullet hole in the victim causes one to search the area for cartridge casings. Further, we would want to turn the body over to see if there is an exit, then we would look for a bullet. The direction of the bullet, in most instances, would be towards the other side of the victim from the casing. These are simple steps in a reconstruction that can end with the entire path of the bullet being elucidated, with the position of both the shooter and the victim determined.

By reconstructing the manner in which a person will behave, we can frequently find fingerprints and other evidence.

> Example
> A burglar came through the roof of a department store. He removed a panel from the ceiling and still had a 10-foot drop to the floor. The identification officer reasoned that if the burglar dropped from that height he probably would have put his hands on the floor to help cushion his fall. He dusted the floor in a 3-foot area directly below the hole. He found two complete handprints. His reconstruction led to the conviction of a previously successful burglar.

Frequently, cases may only be examined for reconstruction evidence during the preparation for trial. The prosecuting attorney may find problems in the progress of the activities leading to the crime. They ask for a reconstruction to aid them in preparing the case for trial. Sometimes they get an answer that is not consistent with their previous theory. Other times a reconstruction will aid them in describing to the jury what they intend to prove in the opening argument and in summarizing what they proved in their closing argument. The same applies to defense attorneys as well.

Not all crimes can be reconstructed at the scene. Many times the results of laboratory tests must be known prior to interpretation. For example, the bloodstains on the wall near a body may be cast-off from the weapon, but they may also be cast-off from the suspect who was also cut. Therefore, documentation of the scene must be as complete as possible incorporating photographs, sketches, measurements, videos, and notes to record as much detail as practical. The reconstruction analyst may have to rely upon those documents to show how the crime was committed. If the reconstruction analyst is not called to the scene, these documents are what the reconstruction must be based upon.

WHY RECONSTRUCT?

Reconstruction is not easy; not everyone is capable of formulating the logic. The good reconstruction analyst can, however, explain the reasoning in such a manner that people can understand and will think the solution is obvious. The question becomes then, "Why do we need to have someone reconstruct a crime?"

The most obvious and important reason is to prevent miscarriages of justice. For example, in the following case the sheriff was convinced that he had a murder.

Example

A woman ran to her sister's home to seek refuge from her abusive husband. When the husband came looking for his wife, the brother-in-law held a rifle and stated that he would shoot the husband if he "didn't behave." The husband was shot – he had a large hole in his chin and a small hole in the back of his neck.

The wife first said that the victim made a lunge at the gun that the brother-in-law was holding. She recanted the next day and stated that the victim was talking to her when, for no reason, her brother-in-law shot the victim.

A visit to the scene with the weapon and a "victim" of the same size, allowed us to show that the back shot was consistent with the evidence. However, when we considered the alternative, the evidence was just as consistent with a frontal shot.

Unfortunately, the doctor who performed the autopsy was not a forensic pathologist. He mistook particles of lead in a section of tissue from the neck as gunpowder. He also gave credence to the observation that the tissue of the neck was "tucked in." He was unaware that the Sheriff had put his finger into the wound and had passed a rod through the head, prior to the pathologist seeing the body. If fact, he had photographed the "angle of the shot" with the probe in place. Faced with these facts, the doctor gave no opinion as to direction.

The body was x-rayed between the funeral service and interment. The x-ray showed a cone of lead particles that radiated out from the chin. Some of the lead was at the back of the neck, over an inch from the hole. It was concluded that the bullet entered the chin and exited the back of the neck.

Another reason for reconstruction is to gain information about the participants and their activities. This can be used for investigative leads or for profiling. And, of course, reconstruction is done to show how a crime was committed. Attorneys need a reconstruction to aid in opening and closing arguments.

HOW TO RECONSTRUCT THE CRIME

To reconstruct, one must understand the role evidence plays. The same evidence may acquire different roles depending upon what is being done with it. Bloodstains, for instance, can be used to reconstruct some of the *actions* at the crime, but they also can be used to establish *who* shed the blood. We can break evidence into many different categories, however for reconstruction purposes we need to categorize the evidence according to its *role*.

Most evidence is collected with the thought that it will be used for identification purposes, or its ownership property. Fingerprints, DNA, bullets, casings, drugs, fibers, and safe insulation are examples of evidence used for establishing *source* or ownership. These are the types of evidence that are brought to the laboratory for analysis to establish the identification of the object and/or its source.

The same evidence at the crime scene may be the evidence used for reconstruction. We use the evidence to sequence events, determine locations and paths, establish direction or establish time and/or duration of the action. Some of the clues that are utilized in these determinations are *relational*, that is, where an object is in relation to the other objects or to the crime; *functional*, the way something works or how it was used; or *temporal*, things based on the passage of time.

Relational evidence has meaning by virtue of its location with respect to the position of other items. The position of cartridge casings combined with the bullet paths gives a "fix" on where the shooter was. The blood droplet under a piece of broken glass may show the glass was broken to stage a burglary. The "evidence" is far more valuable due to the location of these items than in the laboratory examinations.

The relational clues are destroyed when something is moved or collected without proper documentation. Referring again to the chapter by Scott and Conner (1997):

> The patterning of human behavior is key to the concept that the study of the spatial arrangement of artifacts can be used to infer the behavior from which they result. Because of this, the spatial context of artifacts, including their relationship with the natural environment, is more important than the artifact itself. Removing an artifact from its context destroys much of its potential to reconstruct human behavior.

The investigator that moves an object prior to the reconstruction is causing a loss of information that could have been of value due to its location.

Functional evidence is the term used to describe how things work. Even the human body can be considered functional evidence. It can move in certain ways without causing bones to be broken. The actions taken by the victim in responding to the aggression are functional.

Functional evidence refers to the operational condition of an item. The position of the safety on a gun at a suicide, or the number of cartridges present in the magazine may be the most important part of the evidence.

Example
An elderly man stated he went to bed early while his wife watched television. He said that he woke the next morning to find his wife missing. She was on the

living room floor with a shotgun and a bent coat hanger through the trigger. She was shot under the left arm.

When the shotgun was examined, it was found to be fully loaded. The husband confessed to shooting his wife. He forgot that we would check the "function" of the weapon.

Observation and examination of these evidence types provides the basis for reconstruction. However, there is one other classification of evidence: missing or inferred. The things removed from the scene by the suspect are also evidence and can be important to a reconstruction, however, we have to infer what they are by the space left where they were.

Having defined the evidence by the affect time and environment have on the interpretation, we now turn to the types of uses the evidence has in reconstruction:

1 sequential;

2 directional;

3 describes action;

4 defines location;

5 defines ownership;

6 limits the scene.

Sequential evidence aids by establishing the order of the events. The footprint on the tire-track shows the person was present subsequent to the vehicle passing.

Directional evidence aids in determining the actions at the scene. Blood spots with their tails in the direction of travel, the ricochet pattern left by a bullet, and the shoe print, are all examples that show where something was going and, conversely, where it was coming from.

Action evidence shows the motion or actions of the participants. These are sometimes the same as directional, such as blood drops, but can be things such as chips or indentations in a wall showing where items have been thrown, or something as subtle as the indentations in the carpet establishing the normal position of an item of furniture.

Position is established not only by the *location* of various items of evidence but also by their *orientation at the location*. A single fingerprint inside the passenger window could indicate the person was in the vehicle. However, if the fingerprint is pointed down, it may only mean that the person reached inside the glass to speak to the driver. The orientation of the toolmark on a door may show the "burglary" is really an insurance fraud.

Ownership or origin is usually established by laboratory examinations. Whose fingerprint? Blood? Footprint? Which tool? All are questions we are accustomed to having answered by the crime laboratory. The answers to these questions may be crucial to interpretation of the evidence at the crime scene.

Evidence that defines the scene is called *limiting evidence*. Some of these items are not thought of as evidence normally, but we record them on sketches, in photographs, and on video. Walls of a room are limits; the directional evidence may take us beyond the first set of walls into another area or room, for more of the scene or even to a second scene. Whether the walls are real or some artificial points established to keep others out of the scene, we must be ready to expand them if the scene has evidence that indicates another location. It is far easier, of course, to set the limits of the scene larger in the first place and to shrink them later.

The reconstruction analyst must endeavor to go to the scene, even if the crime is months or years old. The spatial relationships are difficult to visualize when only photographs are utilized. A very good sketch with detailed measurements, along with the photographs, can be used to render a three-dimensional model or computer drawing. These are aids in the visualization and may be utilized when there is no possibility of visiting the crime scene.

Sherlock Holmes said, "Eliminate all the alternatives, whatever is left, however improbable, is the truth." Where does the analyst look for alternatives? The first place to look is at the story told by the defendant. We have discussed how the defendant can be shown to be lying by the inconsistencies with the evidence in his story. We must however, prove that these are inconsistencies.

Example
Elmer and Edna had been out drinking heavily one evening. Soon after they left the bar, Elmer called the police to report that he had accidentally shot Edna. When the detectives arrived, Elmer showed them his semi-automatic .22 rifle and told them that Edna had teased him about being impotent, so he was going to commit suicide. She grabbed the gun and it went off, killing her.

His story sounds plausible, however Edna had been shot three times. One shot was in the center of the chest from about 18", one in the right side from about 12", and one in the lower back at about 6". The detectives decided that Elmer was lying, because "no one accidentally shoots someone three times!"

The identification technicians did an extremely thorough job of documenting the scene. This documentation allowed for a reconstruction without visiting the scene. The furniture and the body were arranged such that the only way she could have been shot at these close distances was from a location directly in front of her. In that position, the cartridge casings would be on the dresser to the shooter's right (victim's left). However, the casings were on the opposite side.

Why would the casings be to the left of the shooter? When someone is going to commit suicide with a rifle, they usually rotate it so that their thumb is on the trigger. If the rifle is pulled, it will be upside down, ejecting to the left of the shooter. If the thumb is twisted and caught in the trigger guard, trying to pull it out can cause the gun to fire more than one time.

> Examination of Edna's right sleeve revealed gunpowder flakes, consistent with her grabbing the gun. Unfortunately, no one thought to fingerprint the rifle barrel until it was too late.
>
> Elmer's story appears to be true; there is no evidence to disprove it. To the contrary, the evidence, particularly the location of the evidence, supports his story.

The point of this case is to not dismiss the defendant's story without subjecting the interpretation of the evidence to alternatives. The location of the casings needed to be factored into the solution. If the casings, location of the furniture, etc. had not been documented properly, this case would have resulted in a miscarriage of justice.

The stories presented by "witnesses" to the crime are also alternatives and, as such, should be tested against the physical evidence. There have been numerous studies demonstrating the unreliability of "eyewitnesses." Witnesses often begin to fill in the gaps of what they have seen, with what they have read or heard. Physical evidence does not change. Be cautious when interviewing witnesses to not fill in the gaps for them, by explaining the evidence to them.

The investigators at the scene frequently theorize about what happened. These theories, if incorrect, can lead them in the wrong direction. The crime should be submitted to reconstruction as soon as possible to test these theories.

The prosecutor seeks to convict the defendant by making the crime more heinous in nature. The defense seeks to exonerate the defendant. Both theorize about how the crime occurred with different objectives. Both cannot be correct and, lacking a reconstruction, both are probably wrong. The theories are alternatives and should be examined against the evidence.

When discussing alternatives, someone is bound to say: "Yes, we have to consider that an alien landed in the backyard and committed this crime." This is an imaginative alternative, which is dismissed immediately, however, the use of imagination to seek alternatives *is* legitimate. Brainstorming for alternatives with the entire homicide team is an approach that has proven valuable in the solution of many crimes.

Any theory of the crime must be based on logic – explaining the physical evidence *and its location* at the scene. It is through such analysis that the behavior of the perpetrator is revealed to the profiler, allowing an interpretation of the motivations and intent behind that behavior.

REFERENCES

Gross, H. (1924) *Criminal Investigation*, 4th edn, : 2.

Kuhn, T. S. (1997) *The Essential Tension, Objectivity, Value Judgment and Theory Choice*, : 320.

Peterson, J. (1973) Monograph on Crime Scene Technician.

Rynearson, J. and Chisum, W. J. (1997) *Evidence and Crime Scene Reconstruction*, 5th edn, Sacramento, C. A.: National Crime Investigation and Training.

Scott, D. and Conner, M. (1997) *Forensic Taphonomy*, Haglund and Sorg, Eds, Ch. 2, New York: CRC Press.

CHAPTER 8

WOUND PATTERN ANALYSIS

Brent E. Turvey, M.S.

In homicide cases justice may not be properly served unless meticulous attention to detail is observed. The smallest mark on the body may be of critical importance when all of the facts become known.

(Dr L. Sathyavagiswaran, *Deputy Medical Examiner and Procedure Manual*, 12th edn, Los Angeles County, California.)

Wounds sustained by a victim or an offender can be the result of intentional or accidental behavior on the part of either. They vary in severity, extent, and appearance relative to the amount of force delivered, the time over which force is delivered, the area of the body receiving force, and the characteristics of the object or weapon delivering force (DiMaio and DiMaio 1993). They are a physical manifestation of both behavior and motive, and are therefore a form of behavioral evidence.

Wound pattern analysis involves the recognition, preservation, documentation, examination and reconstruction of the nature, origin, and intent of physical injuries. Whether a case involves homicide, sexual assault, abuse, or any other act of interpersonal violence, wound pattern analysis can play a crucial investigative and reconstructive role. The recognition, preservation, and documentation of wounds will most commonly be found in reports and documentation made by medical personnel in cases of sexual assault and abuse, or in reports and documentation made by the coroner or medical examiner in cases where a death has occurred. Due to the widely varying levels of training and expertise of those involved at this stage, an equivocal forensic analysis of all wound documentation is urged for missed, and misinterpreted, wound patterns.

For the purposes of this book, we will be focusing primarily on wounds associated with violent interpersonal crime. This is done with the full awareness that other criminal and non-criminal events can result in a wide range of injuries beyond what will be discussed here.

GENERAL GUIDELINES

- Wound pattern analysis relies upon competently, thoroughly documented injuries, as well as the same for the environments in which any injuries occurred. This should also include negative documentation, or a record of areas where no injuries exist on a subject, and of associated environments which are believed to contain none of the items responsible for injury.

- It is useful to perform wound pattern analysis not only on victims, but also on offenders, and suspected offenders.

- It is important not to interpret wounds, or any behavior, in a fact vacuum. A wound should be examined and interpreted in the context of the event in which it occurred (as part of a particular history, as part of an environment, and as part of a sequence of events).

- It is important to establish whether an injury was inflicted ante-mortem, peri-mortem, or post-mortem.

- It is important to establish the origin of an injury. What likely caused it and how, and what behavior(s) that it may represent. This means extensive training and experience in different types of wound pattern analysis.

- One person cannot be expected to recognize every form of wound pattern in existence, no matter how well trained or experienced. It is advised that multiple forensic disciplines be involved in any analysis involving extensive, complex, and/or questioned injury patterns. This provides multiple perspectives and experience bases in order to reduce the possibility of overlooking or misinterpreting wound patterns [1].

- It is important to establish the motivation, or, intent of an injury in its context. That means determining whether or not the injury was accidental or intentional. If it was intentionally caused, then we need to further examine it and try to understand what the person inflicting the injury believed they would accomplish by doing so. Again, this cannot be done reliably out of the context of an event, and in the absence of thorough histories.

- Wound pattern analysis is reliant upon physical evidence. Physical evidence may be concealed, poorly documented, undocumented, lost, or otherwise unavailable. Therefore competent and certain conclusions regarding origin, intent, and motivation may not always be possible. The certainty of all conclusions regarding wound patterns should be commensurate with the known facts of the case.

[1] Even the most well trained forensic scientist, arguably a Board Certified Forensic Pathologist, is capable of overlooking and/or misinterpreting wound patterns.

The reason for this will commonly be stated as: "I did not see it because I wasn't looking for it." The actual reasons may include distraction, investigative bias, or lack of familiarity with a certain type or constellation of wound patterns.

Most often the reason is, in my opinion, investigative bias. Forensic pathologists often fall into the habit of not visiting death scenes first hand, and may rely upon law-enforcement investigators to tell them what occurred and how. This is an enormous mistake and results in all kinds of problems, not just those relating to wound pattern analysis.

For specific texts devoted in part or whole to the concepts and procedures involved in the major types of wound pattern analysis, the author strongly recommends that readers reference the following textbooks:

- Adelson, L. (1974) *The Pathology of Homicide*, Springfield, Ill: Charles C. Thomas, Pub.
- DiMaio, D., and DiMaio, V. (1993) *Forensic Pathology*, Boca Raton: CRC Press.
- DiMaio, V. (1993) *Gunshot Wounds: Practical Aspects of Firearms, Ballistics, and Forensic Techniques*, Boca Raton: CRC Press.
- Geberth, V. (1996) *Practical Homicide Investigation*, 3rd edn, Boca Raton: CRC Press.

- Gresham, G. A. (1975) *Color Atlas of Forensic Pathology*, Chicago: Year Book Medical Publishers.

- Hazelwood, R., Burgess, A. and Dietz, P. (1983) *Autoerotic Fatalities*, Lexington, Mass: D.C. Heath & Co.

- Knight, B. and Simpson, K. (1985) *Forensic Medicine*, 9th edn, London, UK: Edward Arnold Publishers, Ltd.

- Monteleone, J. (1996) *Recognition of Child Abuse for the Mandated Reporter*, 2nd edn, St. Louis: G.W. Medical Publishing, Inc.

- Vanezis, P. (1989) *Pathology of Neck Injury*, Somerset, UK: Butler & Tanner Ltd.

- Whelan, M. (1997) *Color Atlas of Sexual Assault*, Mosby: New York.

TYPES OF WOUNDS

The first thing to establish when examining any wound, after it has been thoroughly documented (measured, photographed in context, photographed with and without a scale, etc.) is what type of wound it is. For that we need to have the right language at our disposal. Descriptors for wounds are very specific in their meaning, having a basis primarily in medical terminology. The following is a list of general wound types adapted from DiMaio and DiMaio (1983). It is not an all-inclusive or detailed list, but rather a cursory overview for readers to begin familiarizing themselves with the language of wounds.

For more complete information regarding the precise interpretation of wound patterns, readers are again admonished to reference the recommended texts above.

BLUNT FORCE TRAUMA

These are divided into the categories of:

- *Abrasions*. An excoriation, or circumscribed removal of the superficial layers of skin, indicates an abraded wound. Examples include ligature furrows where movement causes the skin to break and redden, and the long marks that can be left behind on a body from dragging it across a rough surface like concrete.

- *Contusions*. These are injuries (usually caused by a blow of some kind) in which blood vessels are broken, but the skin is not. They can be patterned (imprinted, not directional) and non-patterned. They include things like bruises and hemorrhages.

- *Lacerations*. These are torn or jagged wounds, and tend to have abraded and contused edges. They can be differentiated from sharp force injuries by the recognition of tissue bridging from one side of the laceration to the other (indicating shearing or crushing force).

- *Fractures* of the skeletal system. Focal fractures are the result of a limited amount of force applied to a localized area. Crush fractures are the result of a lot of force applied to a large area. Penetrating fractures are the result of a great deal of force concentrated on a small area.

BURNS

These include injuries caused by:

- direct exposure to open flame;
- contact with hot objects;
- radiated heat waves;
- scalding hot liquids;
- chemical burns;
- microwave burns.

SHARP FORCE INJURY

These are divided into the categories of:

- *Stab* wounds. These injuries are the result of being pierced with a pointed instrument. The depth of the injury into the tissue is usually greater than its width in the skin.
- *Incise* wounds (cuts). These injuries are the result of sharp instruments being drawn across the surface of the skin, even into the tissue, and are longer than they are deep.
- *Chop* wounds: These injuries are the result of heavy instruments with a sharp edge. They go deep into the tissue, can be associated with bone fractures, and can have a combination of incised and lacerated characteristics. Examples include injuries inflicted by axes, hatchets, machetes, swords, and meat cleavers.

GUNSHOT WOUNDS

The purpose of a firearm (rifle, handgun, or shotgun) is to deliver force from a distance with a single projectile or multiple pellets. These will generally arrive at a target with enough force to be either penetrating (entrance wound only) or perforating (entrance wound and exit wound). They include *entrance* wounds, which are divided into the categories of contact, near contact, intermediate, and distant. They also include *exit* wounds, and *atypical* entrance wounds (DiMaio 1993).

THERAPEUTIC AND DIAGNOSTIC WOUNDS

These are injuries inflicted by Emergency Medical Service (EMS) personnel during treatment. They include things like needle marks, various incisions and puncture marks, and even bruising caused by rough handling or transport. It is important, when interpreting wounds, to get a complete record of the activities of EMS personnel so that those injury patterns unrelated to crime-scene behavior between the victim and the offender can be separated out.

POST-MORTEM V. ANTE-MORTEM WOUNDS

An important, but often overlooked, behavioral consideration in wound pattern analysis is whether or not wounds were inflicted before, during, or after the onset of death. This is an involved, often imprecise, process that may require more than just examining the wound. If an injury was inflicted just before or just after death, it may not be completely possible to determine when it indeed occurred. Hence the use of the imprecise term *peri-mortem*.

- *Ante-mortem* wounds are those which occurred during the period before death. They tend to be associated with injuries that resulted in a lot of bleeding either internally or externally. When large vessels are broken ante-mortem, as in gunshot wounds or deep stab wounds, this might result in what is referred to as arterial spray, or arterial gushing. When smaller vessels are broken ante-mortem without perforation or penetration, as in wrist or ankle ligatures, there will be internal hemorrhaging into the surrounding cells.

- *Post-mortem* wounds are those which occurred during the period after death. They are commonly associated with very little or almost no bleeding from broken arteries and veins. This is not a hard and fast rule, as every injury has its own peculiarities.

Given the difficulty of interpreting whether certain wounds were post-mortem or ante-mortem, it is advised that multiple perspectives (ME, reconstruction criminalist, arson investigator, etc.) be involved in any case of equivocal wound analysis (where the precise nature and timing of a wound is questioned).

THE PHYSICAL ORIGINS OF WOUNDS

As already discussed, wound patterns originate from a variety of intentional and accidental sources. In some cases, the source may be readily apparent or inferred by the distinctive pattern of the wound, and the distinctive nature of the environment the wound was received in. In other cases, the source of wound patterns may not be so readily apparent. Injuries whose source is disputed, or where there is more than one potential source, may be referred to as *equivocal wound patterns*.

To approach the analysis of an equivocal wound, it is important to keep in mind all of the potential relationships in a crime scene. Crime-scene reconstruction in general, and wound pattern analysis and behavioral evidence analysis in specific, involve an appreciation of those relationships. They rely on the process of eliminating possibilities to understand the nature of a relationship in a given instance. To that end, consider that wound patterns are most often the result of the following Locardian evidence transfer relationships.

WEAPON TO VICTIM/OFFENDER

This refers to any item found in the crime scene (available materials), or brought to the crime scene by the victim or the offender, that is used for the purposes of administering force (see Motivational Origins of Wounds section below). Examples include:

- A rock used to strike a victim in the head that leaves behind lacerations, abrasions, and contusions.
- A gun used to shoot a victim that leaves behind a contact wound to the forehead.
- A kitchen knife used to ward off an attacker that cuts the attacker's forearm.
- A lamp cord used to bind a victim that leaves behind a flat, smooth ligature furrow around their wrists.
- A shirt collar used to control a victim that leaves behind material compression abrasions.

RESTRAINT TO VICTIM

A *restraint* is any item found in the crime scene, or brought to the crime scene, which is used to physically control, limit, contain, or restrict a victim. Among other things, restraints are used to make living victims more compliant, and less of a threat to the offender. They are also used to make deceased victims less unwieldy and more compact for transport. When the victim is compliant, unconscious, or dead, a restraint is likely to leave only a smooth transfer impression, or cause only minor reddening of the skin depending upon how tight it is. When the victim is noncompliant, combative, or attempting to evade an attack they will likely move around. This will cause movement of the restraint, and subsequently abrading and contusing of the tissue beneath and around the restraint. It can also result in multiple restraint wound patterns, again, depending upon how tight the restraint is and how much the victim moves around.

Examples include:

- A shirt collar pulled up around a victim's neck to control their movement that leaves a material compression abrasion.
- Handcuffs on a victim's wrists to keep their arms together in front or behind their back leaving a circular abraded and contused pattern.
- A victim's jeans pulled down around her ankles during a sexual assault to gain access to her sexual areas and also restrain her legs. Metal zippers or buttons can cause superficial lacerations on the thighs and calves; jean material can cause material compression abrasions on the ankles.
- A garrote placed around a victim's neck at the onset of a sexual assault that leaves an abraded and contused ligature furrow.

ENVIRONMENT TO VICTIM/OFFENDER

Environmental wound patterns can result from any item in the crime scene that was not taken in hand for use as a weapon, but which did come in contact with the victim/offender in such a manner as to cause an injury. That is to say, these items are simply a part of the scene and the fact that they caused wound patterns on a victim or an offender is an unintentional result of victim–offender behavior.

Keep in mind that crime scenes can be indoors, outdoors, or in a vehicle. The nature of any environments involved in a crime may be determinable by the nature of the wound patterns left behind. (Carpet patterns can suggest an indoor or vehicle scene somewhere; vegetative patterns can suggest an outdoor scene.)

Examples include:

- Carpet in a trunk that transfers a material pattern onto the skin of a nude, deceased victim during transport.
- Leaves in a field leaving their imprints on a body disposed of at that location.
- Drag marks left behind on skin from pulling a body across a gravel road.
- Lacerations and abrasions inflicted to the bottom of a victim's bare feet from running across rocks in an effort to escape captivity.
- Mosquito bites received by an offender while disposing of a body in an outdoor scene.
- Poison ivy received by an offender while attacking a victim in a wooded area.
- Trade names from raised lettering on products that come into forceful contact with the victim or offender.

VICTIM TO OFFENDER AND OFFENDER TO VICTIM

Person-to-person wound patterns result when a victim, or an offender, causes direct injury to the other using a part of their body as a weapon. Body parts can leave their own, distinctive wound patterns on another when used as a weapon during an attack. In addition, items worn on the body can be a defining part of the wound pattern and add not only to its recognizability, but to its distinctiveness as well.

Examples include:

- A fist used to punch a victim in the face causing a black eye.
- An open hand used to slap a victim's face causing a distinctive, hand-shaped welt.
- Fingers around a victim's throat which can leave distinctive abrasions and contusions in the skin from fingernails.
- A victim's own necklace or scarf caused to make distinctive compression patterns on the victim's neck as the result of manual strangulation.
- An offender punching a victim in the forehead while wearing a distinctively shaped ring, which leaves behind an equally distinctive wound pattern.

- An offender stomping on a victim's back, leaving behind a compression abrasion representative of footwear treads.

- A victim biting an offender on the arm during an attack, leaving behind a unique bitemark impression.

- An offender biting a victim on the shoulder to achieve compliance, leaving a unique bitemark impression.

THE MOTIVATIONAL ORIGINS OF WOUNDS

Once the nature and physical origin of a wound pattern have been determined, it may be possible to make an assessment as to the general motivation for inflicting that wound (the intent). Remember the assertion of Dr Wynne E. Baxter, from Chapter 1:

> The object of the inquiry is not only to ascertain the cause of death, but the means by which it occurred. Any mutilation which took place afterwards may suggest the character of the man who did it.

Wounds are the result of behavior involving the use of force. As behavioral evidence, wounds can help to suggest offender motive and intent, among other characteristics. The precise mechanisms for interpreting motive and intent, let alone physical reconstruction, tend to involve both science and art. When any professional opines as to the motivation or intent of a victim or an offender's behavior, based on wound patterns inflicted, or anything else for that matter, that professional is engaging in no small part in the fuzzy process of criminal profiling [2].

As already mentioned, some wound patterns are caused by the unintentional or unconsidered application of force. They can be the result of accidental behavior, or environmental elements. These are not grounded in, or reflective of, a functional (*modus operandi*) or psychological (signature aspect) need.

Other wound patterns can be caused by the intentional use of force. Planned or not, they are grounded in, and reflective of, functional and/or psychological needs. The types of intentional force most commonly found in criminal cases include the following.

[2] MEs, coroners, detectives, patrol officers, and psychologists are among the many whom have been allowed to opine, in court, often sometimes without demonstration of any relevant specialized knowledge, as to motive and intent based on injuries inflicted. When courts begin to realize that this is behavior evidence analysis, or criminal profiling, there may be some new restrictions placed on testimony.

Or it might open the floodgates.

DEFENSIVE FORCE

Defensive force is a term that should be used to describe physically aggressive behavior that is intended to protect the individual administering it from attack, danger, or injury. The application of this term to a behavior does not imply, by its nature, that the behavior was legally or morally justified. Rather it is meant to describe behavioral intent.

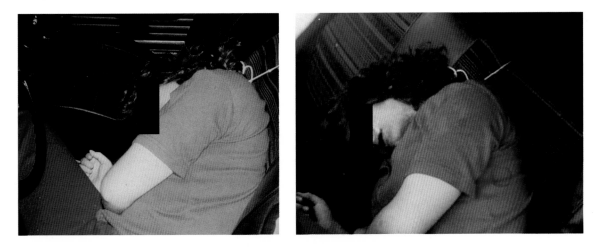

Deceased 15-year-old white female. Victim was abducted and driven in her own car to a location less than two miles away. She had been struck in the back of the head, raped anally and orally, then placed in her vehicle. The scene may have been intended to appear like a suicide at first blush (staged), to misdirect the investigation. She was discovered on the day of her abduction, locked inside her vehicle. Her own weight tightened the ligature (a white cord tied to the seat of the car) around her neck. She bore no defensive-type injuries.

Neck injuries on the victim from the photos above. Note the presence of deep fingernail marks below her chin, as well as a patterned abrasion running along the upper neck, consistent with having been made by some kind of material, such as the collar of her shirt. The ligature furrow itself is quite deep, as well as being abraded, which suggests active victim movement/ resistance at some point. Though it may appear otherwise, the skin was not broken anywhere along the ligature furrow. The dark, indented area of the furrow is where her neck was bent, folding over the knot in the ligature and causing the deep irregular pattern.

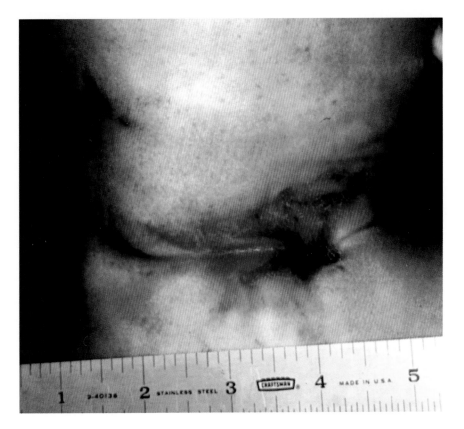

*Multiple petechial
hemorrhages over the face
and extensive petechial
hemorrhages over both the
palpebral and orbital
conjunctivae. The result of
sudden trauma associated
with ligature strangulation
(as opposed to hanging, which
was how she was found).*

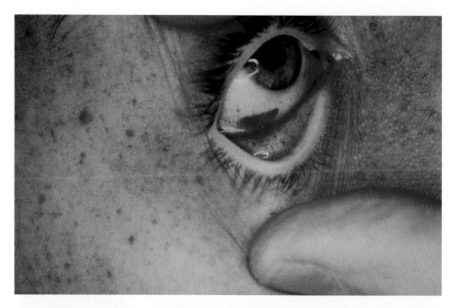

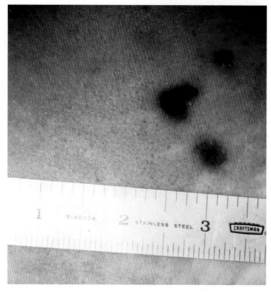

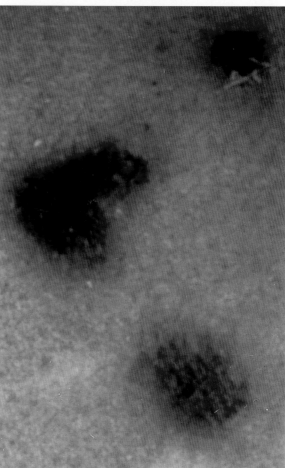

*Three injuries on the victim's posterior right shoulder, just above
the bra line. These compression abrasions are consistent with
having been caused by an offender's index, middle, and ring
finger during the application of coercive or controlling force.
Upon close examination of the injuries, a fabric pattern can be
seen in the abrasion. This pattern was likely to have been caused
by the material from the victim's shirt pressing between the
offender's fingertips and the victim's skin when this injury was
inflicted: this suggests that her shirt was on at the time.*

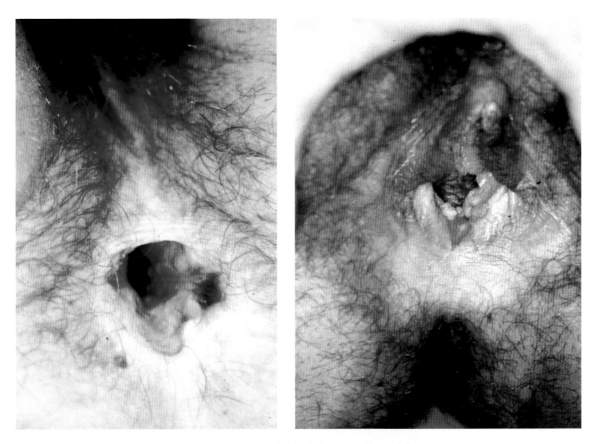

Examination of the victim's anus (left) and vagina (right) revealed similarly patterned lacerations. The author believes that a ring worn by the offender during forcible, digital penetration may have caused these injuries. The image of the anus clearly shows that it is gaping, which is quite common in the deceased, and by itself is not an indicator of sexual assault.

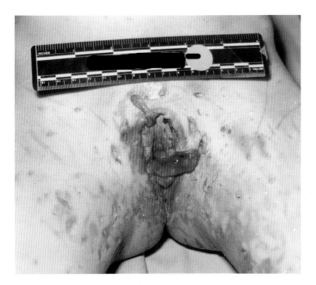

Emasculated genital area of a male child victim. A sharp instrument of some kind was used to perforate the edges of his sexual organs, and then they were removed.
The remainder of the groin area is marked by repeated sharp force injuries. These wounds evidence an anger, or retaliatory, aspect.

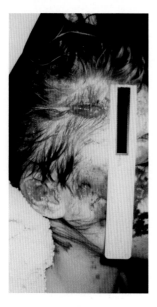

College age female victim of a rape-homicide. She was beaten, and assaulted vaginally and anally. The irregular pattern injuries shown were caused by a hammer. Her death was caused by injuries resulting from blunt force trauma to the head. The offender disposed of the victim's body in a river. The photos show her at autopsy, before cleaning (above), and then after some of her hair has been shaved to allow better discrimination of the wound patterns (right). Aside from the variety of injuries sustained from the hammer, note the row of contusions visible on the right side of the victim's neck, likely to have been caused by the offender's fingers or fingernails.

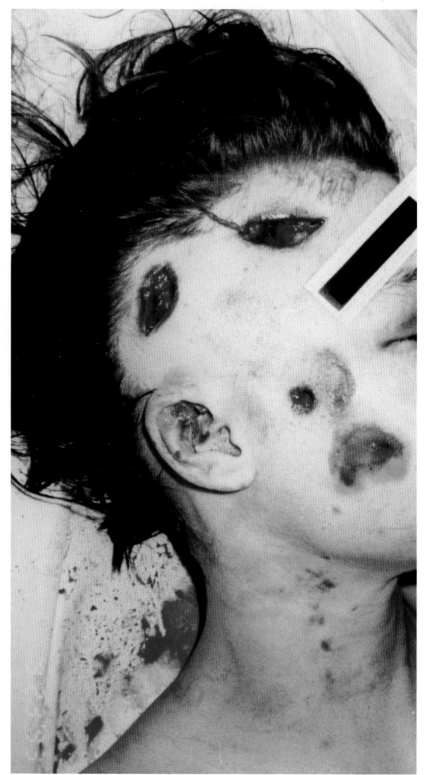

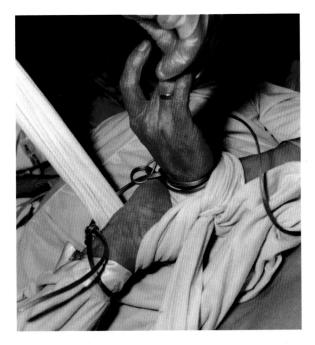

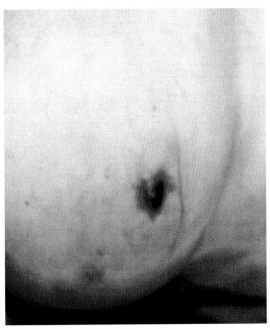

Older female victim. Found deceased in her home, hands bound behind her back with both telephone wire and the cloth belt from her robe. The offender used available materials to bind, sexually assault, and kill her. The cause of death was strangulation.

Breast of same female victim. Nipple has been removed by the offender. This injury appears to have been inflicted premortem, however it is unknown if it was inflicted while the victim was conscious.

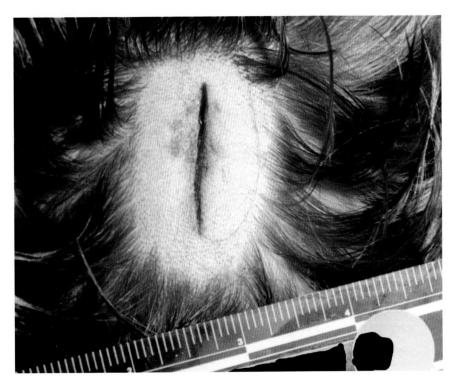

Top view of a victim's head. Laceration caused by blunt force trauma originally misinterpreted as a stab wound by the coroner. Close external examination alone quickly reveals multiple points of tissue bridging, which would not be the case for injuries inflicted with sharp force.

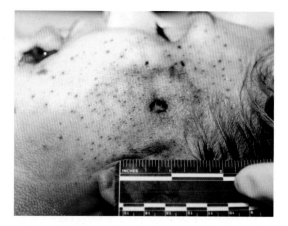

Gunshot entrance wound on the female victim of a domestic murder-suicide carried out by husband. Shows stippling, powder residue, and abrasion collar. This is the wife from the example given in Chapter 7, who also suffered a gunshot wound to the left wrist through to her chin.

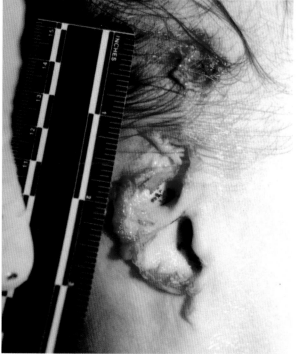

Photo of same victim from the right side showing exit wound and missing ear. Though the victim had only been dead a few hours, the family's 18-month-old kitten still had enough time to come in and devour the deceased woman's ear.

Photo of the bottom of a victim's foot. The irregular abrasions on the bottom of the foot are the result of walking around barefoot on gravel at an outdoor location. The victim was made to strip off all of his clothes, as well as his shoes and socks, partially as a precautionary act so that he could not run away. He was shot to death not long after. The black material covering the skin and autopsy table is fingerprint powder.

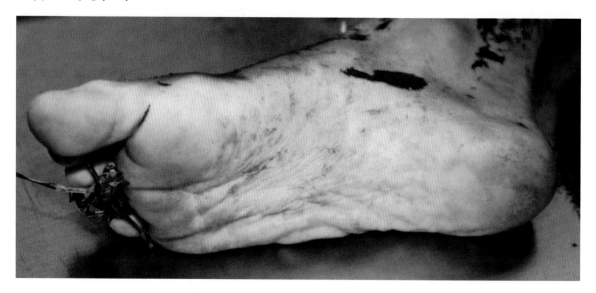

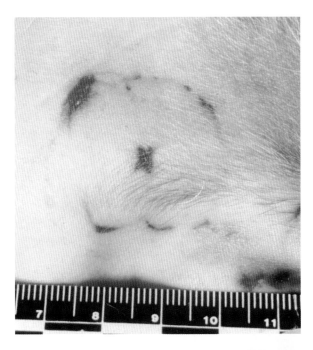

Human bite mark on the forehead and eye socket of an eight year old male victim. In July of 1997, this author was asked by defense attorney Daniel J. Stidham to prepare a criminal profile of a triple homicide case in West Memphis, Arkansas (see Appendix 3a). His client, Jesse Misskelly, had been previously convicted of the crimes in that case along with two other defendants, Jason Baldwin and Damien Echols. Among the recommendations made in the profile was that a forensic odontologist be asked to examine photographs of a particular area of one victim's face, as there appeared to be bite mark evidence that was not recognized and examined at the time of the first trial. As a result of that recommendation, the defense consulted with Dr. Thomas J. David, a Board certified Forensic Odontologist from Atlanta, Georgia. After careful examination, Dr. David determined that the above pattern was indeed a human bite mark. He then acquired dental casts from all three convicted defendants in the case for comparison with the unknown bite mark and was able to exclude them as contributors.

Rust-coated hunting knife found in a lake behind convicted defendant Jason Baldwin's home. This item was admitted into evidence in the West Memphis case. It was never determined by any expert to be consistent with wounds on any of the three murdered victims. There is also no demonstrable chain of physical evidence relating it to the case at hand.

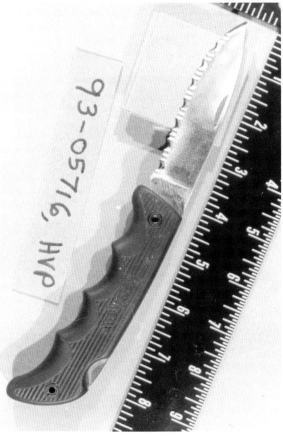

Serrated knife originally owned by John Mark Byers, step-father of victim Christopher Byers. Mr Byers gave this knife to a Home Box Office (HBO) film crew member that he had befriended, as a gift, while HBO was filming the trial in the West Memphis case for the documentary Paradise Lost, Produced by Joe Berlinger and Bruce Sinofsky. The crew member immediately handed this knife over to the authorities, and it was entered into evidence.

Sticks collected from the outdoor location close to the drainage ditch where the victims' bodies were found in the West Memphis case. Investigators returned to the scene many days after releasing it in order to collect these sticks. They were admitted as evidence and it was argued that they were used to inflict wounds on the victims. No hair or tissue were found on these sticks to associate them with victim injuries. No chain of evidence exists to confirm their origin or presence in the scene at the time of the murders. However, these unrelated sticks were shown repeatedly to the jury during the course of the trial as powerful visual "evidence" of the attack on the victims.

Drainage ditch in West Memphis, Arkansas, in woods near the Blue Beacon Truck Stop. The deceased bodies of three eight year old boys were found here on the afternoon of 6 May 1993. Crime scene personnel pumped water out of the ditch to facilitate the search for additional physical evidence.

Examples of defensive behaviors that leave behind wound patterns could include:

- A victim kicking an attacker in the groin in order to facilitate their own flee to safety.
- A victim shooting an attacker out of fear for their own safety, or the safety of another immediate victim.
- A victim biting an offender on the penis during the course of a sexual attack.
- An offender pushing a victim out of the way after they have kicked him in the groin.

PRECAUTIONARY FORCE

Precautionary force is a term that should be used to describe physically aggressive offender behavior that results in wound patterns which are intended to hamper or prevent the recognition and collection of physical evidence, and thwart investigative efforts.

Examples of precautionary acts that leave behind wound patterns include:

- Burning a victim's pubic area to destroy evidence of sexual assault.
- Chopping off a victim's hands and head to obscure future investigative efforts at identification.
- Inflicting misleading injuries to a victim, post-mortem, to mislead investigators into believing that an accidental or punishment oriented homicide by a family member was a sexual homicide committed by a stranger.

EXPERIMENTAL FORCE

Aggression is defined as hostile behavior that is intended to distress or in some way emotionally afflict others. The requirement here is an object that one is being aggressive towards, and in most cases this would be a living and conscious victim. *Experimental force*, then, is a term that should be used to describe behaviors involving force that fulfill non-aggressive, often psychological, and fantasy-oriented needs. It does not require a conscious or living victim.

Examples of experimental behaviors that leave behind wound patterns could include:

- Post-mortem evisceration of a victim's entrails.
- Post-mortem biting of a victim's breasts.
- Post-mortem removal of victim's breasts.
- Peri-mortem stab wounds of repeated, symmetric nature or of varying depths.
- Post-mortem or peri-mortem insertion of large foreign objects into victim's orifices.
- Violent ante-mortem sexual activity with a chemically (drugs or alcohol) unconscious victim.

CORRECTIVE FORCE

Corrective force is a term that should be used to describe physically aggressive offender behavior that is intended to admonish a victim for noncompliance or poor compliance to commands, and subsequently encourage their future compliance. This type of force is reactive in nature, and meant to let the victim know that what they are doing, or failing to do, is unacceptable and must change.

Examples of corrective behaviors that can leave behind wound patterns could include:

- Striking a victim in the back of the head with a firearm for failure to be forthcoming with valuables during a robbery.
- Punching a victim's breast for failing to remove their clothing as directed during a sexual assault.
- Slapping a victim very hard across the face for looking out from behind a blindfold during a sexual assault.
- Pushing a victim onto the ground from behind, for failure to increase their walking speed during an outdoor abduction.
- Biting a victim on the back of their shoulder to keep them from struggling during a sexual assault from behind.

CONTROL-ORIENTED FORCE

Control-oriented force is a term that should be used to describe physically aggressive offender behavior that is intended to manipulate, regulate, restrain, and subdue victim behavior of any kind. It is often found in combination with corrective force. It differs from corrective force, however, in that it involves behavior that is proactive in nature, done to control the victim directly. By itself, control-oriented force does not involve victim compliance without the hands-on involvement of the offender. In other words, by itself corrective force involves getting the victim to comply with commands. Controlling force involves "forcing" victims to comply.

Examples of control-oriented behaviors that can leave behind wound patterns could include:

- Violently tearing off a victim's bra when they fail to do so themselves during a sexual assault.
- Binding a victim's wrists behind their back with the belt from their own robe.
- Garroting a victim at the onset of an attack, and using it to steer them to a preselected site off a wooded trail in a sexual assault.
- Hog-tying a living victim, wrists to ankles with their own shoelaces, to immobilize them while the offender engages in other activities.

PUNISHMENT-ORIENTED FORCE

The differences between corrective force and punishment-oriented force are often subtle, and are not always recognizable. Like corrective force, punishment-oriented force tends to be reactive. The offender is repaying the victim for real or perceived wrongs. The defining characteristic of *punishment-oriented force*, however, is that it involves more physically aggressive force than is necessary to achieve victim compliance. Corrective force involves only as much force as the offender deems necessary in order to get the victim to follow commands. Punishment-oriented force, however, contains a retributive, retaliatory aspect that is not necessarily interested in victim compliance. Punishment-oriented force is about expressing rage. That rage may be a product of events that occurred in the crime scene, or in the offender's past.

Punishment-oriented force is characterized by brutal and short-lived levels of force that are reflected in extensive, severe wound patterns. In cases where brutal force is used, it is not uncommon for the victim to require hospitalization, or to die, as a result of the injuries inflicted. It must be made clear that homicide was not necessarily the desired result in such cases.

Examples of punishment-oriented behaviors that can leave behind wound patterns could include:

- Repeated lashings to a child with a belt.
- Beating the face of a victim with a rock, many times, during a sexual assault.
- Stabbing a victim many times in the chest with an ice pick as the result of a verbal altercation.
- Biting a child multiple times on the face and arms for soiling their diapers.
- Shooting a victim more times than is necessary to disable or to kill them, in a single event (this tends to involve expending all immediately available ammunition and can be indicated by reloading).

SEXUALLY-ORIENTED FORCE

Sexually-oriented force is a term that should be used to describe physically aggressive offender behavior that is intended to satisfy sexual needs. The best way to determine whether this is true for any particular behavior is to note whether it occurs in concert with traditional sexual behavior, with clearly eroticized behavior, in association with sexual materials, or in a sexual context. Though these things by themselves are by no means conclusive indicators.

It is also important to keep in mind that not every physically aggressive behavior associated with the traditional sexual regions of the body such as the vagina, anus, penis, breast, and mouth are intended to satisfy sexual

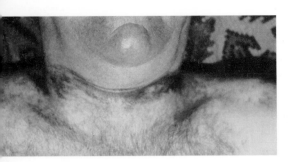

Figure 8.1

Ligature furrow with associated abrasions and contusions on the neck of a deceased 50-year-old male. The cause of this ligature pattern was the tightening of a weave-patterned black belt around the victim's neck from the rear by a sexual partner, during consensual sexual activity. The cause of death was asphyxia by ligature strangulation, but the victim's death itself was unintentional (accidental use of lethal force during sexual asphyxiation).

needs. They may involve the satisfaction of precautionary, experimental, control-oriented, and/or punishment-oriented needs. Each behavior must be evaluated in its own context to determine which needs are being satisfied (see Chapter 17) (see Figure 8.1).

Examples of potentially sexually oriented behaviors that can leave behind wound patterns could include:

- Repeatedly inserting a hammer handle into the anus of a conscious victim during a sexual assault.
- Repeatedly pinching a conscious victim's nipples with pliers and commanding them to scream during an abduction-sexual assault.
- Binding a victim with extremely tight leather handcuffs, and taking pictures of them in sexually provocative poses as part of an abduction-sexual assault.
- Sexual asphyxiation.
- Whipping a naked victim's breasts with a cord as part of a sexual assault.

LETHAL FORCE

Lethal force is a term that should be used to describe physically aggressive behavior that is primarily intended to result in death. By itself, it is distinguishable from punishment-oriented force in that it involves only the amount of force necessary to cause death. It does not have to involve overkill. So, punishment-oriented force can involve lethal force, and lethal force can have a punishment aspect, but they are not mutually inclusive or exclusive.

Examples of lethal-force behaviors that leave behind wound patterns include:

- Shooting a victim twice in the head at close range with a handgun.
- Cutting a victim's throat with a straight razor.
- Placing a plastic bag over a victim's head and tying it off, with no release mechanism.
- Ligature strangulation of a victim to dispose of them as a witness after a sexual assault.

Arguably, some of these lethal force behaviors could include a punishment or sexually oriented aspect, depending on their context.

GUIDELINES REGARDING BEHAVIORAL MOTIVATION

Do not forget that a single behavior involving the use of force can easily be described by more than one of these motivational categories as they are by no means exclusive of each other. There is no bright yellow line between them.

Also keep in mind that one weapon, object, or item may be used for any or all of the above-mentioned purposes. Interpreting the purpose for which a weapon, object, or item was used in a crime scene is dependent upon the nature, extent, and severity of the injuries inflicted with it (i.e. superficial v. overkill v. torture). It is also dependent upon the context of use (i.e. during a heated argument, over the course of a prolonged captivity, during the commission of a violent rape, etc.).

INVESTIGATIVE NOTE ON LIGATURES

This section is adapted from materials originally presented by this author in an article on homicidal ligature strangulation (Turvey 1996).

A *ligature* is anything that is used to tie or bind something. For our purposes, this term applies to cases where an assailant has placed a ligature around a victim's body (often the neck or parts of the extremities) and has tightened it for purposes of controlling, silencing, transporting, and/or killing the victim[2]. Commonly documented examples of ligatures include, but are by no means limited to:

- ropes;
- neckties;
- scarves;
- stockings;
- metal wires;
- shoe/boot-laces;
- necklaces;
- clotheslines;
- clothing;
- brassieres;
- belts;
- telephone wire;
- electrical cords.

[2] It is important to note that in cases of ligature homicide, where the ligature is tightened around a victim's neck, the mechanism of death is occlusion of the vessels supplying blood oxygen to the brain. The victim loses consciousness in between 10 and 15 seconds (DiMaio 1993).

When ligatures are suspected or alleged, begin the investigation with a surface examination of the victim's neck and extremities. It sounds simplistic, but there is a reason for specifically working from the body out to the rest of the crime scene in these cases. If the ligature is not immediately present (i.e. around the victim's neck, wrists, or ankles), the distinctive pattern of the ligature may tell investigators what kind of ligature to search for at the scene or at other connected scenes. Distinctive ligature patterns may also be used to tell whether purported devices could have caused the ligature pattern that the profiler is presented with (see Figures 8.2, 8.3, 8.4 and 8.5).

Figures 8.2, 8.3, 8.4 and 8.5
Body of male child bound wrist to ankle with shoe-laces. Buttocks covered with leaves, mud, and feces. Body was found in a drainage ditch, in shallow water. The victim was most likely killed at another location and then bound hand and foot for transport.

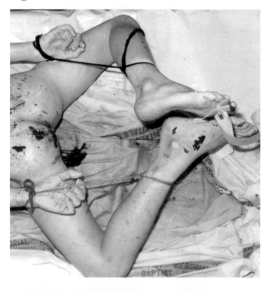

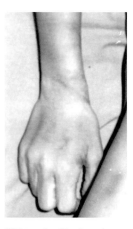

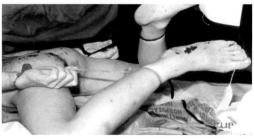

What should be recognized as a ligature-pattern abrasion on a victim's skin, also referred to as a ligature furrow, is sometimes best thought of in terms of what is not a ligature-pattern abrasion. Beware to exclude from recognition as ligature patterns the following post-mortem features (Vanezis 1989):

■ normal skin creases (especially infants and the elderly);

■ collar marks;

■ necklaces and other items found around the victim's neck, which leave marks during the decomposition process.

Wrist and ankles from the child victim that was discovered bound with shoe-laces. Shows ligature furrows without significant abrading or contusing, suggesting that the victim was no longer resistant after the ligatures were in place.

These should all be carefully distinguished from articles that were intentionally tightened around the victim's neck, body, or extremities by an assailant.

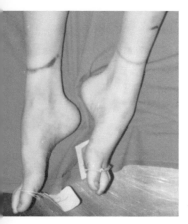

There are associated physical evidences of traumatic asphyxia, which can often be easily visibly identified in conjunction with ligature strangulation. Petechiae are often present on the victim. Because veins are normally at lower pressure than arteries, traumatic injuries from an offending force to the neck (i.e. ligature strangulation) cause an increase in venous pressure and an increase in capillary pressure that then causes damage to the inner walls of those capillaries. This damage produces minute points of bleeding which can be visible as pinpoint hemorrhages in the softer tissues. These minute points of bleeding are called petechiae (DiMaio and DiMaio 1993).

Look for scleral hemorrhage and petechiae in the eyes and insides of the eyelids. Also look for petechiae in the cheeks and neck at or above the ligature furrow. Another place to look for petechiae is inside the nostril on the nasal membrane. The nasal mucosa is often overlooked by even trained pathologists for presence of petechiae.

Petechiae are not to be confused with freckle-like Tardieu spots. These are seen in hanging cases as, with time, punctate hemorrhages occur due to hydrostatic rupture of the vessels from blood pooling in the forearms, hands, and legs. Petechiae are much more minute, and associated with the soft tissue areas in the neck and head.

Also possible, but not necessary, is a bloody discharge from the nose and mouth of the victim. The presence of such a discharge is indicative of some kind of trauma. Absence of such a discharge from the victim should not be given a great deal of investigative weight in either direction.

SPECIAL CONSTELLATIONS OF INJURIES

It is highly unlikely that a single wound pattern will point to a specific suspect. What is common, however, is for general constellations of associated injuries to indicate the need for investigative attention into a particular type of crime. These special constellations can act as red flags for the alert criminal profiler, and other investigators, when interpreting wound patterns and suggesting investigative strategy.

For our purposes, we are going to discuss the recognizable constellations of injuries associated with child physical abuse and other forms of domestic violence. While these special constellations of injuries are not proof positive of criminal activity, they are, again, investigative red flags and we are admonished to heed them.

DOMESTIC/CUSTODIAL ABUSE

The following is a combined list of injuries associated with child physical abuse, and other types of domestic violence taken from DiMaio and DiMaio (1993) and Monteleone (1996). The wound patterns and history associated with custodial abuse and domestic violence are often easily distinguishable. These are wound patterns that, if seen in concert with each other and documented over time, suggest the physical abuse of the victim. They do not suggest who is responsible. However, the investigative implication should be that persons with access to the victim, who are trusted by friends and family to give care or supervision, or who are in relationships with them, should be eliminated as suspects first. This means working first to exclude parents, siblings, caretakers, friends, extended family, and so on.

GENERAL TYPES OF INJURIES

- bruises/welts;
- contusions;
- lacerations;

- abrasions;
- ecchymosis;
- stab wounds;
- burns;
- human bitemarks;
- fractures (particularly of the nose and orbits and spiral wrist fractures);
- multiple injuries in various stages of healing.

UNEXPLAINED BRUISES AND WELTS

- on face, lips, mouth;
- on torso, back, breasts, buttocks, thighs, arms;
- in various stages of healing;
- clustered, forming rectangular patterns, reflecting shape of article used to inflict (example: electric cord, belt buckle);
- on several different surface areas;
- regularly appear after absence, weekend, or vacation.

UNEXPLAINED BURNS

- immersion burns (sock-like, glove-like, doughnut shaped on buttocks or genitalia);
- patterns like electric burner, iron, etc.;
- rope burns on arms, legs, neck, or torso;
- infected burns, indicating delay in seeking treatment.

INTERNAL INJURIES

- blunt trauma to the abdomen with injury to the liver, spleen, or other abdominal organs without an adequate history.

UNEXPLAINED FRACTURES/DISLOCATIONS

- to skull, nose, facial structure, ribs, or long bones;
- spiral fractures;
- corner or chip fractures of the long bones;
- fractures in various stages of healing;
- multiple fractures;
- old fractures.

UNEXPLAINED LACERATIONS OR ABRASIONS

- to mouth, lips, gums, eyes;
- to external genitalia;
- in various stages of healing.

HEAD INJURIES

- absence of hair and/or hemorrhaging beneath the scalp due to vigorous hair pulling;
- subdural hematomas, subarachnoid blood, or blood within the brain (due to shaking or hitting);
- retinal hemorrhages or detachments (due to shaking or impacting);
- jaw and nasal fractures.

COMPLAINTS OF

- pain in the absence of tissue injury;
- sexual assault with multiple injuries in various stages of healing and explanations by those injured that fail to account for the type or pattern of injuries sustained.

INJURIES DURING PREGNANCY

- vaginal bleeding;
- threatened abortion;
- spontaneous abortion.

PREVIOUS EMERGENCY ROOM VISITS FOR TRAUMA

The three most important parts of any investigation into a pattern of abuse are:

- history;
- history;
- history.

OTHER FACTORS TO CONSIDER WHEN ASSESSING INJURIES

- injuries inconsistent with medical history;
- injuries inconsistent with explanation for injury;
- injuries inconsistent with developmental abilities of the child to injure itself.

THE NATURE OF WOUND PATTERN ANALYSIS

As with any type of physical crime scene reconstruction, wound pattern analysis is partly science and partly art (Lee 1994). It requires not only rigorous methodology, but multi-disciplinary expertise. Above all, however, it is firmly grounded in the principles of scientific analysis and the Locard's Exchange Principle, which asserts that anyone, or anything, entering a crime scene both takes something of the scene with them, and leaves something of themselves behind when they leave (Saferstein 1998). Any victim, and the injuries that they suffer (or do not suffer), should be treated as an extension of that crime scene.

REFERENCES

DiMaio, V. (1993) *Gunshot Wounds: Practical Aspects of Firearms, Ballistics, and Forensic Techniques*, Boca Raton: CRC Press.

DiMaio, D. and DiMaio V. (1993) *Forensic Pathology*, Boca Raton: CRC Press.

Lee, H. (1994) *Crime Scene Investigation*, Taiwan: Central Police University.

Monteleone, J. (1996) *Recognition of Child Abuse for the Mandated Reporter*, 2nd edn, St. Louis: G.W. Medical Publishing, Inc.

Saferstein, R. (1998) *Criminalistics: An Introduction to Forensic Science*, 6th edn, Upper Saddle River: Prentice Hall.

Turvey, B. (1996) "A Guide to the Physical Analysis of Ligature Patterns in Homicide Investigations," *Knowledge Solutions Library*, www.corpus-delicti.com/ligature.html, Winter.

Vanezis, P. (1989) *Pathology of Neck Injury*, Somerset: Butler & Tanner Ltd.

CHAPTER 9

VICTIMOLOGY: PROFILING THE VICTIM

Brent E. Turvey, M.S.

Assessing the victimology of the deceased is standard operating procedure for any good homicide investigator. Many times the detective ends up learning more about the deceased than the victim knew about him or herself.

(Geberth 1996)

In the rush to examine a criminal's behavior, it is not difficult to become distracted by the dangling carrot of that criminal's potential characteristics and forget the value of understanding their victims.

Those with a beginner's interest in criminal profiling often raise the question of how emotionally taxing and intellectually challenging it is to see through the eyes of an offender. They have often been educated about profiling, sex crime investigation, and death investigation through the popular media and academic criminologists who have no practical knowledge of criminal profiling and what it actually involves. Subsequently, they perceive that the work may transform them into the dark, brooding characters of fiction that a few of them so desperately desire to become [1]. They perceive that profiling requires one to view the world through the eyes of the offender, who must be a monster, and that this view may ultimately lead to an isolated, emotionally alienated madness.

In point of fact, it is not difficult to see through the eyes of a given offender as long as one has the discipline to do the following:

1   Purge oneself of one's own tastes, desires, fantasies, needs, and sense of morality when considering the actions of another.

2   Accept that any behavior or feeling can be enjoyed and/or eroticized.

Again, this is not difficult if one cultivates the above skills.

However, the most emotionally difficult part of the criminal profiling process, for many, is conducting a thorough victimology.

The emotional coping mechanisms of a large number of detectives, investigators, and forensic personnel involve continuous doses of personal detachment and dissociation from the victim. The victim is seen as an object. Their body, living or deceased, and all of the terrible things done to it, are

[1] *It never ceases to amaze me how often I get approached by those that I have come to refer to as "ghouls." I'm referring to "true crime" junkies – who have delusions of psychic intuition, possess no actual insight or discipline, and whose only interests are prurient or self-serving. They are excited, in a voyeuristic sense, by the aspects of human suffering that criminal profilers seem to be privy to.*

It's actually kind of horrifying.

regarded as things to be examined and analyzed. The advantage of this coping mechanism is that there is no emotional investment, no opening up to be affected by the pain and suffering of something that is only an impersonal object of analysis. However, the disadvantage is that we risk surrendering our humanity when we regard victims, and their suffering, in this way.

We risk losing our humanity because this type of coping mechanism continually demands that we do things to reinforce our view of the victim as an object. If we humanize victims, we know that there is the risk of recognizing that they are not unlike our own daughter, son, mother, father, sister, brother, wife, husband, or friend. In order to maintain this necessary detachment, we actively deprive ourselves of knowledge about the victim as a person. We do not get to know them; we do not want to familiarize ourselves with their personal lives outside of the crimes committed against them. We do not wish to make time to see them as people – all of this because it might affect us emotionally.

This is, in the author's view, why the performance of a thorough victimology is not routine practice for many detectives, investigators, and forensic personnel. When done competently, victimology forces us to get to know the victim better than we know most of the people in our own lives. It opens us up to potential emotional internalizations, where we make a victim's personal feelings our own. It also opens us up to potential emotional transference, where we shift our thoughts and feelings about other people onto the victim. Getting to know the intimate details of a victim's history and personality is not emotionally safe.

But it is necessary.

WHY PROFILE THE VICTIM?

The competent criminal profiler will spend at least as much time examining victim history, as they will any related offender. Victim profiles can help provide three things: context, connections, and investigative direction.

We have to begin by asking ourselves, for a particular case, "What are the offender needs that victim selection satisfies?" Remember that offenders, in general, do not commit their crimes by accident. They are in possession, however elusive, of their own reasons for the behavior they act out with a victim (Turvey 1995).

If we can understand how and why an offender has selected known victims, then we may also be able to establish a relational link of some kind between the victim(s) and that offender. These links may be geographical, work related, schedule oriented, school related, hobby related, or they may even know each other somehow. The possibilities are without limit.

Furthermore, if we can understand how and why an offender has selected their previous victims (by studying the complete victimology, as it changes or fails to change over time and throughout incidents), then we have a better chance of predicting the type of victim that they may select in the future. This gives us investigative direction.

Even if we come to understand that an offender's victim selection process is random, or even more likely, opportunistic (both of which are possible), that is still a very significant conclusion (see Chapter 11).

Victimology is all about getting to know the victim as a real person. Unless we know *who* a victim is, or was, and how they lived, we cannot say that we truly know the context of their demise, or the events leading up to it.

THE VICTIM AS A REAL PERSON

There is a tendency with some investigators, detectives, and forensic personnel to deify or vilify the victim in a given case.

Deification comes in the form of idealizing victims, who are perhaps young school children, missing adolescents, or those who arrive pre-deified by the press and public opinion. Because of the political or public culture of a certain area or region, certain victim populations tend to be more politically or publicly sympathetic. This view facilitates rationalizations about time expended on the case while other investigations suffer, and does not allow for an unbiased victimology by virtue of depriving the crime, and the investigation, of true victim context.

> Example
> Two nine-year-old girls are abducted from a bus stop. Both are found dead in a drainage ditch the next day, disposed of less than 100 yards away. The press refers to the victims as "fallen little angels," and investigators do not conduct an investigation into the victims' family histories, focusing instead on a possible serial murderer. No leads are developed and the case grows cold. When a cursory victimology is performed one year later, it is learned that one victim had a history of starting fires, getting into fights with other children, and was on the prescription drug Ritalin for Attention Deficit Disorder. Through further investigation of these facts, interviews with the family, and medical and psychiatric records, it is learned that a relative had been molesting one of the victims for some time [2]. Suddenly the investigation takes a whole new direction.

Vilification comes in the form of viewing certain victim populations as worthless or disposable by their very nature. This view presumes that it is okay, or not as bad, to commit crimes against people of certain lifestyles, races, religions, or creeds. This can include people of a certain ethnic origin, people of a certain social class, prostitutes, drug dealers, drug addicts, or

[2] This does happen with some frequency. There is a dangerous, pervasive need to believe that all children are perfect and that all families with murdered children are perfect. Both the public in general and investigators in specific may ignore anything that disrupts this view.

People do not like to believe that this type of activity goes on, and this disbelief can affect an investigation negatively.

even runaways. Ultimately, this tends to be defined by an investigator's subjective sense of personal morality. This view facilitates investigative apathy. Detectives and investigators who hold this view of certain victim populations may not feel the need to investigate any crime committed against them thoroughly. The irony is that some of the most skillful serial offenders exploit these attitudes of law enforcement, and can learn to select victims by how disposable local law enforcement views them.

> Example
> A prostitute is raped in one part of the city. Three days later, another is raped six blocks away. Two weeks later, another is raped in the same area. All of the rapes are reported, no evidence is collected, and none of them are linked together, though they are related. The cases go uninvestigated until a more sympathetic victim is raped or killed.

The reality is that victims of crime are human beings. They are not the fictional constructs of our prejudices and biases born of our own morality, true crime novels, or Hollywood films. As we have always secretly feared, and must be willing to admit, they are not unlike our own daughters, sons, mothers, fathers, sisters, brothers, wives, husbands, or friends. They are no more or less deserving of our attention because of their lifestyle choices or situations.

If we idealize them, or vilify them, we will not learn who they were. We will not have the context for a complete profile, and will not be able to provide investigative direction based on victim–victim and victim–offender connections. Subsequently, if we proceed with the mindset that any victims are more or less deserving of our attention, then we do so at the risk of failing to serve justice. And we will most certainly speed ourselves away from our own humanity.

INPUTS

Criminal profiling inputs are all of the case materials that are necessary for the rendering of a competent profile. In terms of what is required for a thorough victimology, the NIJ's *National Guidelines for Death Investigation*, Section E (abbreviated): "Establishing and Recording Decedent Profile Information," as listed in Chapter 6 of this book, is a good place to start. But add to that list documenting the victim's criminal history.

However, the author does not recommend that readers confine themselves to any single victimology checklist. Rather, a criminal profiler should treat nothing about a victim as trivial. This means analyzing each characteristic that presents itself until it is an exhausted possibility, to see how it relates to the rest of the victim information.

Two general suggestions:

1 Spend time, when possible, with the victim's personal items, in their personal environments (hangouts, work, school, home/bedroom, etc.). Read any available diaries or journals. Make note of music and literature preferences. Do this to find out who they seemed to believe they were, and what they wanted everyone to perceive, and how they seemed to feel about their life in general.

2 Travel the last known route taken by the victim in whatever manner they did. See that route from their perspective, and then the perspective of the offender.

CREATING A TIMELINE: THE LAST 24 HOURS

Retracing a victim's last known actions and creating a timeline are critical to understanding the victim as a person, understanding their relationship to the environment, understanding their relationship to other events, and to understanding how the victim came to be acquired by an offender.

The general purpose here is to familiarize the profiler with the last known activities of the victim and subsequently determine, if possible, how a given victim got to a place and time where an offender was able to access them. This picture needs to be built from the ground up. It is a rewarding and illuminating process that is not to be overlooked.

A good approach to creating this timeline of locations and events includes at least the following steps:

- Compile all available forensic and factual data.
- Compile all of the crime scene photographs.
- Compile all witness data.
- Create a linear timeline of events and locations.
- Create a map of the victim's route for the 24 hours prior to the attack, as detailed as possible.
- Physically take yourself on a walk through the victim's last 24 hours using the map and forensic evidence as a guide.
- Document expected background elements of the route in terms of vehicles, people, activities, professionals, etc. for the time leading up to, during, and after the victim was acquired. It is possible that the offender is, or was masquerading as, one of those expected elements.

Attempt to determine the following:

- The point at which the offender acquired the victim.
- The place where the offender attacked the victim.
- How well the attack location can be seen from surrounding areas.
- Whether or not the offender would need to be familiar with the area to know this location, or to even get to it.

- Whether or not the acquisition of the victim was dependent on some sort of routine or schedule, and who could be aware of that schedule.
- Whether or not knowledge of the route would require or indicate presurveillance.
- Whether or not this route placed the victim at higher risk or lower risk.
- Whether or not the acquisition of the victim on that route placed the offender at higher risk or lower risk.

INVESTIGATE THE OBVIOUS

It is very important to investigate the obvious. Offenders of any kind may know, be acquainted with, or have some type of uninvestigated connection with their victims. These connections exist far more often than we have been led to believe by the published research, especially in the first crimes committed by an offender.

Investigate the obvious connections between all victims, and potential suspects. Proceed by questioning all investigative assumptions related to the established victimology when first presented with the facts of a case[3]. If a fact cannot be established, then it should not be assumed.

PSYCHOLOGICAL AUTOPSY

An important part of any investigation into a death that is questioned, or that occurs in association with sexual activity (a *sexual fatality*), is the performance of what is referred to as a *psychological autopsy*[4]. Psychological autopsy is a term that refers to the process that death investigators and mental health experts use, in collaboration with each other, to determine the state of mind of a person before they died (Geberth 1996).

The questions that most commonly arise in a case involving a person who appears to have been alone at the time of death, include whether or not their death was natural, accidental, suicidal, or homicidal, or whether any of these were staged to look like any other. It is believed that by making a very thorough examination of the victim's lifestyle and history (victimology), a more accurate determination can be made. The question is not always answerable with the information available in a given case, but it most certainly cannot be answered without detailed information about both the death scene and the victim's history.

There are three major areas of investigative consideration when performing a psychological autopsy: wound pattern analysis, victim state of mind, and victim mental health history (Turvey: in press).

To evaluate wound patterns on the victim, a complete analysis is required. That means examining the injuries in the crime scene (in the environment

[3] If someone tells me that the victim and suspect are not related in any way, I can't afford to take their word for it. Thoroughness demands that we determine these things to be true firsthand.

[4] Some people groan when they hear this term. I am among them. But the performance of a psychological autopsy is really no different than establishing and recording decedent profile information as outlined in the National Institute of Justice's National Guidelines for Death Investigation.

The NIJ guidelines aren't alone, either. The importance of establishing victim history is argued in every death investigation or forensic pathology text I've ever read. But even basic investigations into victim history rarely happen. Investigators frequently believe that they know what happened, and therefore shouldn't spend their time establishing factual information that it is easier to assume.

that they were created in) and at autopsy (after they have been cleaned up) whenever possible. This also means, at the very least, making an examination of all documentation relating to the crime scene and the autopsy (sketches, photos, videos, reports, notes, etc.). Key questions that are asked of the wounds include whether or not there are hesitation marks, whether or not the deceased could have caused the injuries, where any weapons that were used were found, and the precise causes of death (Geberth 1996).

To evaluate the victim's state of mind prior to their death, a complete background study of the victim's history, habits, and personality (victimology) is required. This requires conducting extensive interviews of the victim's friends and family, including close personal friends and any current or past intimates. Death investigators should also look for any of the classic warning signs of suicidal behavior in the victim's immediate history. These warnings signs include giving away possessions, sudden cheerfulness or emotional calm after a prolonged depression, speaking of life in the past tense, social isolation, extreme changes in regular habits or activities, recent stressful events, an accumulation of stressful events, or recent deaths of friends and/or family (*ibid.*). If there is a suicide note, this should be analyzed and compared to a sample of the victim's handwriting by a questioned document examiner. If a note is not found, handwriting samples should be taken anyway in case a note is found later. If a note is determined to have originated from the victim, then the contents of the note may reveal their state of mind and possible motives for their behavior. In other less common instances, victims may have written letters to friends or family, or made entries in personal journals that can be examined to the same end.

To evaluate a victim's mental health history, a full and complete analysis has to be made of their medical and mental health interactions. This means taking into account things such as whether or not the victim was or had been under any professional care (and subsequent reports and notes), whether or not they were on any medication, and whether or not they had attempted suicide in the past (*ibid.*).

These types of intensive background studies of the victim by law enforcement or medico-legal death investigators are routinely not made in sexual fatalities of any type (including sexual homicides), and as a result, accidental autoerotic deaths can go unreported or mislabeled as homicidal, suicidal, or undetermined deaths. Similarly, a homicide staged as an accident or a suicide may go unnoticed. As stated very clearly and very succinctly in the NIJ's (1997) *National Guidelines for Death Investigation*:

> Establishing a decedent profile includes documenting a discovery history and circumstances surrounding the discovery. The basic profile will dictate subsequent levels of investigation, jurisdiction, and authority. The focus (breadth/depth) of further investigation is dependent on this information.

REFERENCES

Geberth, V. (1996) *Practical Homicide Investigation*, 3rd edn, New York: CRC Press.

National Institute of Justice (1997) *National Guidelines for Death Investigation*, Research Report 167568, Washington DC: NIJ.

Turvey, B. (1995) "The Impressions of a Man: An Objective Forensic Guideline to Profiling Violent Serial Sex Offenders," *Knowledge Solutions Library*, March.

Turvey, B. (in press) "Autoerotic Death," *The Encyclopedia of Forensic Science*, London: Academic Press.

CHAPTER 10

VICTIMOLOGY: RISK ASSESSMENT

Brent E. Turvey, M.S.

Nothing was changed, everything was changed, by my having seen the dragon.

(John Gardner, *Grendel*)

One of the many lenses that may be used to examine the victim–offender relationship is in terms of the *risk* involved. The amount of risk is defined by the amount of exposure to a possibility of suffering harm or loss. In terms of criminal profiling, the question of risk becomes a matter of perspective. That is to say, there is victim risk and there is offender risk. Both must be considered when performing any type of victimological assessment.

RISK ASSESSMENT, NOT BLAME ASSESSMENT

The terms and definitions provided in this chapter are designed to help criminal profilers describe the relationship of a victim to their lifestyle and environment, and subsequently of a given offender to that victim. They provide the profiler with a language to characterize the facts of the case as established by the behavioral evidence. They ultimately provide insight into the defenses that a given offender is willing to try to defeat in order to achieve their goal.

VICTIMOLOGY RELATED RISK ASSESSMENTS ARE NOT ABOUT ESTABLISHING BLAME FOR THE VICTIM

It is important to remember that victims are not responsible for the predatory acts of offenders. This may seem like an obvious concept, but unfortunately, many people do blame the victim as being partially or wholly responsible for certain crimes committed against them. Consider the following:

> Example
> A person travels to a "bad part of town" and gets mugged. Somebody suggests that it is the victim's fault for going there in the first place because, "they should have known better."

This manner of judgmental, and often moral, reasoning has no place in criminal profiling.

To help further elucidate this concept of inappropriate bias and judgmental reasoning, we can contrast the risk of a prostitute with that of a student who lives in a secure building:

> Example
>
> A prostitute, working in a major metropolitan city, lives a lifestyle that exposes them to a relatively high possibility of suffering harm or loss at any given moment. The risk-increasing hazards involved with such work include the overall criminal environment, the hours of operation (night-time), the exposure to a constant barrage of strangers with potentially violent intentions, and the association of prostitution with the drug culture, to name but a few.
>
> A student living in a college town, in a secure building, may live a lifestyle that conversely exposes them to a relatively low possibility of suffering harm or loss at any given moment. However, there are moments of vulnerability for the student. One such moment would be the five to seven seconds that the student takes to get from a vehicle, through their locked front door, into their secured building, or vice versa into a locked vehicle. In either case there is a moment of distraction, when all attention is focused on finding one's keys and using them to open the door of the building or vehicle. There are many offenders who literally plan to lay in wait for those moments of vulnerability in such instances, and then exploit them for some criminal gain (robbery, sexual assault, etc.).

The above contrast demonstrates that choices made by a victim to ensure personal safety, despite their best efforts, are only going to be sufficient for an offender of a certain skill level. Put another way, whether or not a victim is going to fall prey to an offender is not exclusively a function of their efforts to maintain personal safety. It is also a function of the amount of skill and time a particular offender is willing to put into their method of approach and their method of attack (see Chapters 11 and 15)[1].

A detective might blame the prostitute in the above example for allowing themselves to become the victim of a violent crime. The same detective might view the student in the above example as an unfortunate victim of circumstance. However, establishing victim "blame" does not add anything to the investigative effort. All citizens have moments of vulnerability, no matter what type of lifestyle risks they take. Criminals are not entitled to commit crimes just because citizens have these moments of vulnerability. As we will discuss, this begs understanding the difference between *lifestyle risk* and *incident risk*.

RISK: THE VICTIM'S POINT OF VIEW

Victim risk is the amount of exposure to a possibility of suffering harm or loss that we as criminal profilers perceive for a given victim. It is not necessarily

[1] *An attorney contacted me who represented a rape victim involved in a civil suit against the owners of the building where the attack took place. He wanted to know whether or not, in general, a locked door at the front entrance of an apartment building would be more likely to prevent a rapist from gaining access than an unlocked one.*

My response was that it depended upon whether or not the rapist in question had a key.

My point was that the appropriate question is not whether a locked door will deter all rapists or typical rapists (since such creatures exist only in fiction). The appropriate question is whether a locked door would have deterred the rapist at hand. If a rapist somehow acquired a victim's keys prior to his attacks, or had their own key by virtue of working for the property management company, a locked door would be very little deterrent.

All risk is relative to the person taking it.

the victim's perspective. It is also very subjective, depending upon the knowledge and experiences of the profiler examining a given case.

Surprisingly, differences in profiler knowledge and experience do not tend to account for the majority of the varying opinions that can exist regarding victim risk in a particular case (though they certainly are factors). When there is a disagreement regarding victim risk between two criminal profilers, the biggest difference between them tends to be the thoroughness of the examination of victim history. Many criminal profilers are in the habit of approaching a victim with a great deal of prejudice, born out of a-priori investigative bias developed from initial victim information. This initial information, if unchecked by a thorough victimology, can easily become the basis for under-informed assessments of victim risk.

Another influence on a criminal profiler's victim risk assessment, sadly, may be the political kind. If the profiler feels that a certain victim risk suggests a certain offender type (the type that is suspected by others involved in the case), there is the danger that the criminal profiler may tailor the risk assessment by ignoring risk factors in their assessment.

To guard against any of these pitfalls and projections, the best defense is always going to be thoroughness and reliance upon fact, rather than supposition, as the basis for all conclusions in an assessment. The veracity of an interpretation, or conclusion, should always be judged by how well it accounts for the facts.

CATEGORIZING VICTIM RISK

The terms and definitions in the next paragraph are adapted from, but not identical to, terms from Burgess and Hazelwood (1995).

The term *low-risk victims* refers to individuals whose personal, professional, and social lives do not normally expose them to a possibility of suffering harm or loss. The term *medium-risk victims* refers to individuals whose personal, professional, and social lives can expose them to a possibility of suffering harm or loss. The term *high-risk victims* refers to individuals whose personal, professional, and social lives continuously expose them to the danger of suffering harm or loss.

But know that victim risk is relative.

The question to be investigated and answered here, is what a particular victim is at risk for, in specific. Ask how a particular victim's lifestyle places them in harm's way, if at all. For example, a young teen male may have a high victim risk of domestic violence by virtue of living with a parent who is an abusive alcoholic. At the same time, they may have a low victim risk of being abducted, raped, and killed by a stranger, by virtue of a very fixed schedule with a great deal of group activity and adult supervision.

If that is not complicated enough, victim risk can, and should, be categorized even further still in terms of *lifestyle risk* and *incident risk*.

VICTIM LIFESTYLE RISK

Lifestyle risk is a term that refers to the overall risk present by virtue of an individual's personality, and their personal, professional, and social environments. The belief is that certain circumstances, habits, or activities tend to increase the likelihood that an individual will suffer harm or loss. Furthermore, it is also affected by the personality traits possessed by the victim. Lifestyle risk, then, is a function of who the victim is and how they relate to the hazards that their environment contains. The following is a list of general personality traits that can increase victim lifestyle risk. It is not an all-inclusive list but rather a place for the criminal profiler to begin. The more prevalent or intense the trait in the victim's history, the greater the overall lifestyle risk:

- aggressiveness;
- anger;
- emotional outbursts;
- hyperactivity;
- impulsivity;
- anxiety;
- tendency towards addictive behavior;
- tendency towards self-destructive behavior;
- phobias or irrational or inexplicable fears;
- difficulty with authority;
- personal space or privacy issues;
- passivity;
- low self esteem;
- depression or hopelessness;
- negativity;
- emotional withdrawal;
- listlessness;
- need for attention or sympathy;
- history of self injury;
- history of suicide threats and/or attempts;
- aberrant sexual behavior.

These traits should be viewed in the context of the victim's age, occupation, criminal history, and any previous history of being a victim of crime.

VICTIM INCIDENT RISK

Victim incident risk is a term that refers to the risk present at the moment an offender initially acquires a victim, by virtue of the victim's state of mind, and the hazards of the immediate environment.

Factors that can increase victim incident risk include, but are not limited to, the following:

VICTIM LIFESTYLE RISK
This must be established to help place the incident in context, and begin to assist in establishing victim state of mind.

VICTIM STATE OF MIND
This refers to the victim's emotional state before, throughout, and subsequent to an attack (when applicable) as evidenced by convergent patterns of behavior and any reliable witness accounts. An agitated or distressed emotional state, for example, may increase victim incident risk. Additionally, a victim who feels safe in a particular environment or situation will act differently than a victim who does not.

TIME OF OCCURRENCE
Certain times of day can be more risky than others, but the interpretation of the impact of this factor is highly dependent upon the location of the occurrence. It can affect elements such as available light for certain activities and the amount of people present in public environments.

LOCATION OF OCCURRENCE
Location is one of the most important factors to affect victim incident risk. Certain environments contain more criminal activity, others may place a victim out of the immediate reach of assistance, and still others may physically isolate the victim, all of which can increase the incident risk of victims at the lowest lifestyle risk.

NUMBER OF VICTIMS
It is generally true that there is safety in numbers. Those who engage in activities with others are often at lower victim incident risk. This tends to be true as long as the people that an individual is with are not at a high lifestyle or high incident risk.

DRUG AND ALCOHOL USE
The use of mind-altering substances may decrease one's physical reaction time and impair one's judgement. In either case, victim incident risk is increased dramatically, even for otherwise low-risk victims.

The above factors inform the overall context, and each one on its own has meaning only when placed in the context of all of the known facts in a case. The interpretation of one factor alone, or the manipulation of one factor alone, cannot in itself be used to gauge victim incident risk.

Additionally, victim incident risk cannot be adequately assessed without full insight into victim lifestyle risk.

RISK: THE OFFENDER'S POINT OF VIEW

Offender risk is the amount of exposure to a possibility of suffering harm, loss, or identification and capture, that an offender perceives when attempting to acquire a victim. It is not the same as the criminal profiler's perspective, or the victim's perspective, as an offender can only evaluate a given situation using his or her own knowledge and experience. This should be gauged and assessed by an evaluation of the behavioral facts of the case as indicated by the physical evidence.

Like victim risk, offender risk is also relative.

The question to be investigated and answered here is what obstacles did the offender perceive, or consider, in terms of acquiring a particular victim and avoiding identification and capture. And how did the offender subsequently plan to defeat those obstacles, if at all. Ask of each incident, how much risk did the offender believe they were taking.

To fully understand the nature and extent of offender risks taken in a given incident, they should be categorized in terms of *modus operandi risk* and *offender incident risk*.

MODUS OPERANDI RISK

Modus operandi risk is a term that refers to the nature and extent of the skill, planning, and precautionary acts evidenced by an offender before, during, and after a crime to achieve their goal, and avoid detection by law enforcement (see Chapters 11 and 13). The more skill, planning, and precautionary acts evidenced by an offender, the lower they may perceive their own risk to be.

LOW MO RISK

Low MO risk is a term that applies to offenders who evidence a high amount of skill, planning, and precautionary acts before, during, and after a crime.

This term can refer to incidents where victims are selected who will not be immediately missed should they fall prey to misfortune, if they are missed at all. It may also be applied to incidents where the offender has more control, or where there is a low possibility of the offender being noticed and later identified. Examples include:

- dark or poorly lit locations;
- times during the day; late at night or early in the morning when few people are around to witness offender activity;
- offense locations far away from where an offender resides;
- offenses where an offender abducts a victim to a remote or secluded location;
- offenses where a stranger victim is selected by virtue of lifestyle;
- availability (i.e. a runaway or prostitute).

It is important to keep in mind that high-risk victims are not necessarily low MO risks (i.e. unattended children are high-risk victims, but they can also be a high risk to an offender because they are missed almost immediately by parents, caregivers, or guardians).

HIGH MO RISK

High MO risk is a term that applies to offenders who evidence a low amount of skill, planning, and precautionary acts before, during, and after a crime.

This term may be applied to offenders who acquire victims who will be immediately missed should they fall prey to misfortune, and who are very well monitored by their environment and/or those who care for them. It may also be applied to incidents where there is a high possibility of the offender being noticed, and later identified, when acquiring a victim (like someplace very public during the daytime, or where there are security monitors).

High MO risk is a term that also describes instances where an offender increases their chances of being recognized, identified, or apprehended by commission or omission. This can include, for example, actions such as allowing the victim to see their face, letting the victim survive an attack, and attacking victims who are known to the offender and can easily be linked back to them.

The offender's perceptions of risk regarding offense behavior can dictate their actions during any offense planning, during the offense itself, and after the attack has been completed. It is important to recognize that the offender's perceptions regarding an offense can be incomplete or downright wrong. In any case, assessing *modus-operandi* risk gives a criminal profiler direct insight into the offender's perspective regarding what planning, skill, or precautionary acts are necessary and what are not.

OFFENDER INCIDENT RISK

Offender incident risk is a term that refers to the amount of exposure to a possibility of suffering harm or loss that we as criminal profilers perceive for a given offender. *It is not necessarily the offender's perspective. The offender does not necessarily operate with the same insights into victimology and crime scene characteristics as the criminal profiler.*

Example

The author was asked to consult on a case where a 21-year-old female victim, dressed in tight pants, a gold chain belt, lots of make-up, and glamour nails, was walking back and forth on a street just after midnight on a cold winter evening.

The offender, who just happened to be driving by after an evening of drinking at topless bars up the freeway, believed that she was a prostitute. He drove around the block once, parked his van in a quiet residential area, and then made his approach on foot. He engaged her in some initial conversation and then attacked her, dragging her down the block, back into the residential area. He then proceeded to bind her, sexually assault her, and torture her over the next two hours inside of the van. When he was through he wrote down the information from her ID, helped adjust her clothing and jewelry (which he had torn), warned her not to tell anyone, let her out, and then drove off.

In point of fact the victim was not a prostitute, but rather a young lady who was on her way to a nightclub when her vehicle had broken down. The offender perceived that this victim put him at low risk. He perceived that she would not likely report the incident, as she was a prostitute. He also perceived that she would not be missed by anyone, so he did not have to take her to a remote location to engage in a prolonged assault, even though he could have easily done so.

The lesson here is to try to understand the offender's perspective. What does the offender see, and how does that influence their behavior (if at all)? Establish the offender's MO risk level. Then compare those behaviors with the offender incident risk and determine the level of knowledge that the offender appeared to be operating with.

It should be noted that not all offenders will tender themselves to the considerations of blatant or obvious risks, and in such cases that information can be very useful. What kind of risk an offender is willing to take in order to acquire a certain victim tells you not only a great deal about what that offender desires, but what the offender is willing to do in order to achieve that desire.

REFERENCE

Burgess, A. and Hazelwood, R. (eds) (1995) *Practical Aspects of Rape Investigation: A Multidisciplinary Approach*, 2nd edn, New York: CRC Press.

CHAPTER 11

CRIME-SCENE CHARACTERISTICS

Brent E. Turvey, M.S.

...solve the riddle that pursues me through this dark place and leaves my mind perplexed:

you seem to see in advance all time's intent,

if I have heard and understood correctly;

but you seem to lack all knowledge of the present...

(Dante Alighieri, *Canto X, Circle 6: The Heretics* in
reference to the *Knowledge of the Damned*)

You never know what is enough unless you know what is more than enough.

(William Blake, *The Marriage of Heaven and Hell*)

Once a competent forensic analysis of the physical evidence has been made, with the requisite reconstructive efforts, and the victimology has been established, the criminal profiler can focus their efforts on determining the characteristics of a particular crime scene.

Crime-scene characteristics are the distinguishing features of a crime scene as evidenced by an offender's behavioral decisions regarding the victim and the offense location, and their subsequent meaning to the offender.

While it is true that individual crime-scene characteristics, and victimology, will be reflective of the personality traits of the person responsible for the offense, readers are cautioned not to make the mistake of confusing the process of establishing crime-scene characteristics for completing a criminal profile. A criminal profile (a logical argument regarding the characteristics of an offender responsible for a particular crime or series of crimes) is deducted from victimology and crime-scene characteristics as established by a convergence of the physical and behavioral evidence. As such, crime-scene characteristics are still only a language for expressing or explaining the victim–offender behavior as it has been established by forensic evidence or victim and witness interviews (see Chapter 24).

As a part of the forensic reconstruction, criminal profilers are warned that they, or others, may not be able to establish these characteristics with any level of accuracy or certainty. The physical evidence may not be there to inform an interpretation. If the evidence of a behavior is not there, we are admonished not to assume it as part of our examination and analysis, no matter how convenient. This sounds very basic, but for some reason it is often ignored in the investigative zeal to come up with hypothetical scenarios.

Criminal profilers are also warned not to use the characteristics discussed below as a firm template for a criminal profile. Every offense profiled will be different. Even the same offender leaves behind a crime scene that is distinct in its own way from all others by virtue of environmental influences, the victim–offender interaction, and the subsequent physical evidence that is left behind. A criminal profile should reflect the variation between offenses, the subsequent variations in the available evidence, and what those can reliably tell us.

The discrimination of a number of the crime-scene characteristics reviewed here is owed in no small part to *Practical Aspects of Rape Investigation: A Multidisciplinary Approach* (Burgess and Hazelwood 1995).

These are so noted where they occur. However, the author has expanded on this framework significantly and has covered the characteristics in a different manner.

LOCATION TYPE

The location type refers to the type of environment that a crime scene exists within. There are four general types (these are not always exclusive), and each determines the nature and extent of evidence that one can potentially recover there.

For an excellent reference on this subject, please see Geberth (1996) *Practical Homicide Investigation*, Chapter 8, "The Homicide Crime Scene Search".

- *Indoor crime scenes.* Refers to crime scenes inside of a structure with some form of cover from the elements of nature. Houses, apartments, buildings, sheds, garages, warehouses, cabins, tents, caves and so on.
- *Vehicle crime scenes.* Refers to crime scenes that are mobile. Cars, trucks, boats, ships, trains, airplanes, motorcycles, blimps, and so on.
- *Outdoor crime scenes.* Refers to crime scenes that are exposed to the elements of nature. Fields, forests, ravines, canyons, ditches, roadsides, deserts, and so on.
- *Underwater crime scenes.* Refers to crime scenes that are beneath the surface of any body of water. Lakes, ponds, creeks, rivers, oceans, reservoirs and so on.

CRIME-SCENE TYPE

One of the most important considerations of crime-scene investigation, reconstruction, and criminal profiling is determining what type of crime scene we are presented with. By this we are referring to establishing the crime scene type: the relationship of the crime scene to the offender behavior, in the context of the offense.

A *crime scene* is defined as an area where a criminal act has taken place (Lee 1994). A criminal offense, however, can take place in not just one, but multiple locations. This can create many crime scenes that are related together within a single offense, by virtue of the role they played in the crime. Consider the following types of crime scenes. These are not mutually exclusive categories.

Caution
When trying to figure out the crime-scene type in a particular case, do not use intuition or experience as a guide. Let the physical evidence tell the story. Work from the physical evidence out to a sound reconstruction, not from biased theories into a corner.

POINT OF CONTACT

The location where the offender first approached or acquired the victim. This is a neutral term because it includes locations where the victim was encountered under some ruse devised by the offender, as well as locations where the offender may have attacked the victim and dragged them to some other pre-selected *primary* or *secondary scene.*

PRIMARY SCENE

The location where the offender engaged in the majority of their attack/ assault upon the victim or victims. This is the location where the most time was spent, and where the most physical evidence was deposited during the offense. It is possible for there to be one primary scene per victim, if attacks on separate victims within a single offense occur in separate locations. It is possible for the primary scene to also be the disposal site.

SECONDARY SCENE

The location where some of the victim–offender interaction occurred, but not the majority of it. If it is the location where the body is found, a secondary scene is also the disposal site. There can also be several secondary scenes associated with a single crime. Essentially, the term 'secondary scene' encompasses any place where there may be evidence of criminal activity outside of the primary scene.

All crime scenes may be categorized as primary scenes or secondary scenes.

INTERMEDIATE SCENE

This is any crime scene between the primary scene and the disposal site, where there may be evidence transfer. This includes vehicles used to transport the body to a disposal site, after a homicide, and locations where a body has been stored prior to final disposal. Intermediate scenes are generally secondary crime scenes.

DUMP-SITE/DISPOSAL SITE

This term is used to refer to the place where a body is found. More often than not, the use of this term implies that the victim was assaulted somewhere else and transported to this location after or just prior to death. That is an unfortunate and very dangerous investigative assumption to make. As a disposal site may also be the primary scene, this possibility must not be excluded by virtue of an investigator's subjective experience.

Many of the criminal profilers and homicide investigators encountered by this author seem to have a nearly pathological problem with interpreting the relationship of outdoor locations to the bodies of victims found within them. Very often, they will assume that an outdoor crime scene is a disposal site only, when in fact it is *also* a primary scene (and subsequently fail to direct investigators to look for certain types of evidence). Or they will assume that an outdoor crime scene is both a primary scene and a disposal site, ignoring other nearby potential underwater, indoor, or vehicle locations.

In terms of criminal profilers, this occurs generally for three reasons:

- The profiler in question has not visited the crime scene.
- The profiler in question has not questioned the assumptions of law enforcement, and is taking their word for the relationship of the crime scene to the crime.
- The profiler in question has little or no knowledge, training, and experience in crime scene investigation and the forensic sciences.

The remedy for this problem is avoiding a-priori investigative bias by not opining firmly without physical evidence, questioning all investigative assumptions no matter how firmly they are "believed" by others, and adequate education and training in the forensic sciences.

LOCATION OF THE SCENE

Determine the physical location of each crime scene, and its relationship to the surrounding environment. In urban and suburban locations, make sure to determine precise addresses and cross-streets. In rural, outdoor, or underwater scenes, determine latitude and longitude using a *global positioning* (GPS) device. For the criminal profiler, key questions to address include:

- Who frequents the location and the surrounding area?
- How can it be reached/terrain (vehicle, walking, hiking, airplane, etc.)?

- What is located at that scene? What belongs there?
- What activities normally occur in the crime scene?
- What is the criminal activity like in the areas surrounding the scene?
- Where is that scene located relative to other crime scenes?
- How did the offender get into the scene (transportation, point of entry, etc.)
- Why did the offender choose that scene (intentional, accidental, convenience, etc.)?
- How well would an offender have to know the area to find the scene? Is it something a stranger could notice who was just passing through, or does getting there require a level of familiarity?

METHOD OF APPROACH

The *method of approach* is a term that refers to the offender's strategy for getting close to a victim. It is usually described as a blitz, a surprise, or a con (Burgess and Hazelwood 1995). These methods of approach are not mutually exclusive.

SURPRISE

The surprise approach is characterized by an offender who gets close to a victim by laying in wait for a moment of vulnerability. This can mean waiting for victims at a particular location commensurate with the victim's schedule, which is suggestive of some type of preselection (*ibid.*). But it can also mean acquiring a victim and waiting to approach them until they are distracted, preoccupied, or asleep.

This term describes the approach only, and does not include the method of attack.

CON

The *con* approach is characterized by an offender who gets close to a victim by use of a deception or a ruse (*ibid.*). This can be a simple ploy to divert attention momentarily, or it can involve a more complex scheme whereby the offender requires the offender's immediate or prolonged trust.

This term describes the approach only, and does not include the method of attack.

THE TROUBLE WITH BLITZ

According to Burgess and Hazelwood (1995) an offender who gets close to a victim and delivers an immediate application of overpowering force (in other words, an attack) characterizes the blitz approach (*ibid.*). The intention is to deprive the victim of any reaction time, and give the offender immediate control of the situation. Burgess and Hazelwood also state that this definition has everything to do with the amount of damage inflicted, and nothing to do with the suddenness of onset.

This author finds the concept of a blitz approach without the element of suddenness in onset difficult to imagine. This author is also of the opinion that the term *blitz* describes an attack only, and not an offender's approach. Blitz *attacks* often involve the offender lying in wait for the victim (a surprise approach), especially in cases where the victim has been preselected in some general or specific fashion. Readers are encouraged to come to their own conclusions regarding the use of this term, but then to use it consistently.

This author advocates its use as a descriptor for an offender's method of attack when there is an immediate, brutal application of controlling, sexual, punishing, or lethal physical force which is aimed at incapacitating or killing the victim.

METHOD OF ATTACK

The *method of attack* is a term that refers to *the offender's mechanism for initially overpowering a victim once they have made their approach.* It is also usually described as a blitz, a surprise, or a con. While the term 'blitz' may be useful here, the terms 'surprise' and 'con' are not appropriate. These last two are descriptive of methods of approach, and not suggestive of the nature or the extent of any subsequent attack.

It is more appropriate to describe a method of attack in terms of the weapon, and the nature of the force involved. Examples include:

- verbal threat of lethal force. "Do what I say or I'll kill you";
- verbal command and threat of lethal force; controlling force with a gun. "Do what I say or I will shoot you";
- blitz attack from behind; controlling force with a wire garrote around the neck;
- verbal command; controlling force with a knife. "I have a knife in your ribs. Do exactly as I tell you".

As already suggested, an offender's method of approach may include the offender's method of attack, but if it does not, then it is only an approach. The method of attack may be entirely separate and must be examined separately.

For example, in a surprise attack an offender may lie in wait for hours and then jump out of the bushes in a park and gain control over a victim from behind with a knife and verbal threats. If he does not use the knife to inflict injuries on the victim right away or at all, then this whole event can be called a surprise attack. If he uses the knife to immediately cut the victim in some way, then this could be referred to as a surprise approach with a blitz attack involving a knife.

In another example, an offender may approach a different victim in the same park with a ruse. They may spend a few minutes together before the offender decides to make their move. The ruse itself is not the attack; it is only an approach. The attack comes later when the offender begins to coerce the victim into non-compliant behavior. At that point the offender may use commands, threats, his fists, and/or a knife to deliver corrective, controlling, or lethal force.

The method of attack, then, does not always come with the initial method of approach. This concept is key to understanding what the offender is capable of, and what they are comfortable with, in a given environment with a given victim.

METHODS OF CONTROL

An offender's *methods of control* are those means used to manipulate, regulate, restrain, and subdue victim behavior of any kind throughout the duration of an offense. This can include the use of:

CONTROL-ORIENTED FORCE

- slapping a noncompliant victim;
- choking a combative victim;
- biting a combative victim;
- use of ligatures to bind or secure the victim's body;
- use of handcuffs;
- use of a gag to quell the victim's verbal activity.

VERBAL THREAT OF CONTROLLING, PUNISHING, SEXUAL, OR LETHAL FORCE

- "Quit moving around or I'll tie your hands behind your back."
- "Do that again and I'll kill you."
- "Do what I say or I'll put this in your ass."
- "Keep walking or you'll really be taught a lesson."

UNARTICULATED PRESENCE OF THE PHYSICAL THREAT OF CONTROLLING, PUNISHING, SEXUAL, OR LETHAL FORCE

- presence of a gun;
- presence of a knife;
- presence of a bat;
- clenched and raised fists;

- physical intimidation by virtue of size;
- presence of handcuffs.

When describing an offender's methods of control, the criminal profiler is admonished to be very specific about the physical mechanism of control, and precisely how it manipulated, regulated, restrained, and/or subdued victim behavior.

WEAPONS

The term *weapon* refers to any item found in the crime scene (available materials), or brought to the crime scene by the victim or the offender, that is used for the purposes of administering force (see Chapter 8).

Not all offenders use a weapon in their offenses. Some because they do not have it within them to use a weapon; some because they do not have access to a weapon; some because they do not feel that they need a weapon; and some because the nature of their perception does not allow them to use a weapon (such as having a reassurance-oriented fantasy that the attack involves the consent of the victim, and is therefore not actually a criminal act).

For the criminal profiler, key questions to address regarding any weapons include:

- What is the nature of the weapon? (i.e. knife, gun, rope, rock, shovel, etc.)
- Who does the weapon belong to? (i.e. victim, offender, third party, etc.)
- How did that weapon get into the crime scene?
- Where was the weapon found? (i.e. on/near victim, discarded nearby, other related crime scene, not found, etc.)
- When during the crime was the weapon used? (i.e. during the offender's approach, during the physical attack, during sexual attack, etc.)
- How was the weapon used? (i.e. defensive, precautionary, experimental, corrective, controlling, punishing, sexual, or lethal force)

USE OF FORCE

The amount of force that an offender is willing to use throughout their offense tells us a great deal about their potential needs and motives (Burgess and Hazelwood 1995). For a review of the motivational origins of wounds – and by extension the motivational origins of the force that can cause them – refer back to Chapter 8.

This includes an assessment not only of the force used in the method of attack, but also how that relates to the rest of the offense behavior. It should include a breakdown of when the offender used force, and the intention of that force. But it can also include an assessment of what force was not used (this may not be possible without a living victim and a behaviorally oriented interview, or a linear record of the event made by the offender such as audio or videotape).

Regarding the use of force – there may be no sign of physical injury on the victim. It is important to document this and review it as part of forming opinions about the use of force. However, keep in mind that the absence of injuries reflecting physical force does not exclude the use of physical force. It merely excludes the more violent forms.

It also does not automatically mean that the victim did not resist the offender. See Victim Resistance below.

VICTIM RESISTANCE

Burgess and Hazelwood (1995) provides three very useful categories of victim resistance, and gives a well-made warning not to define resistance merely as physical or verbal, but as passive as well (see below). In defining victim resistance, however, Burgess and Hazelwood does not list the extreme end of the behavioral continuum, which would be victim compliance. It also fails to explain how these are not exclusive categories and that each type of victim resistance may exist within an offense and should be looked for.

This author offers the caution that the below descriptors are not about victim blame or victim responsibility. Victims respond to an offender according to their own life history, their own experiences, and their own understanding of the world as expressed through their individual personality. What is extreme behavior for one victim may not be for another. This speaks to developing a full victimology before assessing victim resistance. Find out who they are first, and that will provide insight into why they reacted the way that they did[1].

VICTIM COMPLIANCE

This term refers to when a victim acquiesces to an offender demand, readily and without hesitation. Certain victims may even proactively ask what they can do to please the offender so that they will be on their way. This does not mean that the event was consensual, or that no actual crime took place. What it can be the result of is a fear of harm, or a resignation to the events that are about to take place.

PASSIVE RESISTANCE

This term refers to when a victim defies an offender by non-aggressive means, such as the refusal to comply with offender commands or the refusal to eat or drink if in captivity for prolonged periods of time (Burgess and Hazelwood 1995). That work admonishes us to remember that victim

[1] In graduate school, a female classmate once said to me, "Isn't it true that if you can prove that the victim gave the guy oral sex (like finding semen in her mouth) then it wasn't rape?"

I told my classmate that this was not the case at all. There was still disbelief.

The reality is that no one knows what they are capable of until they are confronted with very real, very present physical danger, including the threat of death.

However, for some reason, this myth about fellatio being necessarily consensual persists, especially among females.

non-compliance is a form of resistance, and may be all that certain victims are capable of (physically or psychologically).

VERBAL RESISTANCE

This term refers to when a victim defies an offender with words. This can include a victim who shouts for help, screams when attacked, pleads for mercy, verbally refuses to follow commands, or who tries to negotiate or bargain. Examples include:

- "Don't touch me."
- "I'm not going anywhere with you."
- "You'll have to kill me to rape me."
- "I don't want to die."
- "Please, I just don't want you to hurt me."
- "Let me go and I won't tell anyone."

PHYSICAL RESISTANCE

This term refers to when a victim defies an offender with physical force. This can include punching, slapping, scratching, biting, struggling, kicking, and running away.

If a victim claims that physical force was used, there should be an attempt made to confirm this with an examination of their body, and the area of the offender's body that would have been affected or injured. Absence of offender injury is not always an indication that physical force was not used, or that the victim is being untruthful.

> Example
> An offender attacks a victim in her apartment building, in an elevator. She claims that she drew a knife, stabbed her attacker in the ribs through his leather jacket, and then fled the elevator to safety where she then called the police. She makes a positive identification of her attacker, but he is not arrested because he has no stab injury to his abdomen. In fact he has no injuries and no blood on his clothing at all. Later, after adamant protests are made, a search warrant is served and a leather jacket is recovered from his home. It is cut precisely in the location indicated by the victim's account.

NATURE AND SEQUENCE OF SEXUAL ACTS

A *sexual act* is any offender behavior involving sexual organs, sexual apparatus, or sexualized objects. Establishing their nature and sequence within an offense gives insight into offender *modus operandi* (see Chapter 13), and signature (see Chapter 14). This can be done to a limited extent (nature, often without definite sequence) with physical evidence, but often relies heavily on witness accounts or victim interviews.

Sexual acts are an extension of offender force, and should be evaluated similarly as being used for defensive, precautionary, experimental, corrective, controlling, punishing, sexual/fantasy, or lethal purposes (see Chapter 8).

They can include, but are not limited to, behaviors such as the following (readers are encouraged to seek out as many sources as they can of material relating to human sexual behavior and rituals):

- anal sex;
- analingus;
- bestiality;
- cunnilingus;
- fellatio;
- fetishism;
- flagellation;
- frottage;
- infibulation;
- kissing any body part;
- licking any body part;
- masochism;
- masturbation;
- necrophilia;
- sadism;
- scatophilia;
- sexual bondage;
- sexual immolation;
- sucking on any body part;
- urophilia;
- vaginal sex;
- voyeurism.

PRECAUTIONARY ACTS

Precautionary acts are behaviors committed by an offender before, during, or after an offense that are consciously intended to confuse, hamper, or defeat investigative or forensic efforts for the purposes of concealing their identity, their connection to the crime, or the crime itself.

Examples include and are certainly not limited to:

CLOTHING/DISGUISE

The offender may change their appearance using disguises, masks, or bulky clothing. This conceals their physical features, and makes later identification by a living victim or witness difficult or impossible.

ALTERATION OF VOICE

The offender may deepen their voice, increase the pitch, or affect an accent.

BLINDFOLD

This prevents the victim from seeing the offender's physical features.

TIME OF DAY

The offender may choose a time of day when the scene is very dark, to obscure their own physical features and to increase victim vulnerability.

LOCATION SELECTION

A location may be determined by a rapist to be somewhat secluded and untravelled, and out of the visual range of any local residences. This would make his willingness to seize the opportunity to rape more likely.

VICTIM SELECTION

The offender may select complete strangers as victims, decreasing the likelihood that they may be connected to the crime at a later date.

USE OF GLOVES

This prevents the transfer of fingerprint evidence during the commission of a crime.

USE OF CONDOM

Inhibits the transfer of sperm (and subsequently DNA evidence) to the victim or the crime scene. Can be taken from the scene by the offender and disposed of elsewhere.

USE OF FIRE

Fire can be used to damage or destroy the victim, the crime scene, and/or evidence of the offense. It may also be an expression of anger.

DISPOSING OF THE VICTIMS' CLOTHING

The offender may throw some (i.e. shirts, shoes, and socks), or all of the victim's clothing away. This serves the purpose of increasing victim shame, leaving them without protective footwear, and ultimately delays the victim's ability to get help or contact authorities. It also disposes of potential physical evidence.

LOOKING AT OR COLLECTING VICTIM IDENTIFICATION

The offender may examine, record, or take the victim's personal identification to learn the victim's name and address. This can be used as a threat of future violence to intimidate the victim from reporting the incident, or at least delay reporting.

ITEMS TAKEN

This refers to anything that originally belonged to a crime scene, which the offender took with them when they left. This can be established by a competent forensic examination of the scene. When possible, compare a crime scene as it exists to how it existed before the crime occurred there. Look for things that are:

- new;
- missing;
- the same.

Once that has been done, account for why those things are new, missing, or the same.

To make this comparison, the criminal profiler and forensic personnel will need solid documentation of the scene prior to the crime occurring. Use photos from recent events held at the location, ATM machine cameras, security cameras, etc. Then develop a list of potential witnesses who know the area well and interview them extensively ... the rule here is to be creative and to be thorough.

Burgess and Hazelwood (1995) places items taken into three categories.

EVIDENTIARY

These are items that the offender believes may link them to the victim and/or the crime. Examples include, but are not limited to:

- victim clothing with bloodstain patterns, fibers, or semen on them;
- gifts, valuable items, or jewelry given to the victim by the offender;
- photographs of the victim and the offender together;
- letters written by the offender in the victim's possession.

Taking these types of items from a crime scene would be considered a precautionary act.

VALUABLES

These are items taken from the crime scene that the offender believes may have financial value. The type of item taken by an offender for profit is suggestive not only of the skill level and transportation capabilities of the offender, but the level of offender financial need as well.

Examples include, but are not limited to:

- credit cards;
- jewelry;
- cash;
- TVs;
- computer equipment;
- stereos;
- VCRs;
- cell phones;
- pagers;
- drugs.

Taking this type of item from the crime scene is a profit-motivated behavior, and is suggestive of offender involvement in other types of equivalent profit-motivated offenses.

PERSONAL

These are items taken from the victim or the crime scene that have sentimental value to the offender. These types of items often have no financial value attached to them, but if they do, that value is ancillary or incidental.

These items are divided into two subjective categories. The precise nature of each item must be determined on an item-by-item basis, and cannot be done without knowing how the offender acquired it (context), and the offender or victim behavior that it is associated with. Note that items given as examples from either category could fit into both, and they are not mutually exclusive categories.

TROPHY

A symbol of victory, achievement, or conquest. Associated with force, victim resistance, and/or victim subjugation and humiliation.

- a torn garment worn by the victim;
- a lock of victim hair;
- victim personal identification;
- pictures taken of the victim during the attack;

- a weapon used on the victim, taken from the scene;
- a victim body part.

SOUVENIR

A reminder or token of remembrance representing a pleasant experience. Associated with reassurance-oriented needs (see Chapter 15).

- victim undergarments taken from their clothes hamper;
- victim school identification;
- pictures taken from the walls of the victim's home, or taken out of the victim's personal photo albums;
- a ribbon worn by the victim;
- pictures taken of the victim during preselection activity, before the offense.

Taking these types of items from a crime scene are signature behaviors, and are suggestive of offender motivation (see Chapter 14 and 15).

THE BODY

In all cases, whether a victim is living or dead, the body is an extension of the crime scene. For an excellent reference on this subject, please see DiMaio and DiMaio (1993).

For the criminal profiler, key questions to address regarding the body of the victim include:

- At what point during the offense was the body put in the scene?
- How did the victim or body physically get into the crime scene?
- How did the victim or body physically get into its final position at the crime scene?
- Why was the body left in that particular scene?
- What condition is the body in?
- Is the positioning of the body in keeping with the established facts of the offense?
- Is there evidence to suggest that the offender placed the body in a particular position?
- If the body was placed in a particular position, how is that posing meaningful?
- To whom is the posing meant to be meaningful? (i.e. the offender, whoever finds the body, the victim, etc.)

VERBAL BEHAVIOR – SCRIPTING

Scripting is a term that refers to the language used by an offender during an offense, as well as the language that they command the victim to use. Scripting is used to direct the victim verbally and behaviorally. This speaks to the offender's ideal fantasy regarding the nature of the offense – what will happen, what they will say, and what the victim will say in return (if anything at all).

Language, then, is an extension of both psychological needs and force (or an extension of a lack of psychological/emotional need and a lack of force). According to Burgess and Holmstrom (1979), there are 11 major themes in offender verbal behavior, which must be evaluated not only for content, but also for tone, attitude, and timing in the context of the attack. Due to the fact that these initial eleven themes only cover certain kinds of selfish rapist motivations, totally ignoring others, the author has made additions to these themes in bold. They include the following:

- **MO-oriented orders and commands**. "Don't look at my face."
- **Signature-oriented orders and commands**. "Shake your ass for me. I want to see it move."
- Threats. "Don't look at my face or I'll kill you."
- Confidence lines. "I'm going to show you how a man feels."
- Personal inquiries of the victim. "What is your name? How old are you?"
- Personal inquiries regarding the victim's sexual enjoyment. "Does that feel good?"
- Personal revelations by the offender. "I love the way this feels."
- Obscene names and racial epithets. "Bitch. Nigger."
- Soft-sell departures. "I'm not going to hurt you."
- Sexual insults. "You're barely worth raping."
- Possessive. "I own you."
- Taking property away from others. "You think that you can't be had by someone else?"
- **Intentional deceptions**. "My name is Paul. I live very close by so don't watch me while I'm leaving."
- **Reassurance-oriented truths**. "My name is Paul. I won't hurt you."
- **Apologies**. "I'm sorry. This wasn't me."
- **Bargaining**. "If you do this, I'll let you go."
- **Personal compliments**. "You look so pretty."
- **Sexual compliments**. "You have really nice tits."
- **Self-deprecation**. "I am such a loser."

Note that offender verbal behavior can include commands to the victim to repeat certain phrases or words, or perform particular behaviors, that have a special meaning to the offender. This, and any other offender verbal behaviors beyond the use of commands to gain compliance, are signature behaviors (see Chapter 14).

CASE EXAMPLE OF AN OFFENDER VERBAL ACTIVITY EVIDENCING MULTIPLE SIGNATURE ASPECTS
(See Chapter 15, Behavior-Motivational Typologies)

An offender abducts a stranger victim from her broken-down vehicle. He tortures her in a van, parked a few blocks away, with tools, and yells at her to scream so that he can hear it. Between attacks on this same victim within the space of a few hours, he engages in caressing and fondling behavior, while apologizing. He finally releases her, after helping her put her clothes back on. The evidence of torture suggests a sadistic signature aspect, while the caressing, fondling, and apologizing suggest a reassurance-oriented signature aspect.

Throughout the assault on the victim, the victim recalls the offender using the following phrases, in the following order:

"Where's Bill?"

"Where's Bill?"

"Yeah."

"Pull your pants down!"

"Keep your pants down!"

"I don't give a fuck!"

"Shut up, shut the fuck up!"

"Shut up! Keep walking; shut up or I'll kill you!"

"Stop fucking around!"

"Get in, get in!"

"Take your fucking clothes off!"

"Take it off, take it off. Take it off right now!"

"Take you're pants off!"

"Don't you like being naked?"

"Take the fucking boots off!"

"Take them off. Take them off!"

"Let me see something."

"What the fuck are you trying to do?"

"Do you like this?"

"Stop fucking lying to me!"

"I want to see how deep it goes!"

"Do you like being naked?"

"Do you want me to be naked?"

"What are you laughing at?"

"Stop lying!"

"I want you to cum!"

"Stop lying, I know you're lying to me! I know you're not cumming!"

"What?"

"Okay."

"Keep your hands up to the front where I can see them!"

"Lift up higher!"

"I said higher!"

"What the fuck are you doing? Trying to look at me?"

"I want you to take it deeper. I want you to take it deeper; your life depends on it!"

"Loosen your teeth!"

"I said loosen your teeth!"

"You liar!"

"Whore!"

"You know how to do it!"

"How old are you?"

"Oh, you're old enough then."

"I want you to do it again; your life depends on it!"

"You're a liar. You were sucking on it pretty good last time!"

"Do you want me to cum in your mouth?"

"I'm gonna cum!"

"Swallow it!"

"Shut up; don't ask me any questions!"

"Do you have any ID on you?"

"Where is it? In the car?"

"What is your name?"

"What is your last name?"

"I'm gonna go out there and get your wallet and if the name doesn't match, I'm gonna kill you! What is your name?"

"It's okay baby."

"Are you trying to look at me?"

"Shut up!"

"I love to lick you."

"I want you to say this. I want you to tell me that you want me to fuck you in the asshole real good."

"Say it slowly."

"I want you to say it over and over again, like you mean it!"

"Say it!"

"Say it!"

"What the fuck do you think this is, put your leg up there! Higher! I want your leg up higher!"

"Did you take a look at me? I know you saw me!"

"Stop lying! That's what they all say!"

"They didn't like the outcome after they told."

"Get on your knees, put your hands behind your head, and shake your breasts back and forth."

"You have a great-looking chest. You have that going for you."

"Do you want your underwear back? I'll take it if you'll let me have it."

"It doesn't matter. What do you need it for?"

"This is a machete and I want you to stay still; I'm going to cut the tape off your hands."

"Do you want me to stitch it for you? I'll do it if you want me too."

"Are the boots zipper or laces?"

"No, I don't want you to go outside without shoes."

"Here is your necklace; I'll put it on for you. I want you to look pretty again."

"Now I'm going to take you to my house. Do you have a problem with that?"

"I'm going to let you go because you're so nice to me and you did everything I told you to do."

"That's a whole lot of shit!"

"What are you doing down here?"

"Don't you know this is the worst neighborhood to be in? You know you don't belong here."

"I want you to turn around. I don't want you to see my face. I'm going to leave you at the corner and I'm going to drive off. I'm gonna beep the horn and you're gonna' start walking. Take the tape off your head but if you turn around before I beep the horn, I'm going to come back and put you in the truck again."

MOTIVE

The purpose of an attack is the general motivation evidenced by a convergence of the behavioral evidence. It can also include the specific goals of the offender during the offense, if they are known. See Chapter 15, The Behavior-Motivational Typology.

VICTIM SELECTION

Victim selection is a term that refers to the process by which an offender intentionally chooses or targets a victim. Each offender has their own selection criteria, which satisfies their specific needs. The need for a victim can be primary to the purpose of the offense (the offender's motive), or it can be ancillary. Put another way, a particular victim can be the whole reason for the offense, or they may be chosen by other criteria as an object, selected for verbal and behavioral scripting into an offender fantasy.

The major factors that can influence this decision-making process (which are not mutually exclusive) include:

AVAILABILITY

This refers to a particular victim's accessibility to the offender. It is related to the concept of offender risk (see Chapter 10).

LOCATION

This refers to the victim's particular locality in contrast to the offender's. It is often a function of both offender and victim activities and schedules, and is also related to the concept of offender risk (see Chapter 10).

VULNERABILITY

This refers to the offender's perception of a how susceptible a particular victim is to their method of approach and attack. It is also related to the concept of offender risk (see Chapter 10).

RELATIONSHIPS

This refers to victims who are selected by virtue of being in a relationship with the offender. (Spouse, parent, family member, co-worker, friend, roommate, therapist, teacher, etc.)

SYMBOLIC CRITERIA

This refers to victims who are selected by virtue of sharing characteristics of those in a relationship with the offender. (Spouse, parent, family member, co-worker, friend, roommate, therapist, teacher, etc.)

FANTASY CRITERIA

This refers to victims who are selected by virtue of having traits that a particular offender views as desirable or necessary for the satisfaction of a particular fantasy. The nature of those desireable or necessary traits will be born out in the victimology and the offender signature behavior.

Remember that each of these can be, but are not required to be, an influence on the offender's decision to choose or target a victim. The criminal profiler must determine what selection criteria are at work for the offender at hand, as evidenced by a convergence of the behavioral evidence. This is best born out in a thorough comparison of victimology and offender motive. (Determining who the victim really was, in light of what the offender believed they were doing with that victim, in that crime scene.)

OPPORTUNISTIC ELEMENTS

The term *opportunistic* refers to any unplanned element that is seized upon by the offender for inclusion in an offense. It can refer to an opportunistic victim, an opportunistic offense, an opportunistic weapon, or an opportunistic location – anything that was not planned for but was utilized during the offense.

Evidence of opportunistic elements or behavior in an offense does not necessarily imply an unplanned or unimagined offense.

In assessing whether or not a behavior or element (victim, location, etc.) is opportunistic, remember to look for any associated behavior or element that indicates preplanning. These include, but are not limited to:

- evidence of victim surveillance;
- items brought to the crime scene specific to the crime committed (rape kit, lock picks, disguise, weapon, etc.);
- strange calls to the victim prior to the attack;
- intimate knowledge of victim's residence and personal schedule.

It is not uncommon for investigators to mistakenly theorize that an offender is generally opportunistic when a victim appears to be one of opportunity (a mistake often made when an inadequate victimology has been done). They may therefore reason that the offender is less dangerous, or less likely to offend in the future. This can result in a-priori investigative bias which results in the failure to recognize offender preplanning behavior, or the pattern of a serial offender.

MO INDICATORS OF OPPORTUNISTIC BEHAVIOR

- offense occurs during the commission of another offense or other offender activity;
- offense lasts a very short period of time;
- offense is committed hastily – lots of evidence left at the scene;
- available materials used by offender to disable victim;
- offense is controlled by the context it occurs in.

CRIME-SCENE STAGING

Crime-scene staging is a term that refers to a conscious criminal action by an offender to thwart an investigation; not extended to families attempting to preserve the dignity of their loved ones (Geberth 1996). Evidence of "staging" indicates a criminal or precautionary intent. When people alter a crime scene to preserve a loved one's dignity, they do so for personal reasons and not to harm the investigative effort.

Geberth notes that the most common type of staging occurs when offenders alter the elements of a crime scene to make it appear as though a death scene is a suicide, or an accident, when in fact what took place was actually a homicide.

Some simple methods of crime-scene manipulation in these cases include:

- intentionally destroying or hiding physical evidence;
- situating a murder weapon (i.e. shotgun) into the hands of the victim;
- relocating a body, after death, to a secondary crime scene where accidental death is possible (i.e. the bottom of a cliff, into a body of water, etc.);
- giving false statements to witnesses or authorities during an investigation;
- preparing a suicide note.

Geberth also notes that the other common form of staging is when an offender, attempts to redirect the homicide investigation by manipulating evidence in such a way that it suggests a sexual homicide. Commonly, this is an attempt to conceal something anger related (like a domestic situation that explodes into violent homicide).

Some methods of crime scene manipulation in these cases include:

- alteration/ripping of victim clothing;
- removal of victim clothing;
- disposing of the victim at a remote, outdoor location unrelated to the victim or the offender;
- post-mortem sexual display of body.

Recognizing red flags for crime-scene staging requires an investigation into the following questions (Burgess *et al.* 1997):

- If profit was the motive, did the suspect take the appropriate items from the crime scene?
- Did the point of entry to the crime scene make sense?
- Did the perpetration of the crime pose a high risk to the offender?
- Did the injuries to the victim fit the crime?
- Do witness accounts conflict with each other, or with the forensic evidence?
- Is there evidence of paradoxical witness behavior or statements (witnesses who joke with investigators at the death scene of their loved ones, excessive or misdirected anger, etc.)?

REFERENCES

Burgess, A., Burgess, A., Douglas, J. and Ressler, R. (1997) *Crime Classification Manual*, San Francisco: Jossey-Bass, Inc.

Burgess, A. and Hazelwood, R. (eds) (1995), *Practical Aspects of Rape Investigation: A Multidisciplinary Approach*, 2nd edn, New York: CRC Press.

Burgess, A. and Holmstrom, L. (1979) "Rapist's Talk: Linguistic Strategies to Control the Victim," *Deviant Behavior*, Vol. 1, Washington DC: Hemisphere.

DiMaio, D. and DiMaio V. (1993) *Forensic Pathology*, Boca Raton: CRC Press.

Geberth, V. (1996) *Practical Homicide Investigation*, 3rd edn, New York: CRC Press.

Lee, H. (ed.) (1994) *Crime Scene Investigation*, Taiwan, R.O.C.: Central Police University Press.

CHAPTER 12

ORGANIZED V. DISORGANIZED – A FALSE DICHOTOMY

Brent E. Turvey, M.S.

He has observ'd the Golden Rule, Til he's become the Golden Fool.

(William Blake)

It should be emphasized that the crime scene rarely will be completely organized or disorganized. It is more likely to be somewhere on a continuum between the two extremes of the orderly, neat crime scene and the disarrayed, sloppy one.

(Burgess *et al.* 1997: 9)

Dichotomy is a term that refers to a division into two polarized or contradictory parts or opinions. The *organized* and *disorganized* crime-scene classification theory represents such a conceptual division.

The FBI's Behavioral Sciences Unit (BSU) developed the organized and disorganized dichotomy in the 1980s as an attempt to more effectively communicate and teach profiling tools. This was in response to overwhelming requests from law enforcement for investigative assistance, insight, and criminal profiling services. The organized and disorganized dichotomy, based on the collective experiences of those in the BSU (Burgess *et al.* 1988), was intended to simplify the language of crime scene profiling for unsophisticated law enforcement agencies requesting profiles. It also leant itself very effectively as a teaching tool for FBI students of criminal profiling techniques (who, again, were intended to be law enforcement).

> Amassing this knowledge was one thing. Communicating it to our audience – those police officers who sought our help in tracking down violent criminals – was another. To characterize the types of offenders for police and other law enforcement people, we needed to have a terminology that was not based on psychiatric jargon. It wouldn't do much good to say to a police officer that he was looking for a psychotic personality if that police officer had no training in psychology; we needed to speak to the police in terms that they could understand and that would assist them in their searches for killers, rapists, and other violent criminals. Instead of saying that a crime scene showed evidence of a psychopathic personality, we began to tell the police officer that such a particular crime scene was 'organized,' and so was the likely offender, while another and its perpetrator might be 'disorganized,' when mental disorder was present (Ressler and Shachtman 1992).

It is a very simple concept. A crime scene that is messy, with a lot of physical evidence, can be labeled, "disorganized," and is used to suggest a disorganized, psychotic offender. A crime scene that has very little evidence, and appears less chaotic, can be labeled, "organized," and is used to suggest an organized, psychopathic offender.

This classification system is very easy to use, and can be applied almost without thinking, making it especially seductive to those without any actual education in, or knowledge of, human psychology (i.e. the majority of law enforcement). In fact, that is the type of person it was designed for. The organized and disorganized dichotomy gives law enforcement personnel without any other real education and training in human psychology or human emotional and psychological development, ready access to unsophisticated, simple labels with forensic mental health implications.

PSYCHOPATHIC (ORGANIZED) V. PSYCHOTIC (DISORGANIZED) CRIME SCENES

In reading the chart below, it should be clear to readers just how much room for variability there is between these two classifications.

Adapted from Burgess *et al.* (1988), the characteristics in Table 12.1 show the theoretical differences between organized and disorganized crime scenes observed by those authors, suggested by their research. This dichotomy is the epitome of inductive profiling. If a crime scene has organized characteristics, it is assumed that the offender must also be organized. If a crime scene has disorganized characteristics, it is conversely assumed that the offender must also be disorganized.

Readers may recognize some of these offender characteristics from the boilerplate checklists that are routinely released by FBI-trained profilers to police departments and news agencies as the profile of an unknown offender in a given case. This is one of two major sources that those boilerplate characteristics originate from. The other source is the Groth (1979) Rapist Motivational Typologies (see Chapter 15).

The profiling implications of this classification system are that disorganized offenders are, as discussed, inferred to be psychotic. That is to say, by virtue of a messy crime scene, they are determined to be suffering from a mental illness that afflicts them with a psychosis that is evidenced by a deterioration of normal intellectual and social functioning, and by a partial or complete withdrawal from reality.

Conversely, organized offenders are, as discussed, inferred to be psychopathic. That is to say, by virtue of a relatively clean crime scene, they are determined not to be suffering from a mental illness that afflicts them with

TABLE 12.1 Theoretical differences between organized and disorganized crime scenes

PSYCHOPATHIC (ORGANIZED) CRIME-SCENE CHARACTERISTICS

- Offense preplanned
- Victim a targeted stranger
- Personalizes victim
- Controlled conversation
- Crime scene reflects overall control
- Demands submissive victim
- Restraints used
- Aggressive acts prior to death
- Body hidden
- Weapon/evidence absent
- Transports victim or body (Attack occurs at primary scene; victim dumped at secondary scene)

PSYCHOPATHIC (ORGANIZED) OFFENDER CHARACTERISTICS

- Average to above average intelligence
- Socially competent
- Skilled work preferred
- Sexually competent
- High birth order status
- Father's work stable
- Inconsistent childhood discipline
- Controlled mood during crime
- Use of alcohol with crime
- Precipitating situational stress
- Living with partner
- Mobility with a car in good condition
- Follows crime in news and media
- May change jobs or leave town

PSYCHOTIC (DISORGANIZED) CRIME-SCENE CHARACTERISTICS

- Spontaneous offense
- Victim or location known
- Depersonalization of the victim
- Minimal conversation
- Crime scene random and sloppy
- Sudden violence to victim
- Minimal use of restraints
- Sexual acts after death
- Body left in view
- Evidence/weapon often present
- Body left at death scene (primary scene only)

PSYCHOTIC (DISORGANIZED) OFFENDER CHARACTERISTICS

- Below average intelligence
- Socially inadequate
- Unskilled work
- Sexually Incompetent
- Low birth order status
- Father's work unstable
- Harsh discipline as a child
- Anxious mood during crime
- Minimal use of alcohol
- Minimal situational stress
- Living alone
- Lives/works near crime scene
- Minimal interest in news media
- Significant behavior change (drug/alcohol abuse, religiosity, etc.)

a psychosis. They are determined to be aware of, and understand the nature and quality of, their behavior.

Both of these inferences, key to the profiling applications of the organized and disorganized crime scene classification theory, are predictions masquerading as conclusions.

THE FALSE DICHOTOMY

This author does not agree with or advocate the use of the organized and disorganized dichotomy[1]. That is because it is a false dichotomy. It arises from mistaken ideas about the developmental nature of criminal behavior and the value of crime-scene reconstruction. There are some very straight-forward arguments that evidence this.

First, the majority of crime scenes will present somewhere on a continuum between the two extreme classifications of organized and disorganized, not as simply one or the other. Even the *Crime Classification Manual* (Burgess *et al.* 1997) states this quite plainly on page 9. This fact has not kept the ignorant, as well as the unqualified, from attempting to cram crime scenes, and subsequent offenders, into these classifications. Clearly this has been one of the most overlooked passages in the CCM.

Second, only a competent forensic analysis, performed by qualified forensic scientists and reconstruction criminalists, can give insight into how and why a crime scene presents the way that it does in a given case. The amount of evidence left behind or not left behind must be viewed in the context of a dynamic series of events. It cannot be interpreted at a glance through an isolating construct.

Third, crime scenes evidencing disorganized characteristics can be created as a result of the following non-psychotic and non-mental-illness-oriented events (this is not an all-inclusive list):

- anger-retaliatory offenders who do not suffer from any kind of mental illness (see Chapter 15);
- domestic-violence-related offenses;
- staged offenses;
- interrupted offenses
- offenses involving controlled substances.

Fourth, a crime scene evidencing organized characteristics does not auto-matically suggest a psychopathic offender. Psychopathy is a very specific personality disorder (see Chapter 17). It is not evidenced merely by a lack of psychotic behavior.

Fifth, labeling an offender using the dichotomy may cause a failure to account for an offender's development over time. Some offenders become more competent and skilled over time, leaving less evidence and engaging in more precautionary acts. Other offenders may become less competent and skillful over time, decompensating by virtue of a deteriorating mental state, or increased use of controlled substances.

For instance, an offender evidencing an anger–retaliatory motivational aspect would leave a crime scene most likely classified as disorganized. However, such offenders have been known to learn to eroticize the pain that they inflict to their victims, over time, and subsequently incorporate sadistic motivational aspects. Sadistic motivations can lead to the evolution of crime scene behaviors that would be classified as organized.

For a classic example of a deteriorating mental state evidenced by the serial murderer Ted Bundy, see Chapter 13.

Sixth, and related to arguments two and five, the organized and disorganized dichotomy quite inappropriately hinges offender classification on *modus-operandi* considerations. It takes into account what appears to have occurred, physically, but does not take into account why it occurred. This bears pointing out because those who constructed the dichotomy at the NCAVC know the difference between offender MO and signature, and they understand the investigative dangers of ignoring signature considerations. However, para-doxically, they have constructed a crime-scene classification tool that appears to completely ignore those concerns.

Seventh, an ethical danger of the organized and disorganized dichotomy is that it essentially, and undeservedly, empowers those who use it to speak from a clinical perspective on issues that have courtroom relevance. This issue will be further elucidated in Chapters 20 and 21.

> Looking at the crime scene photographs and the police reports, it was apparent to me that this was not a crime committed by an 'organized' killer who stalked his victims, was methodical in how he went about his crimes, and took care to avoid leaving clues to his own identity. No, from the appearance of the crime scene, it was obvious to me that we were dealing with a 'disorganized' killer, a person who had a full blown mental illness. (Ressler and Shachtman 1992)

The author of this statement presumes the ability to essentially diagnose a mental illness without the benefit of clinical interviews, years of clinical training, or a competent forensic reconstruction of what he is actually looking at in the photos.

AUTHOR'S SUGGESTION

When approaching a case and examining related crime scenes, we, as criminal profilers and investigators of fact, should purge ourselves of expectation. The physical evidence and its context should be our primary guide. Therefore we cannot, in good conscience, approach crime scenes using the organized or disorganized classifications. To do so is an invitation to be misled by what is no more than a badly thought out set of offender generalizations designed for train-ing those without basic levels of knowledge in the area of human psychology.

The organized and disorganized crime scene dichotomy is a beautiful theory that cannot withstand the scrutiny of critical analysis. As with any theory that cannot be supported by the facts, and that would ultimately harm an investigative effort, it should be abandoned.

REFERENCES

Burgess, A., Burgess, A., Douglas, J. and Ressler, R. (1997) *Crime Classification Manual*, San Francisco: Jossey-Bass, Inc.

Burgess, A., Douglas, J. and Ressler, R. (1988) *Sexual Homicide: Patterns and Motives*, New York: Lexington Books.

Groth, A. N. (1979) *Men Who Rape: The Psychology of the Offender*, New York: Plenum Press.

Ressler, R. and Shachtman, T. (1992) *Whoever Fights Monsters*, New York: St. Martin's Press.

CHAPTER 13

UNDERSTANDING MODUS OPERANDI

Brent E. Turvey, M.S.

This thou must always bear in mind, what is the nature of the whole,
and what is my nature, and how this is related to that,
and what kind of a part it is of what kind of a whole.

(Marcus Aurelius, *Meditations, II: 9*)

Modus operandi (MO) is a Latin term that means, "a method of operating." It refers to the behaviors that are committed by an offender for the purpose of successfully completing an offense (Burgess *et al.* 1997). An offender's *modus operandi* reflects *how* an offender committed their crimes. It is separate from the offender's motives, or *signature aspects* (see Chapter 14), as these have to do with *why* an offender commits their crimes.

An offender's *modus operandi* has traditionally been investigatively relevant for the case-linkage efforts of law enforcement. To the criminal profiler, it is also relevant because it can involve procedures or techniques that are characteristic of a particular discipline or field of knowledge. This can include behaviors that are reflective of both criminal and non-criminal expertise.

INVESTIGATING CRIMINAL BEHAVIOR

Law enforcement has long held to the belief that understanding the methods and techniques criminals use to commit crime is the best way to investigate and ultimately apprehend them. This has traditionally required that the best detectives become a living encyclopedia of criminal cases and criminal behaviors. It has also demanded that they learn to utilize the knowledge and experience of known criminals to inform their investigative strategy.

A strong belief in this way of approaching the process of criminal investigation was well demonstrated in France, in 1817, when a former convict named Eugene Vidocq, who had been working as a police spy, was assigned by the government to form a Brigade de Surete. He organized and led this group of detectives, mostly former criminals themselves, as it grew from four to twenty-eight in number.

Vidocq and his detectives were paid based upon the number of criminals that they apprehended. Within their first year, they had made more than 750 arrests. This led some to believe that Vidocq and his detectives were a perfect solution to the local criminal problem; they understood how criminals operated, had insights into their habits and methods of operation, and were putting that knowledge to work for the good of the state. However, this led others to suspect that Vidocq and his detectives committed many of the crimes themselves, and then framed known criminals or detractors in order to close out the cases. This suspicion was never proven, however, and Vidocq enjoys a largely favorable historical place as the first, and very successful, chief of the French *Surete Nationale* (Symons 1966).

Whether or not Vidocq was a master detective or merely continued his criminal career through the Surete, a philosophy of criminal investigation emerged. To understand criminals, to develop competent investigative strategies, to link their crimes, and to successfully apprehend them, detectives needed to understand the particular methods criminals used to commit their crimes. This is an investigative philosophy that survives on an international level, in one form or another, to the present day.

DEFINITIONS

Modus operandi has been defined as the behaviors that are committed by an offender for the purpose of successfully completing an offense (Burgess *et al.* 1997). A criminal's MO comprises learned behaviors that can evolve and develop over time. It can be refined, as an offender becomes more experienced, sophisticated, and confident (Geberth 1996). It can also become less competent and less skillful over time, decompensating by virtue of a deteriorating mental state, or increased used of controlled substances (Turvey: in press).

In either case, an offender's MO behavior is functional by its nature. It most often serves (or fails to serve) one or more of three purposes:

1 protects the offender's identity;

2 ensures the successful completion of the crime;

3 facilitates the offender's escape.

General types of MO behaviors include actions such as, but are not limited to:

- amount of planning before a crime;
- offense location selection (i.e. in a public park, on a school campus, or in a victim's residence, etc.);
- presurveillance of a crime scene or victim;
- involvement of a victim during a crime;
- use of a weapon during a crime;

- use of restraints to control the victim during a crime;
- offender precautionary acts (i.e. wearing a mask, gloves, covering the victim's eyes during an attack, wearing a condom during a rape, forcing the victim to bathe after a sexual attack, etc.);
- offender transportation to and from the crime scene (i.e. use of a bicycle, use of a motorized vehicle, walking, etc.).

An offender's MO, which is the method employed to commit the crime, is not the same thing as an offender's *motive*, which is their reason for committing the crime. An offender's motives are evidenced by *signature behaviors* that suggest overall *signature aspects*, or motivational aspects of a crime. Signature behaviors are those which satisfy the offender's emotional and psychological needs. They are typically not necessary for the completion of the crime, and tend to show less evolution across offenses than MO behavior (see Chapter 14).

INFLUENCES ON *MODUS OPERANDI*

An offender's MO behaviors are learned, and by extension dynamic and malleable. This is because MO behavior is affected by time, and can change as the offender learns or decompensates. In one case, an offender may realize that some of the things they do during a crime are more effective. They may subsequently repeat them in future offenses, and become more skillful, refining their MO. Furthermore, an offender may recognize a deficiency in their MO, and seek to remedy it in future offenses (Geberth 1996).

However, MO behavior may also change due to a criminal's deteriorating mental state, due to the influence of controlled substances, or due to increased confidence that law enforcement will not successfully apprehend them. These things may cause a criminal's MO to become less skillful, less competent, and more careless.

Over the course of an offender's life or experience, they may learn things that are incorporated into criminal behavior to refine their MO, but which unintentionally reveals something about their personality or experience (Burgess *et al.* 1997). Common ways that any offender can learn how to more skillfully commit crime, evade capture, and conceal their identity include, but are certainly not limited to, those listed below.

EDUCATIONAL AND TECHNICAL MATERIALS

Offenders are human beings with equal access to all of the same learning opportunities of any other citizen. Professional journals, college courses, textbooks, and other educationally oriented media available at the public library or on the Internet can provide offenders with knowledge that is useful towards refining their particular MO. The important lesson for the criminal profiler is that the offender's MO may reflect familiarity or proficiency with specialized knowledge or techniques, and this can be incorporated into the final criminal profile as well as provide investigatively relevant direction.

Arsonists may read *Kirk's Fire Investigation*, by John DeHaan; rapists may read *Practical Aspects of Rape Investigation*, by Burgess *et al*; murderers may read *Practical Homicide Investigation*, by Vernon Geberth; and bank robbers may subscribe to security magazines[1].

TRADE OR PROFESSIONAL EXPERIENCE

Offenders may have been or may currently be employed in trades or professions that utilize special knowledge, or require proficiency with specialized techniques (i.e. electrician, plumber, telephone company, computers, military, law enforcement, pilot, and so on). These may find their way into an offender's MO, and be reflected in their offense-related behavior. Despite any specialization or proficiency, these behaviors are necessarily signature behaviors.

An arsonist may be a volunteer fire fighter and use department-issued flares or techniques duplicated from internal training materials to start their fires. A rapist may be a security guard for the building where they target victims, and as such may have an insider's knowledge of how to circumvent security protocols, as well as using handcuffs to restrain victims. A murderer may also be in the military, and may use government-issue ammunition or weaponry. And a robber may have previously worked for the business that they have robbed, and may subsequently evidence specialized knowledge of shift change times and procedures, security protocols, the locations of valuables, and law enforcement response time.

CRIMINAL EXPERIENCE AND CONFIDENCE

As an offender commits more of the same type of crime, they may become more proficient at it. They may act more confidently, be able to handle the unexpected more smoothly (or even be more prepared for it), or they may have tailored their precautionary acts (see Chapter 11) to the type of criminal activity they expect to engage in. It is important to establish, in any crime, what the offender had planned for by virtue of what they brought with them, and by virtue of the behaviors they engaged in. The first question that criminal profilers need to ask is whether the materials brought and the behaviors committed were appropriate to the crime. The second question is whether or not the materials brought and the behaviors committed are suggestive of proficiency with another type of crime (suggesting a criminal history apart from the crime at hand) (Turvey: in press).

[1] *I often get asked why I would provide training and information to the public that might help a criminal become more proficient. The public availability of such material is not the problem, in my view. I'm not so much concerned that criminals get a hold of books such as these, but that those who are responsible for investigating crimes won't.*

Besides, the law enforcement community has its own share of criminals (as does any profession).

CONTACT WITH THE CRIMINAL JUSTICE SYSTEM

Being arrested just once may teach an offender an invaluable lesson about how to avoid detection by law enforcement in the future. Further still, and with some great irony, a prison term in the United States is referred to by some in both law enforcement and the criminal population as "going to college." This is because younger and less-experienced offenders have the opportunity in prison to network with older and more experienced offenders who have already accumulated a great deal of criminal knowledge. Subsequently, a prison term of only a few years has the potential to advance an offender's skill level far beyond their original MO. Once released, that offender may take their "education" and embark on criminal enterprises that before would have been beyond their ability.

THE MEDIA

Some offenders monitor investigations into crimes by paying close attention to media accounts in the newspapers and on television. It is important that investigators and profilers alike pay close attention to the release of any such information to the media, when it was released, and how that may impact the future crimes of a given offender in serial cases (see Chapter 18). Not only may information relating to a case provide an offender with insight into future precautionary acts, but it may also provide other offenders with adequate information to "copycat" a particular series, and defer investigative suspicion from themselves.

For example, a rapist may commit five different attacks in a single region. They may go unconnected until DNA results come back and demonstrate that the rapes were more than likely committed by the same offender. If the media publishes a headline that reads "Serial rapist linked to five attacks by DNA!" the rapist may alter his MO behavior to prevent law enforcement from linking future cases. The rapist may do so by making temporary changes, such as using a condom during any future rapes. Or, the rapist may decide to make a more permanent change and get a vasectomy. Either way, the rapist may make a conscious attempt to prevent the transfer of a particular type of evidence based on what they have learned from the media coverage in the case or other similar cases.

OFFENDER MOOD

An offender's mood on a given day can influence their aggression level going into an offense, and the manner in which they subsequently react to victim and crime scene influences. For example, if a rapist has a heated argument with their relationship partner an hour prior to attacking a victim, their aggression level is likely to be higher than during previous offenses where such an argument was not a factor. Subsequently there may be less planning or control evident in crime-scene behavior. (Victim injury may also be higher, but this would be reflective of the signature aspect – see Chapter 14).

X-FACTORS

An X-factor, for our purposes, is any unknown or unplanned influence that can affect crime-scene behavior during an offense. The successful completion of any offense, from an offender's perspective, is dependent upon the event conforming to their fantasies or expectations. Under real-life conditions, crime scenes, victims and other extrinsic influences (i.e. weather, witnesses, scheduled events, and so on) may not always conform to offender expectations. The presence of any number of X-factors, such as victims under the influence of controlled substances, unexpected witnesses, and unexpected victim responses (compliance, non-compliance, death, etc.), may force the offender to improvise or to make a hasty retreat, resulting in an interrupted/incomplete offense, or an offense gone wrong.

> Example
> A rapist attacks women in the park by approaching them from behind and dragging them into the nearby woods. He uses one arm around their neck to control them, and puts their shirts up over their face during the attack to conceal his identity. When he is finished, he manually chokes them until they pass out and leaves them unconscious.

An *interrupted/incomplete offense* is one that does not contain enough MO behaviors to complete the offense. An incomplete event might include the following: the victim in the example, instead of being easy prey, turns around and kicks the offender in the groin. The offender may be stunned and limp away or the victim may create an opportunity to flee the scene. Or, during the attack on his victim, the offender might be unwittingly witnessed by a passerby and flee the scene. Either way, the event would not have included the full potential range of offender MO behaviors, and would therefore be incomplete.

An *offense gone wrong* is one that contains unintentional, unplanned MO behavior, which increases the offender's risk or criminal status. An event gone wrong might include the following: in the example given, the offender might accidentally use too much force, or the victim response might be too violent for him, and the offender's control-oriented choking could result in the victim's death. This turn of events can transform a serial rape investigation into a homicide investigation, increasing the offender's criminal status.

THE DE-EVOLUTION OF MO

As discussed, MO behavior does not always evolve to become more competent as the offender progresses through their criminal career. Due to a deteriorating mental state, the use of controlled substances, or increased confidence that law enforcement will not successfully apprehend them, an offender's MO behaviors can de-evolve over time to a *less* competent and *less* skillful level than when they first began.

> Example
> The American serial murderer Theodore (Ted) Bundy, who killed at least 30 victims across five states between 1973 and 1978, began his criminal career with a very competent, very well-thought-out MO. He was polite and friendly, extremely mobile, and often approached his victims in some manner as to appear helpless or weak, and essentially non-threatening. He sometimes accomplished this by presenting himself as a motorist who needed assistance with a disabled vehicle, and would often wear his arm in a false sling. He also tended to select victims who were teenage females, stalking them and selecting a disposal site for their body well in advance of committing an actual crime. But his MO deteriorated remarkably over time.
>
> After being incarcerated and then escaping on two separate occasions in Colorado, he made his way to Florida. He began to drink heavily, and he began to involve the bodies of his victims in rituals (*signature behavior*), including keeping the body for days at a time after death. There was also evidence that Bundy shampooed some of his victim's hair, and applied make-up to their corpses, rather than disposing of them immediately. In short, he began to leave more and more evidence behind, engaged in fewer precautionary acts, and became involved in more ritual behavior. His victim selection also changed; he chose his last victim, a 12-year-old female student from Florida, totally by virtue of her availability. This was a marked departure from his previous MO behavior of carefully stalking victims in advance and selecting victims who were in their late teens and early 20s. (Hickey 1991)

Understanding how and why an offender's MO evolves, or devolves as the case may be, is crucial to the criminal-profiling process and to the subsequent development of investigative strategy. An offender's MO tells the criminal profiler what an offender has considered, what they have not considered, and what they were subsequently prepared and unprepared for. This means that a criminal profiler must be open to considering all possible influences on an offender's behavior, and what those influences may suggest to them.

REFERENCES

Burgess, A., Burgess, A., Douglas, J. and Ressler, R. (1997) *Crime Classification Manual*, San Francisco: Jossey-Bass, Inc.

Geberth, V. (1996) *Practical Homicide Investigation*, 3rd edn, New York: CRC Press.

Hickey, E. (1991) *Serial Murderers and Their Victims*, Pacific Grove: Brooks/Cole Publishing Co.

Symons, J. (1996) *A Pictorial History of Crime*, New York: Bonanza Books.

Turvey, B. (in press) "Modus Operandi," *Encyclopedia of Forensic Science*, London: Academic Press.

CHAPTER 14

UNDERSTANDING SIGNATURE

Brent E. Turvey, M.S.

Those ideas which, in others, are casual or obscure, which are entertained in moments of abstraction and solitude and easily escape when the scene is changed, have obtained an immovable hold upon his mind.

(Charles Brockden Brown, *Weiland*)

The senses' joy is always dependent upon the imagination.

(Marquis DeSade, *Justine*)

Signature is a term that was first coined by the American criminal profiler John Douglas, a special agent with the Federal Bureau of Investigation who was the head of their Behavioral Sciences Unit in the 1980s. He developed the term to help those investigators involved in criminal profiling distinguish offender behaviors that suggest psychological needs and themes, from offender behaviors that are a part of their *modus operandi* (see Chapter 13) (Douglas 1995).

The term signature is used, in theory, to describe behaviors committed by an offender that serves their psychological and emotional needs (Geberth 1996). It is believed that through an analysis and interpretation of a particular offender's signature behaviors, in combination with other elements such as *modus operandi* (MO) and victimology, that criminal profilers may link cases and develop an understanding of an offender's *motive* for committing the crime. However, despite the development of the term, and its adoption by the law enforcement community, there is still a great deal of confusion regarding its applied use on a case-by-case basis.

DEFINITIONS

An *offender signature* is a pattern of distinctive behaviors that are characteristic of, and satisfy, emotional and psychological needs[1]. There are two separate but interdependent parts to the concept of offender signature.

First, there is the general *signature aspect* of a crime. The overall signature aspect represents the emotional or psychological themes that the offender satisfies when he commits an offense. These include, but are not necessarily limited to, the following general motivational categories (see Chapter 15):

[1] This definition is an evolution of the definitions developed by Douglas, Ressler, Geberth, and Keppel independent of each other. It owes them each a great debt, but refines the concept of offender signature to the point where it is actually useful, and can be further broken down into its identifiable parts.

- profit;
- anger/retaliation;
- reassurance/experimentation;
- assertiveness/entitlement;
- sadism.

As we will discuss later in this chapter, these are not mutually exclusive motivational themes.

The second part of offender signature is that signature aspects are manifested or evidenced by *signature behaviors*. Signature behaviors are those acts committed by an offender, which are not necessary to commit the crime, but that suggest the psychological or emotional needs of that offender.

The problem for the criminal profiler is distinguishing between MO behaviors and signature behaviors. The bigger problem is that signature needs and MO needs may be satisfied by the same behavior. This behavioral conundrum is best elucidated by what are perhaps the two most important axioms of criminal profiling and behavioral evidence analysis:

1 Different offenders do similar things for different reasons.
2 Individual offender behaviors are multi-determined; they can be the result of multiple offender motivations and multiple external influences.

Due to the differences in the ways that offenders express their psychological needs, differences between the manifestation of their *modus-operandi* behaviors and signature behaviors are not always readily apparent to even the most competent criminal profilers.

In the case of one offender, for example, the act of covering a victim's face with her own shirt during a rape may be a part of a psychological desire, facilitating a fantasy that the victim is another person. This would be a signature behavior.

In the case of another offender, the act of covering a victim's face with her own shirt during a rape may be a part of a functional need to keep the victim from seeing his face, and identifying him at a later time. This behavior would then be considered a part of the offender's *modus operandi*.

In the case of yet another offender, behavior being multi-determined, the same act could be intended to satisfy both of the above needs, and therefore could be a part of both an offender's MO and signature.

To address the issue of whether a behavior is part of the MO, or part of the signature, criminal profilers must look for behavioral patterns and convergences. They must not fall into the inductive trap of interpreting behavioral meaning based on averaged meanings born from unrelated offenses. They must further not fall into the trap of interpreting a single behavior outside of the context of the facts of a given case, and apart from the other behaviors in the offense. A behavior's meaning to the offender can only be interpreted when it is in context.

THE PSYCHODYNAMICS OF OFFENDER SIGNATURE

Not all offenders are the same. They have different histories, different likes, and different needs. Therefore, as suggested above, similar behaviors committed under similar circumstances by different offenders will not necessarily be for identical or even similar motivations. The reason for this is related directly to theories about normal human development (Turvey: in press).

According to the American psychologist Dr John Money, the explanation for this behavioral–motivational distinctiveness is that offenders have in their mind's eye a pattern of specific behaviors, and subsequent associated feelings, that he refers to as a *love map* (Money 1989). Love map is a term that Dr Money developed to describe an idealized scene, person, and/or program of activities that satisfy the particular emotional and psychological needs of an offender. Love maps, needs, or fantasies develop in all people (not just criminals) as a part of the natural process of human development, and can subsequently be affected by both biological and environmental factors.

Dr Money theorized that criminal behaviors result when the human developmental process is derailed, and a person is able to make pleasurable associations with violent or otherwise criminal activity[2]. These associations, varied and evolving over time, amount to a behavioral distinctiveness in the way that an individual offender seeks to satisfy their emotional or psychological needs during the commission of a crime such as rape, homicide, arson, and other similar or serial offenses.

The specific etiology of offender signature has been described as an offender's fantasies that are progressive in nature, and contribute to thoughts of committing violent or predatory behavior (Keppel 1995). As an offender's fantasy behavior develops over time, so does the need to live out those fantasies. When a violent or predatory fantasy is subsequently acted out, the act itself fuels the fantasy in the mind of the offender and causes it to evolve. The process is complimentary, and can facilitate the evolution of fantasy, signature behaviors, and signature aspect over time.

SIGNATURE BEHAVIOR

The distinctiveness of a particular offender's needs (again, more than one general type of need may be at work) can be manifested by a particular pattern of signature behavior. Signature behaviors, therefore, are best understood as

[2] Now, "derail" is used here to suggest that the process of associating pleasure with violent and criminal activity is not the normal state of human kind. That argument is flawed for two reasons:

It assumes a normal developmental pathway that one can be derailed from.

What is criminal is subordinate to subjective moral considerations from culture to culture.

a reflection of the underlying personality, lifestyle, and developmental experiences of an offender (Turvey: in press). With the potential of being fairly distinct to a particular offender, depending upon the available convergence of physical and behavioral evidence, a specific pattern of signature behaviors and the needs that they represent can be used to distinguish between crime scenes and potentially between offenders.

Examples of general types of individual signature behaviors include, but are not limited to (Burgess *et al.* 1988; Geberth 1996):

- special order or types of sexual activity;
- special type of ligature or binding;
- inflicts special order or types of injuries;
- displays the body for shock value;
- tortures and/or mutilates the victim;
- engages in ritualistic (repeated) behavior;
- domination;
- excessive manipulation;
- excessive control;
- excessive vulgarity and/or abusive language to the victim;
- scripting the victim to say specific phrases or words;
- excessive brutality.

Signature behaviors are the manifestation of offender needs. They are evidenced in the interaction between the victim, the offender, and the crime

Figures 14.1, 14.2 and 14.3

Male and female teen couple, taken to a remote location and then forced to remove their clothing. The male was executed with a firearm. The female was raped and then executed with a firearm. The bodies were arranged postmortem to emulate a consensual sexual "scene" with the deceased female positioned to fellate the deceased male. There was evidence suggesting that the offender had post-mortem anal sex with the female victim. The victims were intended to be discovered in this position, in an effort to further degrade and humiliate them by the offender.

scene itself. A convergence of these offender signature behaviors is used to infer the offender's signature aspect, or motivational theme, for the offense (see Figures 14.1, 14.2 and 14.3).

RECOGNIZING OFFENDER SIGNATURE

An offender's signature is sometimes referred to inappropriately as a "calling card" or a "trademark" (Keppel 1995). Those terms evoke the vision of a static, inflexible psychological imprint on the crime scene by virtue of offense behavior. This is a misleading comparison, not unlike the poorly contrived term "DNA fingerprinting." [3]

It is true that the ability to interpret the behavioral evidence in a crime scene and recognize offender signature has been shown to be extremely beneficial to the investigative process, and there are many examples of the successful investigative use of offender signature in the published literature (Burgess *et al.* 1997; Geberth 1996).

But there are important limitations on the concept of offender signature that must be understood. Many serial or predatory offenders do have a need to engage in personal expressions during an offense that are very distinct to their individually formed personality. However, despite this behavioral distinctiveness, which is a result of the many different variables affecting the human developmental process, it is not truly appropriate to state that two crime scenes related by signature alone are psychologically "identical." The terms "identical" and "match" can be misleading to those who do not fully understand the concept and psychology of offender signature.

The term "match" may be used to suggest "identical", shared characteristics between two things. But by their very nature, as discussed in Chapter 13 under the "Influences on Modus Operandi" section, *crime scenes and crime-scene behavior cannot be precisely the same even when the same offender authors them.* Not only are the locations likely to be different, but the victims are most certainly different people with their own responses to offender behaviors that will in turn influence the offender's expressions, both MO and signature oriented.

One of the other primary reasons for the lack of absolute certainty in interpreting signature behaviors as unique to a specific offender, is the subjectivity of the interpretation itself. While offenders may be psychologically distinct, profilers cannot see through the eyes of an offender with perfect, objective clarity. They can show the most likely perspectives and needs of the offender by demonstrating a strong convergence of the physical and behavioral evidence, but they cannot go so far as to call it a "psychological fingerprint."

In addition, there are many variables to consider when interpreting signature behaviors that must be factored into any complete analysis. It is

[3] *DNA evidence, though potentially highly individuating, is not a fingerprint. That is to say that fingerprints can tell everyone apart, even twins. Even the most discriminating forensic DNA analysis cannot.*

important to understand that it may not always be possible to link or unlink cases with signature, because:

- an offender may not always leave their signature behaviors behind (see Chapter 13 under the "Influences on Modus Operandi" section, as the same things also influence signature behaviors);

- an offender may engage in precautionary acts that conceal the evidence of signature behaviors (burning evidence, removing unknown fantasy items from the crime scene, staging the crime scene, etc.);

- evidence of offender behavior may be lost, overlooked, or destroyed.

When making inferences about offender signature, profilers may not have all of the facts in the case, or may be operating with flawed investigative assumptions, and must consider the following:

- Whether the amount of behavioral evidence is competent and sufficient to make an interpretation of offender signature (i.e. was there a competent crime-scene reconstruction performed, are the forensic protocols that the reconstruction is based on competent, was evidence of wound patterns lost due to bodily decay, etc.?).

- Whether the amount of behavioral evidence is fully representative of the offender's needs (i.e. is there evidence of interruption during the crime, did the offender have the time to do all of the things that he felt were important, etc.?).

- Whether the behavioral evidence suggests a signature that is part of an escalation or evolution in an offender's fantasy continuum, or whether the offender signature appears to be relatively fixed over time.

Given these pitfalls, it is most appropriate to explain the nature of an offender's patterns of signature behavior, subsequent case linkages, signature aspects, or other inferences, in terms of an appropriate level of confidence, addressing the considerations mentioned. Understanding offender signature is an important investigative tool, and an important part of understanding offender fantasy and motivation. However, until such time as a consistent concept of offender signature has been more thoroughly documented in the literature, and is more universally understood in terms of practical application to crime-scene behavior and human development, a level of caution and care is requisite.

CASE EXAMPLE

The author was asked to review the case of a serial murderer for the defense. The prosecution had employed the services of a well-known, high-profile expert to review the case for linkage using signature and for the possibility of sadistic behavior. The expert had submitted a page and a half report summarizing his findings, which contained language that confused the defense.

They requested that this author review the materials submitted to the prosecution expert and determine whether or not the materials were adequate for the opinions given in the report. This is a very typical defense request and an important part of the checks and balances that exist to inform the adversarial process.

The first three paragraphs of the report are as follows (italic text has been highlighted for emphasis, and identifying information has been removed):

> At your request, I have prepared this brief report to summarize my findings in the above-captioned matter. As you know, my findings are based on photographs and documents provided by your office. I have been unable to interview [the defendant], as his attorney declined to make him available for an interview.
>
> In the material reviewed, I found conclusive evidence that the defendant engaged in sexually sadistic behavior with two surviving sexual partners [females, names withheld], and a murder victim [female, name withheld]. The killer of [the female murder victim] engaged in sexually sadistic behavior with her that is *psychologically identical* to the sexually sadistic behavior exhibited in the murder of [the female murder victim].
>
> The significant behaviors demonstrated at the murder scenes are familiar to you and will not be repeated here, but include the use of blunt force trauma to control the victims, sexual bondage behavior through the use of ligatures, insertion of a foreign object … and asphyxiation.

The report continues on to describe five instances of "significant behaviors" committed by the defendant with living sexual partners that are of the same general type committed during the offense (not the exact same behaviors by any means). There are several problems with the conclusions of this report. They are as follows.

THE TERM "PSYCHOLOGICALLY IDENTICAL"

This term is a very specific reference to the concept of offender signature. As already discussed, given the high degree of evolutionary and environmental influences on crime scenes and crime scene behaviors, no two can be precisely the same physically or psychologically, even if planned and executed by the same offender. Offender signature across two separate offenses, comprising behaviors and motivations, cannot be called identical.

However, the expert in the above case did not say that offender signature was identical. He used the term "psychologically identical," when referring to offender behavior with living compliant victims, and the murder victim. "Psychologically identical" behavior is a term that must mean one of two things:

- Precisely the same behaviors were committed in precisely the same type of location with precisely the same type of victim in precisely the same manner by the same offender to satisfy precisely the same needs.
- The offender committed similar behaviors at two different crime scenes, to satisfy the same general psychological needs.

The second meaning is what the expert in the case hopefully meant, as this is what one can really say regarding even the best cases where signature is used to link cases where the behaviors are so different. The first meaning, however, is what is implied by the term used, and what law enforcement or a jury, without adequate explanation, might hear. There was no such explanation or discussion in the expert's report.

LACK OF RECONSTRUCTION/INADEQUATE INFORMATION

There was no forensic reconstruction of the homicide crime scene. This means that a competent, qualified forensic scientist did not establish the behavior of the offender with the victim using the physical evidence. The expert in the case relied solely upon the crime-scene photos and available law-enforcement documentation and opinion to make informed assumptions about offender behavior.

The expert in question was not qualified to interpret behavior from those photos, and in fact did not seek to determine or establish whether or not the injuries to the victim were received pre-mortem or post-mortem. This would be important, as, in absence of a clinical interview, offender behavior with the victim would have to be the basis for the entire opinion regarding offender sadism. To establish sadism with crime-scene behavior one must prove not only that that the injuries reflect intent to torture the victim, but that the offender enjoyed it (see Chapter 17).

DID NOT ACCOUNT FOR THE MAJOR DIFFERENCES IN CRIME SCENE BEHAVIOR

If one is going to opine on the similarity of offender signature between two cases, one must not only look at how behaviors are the same, but at how behaviors are not the same. Furthermore one must be willing to explain it.

In this case, the blatantly obvious difference in crime-scene behavior is that the comparisons of offender signatures are between two living, consensual victims and one that was killed. Consensual victims by their very nature are going to be psychologically different, in terms of feedback during the encounters, than non-consensual victims. This would be especially true in cases involving sadism where the offender's intent is to elicit a certain type of response from the victim. It is not the suggestion of this author that these differences are irreconcilable with the opinion that the same signature behaviors and aspects may exist. However, the expert in this case did not address it.

Furthermore, without a crime-scene reconstruction by a forensic scientist, one cannot be certain of the crime-scene behavior at all. Even when the best possible reconstruction has been done, there are practical limits to conclusions about behavior, which should prevent us from inappropriate levels of certainty.

In this case, the expert was willing to:

- absolutely confirm the linkage between the cases using a term that implies an inappropriately high level of confidence for the subject matter covered;
- form conclusions about offender and victim behavior based on photographs and a few reports without a crime-scene reconstruction, and without visiting the crime scene;
- form opinions about motive and intent based on unconfirmed, potentially misinformed assumptions about crime-scene behavior.

Any one of these items above invalidates the opinions expressed in the report. Fortunately, the judge in the case agreed, to an extent, and let the expert give only very limited testimony. That he was allowed to testify at all is likely owing to his high professional status.

Regardless of the outcome, this is precisely the type of overconfident interpretation of crime-scene behavior and motivation that hurts those in this field, and derides the credibility of all expert witnesses. Not to mention the damage that it does to the criminal justice system and the victims of violent crime. Criminal profilers need to attenuate themselves to appropriate levels of confidence regarding their opinions.

REFERENCES

Burgess, A., Burgess, A., Douglas, J. and Ressler, R. (1997) *Crime Classification Manual*, San Francisco: Jossey-Bass, Inc.

Burgess, A., Douglas, J. and Ressler, R. (1988) *Sexual Homicide: Patterns and Motives*, New York: Lexington Books.

Douglas, J. (1995) *Mindhunter*, New York: Scribner.

Geberth, V. (1996) *Practical Homicide Investigation*, 3rd edn, New York: CRC Press.

Keppel, R. (1995) "Signature Murders: A report of Several Related Cases," *Journal of Forensic Sciences*, Vol. 40, No. 4, July, pp. 670–4.

Money, J. (1989) *Lovemaps: Clinical Concepts of Sexual/Erotic Health and Pathology, Paraphilia, and Gender Transposition in Childhood, Adolescence, and Maturity*, Amherst, N.Y.: Prometheus Books.

Turvey, B. (in press) "Offender Signature," *Encyclopedia of Forensic Science*, London: Academic Press.

CHAPTER 15

MOTIVATIONAL TYPOLOGIES

Brent E. Turvey, M.S.

Consider where each thing originates, what goes into its composition, what it is changing into, what it is going to be after the change...

(Marcus Aurelius, *Meditations, XI: 17*)

WHAT IS A TYPOLOGY?

The term *typology* most often refers to any systematic grouping of offenders, crime scenes, victims, or behaviors by virtue of one or more shared character-istics. For example, a typology might classify offenders based on their relationship with their victim(s). This typology might include a continuum from total stranger to spouse or intimate, with all manner of relationship types in between like acquaintance, neighbor, friend, classmate, co-worker, or supervisor. Another example is the organized and disorganized dichotomy (see Chapter 12) which classifies offenders and crime scenes. It approaches the criminal event by comparing shared crime-scene characteristics. A typology is, in essence, any classification system.

SIGNATURE ASPECTS AND MOTIVATIONAL TYPOLOGIES

A *signature aspect* is an offender's motivational theme, or psychological need, suggested by a convergence of their signature behaviors. It can be a relatively stable element over time, but it is also susceptible to environmental influences (see Chapter 14). It can also be, depending on the offender, vulnerable to the influences of fantasy development.

In order to understand the motivations of violent, predatory offenders, *A. Nicholas Groth*, an American clinical psychologist who worked with both victims and offender populations, published a study of over 500 rapists in 1979 (Groth 1979). The purpose of his work was clinical. He wanted to classify the motivations of rapists for the purpose of the development of effective treatment plans. In his study, Groth found that rape, like any other crime that satisfies emotional needs, is complex and multi-determined. That is to say, the act of rape, and its associated behaviors, can serve a number of psychological needs and purposes (motives) for the offender (*ibid.*).

Those engaged in criminal profiling research adopted the Groth typology and began to use it investigatively. Ultimately, the Groth typology was modified and used as a part of the basis for the *Crime Classification Manual*, a project designed to create a DSM-type reference specifically for criminals (Burgess *et al.* 1997).

From Groth's studies, and the work of those associated with the FBI's NCAVC, Burgess and Hazelwood (1995) developed the rapist motivational typology further, placing offender behavior into one of five classifications:

1   power reassurance;

2   power assertive;

3   anger retaliatory;

4   sadistic;

5   opportunistic.

The author has found that this motivational classification system, with some modifications (see Chapter 11 – Opportunistic Elements), is useful for classifying most criminal behavior. The penal classifications for a crime, keep in mind, are just one name for a group of offender behaviors that express offender needs. The needs, or motives, that impel human criminal behaviors remain essentially the same for all offenders, despite their behavioral expression that may involve kidnapping, child molestation, terrorism, sexual assault, homicide, and/or arson. This is not to say that the motivational typology presented here should be considered the final word in terms of all *specific* offender motivations. But in terms of general types of offender needs that are being satisfied by offender behavior, they are fairly inclusive, and fairly useful.

Below the author gives a proposed typology with examples of offender behavior adapted and expanded from Turvey (1996), admittedly with some input from Geberth (1996). This author takes credit largely for the fresh, extended perspective and for the shift in emphasis from classifying *offenders* to classifying *behaviors* (turning it from an inductive labeling system to a deductive tool).

However, the author owes a great deal to the following individuals for their efforts and published work in the development of this typology:

- Burgess, A., Burgess, A., Douglas, J. and Ressler, R. (1997) *Crime Classification Manual*, San Francisco: Jossey-Bass, Inc.

- Burgess, A. and Hazelwood, R. (eds) (1995) *Practical Aspects of Rape Investigation: A Multidisciplinary Approach*, 2nd edn, New York: CRC Press.

- Geberth, V. (1996) *Practical Homicide Investigation*, 3rd edn, New York: CRC Press.

■ Groth, A. N. (1979) *Men Who Rape: The Psychology of the Offender*, New York: Plenum Press.

■ Thiel, S.A. Max (ret.) (1995) Lecture: "Crime Scene Profiling" given at The University of New Haven on January 14th, for course titled *CJ 632: Advanced Investigation I.*

A special debt is owed to A. Nicholas Groth for his groundbreaking work in *Men Who Rape* (Groth 1979). He laid the ground upon which we are building, and he reminds us that human behavior is multi-determined.

Keep in mind that this typology is constructed as a guide to help criminal profilers classify behavior, in context, in relationship to the offender need it serves. It is not intended for use as a diagnostic tool, where offenders are crammed into one typology or another and conclusively labeled. Therefore, it is not helpful to think of this as an offender typology, but rather as an offender *behavior–motivational* typology.

Also, readers are admonished not to interpret a single offender behavior outside of its context. For example, an offender who says, "Is your boyfriend home?" to a victim during the abduction phase of a sexual assault may be doing so for MO-related reasons. However, if an offender says the same thing while performing a sexual act on the victim, it may very likely be fantasy related, and subsequently related to offender signature. It is not just about what an offender says or does, it is about how and when they say or do it (context!).

THE BEHAVIOR–MOTIVATIONAL TYPOLOGY

POWER REASSURANCE (AKA COMPENSATORY)

These include offender behaviors that are intended to restore the offender's self-confidence or self-worth through the use of low-aggression means. These behaviors suggest an underlying lack of confidence and a sense of personal inadequacy. This may also manifest itself in a belief that the offense is consensual, or that the victim is somehow a willing or culpable participant.

METHOD OF APPROACH
Surprise.

METHOD OF ATTACK
Verbal threat, weapon.

VERBAL BEHAVIOR/SCRIPTS
Examples include signature behaviors:

■ Reassures victim that they do not wish to harm them. "Don't worry, it will be over soon. I'm not going to hurt/rape you. I'm not that kind of guy."

- Compliments victim. "You're beautiful, I bet you have a lot of boyfriends/girlfriends. You have nice breasts. You have a pretty face."
- Asks for emotional feedback. "Do you like me? Tell me that you won't leave me. Tell me that you love me."
- Self-deprecation. "You couldn't love me; nobody could. I'm so ugly, you're so beautiful. I don't have anything to offer anyone."
- Voices concern for victim welfare: "Am I hurting you? Do you need me to move this? Am I on your hair?"
- Apologetic: "I didn't mean it. Please forgive me. I know I wasn't supposed to do this. I hope you will be okay."
- Asks about victim sexual interests. "Are you a virgin? Do you do this to your boyfriend/girlfriend? Does your boyfriend/girlfriend do this with you?"
- "Do you like this? Does this feel good? Are you going to be getting aroused?" Asks victim to evaluate their sexual skills – sexual reassurance.

SEXUAL BEHAVIOR
Examples include signature behaviors:

- Foreplay attempt with victim (kissing, licking breasts, cunnilingus, and analingus, etc.).
- Involvement of the victim in sexual activity.
- Allowing the victim to negotiate sexual activity.
- Not forcing the victim to physically comply with sexual demands.

PHYSICAL BEHAVIOR
Examples include signature behaviors:

- Does not harm the victim, physically.
- Minimal force used to intimidate victim.
- Relies on threats or the presence of a weapon to get victim compliance.

MO BEHAVIOR

- Selects victims who live in the same general area, often near offender's home, work or other places where they feel comfortable.
- Targets several victims in advance.
- Engages in surveillance of victims.
- Attacks occur in late evening or early morning.
- Victims are alone or with small children when attacked.
- Attack lasts a short period of time: duration increased with victim passivity.
- Vicinity of the attacks remains within same general area.
- Terminates the rape if the victim resists.

SIGNATURE BEHAVIOR

- Engages in voyeuristic behavior of victim before or after attack.
- Takes personal item from the victim, such as an undergarment, ring or photograph.
- Keeps a record of attack.
- Makes obscene phone calls to the victim.
- Contacts the victim after the attack (phone calls asking the victim out on a date, flowers sent to their home, messages on their answering machine telling them what a good time they had).

Offenders evidencing this type of behavior may attempt to re-contact their living victims after an attack. They might have expected the victim to respond erotically to their advances. In the offender's mind the victim might even be in love with them, and have enjoyed the attack. From the offender's point of view, it was more of a date.

The core fantasy motivating this rapist is that the victim will enjoy and eroticize the rape, and subsequently fall in love with the rapist. This stems from the rapist's own fears of personal inadequacy, hence the term commonly applied to this rapist is "an inadequate personality." The rape is restorative of the offender's doubts about himself, and therefore sexually and emotionally reassuring. It will occur as his need for that kind of reassurance arises.

POWER ASSERTIVE (AKA ENTITLEMENT)

These include offender behaviors that are intended to restore the offender's self-confidence or self-worth through the use of moderate- to high-aggression means. These behaviors suggest an underlying lack of confidence and a sense of personal inadequacy, that are expressed through control, mastery, and humiliation of the victim, while demonstrating the offender's sense of authority.

METHOD OF APPROACH

Con or surprise.

METHOD OF ATTACK

Verbal threats, physical force, weapon.

VERBAL BEHAVIOR/SCRIPTS

Examples include signature behaviors:

- Does not want the victim to be verbally or otherwise involved in the attack.
- Gives sexual instructions/commands. "Suck this. Bend over. Hold still. Don't move. Shut up."
- Offender's pleasure is primary.
- Acts "macho".

- Uses a great deal of profanity, language is offensive and abusive.
- Demeans and humiliates the victim. "You are a whore. You are a slut. I own you. You're not so pretty now."
- Verbally explicit about sex. "I'm going to put my cock in your cunt. I'm going to cum in your ass. You are going to suck my dick."
- Verbal threats. "Do what I say and you won't get hurt. Shut up or I'll kill you. I don't want to have to teach you a lesson."

SEXUAL BEHAVIOR

Examples include signature behaviors:

- Offender does whatever they want to the victim, sexually or otherwise.
- Lack of fondling foreplay behavior.
- Repeated attacks with a single victim.
- Offender sexually punishes or abuses victims.
- Offender engages in pulling, pinching or biting behaviors.
- Offender's goal is capture, conquer, and control.
- Victim is a prop only; an object for his sexual fantasy.

PHYSICAL BEHAVIOR

Examples include signature behaviors:

- Offender rips or tears the victim's clothing.
- Offender engages in the use of corrective force.
- Offender engages in moderate, excessive, or brutal levels of force that increase with victim resistance or his level of sexual dysfunction during the offense.
- Offender chooses locations for the attack that are convenient and safe.

MO BEHAVIOR

- The victim is pre-selected or opportunistic (too good to pass up).
- Victim chosen by availability, accessibility, and vulnerability.
- The location of the offense is victim dependent.
- Weapon is involved, or substituted with higher levels of force.
- Physical aggression is used to initially overpower the victim.
- Victim is held captive in some fashion while being raped.

Offenders evidencing this type of behavior have absolutely no doubt about their own adequacy and masculinity. In fact, they may be using their attacks as an expression of their own virility. In their perception, they are entitled to the fruits of their attack by virtue of being stronger.

This offender may grow more confident over time, as their egocentricity tends to be very high. They may begin to do things that might lead to their identification. Law enforcement may interpret this as a sign that the offender desires to be caught. What is actually true is that the offender has no respect for law enforcement, has learned that they can commit their offenses without the need to fear identification or capture, and subsequently they may not take precautions that they have learned are unnecessary.

It is not this offender's desire to harm their victims, necessarily, but rather to possess them sexually. Demonstrating power over their victims is their means of expressing mastery, strength, control, authority, and identity to themselves. The attacks are therefore intended to reinforce the offender's inflated sense of self-confidence or self worth.

ANGER RETALIATORY (AKA ANGER OR DISPLACED)

These include offender behaviors that suggest a great deal of rage, either towards a specific person, group, institution, or a symbol of either. These types of behaviors are commonly evidenced in stranger-to-stranger sexual assaults, domestic homicides, work-related homicide, and cases involving political or religious terrorists.

METHOD OF APPROACH

Blitz or surprise.

METHOD OF ATTACK

Brutal physical force, extreme violence, weapons, explosives.

VERBAL BEHAVIOR/SCRIPTS

Examples include signature behaviors:

- Verbally selfish – is not interested in hearing the victim.
- Does not negotiate.
- May blame victim for events and perceived events. "If you wouldn't have struggled I wouldn't have had to beat you like that. You think you are so hot. You think you're better than I am. It's people like you that are the problem. You don't understand; you have to be made to understand."
- Very angry, hostile language.

SEXUAL BEHAVIOR

Examples include signature behaviors:

- Sexually selfish.
- Sex is violent, an extension of the physical attack.
- No foreplay.
- Attempts to force victim to perform acts that they perceive as degrading or humiliating (fellatio or sodomy).

PHYSICAL BEHAVIOR

Examples include signature behaviors:

- Ripping of victim's clothing.

- Dresses for the event (full military dress uniform, face paint, battle dress uniform [khakis or camouflage material], etc.).

- Excessive or brutal levels of force with high amount of injury to the victim.

MO BEHAVIOR

- Attack is unplanned; a result of an emotional reaction on the part of an offender.

- Attack is skillfully planned and focused on a particular victim or victim population.

- Offenses appear sporadic over time, occurring at any location, at any time of day or night (whenever the offender gets pissed off or whenever a particular victim type is accessible).

- Uses weapons of opportunity, or if planned will prepare for the event with excessive weaponry and ammunition.

- Offender knows the victim, or the victim symbolizes something specific to the offender.

SIGNATURE BEHAVIOR

- There is an immediate application of direct physical force to the victim; the offender attacks first, then continues into any other behavior as an extension of that attack.

- Duration of attack is very short – ends when the offender is emotionally spent.

- Results in the offender intentionally surrendering their life as part of a social, political, or personal message to others.

- There is a lot of anger evident in the crime scene.

- Collateral victims in the crime scene as a result of anger and lack of planning, other victims surprise the offender in the heat of the moment or just get caught in the "crossfire" (very often unintentional, but if it is intentional it will be evidenced by offender planning behavior).

Anger retaliation behavior is just what the name suggests. The offender is acting on the basis of cumulative real or imagined wrongs from those that are in their world. The victim of the attack may be one of these people such as a relative, a girlfriend, or a co-worker. Or the victim may symbolize that person to the offender in dress, occupation, and/or physical characteristics.

The main goal of this offender behavior is to service their cumulative aggression. They are retaliating against the victim for wrongs or perceived wrongs, and their aggression can manifest itself spanning a wide range, from verbally abusive epithets to hyper-aggressed homicide with multiple collateral victims.

It is important not to confuse retaliatory behavior with sadistic behavior.

Although they can share some characteristics at first blush, the motivations are wholly separate. Also, a distinct lack of planning and overall offender preparedness will likely be apparent in conjunction with non-terroristic anger retaliatory behavior.

ANGER EXCITATION (AKA SADISTIC)

These include behaviors that evidence offender sexual gratification from victim pain and suffering. The primary motivation for the behavior is sexual, however the sexual expression for the offender is manifested in physical aggression, or torture behavior, toward the victim.

METHOD OF APPROACH

Con.

METHOD OF ATTACK

Surprise, physical force, weapons, explosives.

VERBAL BEHAVIOR/SCRIPTS

Examples include signature behaviors:

- The offender says things meant to gain the victim's trust and confidence – things that will lower the victim's guard. "Can you help me with this? I'm lost. Do I know you? You remind me of a friend I had back in school."
- The offender says things to entice the victim away from safe areas – "I have something I want to show you. Let me offer you a ride. Can I give you help with that heavy load up to your apartment?"
- During the attack, the offender may demand to be called a certain name to indicate victim subservience (Sir, Master, Lord, etc.).
- The offender asks, "Does it hurt? Did that hurt? Can you feel that?" when engaged in rough sex acts or inflicting victim injury.
- Calls the victim demeaning, humiliating names attesting to his view of their worthlessness, "Bitch, slut, whore, cunt."

SEXUAL BEHAVIOR

Examples include signature behaviors:

- The offender has an extensive collective of pornography.
- The offender is sexually stimulated by the victim's response to the infliction of physical and/or emotional pain.
- The offender rehearses attacks in private, and with compliant victims (i.e. wife or girlfriend).
- The offender involves the use of sexual bondage apparatus and behaviors during the attack.
- The offender performs sexual torture on victim, including repeated biting,

insertion of foreign objects in vagina or anus, and the use of sexual torture devices on a conscious victim.

- The offender prefers rough anal sex followed in frequency by forced fellatio.
- The offender prefers ejaculation on specific parts of the victim's body.
- The offender is sexually selfish; the victim's primary function is to suffer, sexually.
- The offender records the attack for later fantasy activity (video, photos, journal, audio, maps, calendars, diaries, media clippings).
- "Souvenirs" and "trophies" are kept and hidden in secret, but accessible places (home, office, vehicle, storage space, etc.).

PHYSICAL BEHAVIOR

Examples include signature behaviors:

- Brutal or high level of force used to inflict victim injury over a prolonged period of time.
- Injuries inflicted against specific areas of the victim's body of sexual significance to the offender (feet, nipples, anus, vagina, mouth, etc.).
- The intensity of specified sexual injury increases with the rapist's anger (i.e. response to a non-compliant victim, or a victim that is too compliant), which increases with the level of sexual arousal.

MO BEHAVIOR

- The offender chooses or impersonates an occupation that allows them to act as an authority figure, placing them in a position to identify and acquire victims (i.e. law enforcement, security guard, youth counselor, coach, etc.).
- Offenses planned in exacting detail – victim type; location for selecting victim; con; location for attack; signature behavior; disposal site – all are thought of in advance.
- Offenses executed methodically.
- Offender assesses and selects victim by emotional vulnerability, and gains their confidence through seduction.
- Victims are vilified by law enforcement (prostitutes, drug addicts, runaways, etc.).
- Victims are non-aggressive and have low self-esteem.
- Victim is lured to a concealed area where the offender has a great deal of control (vehicle, basement, garage, hotel room, etc.).
- This offender increases aggression with each successive attack.
- The offender kills the victim as a precautionary act.

SIGNATURE BEHAVIOR

- Special offense materials brought with offender to the scene, containing weapons, bindings, and any sexual apparatus.
- The sexual attack lasts for an extended period of time.
- Offender is good at presenting the image of a loving and sincere individual (see Chapter 17).

■ Victims are strangers to the offender (facilitates both MO and signature – it is easier to torture and humiliate and make to suffer those that one has no personal connection to, however it is also less likely that law enforcement will link the offender to the crime).

This offense behavior is perhaps the most individually complex. This type of behavior is motivated by intense, individually varying fantasies that involve inflicting brutal levels of pain on the victim solely for offender sexual pleasure. The goal of this behavior is total victim fear and submission. Physical aggression has been eroticized. The result is that the victim must be physically and psychologically abused and degraded for this offender to become sexually excited and subsequently gratified. (See Chapter 17 for more detail.)

PROFIT

These include behaviors that evidence an offender motivation oriented towards material or personal gain. These can be found in all types of homicides, robberies, burglaries, muggings, arsons, bombings, kidnappings, and most forms of white-collar crime, to name just a few. Profit-motivated behaviors are the exceptions that prove the rule of signature aspects, as they do not satisfy psychological or emotional needs.

METHOD OF APPROACH
Any.

METHOD OF ATTACK
Any.

VERBAL BEHAVIOR/SCRIPTS

■ Offender gives simple commands to achieve victim compliance regarding the release of valuables – "Give me the money. Open the safe. Give me all of your jewelry. Where is the cash?"

■ Offender shows an interest in the value of items – "Is this real gold? Are these fake diamonds? This is cheap shit."

SEXUAL BEHAVIOR

■ Offender creates fantasy or pornographic material using victim, which is sold for personal or material gain.

■ Offender sells victim's sexual services for personal or material gain.

■ Offender sells victim to another party as a "sexual slave" for personal or material gain.

PHYSICAL BEHAVIOR

- Engages in that behavior which is necessary to control the victim during the offense.
- Moderate, commensurate force.

MO BEHAVIOR

- Short offense duration.
- Searches vehicles or residences in a targeted fashion for specific types of valuables.
- Shows interest in completing an offense as quickly as possible, and disinterested in activities that may prolong the offense.

SIGNATURE BEHAVIOR

- Special materials with personal meaning brought with offender to the scene to complete the crime, including weapons, bindings, and any other distinctive apparatus.
- Any behavior that was committed during the offense which prolonged the offender's exposure to apprehension without gaining them some sort of financial reward (which would have to be reviewed and assessed in the lens of the other motivational typologies).

This offender behavior is the most straightforward as the successful completion of the offense satisfies the offender's needs. There are no emotional or psychological needs satisfied by purely profit-motivated behavior (if one wants to argue that it is designed for reassurance that one is a good provider, that would have to be followed by a host of other reassurance behaviors). Any behavior that is not purely profit motivated, which satisfies an emotional or psychological need, must be examined with the lens of the other motivational typologies.

For example, if a thief attacks a victim on a public street, stealing their purse and making a quick getaway, this is evidence of profit-motivated behavior. If the same thief brutally beats the victim, in the absence of any victim resistance, before stealing the purse, then this is evidence of retaliatory behavior. It further suggests that more is going on with the offender than just the need to make a quick profit.

MOTIVATIONAL TYPOLOGY V. A COMPLETE PROFILE

The behaviors and characteristics in the behavior–motivational typology given are not representative of fully constructed criminal profiles. They are designed to represent the types of behaviors and characteristics associated with general motivational themes. Motivation is only one aspect of the overall profile. Put another way, the behavior–motivational typology classifies offender behavior, not actual offenders.

The typologies are also not designed as a diagnostic checklist, and they are not characteristically cumulative. That is to say that if an offender evidences 10 characteristics or behaviors from one motivational typology (i.e. power reassurance), and only three from another (i.e. anger retaliatory), it does not necessarily follow that we are dealing with a power reassurance rapist. What it might mean is that there may be more than one motive at work (multi-determination), and we need to be able to accept that motivations can co-exist within an offense or over the course of multiple offenses.

A deductive criminal profile is not an average. It is a document that contains information regarding a specific offense, or offenses, including physical evidence, victimology, and crime-scene characteristics, from which offender characteristics are rendered. A criminal profile is not a list of unsubstantiated declarations regarding typical offenders. It is a logical argument with conclusions that are supported by the facts of a case, as established by physical and behavioral evidence.

Those who would use any motivational typologies as diagnostic tools, rather than investigative ones, are misusing them.

PSYCHOLOGICAL CRIME-SCENE TAPE: THE INVESTIGATIVE USE OF THE MOTIVATIONAL TYPOLOGY

The behavior–motivational typology does not provide a dynamic, developmental scale that measures an offender over time. It is a tool for the assessment of offender behaviors at a particular moment, in a particular setting, with a particular victim. The behavior–motivational typologies are not to be confused with full criminal profiles, nor by any means should they be considered an exclusive list of characteristics and potential signature aspects (motivational themes for behavior patterns). They can be used to provide a psychological snapshot of a rapist during a single instance from which some reliable inferences about motive can be made.

There is also no bright yellow line between the behavior–motivational typologies, meaning that a single offender can evidence behaviors suggestive of more than one motivation. They should be used to help understand the needs satisfied by offender behavioral patterns at one point in time. All too often, investigators and criminal profilers use motivational typologies and other sorts of offender classifications to label a rapist's behavior with a single investigative "diagnosis." Investigators and inexperienced criminal profilers will often issue a report stating that the offender characteristics that are associated with whatever typology appear to "match" the offender. They inappropriately use a typology as a boilerplate replacement for a thoroughly rendered criminal profile.

This practice results in misleading investigative generalizations, and inappropriately pigeonholes an unknown offender into an inductive, inflexible classification. The typology becomes the equivalent of psychological crime-scene tape; a barrier which investigators all too often fail to look beyond in the search for evidence.

For a case example of an offender evidencing multiple signature aspects (motivational typologies), see Chapter 11, Verbal Behavior.

Human behavior and human needs are developmental in nature, not fixed and static. Offender signature behavior is expressive of multi-determined needs. Using the motivational typologies to "diagnose" an offender as a certain type can have limiting effects on an investigation, not unlike improperly placed crime-scene tape. It can result in ignoring other offender motivational patterns, incorrect investigative assumptions, and ultimately overlooked physical and behavioral evidence. All of this working together facilitates the inability of investigators to link and investigate related cases (see Chapter 18). To avoid this pitfall, the motivational typologies should be used investigatively to suggest the motivations of an offender that are apparent in the given patterns of crime-scene behavior, not as rigid diagnostic classifications.

REFERENCES

Burgess, A., Burgess, A., Douglas, J. and Ressler, R. (1997) *Crime Classification Manual*, San Francisco: Jossey-Bass, Inc.

Burgess, A. and Hazelwood, R. (eds) (1995) *Practical Aspects of Rape Investigation: A Multidisciplinary Approach*, 2nd edn, New York: CRC Press.

Geberth, V. (1996) *Practical Homicide Investigation*, 3rd edn, New York: CRC Press.

Groth, A. N. (1979) *Men Who Rape: The Psychology of the Offender*, New York: Plenum Press.

Turvey, B. (1996) "Behavior Evidence: Understanding Motives and Developing Suspects In Unsolved Serial Rapes Through Behavioral Profiling Techniques," *Knowledge Solutions Library*, http://www.corpus-delicti.com/rape.html, June.

CHAPTER 16

OFFENDER CHARACTERISTICS

Brent E. Turvey, M.S.

Between his purpose and his conscience,
Like heralds 'twixt two dreadful battles set:
His passion is so ripe, it needs must break.

(Shakespeare, *King John: Act 4, Scene 2*)

As we stated at the beginning of this text, the general term *criminal profiling* is used to describe any process of inferring distinctive personality characteristics of individuals responsible for committing criminal acts. But we quickly learned that all criminal profiling methods are not the same. There are more than a few ways to extrapolate offender characteristics, each with their own considerations.

In Chapter 2, we reviewed *inductive* methods of reasoning as they relate to the criminal profiling process. This refers to any method that describes, or bases its inferences on, *the characteristics of a typical offender type.* Supporting arguments for inductive offender characteristics will include criminological studies of known offenders, analyst intuition, analyst experience, and broad generalizations. We further explained how subjective this process is, and how subsequent inductive offender profiles may tell us more about the profiler than the offender in question (that is, if any attempt is made to relate the profile to a particular offender at all).

In Chapter 3, we explained the *deductive method* of criminal profiling, which has been the focus of this work. We defined a deductive criminal profile as a set of offender characteristics that are reasoned from the convergence of physical and behavioral evidence patterns within a crime or a series of related crimes. That is to say, the deductive method describes, and bases its inferences on, the *behavioral evidence in a particular case, or a series of related cases.* We further explained that the process of rendering a deductive criminal profile is called *behavioral evidence analysis.*

In this chapter, as well as in Chapter 17, we will focus on creating the deductive criminal profile and how the arguments for a particular offender's characteristics may be formed from physical and behavioral evidence.

Credit should be given to Burgess *et al.* (1997), Cleckley (1976), Geberth (1996), Groth (1979), Hare (1993), and Burgess and Hazelwood (1995) for their published works in this area, as collectively they have assisted the author's development of the concepts in this chapter.

HARD V. SOFT CHARACTERISTICS

Offender characteristics are divided into two categories: *hard characteristics* and *soft characteristics*.

HARD CHARACTERISTICS

Hard characteristics refer to those offender attributes that are a matter of verifiable, uninterpreted fact. They are evident by virtue of demonstrable, unequivocal existence in the form of some kind of permanent, unalterable documentation.

These characteristics may be demonstrable or suggested by the physical or behavioral evidence, or by virtue of victim and witness statements. But, in any case, they may be verified. Examples can include, but are certainly not limited to, such things as:

- offender age;
- offender sex;
- offender DNA;
- offender blood type;
- offender secretor status;
- offender fingerprints;
- offender race (though in certain areas this may actually be a *soft* characteristic);
- offender marital status;
- offender residence history;
- offender formal education history;
- offender employment history;
- offender incarceration history;
- offender medical history;
- offender mental health history;
- offender military history;
- offender vehicle ownership history;
- offender property ownership history.

SOFT CHARACTERISTICS

Soft characteristics refer to those offender attributes that are a matter of opinion. They require some kind of interpretation in order to define them. They also include things that are subject to natural or intentional change with the passage of time, without any kind of permanent, verifiable record.

These characteristics may be demonstrable or suggested by the physical or behavioral evidence, or by virtue of victim and witness statements. But in any case they are potentially alterable, affected by time, and/or subject to interpretation. Examples can include, but are certainly not limited to, such things as:

- offender relationship history;
- offender physical characteristics (clothing, height, weight, eye color, hair color, hair length, breast size, facial features, physical abnormalities, tattoos);
- offender grooming habits;
- offender skill levels;
- offender vehicle type or color;
- offender personality habits;
- offender hobbies;
- offender self-esteem;
- offender empathy;
- offender deceitfulness;
- offender criminal versatility;
- offender acceptance of responsibility for actions;
- offender glibness/superficial charm;
- offender impulsivity;
- offender remorse or guilt;
- offender behavioral controls;
- offender aggressiveness;
- offender motive/fantasy aspect.

DEDUCING OFFENDER CHARACTERISTICS

Deducing offender characteristics is about asking the right question of the offender's behavior. The first part of the question is defining the characteristic (i.e. a sadistic motive). The second part is agreeing upon what type of behavior evidences that characteristic (i.e. evidence of offender sexual gratification from victim suffering). If the crime reconstruction includes those behaviors, then the criminal profiler has a good argument for that characteristic.

Example: Offender Skill Level
An offender enters a second story apartment wearing gloves, a mask, and carrying a bag. He finds a sleeping female in her bedroom, wakes her, ties her up, and rapes her (he removes his gloves during the sexual attack, and places them back on when he is through). He uses a condom that he brought with him. He leaves her tied up and quickly searches through her home. He ends up taking her jewelry, a handgun that was stored in the closet, and all of the cash in her purse.

First, in a case where the crimes of burglary and sexual assault both occur, detectives from both the robbery unit and the sex crimes unit should be involved in the investigation. If the offense had involved a homicide, then a homicide detective should have also been asked to participate in the investigation.

Evidence of offender skill in the crime of rape includes precautionary acts specific to the nature of evidence transfer that commonly occurs. Two things that link a rapist directly to their crime include their physical description as given by a witness and the DNA from their ejaculate. This offender has skillfully prevented either from being a factor by wearing both a mask and a condom.

Evidence of offender skill in the crime of burglary also includes precautionary acts specific to the nature of evidence transfer that commonly occurs. Two things that link a burglar directly to their crime include their physical description as given by a witness (actual or recorded via surveillance cameras), and their fingerprints left at the scene. This offender has skillfully prevented either from being a factor by wearing both a mask and gloves during the entry, search, and exit of the scene.

If the offender had evidenced skill in the crime of burglary, but not in the crime of rape, this would also have provided the criminal profiler with useful information.

Keep in mind that many characteristics may not be deducible by virtue of the available evidence in a given offense, and that one behavior is meaningless outside of the context of all other offender behaviors exhibited. Individual offender behaviors can only be understood in the light of their relationship to other behaviors. For full examples of deductively rendered criminal profiles, please see Appendix IIIa and IIIb.

PROBLEM CHARACTERISTICS

There are three offender characteristics which, to date, have posed a pervasive problem for all criminal profilers: offender age, sex, and intelligence. This author specifically recommends that the first two, age and sex, not be inferred without conclusive physical evidence (when the theory stops working, throw it out). The third, intelligence, should be left out of an assessment altogether.

AGE

If a profiler is going to be wrong, this is one of the most likely places. Estimates regarding age have typically involved inferences based on behaviors that suggest mental illness. If a criminal profiler saw a behavior indicative of a psychotic state, they gave an age above 18 years (as it has been argued that this is the age after which psychosis tends to set in). Age estimates also tend to be based upon what a criminal profiler believes, based on their own experience, is *likely* behavior for different age groups.

This author suggests, given the track record of inferring this particular offender characteristic, and given the increase of violent, aberrant crimes committed by increasingly younger offenders, that it remain out of a criminal profile unless there is conclusive physical evidence.

Consider the following case, and note that some American profilers voiced loud opinions that this particular offender was likely above the age of thirty, and had visited the United States on at least one occasion. The offender turned out to be a 14-year-old boy.

…a severed head was found in front of a junior high school in Kobe with a chilling note stuck in the 11-year-old male victim's mouth that declared "the beginning of the game… It's great fun for me to kill people. I desperately want to see people die." When police announced today that they had arrested a suspect in the murder, the horror that had gripped this relatively crime-free nation turned to relief – but then to horror again as it was revealed that the suspect is a 14-year-old boy.

…Seishi Yamashita, chief investigator, said police questioned the boy and arrested him after he confessed to the crime. According to police, the boy said he beheaded the victim, Jun Hase, with a knife and a saw. Yamashita said police later searched the suspect's home and found the knife and other weapons. The boy told police he knew Hase.

Police declined to identify the suspect and said they were trying to determine the motive for the crime.

Hase's head was discovered May 27 by a school custodian in front of Tomogaoka Middle School in Kobe, a city of 1.5 million that is 300 miles west of Tokyo. His body was found later the same day in a forest near his elementary school. The beheading and the taunting note threatening more murders triggered a massive, four-week manhunt involving more than 500 investigators…

…A few days before Hase's head was found, two dead kittens turned up – one with severed limbs – near the same school. NHK television reported tonight that police tracked down the suspect after investigating the fate of the cats. Days after Hase's head was discovered, the killer sent a letter to the Kobe Shimbun newspaper. He blamed "the compulsory education system and the society that created that system that rendered me invisible, and I will exact revenge."

He said he might kill three people a week, and added, "If you assume I am a childish criminal able to kill only the young, you will be grossly mistaken."

Investigators originally thought the killer was between 20 and 40 years old, based on descriptions of suspicious persons in the area at the time of the slaying. Psychiatrists also concurred that it was probably someone in that age range, based on the writings. Hase's murder came two months after two schoolgirls were attacked in the area. Many residents feared the attacks were linked, although no proof has emerged. (Sugawara 1997)

SEX

Like age estimates, estimations regarding the sex (male or female) of an offender also tend to be based upon what a criminal profiler believes, based on their own experience, is *likely* behavior for different sexes. Females are often regarded, quite erroneously, as a weaker, less aggressive sex that is incapable of complex fantasy motivation. This is an outdated notion that can create investigative bias, resulting in the failure of authorities to investigate potential suspects because they have been eliminated on the basis of the sex.

This author suggests, given the potential investigative misdirection that assumptions can cause, that estimations regarding offender sex also remain out of a criminal profile unless there is hard physical evidence (i.e. a sexual assault, or a competent witness/victim description).

Consider the following case:

> A Tacoma woman has been declared a violent sexual predator, the state's first woman to receive that designation. In Pierce County Superior Court yesterday, Laura Faye McCollum, 39, was ordered to undergo treatment and confinement at the Special Commitment Center in Monroe.
>
> Pierce County Prosecutor Barbara Corey-Boulet said McCollum is "one of a very small number of women classified as violent sexual predators. I know of one other in Minnesota." McCollum was convicted in 1990 of raping a three-year-old girl and completed her 5½-year sentence in November 1995.
>
> …She has repeatedly sent Corey-Boulet letters urging that she be confined and treated because "she knows she is at high risk to re-offend and that she wants treatment," according to an affidavit in her court file.
>
> The affidavit said that her adjustment during confinement has been "marginal" and that she committed 38 major rule violations during that time, including several for assault. No agency in the community was willing to accept her for treatment, the affidavit said.
>
> Michael Compte, one of three sexual-predator-treatment specialists who examined McCollum, reported she is "an obsessive and compulsive child molester who is particularly attracted to preverbal and barely verbal children ages 2 to 4."
>
> McCollum had committed numerous earlier assaults on small children, many of whom she gained access to by providing day-care services, Corey-Boulet said.
>
> In one letter to Corey-Boulet, McCollum allegedly fantasized about living next to a day-care center from which she removed two children, took them "to a wooded area where sexual acts and assault/homicide occurred."
>
> Compte said McCollum "is clearly aroused by sexually violent themes and entertains sadistic and homicidal fantasies. She is an extremely dangerous woman, and in my opinion it is not a matter if she re-offends but when."
>
> McCollum allegedly told Florence Wolfe of Northwest Treatment Associates that her youngest victim was four days old. (Associated Press 1997)

INTELLIGENCE

Intelligence is a term that generally refers to the ability of a person to acquire knowledge and apply it in an effective manner. However, it is a very vague and subjective term that has no actual investigative value. Most often, what the criminal profiler is concerned with is an offender skill level. Very intelligent people may commit foolish or poorly planned offenses. Therefore, evidence of a low offender skill level suggests a lack of criminal experience and poor planning, not a lack of intelligence. Conversely, an offender of low intelligence may, by virtue of criminal experience, acquire a great deal of criminal skill. Therefore evidence of a high criminal skill level is not a sure indication of a high level of offender intelligence.

This author strongly recommends that criminal profilers focus their efforts on the investigatively relevant offender characteristic of offender skill level, and leave the subjective interpretation of offender intelligence to the forensic psychologists and psychiatrists (who are more qualified to make such estimations in the first place).

SUGGESTED FORMAT

A deductive criminal profile should be a written document, not something that was done over the phone, or over lunch on the back of a napkin. It should be rendered as a court-worthy document with probative value that may be subjected to examination by opposing counsel. This structure has proven to be a very effective, logical, argument-oriented presentation of the profiler's behavioral evidence analysis.

Please keep in mind that more elements than are listed below may be a part of the final criminal profile. This is just a place to begin.

I. EQUIVOCAL FORENSIC ANALYSIS

(See Chapters 6 and 7 of this work.)

II. VICTIMOLOGY

(See Chapters 9 and 10 of this work.)

III. CRIME-SCENE CHARACTERISTICS

(See Chapters 8, 11, 12, and 13 of this work.)

IV. OFFENDER CHARACTERISTICS

(See Chapters 14, 15, 16, and 17 of this work.)

V. INVESTIGATIVE STRATEGY

Give investigatively relevant suggestions regarding future strategy. This may include suggestions based on the criminal profiler's knowledge and experiences. But these should be investigative recommendations only, and should not be confused with conclusions regarding offender characteristics. (See Chapters 4, 5 and 18 of this work.)

VI. OTHER

There are a number of issues not addressed by this structure which cannot be anticipated. Some cases may require a specific comparison of MO or signature elements for crime linkage, some may require a field checklist of offender characteristics for law enforcement officers on patrol, and still others might require insight into specific behavioral indicators for things like remorse. Each profile is different. This basic structure, however, should provide an adequate starting point.

THE WRITTEN PROFILE

A fully rendered deductive criminal profile should be a written, court-worthy document. It should not be something that is done over drinks, or done over the telephone. There are several very important reasons for this.

A written criminal profile is less likely to be misrepresented to others. If the conclusions of an unwritten profile must go through several people before they reach those who can use the information, they may suffer brutal revisions. In any case, constructing a written profile is the only way that a criminal profiler can know that their conclusions are going to reach others, in context, without alteration or misrepresentation.

Those who need the information can more easily reference a written profile. It can be photocopied, emailed, and distributed with greater facility, and reduce the amount of time that it takes to convey the information.

A written criminal profile provides for the investigative record of a case. In cases that see no movement in weeks, months, or years for whatever reason, verbal profiles may be forgotten by not only those who requested the information, but by the criminal profilers themselves. Additionally, if an investigation changes hands or jurisdictions, a written profile can follow it.

A written criminal profile represents the methods and subsequent conclusions of a criminal profiler in a given case. This information can be used to validate the criminal profile at a later time. It can also assist the criminal profiler as a feedback mechanism for refining their technique in instances where their profile was in error, for whatever reason.

A written criminal profile is subject to the scrutiny of peer review. Peer review is another mechanism for the criminal profiler to get feedback on the veracity of their profiling methods. In the absence of peer review, which independently seeks to validate or invalidate methods, techniques, and conclusions, a criminal profiler's particular method cannot be trusted by the community that it seeks to serve. A criminal profiler must be willing to submit their work for the scrutiny of their peers.

This can take the form of written profiles that are independently peer reviewed as part of the adversarial process, or by the willingness to openly publish full criminal profiles for criticism by the entire criminal-profiling community. It does not include written profiles that are submitted internally to private groups, or groups with a vested interest in promoting their own competency. Peer review must be public, and it must be independent.

REFERENCES

Associated Press (1997) "Woman held as a sex predator, Designation is state's first," January 22.

Burgess, A., Burgess, A., Douglas, J. and Ressler, R. (1997) *Crime Classification Manual*, San Francisco: Jossey-Bass, Inc.

Burgess, A. and Hazelwood, R. (eds.) (1995) *Practical Aspects of Rape Investigation: A Multidisciplinary Approach*, 2nd edn, New York: CRC Press.

Cleckley, H. (1976) *Mask of Sanity*, 5th edn, St. Louis: Mosby.

Geberth, V. (1996) *Practical Homicide Investigation*, 3rd edn, New York: CRC Press.

Groth, A. N. (1979) *Men Who Rape: The Psychology of the Offender*, New York: Plenum Press.

Hare, R. (1993), *Without Conscience*, New York: Pocket.

Sugawara, S. (1997) "Japanese Arrest 14-Year-Old in Decapitation of 11-Year-Old," *Washington Post Foreign Service*, Sunday, June 29: A26.

CHAPTER 17

PSYCHOPATHY AND SADISM

Brent E. Turvey, M.S.

I have no brother, I am like no brother;
And this word 'love,' which graybeards call divine,
Be resident in men like one another And not in me:
I am myself alone.

(Shakespeare, *King Henry VI: Act 5, Scene 6, 3*)

If criminal profilers are not concerned with, and often not qualified to perform, the diagnosis and treatment of offenders (see Chapter 21), then why should they concern themselves with the diagnostic terms *psychopathy* and *sadism*? The answer is that these two particular offender classifications are behaviorally determined. That is to say, the diagnosis of psychopathy or sadism is dependent upon behavioral evidence. The criminal profiler, in some case, will address behavioral patterns and crime-scene characteristics that may incidentally be a part of a particular clinical diagnosis.

An analogy would be that while criminal profilers may not be allowed to bake the forensic psychologist's cake, they may show up in the kitchen with a few ingredients that the forensic psychologist can use (or at the very least should not ignore).

PSYCHOPATHY

More than two hundred years ago, the phrase *manie sans delire* was used by Philippe Pinel, a French physician, to describe an unusual case of a man who did not fit the expected categories of mental disturbance of the day. Pinel characterized the patient as remorseless, and lacking in restraint. The phrase Pinel chose to describe this patient's condition, when translated to English, means simply "madness without confusion," or as Dr Robert Hare interprets it, "insanity without delirium" (Hare 1993). This was one of the first attempts to describe what today we often refer to as a *psychopath*. An individual capable of enjoying what most would consider horrible, heinous acts, and recognizing the harmful consequences of those acts to others, but incapable of feeling remorse and subsequently unwilling to stop.

Pinel did not consider these individuals immoral (someone whose beliefs are contrary to accepted morality), but rather amoral (someone who does not care about conventional interpretations of right or wrong and gives those issues no weight in decisions). However, there were others who considered these patients quite immoral and subsequently quite evil. The debate persists to this day on the subject.

In 1835, the English alienist J.C. Pritchard came up with the term "moral insanity," which was applied in instances where abnormality or "insanity" expressed itself in a particular field of morality. Then, in 1888 Toch began substituting the term "psychopathic inferiority" for Pritchard's term. But Toch implied a biological predisposition for the disorder rather than a wholly environmental cause (Toch 1979).

In a 1952 revision of the psychiatric nomenclature, according to Cleckley (1976), the term "psychopathic personality" was officially replaced by "sociopathic personality," hence the word sociopath found its way into the literature. Then in 1968, that was replaced by *personality disorder, antisocial type.*

So from the very start there has been a lot of confusion about the diagnosis of psychopathy, the meaning behind the behavioral manifestations, and the causes of the overall disorder. And in the grand tradition of psychiatry and mental health, each person who encountered these related terms has interpreted them in their own unique way with their own subjective measures. Even today, qualified clinicians and the public alike confuse psychopathy with Antisocial Personality Disorder (ASPD):

> The distinction between psychopathy and ASPD is of considerable significance to the mental health and criminal justice systems. Unfortunately, it is a distinction that is often blurred, not only in the minds of many clinicians but in the latest edition of DSM-IV...
>
> Most psychopaths (with the exception of those who somehow manage to plow their way through life without coming into formal or prolonged contact with the criminal justice system) meet the criteria for ASPD, *but most individuals with ASPD are not psychopaths.* Further, ASPD is very common in criminal populations, and those with the disorder are heterogeneous with respect to personality, attitudes and motivations for engaging in criminal behavior." (Hare 1996)

For the purposes of this work, to stem any confusion, the following definitions will apply:

PSYCHOPATHY

A personality disorder evidenced by a distinctive cluster of behaviors and inferred personality traits defined by a Hare's Revised Psychopathy Checklist (PCL-R) (Hare 1991).

PSYCHOPATH

A social predator (diagnosed with psychopathy) who often charms and manipulates their way through life. They are completely lacking in conscience and in feelings for others, taking what they want and doing as they please without the slightest sense of guilt or regret (Hare 1993). This term is used when psychological, biological, and genetic factors have contributed to the development of the syndrome, as well as social forces and early life experiences.

SOCIOPATH

This term is used to describe the same behavior manifestations and inferred personality traits as are evident in a psychopath. The explicit exception is that sociopaths have a syndrome forged entirely by social forces and early experiences (*ibid.*).

PSYCHOPATHIC CHARACTERISTICS

The "distinctive cluster of behaviors and inferred personality traits" that Hare is referring to are found in the Hare PCL-R. They are listed in Table 17.1. This author has divided them up by what may be evidenced in offense behavior, and what are personality traits that require a clinical interview.

TABLE 17.1: Adapted from the Hare Psychopathy Checklist:

INFERABLE FROM OFFENSE BEHAVIOR	REQUIRE CLINICAL INTERVIEW
■ Callous lack of empathy	■ Early behavioral problems
■ Conning/manipulative	■ Irresponsibility
■ Criminal versatility	■ Juvenile delinquency
■ Failure to accept responsibility for actions	■ Lack of realistic long-term goals
■ Glibness/superficial charm	■ Many short-term marital relationships
■ Grandiose sense of self-worth	■ Need for stimulation/proneness to boredom
■ Impulsivity	■ Pathological lying
■ Lack of remorse or guilt	■ Parasitic lifestyle
■ Poor behavioral controls	■ Promiscuous sexual behavior
	■ Revocation of conditional release
Source: Hare 1991	■ Shallow affect

Hare (1991) gave the following instructions regarding the use of these criteria:

> The 20 items of the PCL-R measure behaviors and inferred traits considered fundamental to the clinical construct of psychopathy. Most of the traits are treated as open concepts. That is, the rater is provided with a description of a trait and with some behavioral exemplars and is asked to make a judgement about the extent to which a person has the trait...

> ...Although clinical judgement and inference are required, the scoring criteria are quite explicit, and with some training, the items are not difficult to score.

This gives us a very important piece of information: These traits exist in varying degrees of intensity, thus individual psychopaths will manifest them in varying degrees of intensity. All psychopaths are not equal, and by extension all psychopathic behavior is not equal. Psychopathic behavior exists on a continuum.

The characteristics in the right column of Table 17.1 are such that they most likely will require a clinical interview and a complete history of a known suspect to be inferred.

The characteristics in the left column are such that they may be inferable from unknown offender behavior, depending upon the nature of the offense and the documentation available to the criminal profiler. The reason that this may interest the court at trial, or a parole board later on, is that it can give insight into an offender's personality during the commission of a criminal offense. This is separate from what an offender may have evidenced in a prison environment, in a courtroom before a jury, or during a parole hearing.

As previously stated, criminal profilers are interested in what offenders do in relation to an offense. They are not interested in what the offender has to say about their offense behavior. Information regarding an offender's personality characteristics are derived directly from their offense behavior as established by the physical evidence, and not from offender insights requested from them days, months, and even years after an event.

Below are some sample explanations regarding how these characteristics may be inferred from physical evidence and reconstructed offender behavior by the criminal profiler. They are not the only possibilities. Again, these should only be inferred in the context of other offender behavior, and then only when there is adequate documentation.

LACK OF EMPATHY

A lack of empathy is suggested by the inability to understand the situation, feelings, or motives of others. This characteristic may be inferred, for example, when an offender evidences a total lack of interest in victim response to victim suffering during an offense.

CONNING/MANIPULATIVE

This is suggested by behavior that is intentionally deceptive for personal gain. This characteristic can be inferred when an offender uses a deception or a "con" method of approach (see Chapter 11) to get close to the victim.

CRIMINAL VERSATILITY

This can be inferred when an offender evidences MO behavior that is suggestive of competency with criminal activity other than that typically necessary for a given type of offense. An example would be a rapist who evidences burglary skills like wearing gloves, disabling alarms, and stealing easily turned over, non-traceable valuables. This characteristic may also be inferred when an offender has been linked to other criminal activity by physical evidence.

FAILURE TO ACCEPT RESPONSIBILITY FOR ACTIONS

This refers to an offender who blames everyone but themselves for their situation, or who does not feel obligated to address the consequences of their behavior. This can be inferred when an offender blames the victim or the authorities during the attack.

GLIB AND SUPERFICIAL

Glib and superficial are terms that refer to behaviors that are done with little concern or thought, with intent to be evasive or conceal a lack of emotional depth. In some psychopaths, these behaviors appear contrived, and lack substance. In others, they appear quite sincere. The effectiveness of these behaviors has to do with the skills of the psychopath, as well as the ability of the person perceiving the behavior to recognize deception or secondary gain. This characteristic can be inferred when a verbally facile offender exudes an insincere and superficial charm as part of a con that is used to acquire a victim's trust in their method of approach.

GRANDIOSE SENSE OF SELF-WORTH

This characteristic can be inferred when an offender evidences an inflated view of themselves and their abilities. For example, they may speak in an unrealistically conceited manner, and appear to be indifferent about present or future investigative efforts on the part of the authorities to apprehend them (lack of precautionary acts).

IMPULSIVITY

This refers to behavior that is not thought out, and which does not consider consequences. This characteristic may be inferred when an offender consistently initiates offense behavior in a reactionary fashion, without planning, and when they do not.

LACK OF REMORSE OR GUILT

Remorse and guilt are characterized by moral anguish and regret for actions. This may be inferred when an offender shows no emotion, anger, or delight, in the face of victim suffering. This may also be inferred when an offender is able to engage in extremely violent crimes and then participate in regular, non-violent activities without apparent distress.

POOR BEHAVIORAL CONTROLS

This refers to violent, damaging, or reactionary behavior that is not controlled, even when the consequences may be harmful to the offender. This may be inferred when an offender is easily angered or frustrated, and when they frequently respond with verbal or physical aggression.

MOTIVATIONS

Perhaps the most important thing to understand about the motivation of the *criminal* psychopath is that it is no different from the motivations of other, non-psychopathic criminals. They are susceptible to the same needs and motivations (see Chapter 15) as other offenders.

Where psychopaths may differ from other offenders are in the means that they will use to satisfy their needs. The means that are employed by the psychopath can be particularly brutal, lack sympathy, exploit vulnerabilities, and be carried out in the absence of any remorse whatsoever, as we have previously discussed.

Psychopaths do not place any value on those outside of themselves, other than as a source of pleasure, and view the socialized world of rules and negotiation as an onerous imposition.

It has been said by wise men, that inside every human being is a war between good and evil that can never be won. The psychopath, however, having no remorse regarding the suffering of others to compass their behavior, is not encumbered by this internal conflict. It has been argued that most psychopaths in general lack the ability to take the perspective of others, and therefore do not have access to that information in their decision-making process (Cleckley 1976). In as much as this is true, they necessarily lack the basic building material for a conscience (Hare 1993).

This lack of remorse, this absence of negative emotional consequences, is argued to be a facilitating factor for their violent, destructive behavior. This is what allows psychopaths, existing on any range of the spectra, the psychological and emotional facility to do what the rest of us consider horrible, cruel, and morally wrong. They have no sympathy for the pain of others, no remorse for the harm they inflict, and often a high level of impulsivity. As such, normally socialized people are one of two things to the psychopath:

1 a source of amusement and gratification;

2 in the way.

For all of our discussion so far about psychopathic criminality, we have largely ignored an important truth that is not pleasant for many to consider when trying to understand the motivations of human criminal behavior. Not all psychopaths are criminals (and not all criminals are psychopaths). As Hare (1996) has stated:

> ...we live in a "camouflage society," a society in which some psychopathic traits – egocentricity, lack of concern for others, superficiality, style over substance, being "cool," manipulativeness, and so forth – increasingly are tolerated and even valued. With respect to the topic of this article, it is easy to see how both psychopaths and those with ASPD could blend in readily with groups holding antisocial or criminal values. It is more difficult to envisage how those with ASPD could hide out among more prosocial segments of society. Yet psychopaths have little difficulty infiltrating the domains of business, politics, law enforcement, government, academia and other social structures.

SADISM

The word sadism bears the name of the man whose writings unabashedly associated the concepts of sex, extreme pain, and suffering together in the 1700s. His full name was Donatien-Alphonse-Francois de Sade, better know as the *Marquis de Sade* (de Sade 1965). Though he was not the first to imagine these associations or put them to practice, he was one of the firsts to have written them down in a way that made them immortal.

According to the *Diagnostic and Statistical Manual of Mental Disorders* (American Psychiatric Association 1994), sexual sadism is an adult disorder that is evidenced by:

> Over a period of at least 6 months, recurrent, intense sexually arousing fantasies, sexual urges, or behaviors involving acts (real, not simulated) in which the psychological or physical suffering (including humiliation) of the victim is sexually exciting to the person.

> The fantasies, sexual urges, or behaviors cause clinically significant distress or impairment in social, occupational, or other important areas of functioning.

Here again, as with psychopathy, the criminal profiler is not interested in the diagnostic or treatment considerations of sadism. The criminal profiler is interested in what behaviors are necessary to establish sadism, and their investigative implications.

Sadism is not about killing, and it is not about violence. It is about deliberation, eroticized aggression, and victim suffering. To support the suggestion of sadism as a part of offender behavior with a victim, the following crime-scene characteristics must be established by a convergence of the physical and behavioral evidence. The failure to establish even one of these elements should preclude the forensic psychologist or psychiatrist from diagnosing the offense behavior as sadistic, by depriving them of the behavioral elements of the recipe.

EVIDENCE OF TORTURE

Torture is the infliction of severe pain as a means of punishment, coercion, or sexual gratification. Physically, this is evidenced by the existence of repetitive wound patterns, often to sexualized areas of the body (nipples, anus, vagina, penis, buttocks, mouth, etc.), that are non-lethal in nature. These wound patterns are typified by control-oriented, punishment-oriented, or sexually-oriented force (see Chapter 8). As stated in the *Crime Classification Manual* (Burgess *et al.* 1997):

> The level of violence in a sadistic offender's rape must clearly exceed what is necessary to force victim compliance; the offender's sexual arousal is a function of the victim's suffering, fear, or discomfort; behavioral evidence may include whipping, bondage; violence focuses on the erogenous parts of the victim's body (such as burning, cutting, or otherwise mutilating the breasts, anus, buttocks, or genitals), insertion of foreign objects in the vagina or anus; intercourse after the victim is unconscious; the use of feces/urine in the offense.

> Most often there is high expressive aggression with moderate to severe injury to the victim. Often, the offender uses items to inflict pain/injury (cigarettes, knives, sticks, bottles, etc.); in some cases of muted sadism, however, there is clear evidence of eroticized aggression (insertion of foreign objects, bondage, whipping, etc.) without extensive physical injury.

Psychological torture may also be evident, and among many others, can take the form of extreme verbal or physical threats, displaying materials intended for use in torture, and forcing the victim to witness the suffering of another in some fashion. The purpose of torture in cases of sadism is not just to inflict pain, but to witness the victim's suffering.

A LIVING, CONSCIOUS VICTIM

As stated, sadism is about an offender getting sexual gratification from victim suffering. Suffering is characterized by experiencing harm or pain or distress. To suffer, a victim must therefore be alive and conscious. The feedback that they give while they are suffering (screaming, crying, begging, pleading) is how the offender knows that what they are doing has successfully caused harm, pain, or distress. These are the elements that the sadist craves and is excited by. An unconscious or deceased victim cannot give this type of feedback. Therefore all injuries that are attributed to sadistic motivations must be firmly established as being pre-mortem, and while the victim is conscious.

> This is why neither sexual nor cruel acts committed on an unconscious or dead victim is necessarily evidence of sexual sadism; **such a victim cannot experience suffering**. For this reason, post-mortem injuries alone do not indicate sexual sadism. (Burgess and Hazelwood 1995)

REPETITION AND TIME

Sadism requires not only that the offender tortured the victim, and that the victim suffered, but that the offender also enjoyed it sexually. A competent argument for demonstrating that an offender enjoyed a torture behavior is showing that it was repeated over an extended period of time. Many attacks on victims do not last more than 10 or 20 minutes. A sadist, however, may need to remove a victim to a preselected secondary scene in order to spend the amount of time required to successfully involve the victim in the torture behavior that they have in mind.

SEXUAL GRATIFICATION

The motive of the sadist is sexual gratification. This is a tricky characteristic to determine because different offenders eroticize things differently. The challenge of the criminal profiler is to determine what acts are eroticized to the offender by virtue of their context. One way to do this is by the association of a behavior with a traditional sexual act or area of the body. Another way is by associating an act with erotic materials or apparatus. Yet another is by virtue of what the offender says during certain acts.

> Rapists cause their victims to suffer, but only sexual sadists intentionally inflict that suffering, whether physical or psychological, to enhance their own arousal...Acts of extreme cruelty or those that cause great suffering are often performed for non-sexual purposes, even during sexual assaults. (Burgess and Hazelwood 1995)

These are very straightforward behavioral requirements, but admittedly difficult to establish without all of the physical evidence and without a very thorough, well documented, investigation.

Sadly, not all criminal profilers bother themselves with the onerous task of verifying these behavioral requirements. Sometimes, they make statements or prepare profiles without a reconstruction, and using their own expertise to interpret whatever material they are sent (which may or may not be adequate to the task of competently interpreting an offender's behavior, given the evidence available in a particular case.) Take the following case example.

Example: Jack O. Spillman
The following details are taken from the Chelan County Coroner's Forensic Autopsy Protocol, performed by Dr Gerald A. Rappe, MD dated April 14, 1995.

This case involves the double homicide and post-mortem sexual mutilation of both a 47-year-old mother and her 14-year-old daughter. Both lived together in the same residence in East Wenatchee, Washington. Another daughter of the mother lived down the street.

When Douglas County authorities focused on Jack O. Spillman III as their suspect in the methodical mutilation killings of a Wenatchee woman and her 14-year-old daughter in 1994, they asked **[Dr Robert] Keppel** for a profile so they could devise an interview strategy.

Keppel pegged the 26-year-old Spillman as an 'anger-excitation' sadist acting out a highly ritualized sex-torture fantasy who should be questioned in a precise way. Spillman eventually read Keppel's profile and told the investigator it was dead-on.

"Just looking at the behavior at the scene you could tell that his fantasies were far too developed for this to be the first time – and it wasn't the first time," Keppel said.

Spillman not only pleaded guilty to the murders but also to killing a 9-year-old Tonasket, Okanogan County, girl the year before. He had also been mutilating animals. (Seven 1997)

The daughter who lived down the street last spoke with her mother on April 12, 1995 at 10:00 p.m. According to her, her mother was fine at the time. The next morning at 8:00 a.m., the daughter who lived down the street came over to check on her mother and sister because she could not get them on the phone. She came in through the sliding door in the master bedroom and saw her sister's body, deceased, on the bed. She thought that it was her mother because it was partially covered and it was her mother's bed. She did not go further into the residence, but ran out of the house screaming for help.

The daughter died of massive cranial and cerebral trauma secondary to a blunt impact on the side of the head. She also sustained 16 penetrating stab wounds to the anterior neck, and two stab wounds of the anterior mid chest, among other injuries.

According to the very competent and very thorough report prepared by the forensic pathologist, Dr Rappe:

The stab wounds indicate there was no movement by the decedent at the time she was being stabbed. Also, there are no cuts or stabs on the arms or hands that would suggest that she attempted to defend herself from being stabbed… The stab wounds in the chest caused no serious damage and are associated with minimal bleeding in the soft tissue adjacent to the penetrating wound.

All of the observations noted in the opinion on the previous page would suggest that the stabbings came after the decedent sustained the massive blunt trauma to the left calvarium, which caused instant unconsciousness and respiratory paralysis shortly thereafter. The baseball bat that was jammed up through the top of the vaginal vault is not associated with any hemorrhage in the vaginal vault or abdomen. This indicates that the bat was inserted after she was dead and circulation had ceased completely. Also, the excision of the skin and tissue of the pubis along with the upper half of the external genitalia was all done post-mortem because of the complete lack of hemorrhage.

According to the county's forensic pathologist, all of the stabbing and mutilation injuries inflicted to the daughter (as well as the insertion of the baseball bat into her vaginal vault) were done so after she was unconscious or dead. Not stated is the fact that the excised skin mentioned above was placed over the victim's face.

> The mother died of multiple stab wounds to the upper chest and lower neck with perforations of the left subclavian artery and vein, ascending aorta, and left lung. She also sustained 31 stab wounds to the chest, arms, left leg, and back consistent with defensive type injuries. Furthermore she sustained stab wounds into, or through, the left subclavian artery and vein, and the ascending aorta. And she sustained three stab wounds into the left upper lobe of the lung, among other injuries.
>
> She also sustained post-mortem excision of the breasts, and, similar to her daughter, post-mortem excision of the skin and underlying tissue of the right pubis, vulva, and perineum. The excised skin taken from her pubis, vulva, and perineum was stuffed into her mouth.
>
> Again, according to the very competent and very thorough report prepared by the forensic pathologist, Dr Rappe:
>
>> The decedent put up a vigorous but probably brief defense. It is most likely that she was attacked in the room she was found in and that she was lying on the couch and attacked from behind the couch. Her attacker was above her head and behind her and prevented her from getting up off the couch during the struggle.

It is very easy to become overwhelmed by the details of this case, as they are indeed very horrible. However, the evidence in this case is very clear. Both victims suffered only briefly, and were certainly not tortured. The injuries that might have been confused for torture were all sustained post-mortem.

This is what is referred to as experimental force (see Chapter 8), consistent with reassurance-oriented behavior (see Chapter 15). It is not torture, and it is most certainly not suggestive of a sadistic offender. However, the profiler in this case, according the above mentioned article, "pegged" the offender as a sadist.

It should be noted that the reason an offender might agree with a profiler's assessment is if it casts them in a favorable light. Profilers commonly refer to sadists as the most intelligent, creative, and dangerous offenders (Groth 1979). This plays right into the ego of those with power-reassurance motivations.

As Burgess and Hazelwood (1995) warn us:

> ...Many crimes involve the intentional infliction of physical and psychological suffering; sexual sadism is only one of several motives for such crimes. To avoid misinterpretation, investigators should be aware of those behavior patterns that appear to be sexually sadistic, but which, in fact, arise from different motives and contexts.

INVESTIGATIVE IMPLICATIONS

The whole reason that a criminal profiler is interested in the cluster of behaviors that are requisite for sadism is that they give direct insight into offender motivation, and provide effective arguments for the inference of subsequent offender characteristics (see Chapter 15).

As Burgess and Hazelwood (1995) remind us, not unlike psychopaths, sadists are not necessarily criminals. But they are the products of intense, violent fantasization:

> The behavior of sexual sadists, like that of other deviants, extends along a wide spectrum. Sexual sadists can be law-abiding citizens who fantasize but do not act, or who fulfill these fantasies with freely consenting partners. Only when sexual sadists commit crimes do their fantasies become relevant to law enforcement.

> ...All sexual acts and crimes begin with fantasy. However, in contrast with normal sexual fantasies, those of the sexual sadist center on domination, control, humiliation, pain, injury, and violence, or a combination of these themes, as a means of eliciting suffering. As the fantasies of the sexual sadist vary, so does the degree of violence.

If sadistic behaviors are evident in an offense, then this immediately suggests four things about the offender responsible:

- The offender has an intense fantasy life that has evolved over a number of years to achieve sadistic associations.
- The offender, in some way, preplanned the details of the offense – the victim and the location may have been opportunistic (see Chapter 15), but the offender had a specific series of fantasy related events in mind as well as the facility to engage them.
- There is a very high likelihood that this is not the offender's only offense – it does take some time and some practice to achieve the level of confidence and competence that sadistic offenders evidence by virtue of the behavioral requirement, given previously in this section.
- The offender is not very likely to end offense behavior unless they are acted upon by an outside force.

A NOTE ON OFFENDER EMPATHY AND INTIMACY

EMPATHY

Before we can have this discussion, we need to define our terms:

- Empathy: the identification with and understanding of another's situation, feelings, and motives.
- Sympathy: a relationship or affinity between persons or things, in which whatever affects one, correspondingly affects the other.

It may be true that most psychopaths do lack empathy, or possess it in a lesser form than non-psychopaths. But the most intelligent types, the rarest known breed of criminal psychopath, in this author's experience, lack sympathy while their empathy is fully intact. They understand the consequences of their behavior, they understand their victim's agony and pain; they remain, however, unaffected by it.

At a round-table discussion of the behavioral development of deviant children, one of this author's former professors stated that we (the mental health community) could determine that a child has reached a new stage in moral development when he or she first begins to tease. Teasing requires perspective taking and empathy. The teaser must first assume the role of the teasee and understand what bothers them. Once they know what hurts, they can use it against them. Teasing behavior requires basic empathic skills and is a definite, measurable marker for a new stage of moral development.

The author argues that we can extend this logic. To receive any kind of sexual pleasure from a victim response such as humiliation, pain, and submission, the offender must first understand what humiliates, frightens, and subordinates the victim. Certain types of violent serial offenders are able to accomplish just that. They understand what is humiliating, what is degrading, and what is painful to the victim. They have already taken the viewpoint of the victim into full consideration, and understand it well. In fact they are dependent upon it. That is often how they are able to achieve and maintain control. That may even be where they derive pleasure and satisfaction.

This is further evidence that some violent serial sex offenders have a very clear understanding of the consequences of their behavior towards the victim. They understand that the victim is humiliated and in pain, and in fact that is part of why they are doing it. They feel aroused and powerful when they are assured by victim responses denoting a state of submission and painful humiliation. To be aroused by the pain and domination of the victim, the offender first must understand that the victim is in pain and is dominated. To successfully elicit those victim responses the offender must understand what behavior on their own part causes it. Their behavior is ultimately self-serving, but not born of a single perspective. Their behavior cannot, therefore, be described as purely egocentric. Some violent serial sex offenders use non-egocentric perspective-taking thought processes to arrive at their egocentric pleasure.

For some offenders, it makes them feel good to know that they have made their victims feel bad. It is egocentric entitlement coupled with a necessary empathy. They know that their victims are suffering, and they are affected by it – the suffering only excites them rather than causing them to be distressed. It is easy for us to agree that the offender must be unable to understand what is going on, and must be unable to feel anything, because that is something that our minds can accept with less discomfort.

However, this author would argue that, in some cases, what an offender feels or enjoys is a reflection of their uniquely formed expression of intimacy. And that expression is not subordinate to what is considered to be healthy or preferable behavior by the rest of society. Sometimes the intimate expressions of others require victim suffering.

INTIMACY

Intimacy can be defined as pertaining to or indicative of one's deepest, most essential nature. For those of us who have been socialized, this tends to refer to our healthy, shared expression of emotions, needs, and feelings.

Being a criminal offender of any kind does not mean that one lacks the ability to be intimate. However it may mean that one's expression of intimacy is self-destructive, or destructive to others. As Marshall (1989) points out, sex offenders, for example, probably desire intimacy but lack the skills to achieve it in a healthy form.

What offender's offense behavior may suggest is a sort of one-way, voyeuristic intimacy where the victim is physically revealed to the offender, and completely under their control. Through this forced opening of physical and psychological intimacy an offender perceives his or her own uniquely formed version of emotional and spiritual intimacy. The offender may take pleasure in either the notion that a form of physical intimacy is being forced from the victim, or in the fantasy that the victim actually has a desire for them to experience shared intimacy. The offender may also take pleasure from revealing the victim in a private, intimate, and violent way, devouring the victim's own sense of personal security and control. Though incredibly unhealthy and destructive, this is how an offender may achieve intimacy. That is how they may understand it and experience it; through their offense behavior.

This possibility must not be overlooked.

REFERENCES

American Psychiatric Association (1994) *Diagnostic and Statistical Manual of Mental Disorders*, 4th edn, Washington, DC: American Psychiatric Association.

Burgess, A., Burgess, A., Douglas, J. and Ressler, R. (1997) *Crime Classification Manual*, San Francisco: Jossey-Bass, Inc.

Burgess, A. and Hazelwood, R., (eds) (1995) *Practical Aspects of Rape Investigation: A Multidisciplinary Approach*, 2nd edn, New York: CRC Press.

Cleckley, H. (1976) *Mask of Sanity*, 5th edn, St. Louis: Mosby.

de Sade, M. (1965) *The Complete Justine, Philosophy in the Bedroom, and Other Writings*, New York: Grove Press.

Groth, A. N. (1979) *Men Who Rape: The Psychology of the Offender*, New York: Plenum Press.

Hare, R. (1991) "Psychopathy and the DSM-IV Criteria for Antisocial Personality Disorder," *Journal of Abnormal Psychology*, 100 (3): 391–8.

Hare, R. (1993) *Without Conscience*, New York: Pocket.

Hare, R. (1996) "Psychopathy and Antisocial Personality Disorder: A Case of Diagnostic Confusion," *Psychiatric Times*, February, http://www.mhsource.com/edu/psytimes/p960239.html

Marshall, W. L. (1989) "Intimacy, Loneliness and Sexual Offenders", *Behavior Research Theory*, 27 (5): 491–503.

Seven, R. (1997) "The Profiler: Law enforcement's new darlings blend psychology, computers, probabilities and suppositions to get inside the minds of serial killers," *The Seattle Times*, April 13.

Toch, H. (ed.) (1979) *Psychology of Crime and Criminal Justice*, New York: Holt, Rinehart, and Winston, Chapter 14.

CHAPTER 18

INVESTIGATIVE STRATEGY

Brent E. Turvey, M.S.

Physical evidence can only achieve its optimum value in criminal investigations when its collection is performed with a selectivity governed by the collector's thorough knowledge of the crime laboratory's techniques, capabilities, and limitations.

(Saferstein 1998)

As outlined in Chapter 4 of this work, the goals of deductive criminal profiling are both investigative and adjudicative. First, behavioral evidence analysis may be used to systematically examine and interpret the facts of a case. Then it may be used to assist in the process of settling disputes in a court of law (see Chapters 19, 20 and 21).

The primary responsibility of any criminal profiler is to the objective investigation of fact. Investigatively, this directive subordinates the criminal profiler to achieving justice for the victim (when there is a victim). This can only be achieved by establishing the facts of a case, investigating those who are responsible for any crimes committed, and bringing them before a court of law for the purposes of trial.

It is in keeping with this that the criminal profiler should, as a matter of priority, be able to offer *investigatively relevant* suggestions or insights to a given case effort. Investigatively relevant means that it offers something pertinent to the investigation. This can be in the form of something that sheds new light on facts, that helps provide a useful understanding of the offender's motivations, that leads to new witnesses or new evidence, or that provides for an investigative lead or strategy.

RELEVANT RECOMMENDATIONS

For those who have little or no experience working on an investigation with law enforcement as part of other investigative efforts, the author offers the following general recommendations and insights.

TEAMWORK

A criminal profiler is not a silver bullet. Nor are they a lone wolf. The successful implementation of criminal-profiling techniques requires the ability on the part of the requesting agency to respond to the profiler's needs by competently gathering the necessary information and performing the necessary forensic analysis. It also depends upon the criminal profiler's ability to work as an integral part of the investigative effort – accept and work within real-life limitations, promote information sharing, and be able to explain, in plain language, the investigative relevance of insights into offender behavior.

At no time during an unsolved investigation should a criminal profiler concern himself or herself with getting investigative credit or media attention. In fact, the less of either sought the better. Criminal profilers should concern themselves with the resolution of the case. Anything else is a luxury or, worse, a distraction.

PHYSICAL EVIDENCE FIRST

In many cases there will be numerous tips and leads coming in from the public and other departments. There will also be very firmly felt theories and speculations rising from within. At all times the criminal profiler should respect these possibilities, and be open to investigating each in order of priority. However, *physical evidence alone must be allowed to dictate the known facts of a case.*

This means accepting witness and victim statements with healthy skepticism, as well as any subsequent physical descriptions offered regarding unknown offenders. Different victims and witnesses react differently during different types of events. Some have excellent recollection, some recall only partial information, and still others may recall nothing at all. Working together, the detective and the criminal profiler should determine which statements made by the victim can be trusted, in light of the physical evidence, and which cannot.

More than once in the experience of this author, a physical description given by a witness or victim, as well as the subsequent offender sketch, has been inaccurate and harmed the investigative effort. A good offender sketch informed by a victim or witness who has good recall can help an investigative effort. However, a bad offender sketch informed by a victim or witness with poor recall can increase the number of bad tips and leads coming in from the community and can also cause investigators and detective to focus on the wrong suspect[1].

When the physical evidence does not support a lead, theory, or suggestion, those avenues should not be given investigative priority.

[1] *Am I the only one who has noticed that a lot of witnesses or victims give descriptions of offenders that actually match the sketch artist or the detective in the case?*

I'm not kidding. This really happens.

Example: Professor David Canter and Ripper Diary
According to an article on the subject:

> Psychologists, historians and the police have agreed to disagree about the authenticity of the infamous Jack the Ripper diary after an exhaustive debate.

More than 100 delegates at the International Investigative Psychology Conference at Liverpool University failed to reach a consensus on whether Jack the Ripper was in fact a Liverpool cotton trader called James Maybrick.

The diary of James Maybrick, in which he takes credit for the horrific Ripper murders in the East End of London in the 1880s, was "discovered" by fitter Mike Barrett as he renovated a house in Liverpool in 1992. (BBC News 1998)

It further goes on to explain that:

Author Shirley Harrison, who wrote the academic work *The Diary of Jack the Ripper*, said: "Although I have not been able to prove that it is genuine, I seriously believe the diary deserves serious historical and academic consideration."

She said tests have failed to conclusively date the ink in which the diary was written to the 1880s, but neither could they demonstrate that the ink is not Victorian. (*ibid.*)

In point of fact, Harrison did initially state that there were several scientific tests done on the ink from the diary. It was tested once and was found to be from the 1920s. The ink was tested again at another location and a modern chemical found in ink was discovered. But this information was quickly brushed aside and no one else made a comment about it.

So, while historians and psychologists were stumped, and debated the origins of the diary, the forensic sciences had already offered a conclusion. The document contains ink from a more modern era, and the materials used cannot be placed in the Victorian era (Sugden 1995). Furthermore a man has confessed to writing them. These facts in concert solve the *mystery*.

At this point a criminal profiler cannot go much further in their search for evidence. The item of evidence in question cannot be considered reliable evidence, and can certainly not be used to support conclusions or give valid insights into the Ripper case.

However, Professor David Canter of Liverpool University, which sponsored the conference, disagrees:

…Head of the Liverpool University Centre for Investigative Psychology, Professor David Canter, who hosted the conference, said psychological profiling shows it is "plausible" that the diary may have been written by Jack the Ripper.

He said: "The way it's written – the style of thinking – does reveal some components that are remarkably subtle."

"This was either produced by a very skilled author or someone with detailed knowledge of the Ripper history, or someone with enormous insight into carrying out these crimes and the person most likely to have that is the person who did carry out those crimes." (BBC News 1998)

In his own defense, responding to a colleague who was very offended by the high amount of media attention and the lack of professional ethics involved in the presentation of the Ripper Diary as potentially genuine, Professor Canter stated:

… no forensic evidence has so far refuted the authenticity of the "Ripper Diary" but there is a man who admits he is a lush who claims with some conviction that he wrote it. (Baeza 1998)

He further stated, in the same response:

> Ours was a conference in a University, hosted by a Psychology Department and therefore followed the patterns of science, including the dictum that a wise man can learn from all men, even fools. It was not a conference to teach jobbing cops a few more tricks on how to catch the bad guys. (*ibid.*)

Professor Canter appears to be arguing that the goals of investigative psychology (see Chapter 22) do not lend themselves to providing investigatively relevant insights.

Professor Canter is furthermore selectively ignoring the forensic tests done on the diary that confirm modern origins, as well as the confession of the man who wrote it. This event was apparently not about good science, good psychology, or demonstrating sound profiling techniques. In fact it demonstrated a disinterest in physical evidence that should be of concern.

The lesson for students here is to not make the same error when evaluating evidence. Just because evidence does not fit one's theories does not mean that it can be ignored in subsequent analysis and interpretation.

CULTURAL GUIDE

Whenever a criminal profiler travels to an area where the cultural meaning of behaviors varies from that which they know or understand, they need to get a cultural guide. In most cases, the detectives involved in a case may suffice. However in some cases leads may develop or evidence may suggest a culture or community that is foreign to everyone in the case.

For example, if the criminal profiler were investigating a case that involves suspects who may be Mormon, then it would be wise to consult with someone who has an understanding of the habits, relationships and rituals in the Mormon community. If the criminal profiler were investigating a case involving organized crime, then it would be wise to consult with someone who had an understanding of the habits, relationships, and rituals of organized-crime syndicates in that particular region.

The point is that we should only act as our own investigative guide when travelling in our own territory. Otherwise we are certain to get lost. If we do guide ourselves in foreign territory, and we do get lost, we may not know enough to even be aware of it.

MAJOR CASE TASK FORCES

See Appendix IV of this book.

INVESTIGATIVELY IRRELEVANT

Recall the psychiatric profile offered by Dr James Brussel of the 'Mad Bomber' case in the city of New York, from Chapter 1 of this book. Among other insights into the offender's characteristics was the firm suggestion that the offender would be wearing a double-breasted suit. When finally apprehended, George Metesky was indeed wearing a double-breasted suit. If he had not been, Brussel may have explained this error by saying that although Metesky was not wearing the suit, he probably owned one. That is, if Brussel would have addressed it at all. Since a full written profile was not made publicly available, we cannot be sure which characteristics Brussel accurately inferred, and which he did not.

Regardless, this author questions the investigative relevance of that particular insight (and mentions it due to the amount of attention it is given in the literature), and would hope that law enforcement did not use it to limit their consideration of suspects.

The tradition of offering vague, equivocal, and ultimately irrelevant offender characteristics is held by a number of criminal profilers. Take for example the numerous times that the phrase, "The offender is a loner, and most likely lives alone or with a dominating female," has appeared in newsprint as part of an FBI profile released to the public. This characteristic describes many individuals, and can result in the requesting agency becoming deluged with essentially worthless tips and leads, each of which must be followed up, wasting valuable time and resources. Not only is the characteristic vague, but it has the potential to harm the investigative effort.

Another example would include Dr Micki Pistorius, chief investigative psychologist for the South African Police Service.

> "I assess a crime scene and try to reconstruct in my mind what happened and why. Then I put together a profile of the killer, his background, age, colour, etcetera." Some people call her a forensic psychologist, "but that sounds as if I examine dead bodies, so I prefer the term investigative psychologist", she says.

> "… there's a lot of intuition in it, but anyone can do what I do. I've trained over 100 detectives, mostly men, to be able to investigate such cases.

> …The main thing is to try to focus on the person's sexual fantasy. You have to try to picture that; no matter how grotesque it is, to relive the most minute detail." (Johnson 1997)

She has spoken regarding a case involving an offender who was wearing a suit and tie at the time of capture. Dr Pistorius claims that she predicted that he would be wearing a tie. This evokes images of Dr Brussel predicting that infamous double-breasted suit. Also similar to Dr Brussel is that the investigative relevance of providing that particular insight was not born out in the case.

Dr Pistorius has also spoken regarding Freudian theories as they relate to offender profiling (and she is by no means the only one). For example, she makes the claim that any offender who attacks the womb of a victim may be making a symbolic attempt to get back into the womb, or has been injured in the womb.

The Freudian model of treatment was developed with the idea that the clinician and the patient would build meaningful metaphors to describe the conflicts and issues in the patient's life. In the application of this theory to an investigative process, the clinician is denied the working relationship with the client (the unknown offender), and isolates offender behaviors by interpreting them through inductive generalizations. This means that any insights into offender motives or fantasy, as with all inductive profiling methods, tell us more about the motives, fantasies, and psychological issues at work within the profiler or clinician than those at work within the offender.

The application of Freudian theories of treatment to criminal profiling processes do serve the voyeuristic needs that many Freudian clinicians are accustomed to, but at the expense of valuable investigative time and resources.

The very bottom line is that a criminal profiler should be able to offer investigatively relevant suggestions or insights to a case effort. It is furthermore not on the shoulders of investigators or detectives to demonstrate the relevance of the insights given in a criminal profile. That responsibility is on the criminal profiler[2]. The fact that this ability requires some investigative knowledge, training, and experience on the part of the criminal profiler is a very healthy thing.

[2] The duty to explain investigative relevance is the responsibility of the criminal profiler. However, the duty to act, and to implement the investigative suggestions in the profile, belongs to the detectives and investigators on the case.

Criminal profiles and criminal profilers do not typically solve cases. Detectives and investigators do.

CASE LINKAGE

Most offenses involve a relationship between a victim, an offender, and a crime scene. The way that we establish the nature of the relationship between those elements includes physical evidence, behavioral evidence, and witness or victim statements. These relationships are also our means for *case linkage*, which simply means that they can help us establish a link between two or more previously unrelated cases.

Examples of the most common methods for case linkage include, but are not limited to:

- Physical evidence: similarities between the physical evidence that is collected in relationship to particular cases, as well as the results of any forensic analysis.
- Physical description: similarities between the physical descriptions of an offender given by a witness or victim and potential suspects.
- Modus operandi: similarities between actions taken by an offender that are necessary for the successful completion of the crime.
- Signature behaviors: similarities between actions taken by an offender that are unnecessary for the successful completion of the crime. These actions suggest a psychological or emotional need.

- Victimology: similarities or connections between victims, or the way that victims appear to be selected.

- Wound pattern analysis: a review of the autopsy or hospital protocols for a victim that finds similarities between the nature and extent of injuries sustained during an attack.

- Geographic region or location: offenses that have occurred in the same area, or the same type of area.

There is a large amount of published information regarding the limitations of using a single commonality, such as MO behavior or victim characteristics, as the sole basis for linking unsolved criminal cases (Burgess *et al.* 1997; Burgess and Hazelwood 1995; Geberth 1996). However, for some unknown reason many law-enforcement database initiatives tend to focus on links between MO behavior only.

LINKAGE BLINDNESS

The MO behavior demonstrated by an offender, as well as any associated physical evidence, can indeed play an important role in law enforcement's linkage of related crimes. However, it is the tendency of law enforcement to rely solely upon an offender's MO for the development of investigative strategy. Because MO behaviors can change over time, and because physical evidence often goes unrecognized and uncollected, this can lead to what has been termed *linkage blindness*; the failure to recognize a pattern that links one crime with another crime in a series of cases (Egger 1997).

Specifically, there are three very important factors that can act individually or in concert to facilitate linkage blindness:

1   The tendency of law enforcement to rely solely on MO behaviors such as offense type, victim type, weapon selection, and location type as a basis for case linkage.

2   The possibility that one predatory offender is operating in or near the same general area as another, confusing law enforcement efforts.

3   Interpersonal or interagency conflicts or resource deficiencies that lead to communication breakdowns and poor or non-existent information sharing[3].

USING CASE-LINKAGE SYSTEMS

In the pursuit of investigative solutions to difficult cases, there seems to be a pervasive belief in a Holy Grail of some kind. That Holy Grail is something along the lines of a big red button for investigators to push that will provide them with the name, address, and phone number of an offender, as well as an uncontestable list of all the solved and unsolved crimes they have committed.

In the absence of a big red button, many different types of computerized

[3] *The lack of interagency cooperation and communication is without a doubt one of the most limiting, constraining factors on the successful investigation of serial crimes, at least in the US. Few neighboring agencies talk to each other, and even less share information.*

The reasons tend to be political. Practical politics consists of ignoring facts. There is no excuse for this. Only the offender benefits.

case-linkage systems have been developed. The term *case-linkage system* refers generally to a database of cases or case-related information that is designed to assist in the process of case linkage. Case-linkage systems to date have focused on both physical and behavioral evidence. Examples include, but are by no means limited to, the following systems:

- AFIS: Automated Fingerprint Identification System (United States).
- BADMAN: Behavioural Analysis Data Management Auto-indexing Networking (Surrey, UK).
- CODIS: The Combined DNA Index System (United States).
- Drugfire: A computer technology that matches firearm evidence (bullets, cases, and test-fires from recovered guns) from serial shooting investigations (United States).
- HITS: The Homicide Investigation and Tracking System (Washington State).
- IBIS: Integrated Ballistics Identification System (United States).
- ViCAP: Violent Criminal Apprehension Program (United States).
- ViCLAS: Violent Crime Linkage Analysis System (Canada).

Two major contributors to current and future case-linkage efforts using the analysis of offender behavior are ViCAP and ViCLAS.

ViCAP

The basic ideas surrounding case linkage were first brought to a more modern level of offender databasing by the late Pierce Brooks, an American law-enforcement officer. Brooks joined the Los Angeles Police Department in 1948 and served in the vice, narcotics, and homicide divisions. In 1958, Brooks was assigned two homicides that, although clearly unrelated, appeared to be the work of individuals who had killed before. He looked for resources to assist him in linking either of his homicides to any other cases in other parts of the country. There was nothing like that available on a national level. So Brooks used the only national information system available to him – he went to the local library for hours at a time and sifted through newspapers from around the country in the hopes of finding stories that related cases with similar *modus-operandi* behavior (Burgess *et al.* 1988).

Brooks quickly came to realize that what was needed was a national database and information center that collected information on the *modus operandi* of those killers that crossed jurisdictional boundaries. As early as 1958, he also knew that a computerized database of such information was the most effective way to make it nationally accessible. His technique of searching through library newspaper archives for related cases, born out of extreme necessity, was the basis for what was to become the Federal Bureau of Investigation's Violent Criminal Apprehension Program (ViCAP) (Geberth 1996).

In 1983, Brooks testified before congress about the possibility that unsolved murders around the country might be attributed to anonymous serial murderers. He explained that the only way to investigate the crimes and link the cases to ultimately apprehend these individuals was to put all of the information about each case into a computer database system that everyone in law enforcement could have access to. In 1984, with Brooks' help, the FBI's National Center for the Analysis of Violent Crime (NCAVC) was officially established. ViCAP went online in 1985, with Brooks as the first program manager (Burgess *et al.* 1988).

ViCAP remains a nationwide data information center, specifically designed for collecting, sorting, and analyzing solved and unsolved homicides, as well as missing persons cases where there is a strong possibility of foul play. According to the FBI, ViCAP's mission remains to facilitate cooperation, communication, and coordination between law enforcement agencies and provide support in their efforts to investigate, identify, track, apprehend, and prosecute violent serial offenders (Geberth 1996).

The current form of ViCAP suffers greatly from under-utilization by law enforcement. The primary complaint tends to be that the form is too long and too inconvenient to fill out for every case. Recently the FBI updated its ViCAP form, reducing the number of questions from 189 questions on 15 pages, to 95 questions on 26 pages. This was not actually an improvement in the eyes of end users (law enforcement), as each question on the new form includes many sub-questions.

End users of ViCAP further complain that the database is too small, and that it should contain information regarding other types of interpersonal crime as well, such as rapes and sexual assaults. To augment the limited number of cases in the database, ViCAP analysts have, for some time, taken a page from the book of Pierce Brooks, and have populated it with information on solved and unsolved cases obtained from newspaper articles. This has untold effects on the quality of any professional research conducted using this database, and the veracity of any linkages made.

Another criticism includes the fact that the old ViCAP form was sent off to a remote database that local law enforcement did not have direct access to. A newer, Microsoft Windows® interfaced SQL version of ViCAP is in beta testing now. It is reportedly a PC-network-based system that can maintain a local database as well as communicate with the national-level network at NCAVC.

Currently, the new ViCAP Crime Analysis Report Form is designed to collect information regarding the following types of crimes, whether or not the offender has been arrested or identified:

- solved or unsolved homicides/attempted homicides;
- missing persons/kidnapping;
- unidentified dead bodies.

Future enhancements are hoped to include:

- an integrated mapping tool;
- create store, and search offender timelines;
- scan images and associate them with a particular case;
- include digital video clips and associate them with a particular case;
- download data into case matrix format. (FBI 1998)

Regarding these future enhancements, it should be noted that ViCAP is currently nowhere near anything like this. It represents a wish list that will only be investigated if the new beta testing performs up to expectations.

It should also be noted that there is no current plan for ViCAP to include crimes relating to sexual assault, arson, bank robberies, or other sexual or violent but non-homicidal crimes. In the view of this author, that makes this tool woefully inadequate to the task of investigating serial crime.

ViCLAS

Following research into the FBI's ViCAP system, the Canadian law-enforcement community developed what was referred to as the Major Case File (MCF). It was Canada's first attempt to link homicide cases on a national level. Much like the ViCAP report, investigators filled out their forms and submitted them to regional MCF analysts who would manually input the data into the system. The MCF database was searchable by key words and phrases, and detectives would attempt to link offenses largely by *modus-operandi* behaviors. Despite the approximately 800 cases in the MCF database, no linkages had been made with the system as late as 1990 (Turvey: in press).

In 1991, a RCMP inspector named Ron MacKay who had recently received training through the FBI's profiling fellowship program in Quantico, Virginia helped to develop a new linkage system for Canada. It was to become the Violent Crime Linkage Analysis System (ViCLAS). Its development was the result of analyzing not only the FBI's ViCAP database, but other statewide linkage systems in the United States as well (*ibid.*).

A far more ambitious and robust tool than the FBI's ViCAP, ViCLAS attempts to input information from the following sources:

- all solved or unsolved homicides and attempted homicides;
- solved and unsolved sexual assaults;
- missing persons, where there is a strong possibility of foul play and the victim is still missing;
- unidentified bodies, where the manner of death is known or suspected to be homicide;
- all non-parental abductions and attempted abductions.

An emphasis was also placed on the training and qualification of ViCLAS analysts as an integral part of the system. Submissions still occur via a questionnaire that is filled out by an investigator and is then sent to one of 10 ViCLAS centers servicing the various Canadian regions. However, there are numerous quality-assurance reviews in place, and the ViCAP analysts may return forms to detectives if something is questioned. ViCAP analysts are trained to conduct structured queries of the system based on their own expertise, and arrive at potential linkages based on their own analysis of victimology, offender behavior, *modus operandi*, and forensic information. They are also trained to understand the concept of offender signature. Regardless of the results of their analysis, investigators in the field are charged with ultimately confirming or rejecting the links based on the substance of their own investigation (*ibid.*).

The Canadian ViCLAS initiative has become a popular model for law-enforcement agencies involved in violent crime case linkage. Similar systems to ViCLAS, though not directly connected, have been adopted in countries including Australia, Austria, Belgium, Holland, and the United Kingdom. This speaks to a trend in the international law-enforcement community to both admit that they have serial crime, and that an understanding of the relationship between *modus operandi* and other elements that comprise criminal patterns, is necessary to successfully link and investigate them.

RECOMMENDATIONS FOR A CASE-LINKAGE SYSTEM

As previously suggested, there are no big red buttons for investigators to push which solve cases. Current case-linkage systems tend to be built to link cases by specific characteristics such as MO behavior, physical evidence, and penal designation (type of crime; rape, robbery, homicide, etc.).

Four constraints limit or impede the success of most case-linkage systems:

- The quality of the nature and quality of the information that is being collected and stored in the database.
- The physical and conceptual limitations placed on what is stored in the database and how it may be collated, organized, or searched.
- The quality of the searches being performed by analysts.
- The inability to communicate with other case linkage systems.

Though a good case-linkage system can be part of an investigative solution, it cannot be the only part. It cannot be separated from good detectives, good forensic scientists, and competent analysts. To work towards limiting the power of the constraints listed, this author recommends the following.

First, train all detectives to collect factual case information in a systematic manner. Train them to separate facts from opinions in their reports. Also, train them to elucidate behavior. Do not refer to an incident by its penal designation (i.e. rape), but rather by what specific events are known to have occurred.

Second, do not create databases that exclude certain types of crimes. Database all case materials from all cases, and populate it with the uninterpreted facts, behaviors, and opinions gathered by detectives and investigators.

Third, train all database analysts to work as part of the investigative effort. The ViCLAS model is very good in this regard, and treats the analyst as an integral part of the database. It is not enough to populate the database with good data. Analysts must be trained to search it and ask investigatively relevant questions of it.

Fourth, provide the facility for full text searches of all departmental, interdepartmental, and interagency documents that are known to be related to a case. This includes relating case materials such as photos, video, sketches, and diagrams in some fashion within the system.

Fifth, and in accordance with number four, design databases that can speak with, or be searched in tandem by, other databases in other jurisdictions, both national and international, that contain both physical and behavioral evidence.

Sixth, design database software that monitors the trends, patterns, and associations between cases as new data is updated in the system (this already exists in numerous forms). The system should be able to self-monitor, and notify analysts of trends and patterns that are evident.

Seventh, design systems with the capacity for generating reports that can be customized to a particular agency's standards so that it is not a waste of the detective's or analyst's time to use them.

And eighth, the system should be remotely accessible, 24 hours a day, seven days a week, at authorized terminals, which would be both stationary and portable.

Of course, these recommendations are physically and politically impossible to implement immediately (more politically impossible than anything else). But it is the belief of the author that the only way to get something like this up and going is to just start doing it. To those crime analysts or computer operators who would say that the above is impossible, this author has the following response: Where information databasing and retrieval are concerned, computer programming should be done code independent. The trick is to decide what it is that we want up front. Then we just design a program that does it. It *can* be done – the tools are there.

REFERENCES

Baeza, J. (1998) *Personal communication with the author*, September 26.

Burgess, A., Burgess, A., Douglas, J. and Ressler, R. (1997) *Crime Classification Manual*, San Francisco: Jossey-Bass, Inc.

Burgess, A., Douglas, J. and Ressler, R. (eds) (1988) *Sexual Homicide: Patterns and Motives*, New York: Lexington Books.

Burgess, A. and Hazelwood, R. (eds) (1995) *Practical Aspects of Rape Investigation: A Multidisciplinary Approach*, 2nd edn, New York: CRC Press.

Egger, S. (1997) *The Killers Among Us*, Englewood Cliffs: Prentice Hall.

FBI (1998) "ViCAP: Violent Criminal Apprehension Program," US Dept. of Justice Publication.

Geberth, V. (1996) *Practical Homicide Investigation*, 3rd edn, New York: CRC Press.

Johnson, A. (1997) "The Woman Who Stalks The Killers," South Africa, *Electronic Mail & Guardian*, October 8.

"Ripper diary has historians stumped," *BBC News*, September 16, 1998

Saferstein, R. (1998) *Criminalistics: An Introduction to Forensic Science*, 6th edn, Upper Saddle River: Prentice Hall.

Sugden, P. (1995) *The Complete History of Jack the Ripper*, New York: Carroll and Graf Publishers, Inc.

Turvey, B. (in press) "Modus Operandi," *Encyclopedia of Forensic Science*, London: Academic Press.

CHAPTER 19

TRIAL STRATEGY

Brent E. Turvey, M.S.

The Utopians think it most unjust that any men should be bound by laws that are either too numerous to read or too obscure to understand. Moreover, they exclude absolutely all lawyers since these plead cases with cunning and slyly dispute the laws. For they think it useful that each man should plead his own case and repeat to the judge what he would have told his counsel.

(Sir Thomas More, *Utopia*)

The purpose of this chapter is to discuss the deductive criminal-profiling process, and how it directly lends itself to the development of trial strategy. Specifically, it will address how the deductive criminal-profiling process outlined in this text can help attorneys understand the nature and quality of the forensic evidence in a case, the circumstances of the offense, and an offender's motivation and intent.

It should be noted that this chapter addresses the type of behavioral evidence that is already deemed admissible by the court, though it is not referred to as "profile" evidence. In as much as this is true, a secondary purpose of this chapter is to elucidate just how different deductive criminal profiling is from the inductive profiling techniques associated with psychological syndrome evidence. Deductive criminal profiling, it must be understood, concerns itself with the particular behavioral evidence of a case, as it has been established by the physical evidence. Inductive, or statistical profiles, and syndrome evidence, however, are often nothing more than weakly supported generalizations that have little or no rational bearing on the issues before the court (Edwards 1998).

THE PROBLEM

Many of the agencies requesting criminal profiles, including law-enforcement agencies, prosecutorial bodies, or defense attorneys, are under the misconception that criminal profiling will answer specific questions about offender behavior, but circumvent the work required to analyze complex physical evidence. Just to add to the confusion, there are a number of people calling themselves criminal profilers who think this way as well. This is not surprising, given that most criminal cases do not involve the use of physical evidence of any kind, and, even when available, physical evidence is seldom seen by anyone involved as having any intrinsic value. In fact, a literature review conducted by Horvath and Meesig (1996) showed that physical evidence is used in less than 25 percent of the cases prosecuted in the United States, with the percentage in some regions dipping to less than five percent.

As stated, the notion that physical evidence does not have intrinsic value is a popular misperception, but not one shared by the deductive criminal profiler. For them, physical evidence and its proper documentation in a given case are the very basis for any and all arguments about an offender's characteristics.

This points to a real issue that needs to be confronted in criminal investigations and subsequent judicial proceedings, which is that in crimes involving violent, aberrant, sexual and/or predatory behavior, the physical evidence has generally not been fully examined by qualified investigators or forensic experts. The necessary result of this nearly pathological failure to recognize the intrinsic value of physical evidence is a failure to recognize the importance of, and even gross misinterpretations of, the nature and intent of even the most basic criminal behaviors. The use of competent criminal profilers, who are trained to examine physical evidence and exploit it to its fullest natural conclusion, can be an effective after-the-fact solution to this problem, even years after the crime has been committed (See Chapters 6 and 8).

FINDING AN EXPERT

EXPERTS

The term "expert," in the legal arena of the United States, refers to anyone with more knowledge than the general public. It does not by any stretch of the imagination imply actual demonstrable expertise. Therefore, just because someone has qualified in the courtroom as an "expert," this in itself is not an indication of expertise. It may just be an indication of the laziness, or the ignorance, of the courts.

Charlatans, frauds, and con artists frequently grace the courtrooms with phony credentials, often for years, without being discovered. Then one day someone asks a simple question about their curriculum vitae, and the whole world comes crashing down around every case that the "expert" has worked on. Always check professional references, and be certain that those references and qualifications are commensurate to the questions that are going to be put to the expert.

Consider the following example:

Example

Howard Bruce Ollick's sometimes $200-an-hour job was to testify in Broward County criminal courts as an expert on the effects of drugs on the mind. He showed Broward prosecutors and defense lawyers numerous credentials, including master's and doctorate degrees in organic chemistry from Florida Atlantic University. But Ollick's degrees are bogus, and he is under investigation by the Broward State Attorney's Office, said Assistant State Attorney John Countryman.

... because Ollick, 50, has been an expert witness since 1989, his charade could send defense lawyers scrambling to overturn convictions in cases where he played a role.

...Ollick, of Weston, describes himself in one of his resumes as a "forensic toxicologist with PhD degree in organic chemistry." In reality, he is a laboratory technician licensed by the Florida Department of Health, state records show.

Questions about Ollick's credentials surfaced on Monday during the first-degree murder trial of Richard Chambliss. Prosecutor Tony Loe said the credentials "are not what they appear to be," and Ollick was dropped as a $125-an-hour defense witness.

Robert Ullman, Ollick's attorney, said his client denies the accusations.

A Sun-Sentinel examination of his resumes found: Ollick claims master's and doctorate degrees from Florida Atlantic University. But the registrar's office has no record of his attending the university or receiving a degree there.

Ollick lists a bachelor's degree from Ohio State University. He attended the College of Continuing Education from June 1966 through September 1966 but received no degree, according to the registrar's office there.

Ollick writes he is a "certified NIDA (National Institute of Drug Abuse) scientist." That division of the US Department of Health and Human Services certifies laboratories, not people, a spokesman said.

...Assigned to prosecute Chambliss for the 1994 stabbing death of Felicia Cooley, 26, in Lauderhill four years ago, Loe saw Ollick's name on a list of defense witnesses. He had not come across that name before. Loe looked at Ollick's written credentials and noticed a discrepancy between two resumes: In one, Ollick claimed a bachelor of science degree from the school of education at Ohio State University; in the other, it was a bachelor of arts from the school of business administration at Ohio State. Ollick had also handed out his Florida Atlantic University master's certificate dated 1971. It was signed by, among others, 'Lawton Chiles, Governor.' Chiles was a senator in 1971.

And then there was Ollick's 1973 PhD in organic chemistry from FAU. The university does not offer that degree. (Fitzgerald and Marcus 1998)

THE PROFILING COMMUNITY – A LAYMAN'S GUIDE

Criminal profiling, as defined in this text, is a systemic method developed for analyzing forensic evidence at a more thorough and complete level than traditional forensic methods, in order to elicit the highest amount of relevant behavioral information from it.

It involves the analysis of *physical and behavioral evidence, victimology*, and *crime-scene characteristics*, from which specific offender characteristics are inferred. Any process used to infer offender characteristics which does not take into account at least these three considerations should not be referred to as criminal profiling, in the view of this author.

However, the profiling community, meaning those who put themselves forward as profilers (since no universally accepted standards of education, training, or methodology exists), comprises professionals with all types of backgrounds. Some criminal profilers are very qualified. Some are very qualified, but not to be criminal profilers. And some are not very qualified at all.

Historically speaking, criminal profilers can be placed into a wide range of categories that include the following:

CURRENT AND FORMER FBI AGENTS

Not all FBI and ex-FBI agents are trained to be criminal profilers. In fact, an FBI agent who operates outside of the NCAVC (National Center for the Analysis of Violent Crime) will rarely even work a homicide investigation or a sex crime, unless it happens to occur in a federal building or on an Indian reservation.

For an analysis of a recent FBI profile, please refer to Appendix IIb of this work regarding the Kristen and Kati Lisk case. For an analysis of a recent profile rendered by an ex-FBI profiler, please refer to Appendix IIa of this book, regarding The JonBenet Ramsey case.

FBI FELLOWSHIP PROGRAM

The FBI has trained law-enforcement officers working for a number of state and federal agencies in the United States and around the world as inductive criminal profilers. Some have a formal education, and some have strong investigative backgrounds.

FORENSIC PSYCHOLOGISTS

These are generally individuals with PhDs in psychology, and may or may not be board certified as forensic psychologists by the American Board of Forensic Psychology. Some individuals with PhDs in psychology refer to themselves as forensic psychologists. Some prison psychologists with MA and BS degrees also refer to themselves as forensic psychologists.

In any case, their training lies in the ability to perform clinical interviews for the purposes of diagnosis, treatment, and courtroom competency/sanity assessment. They are not typically trained in any of the forensic sciences relating to physical evidence, and are not often experienced in interpreting crime-scene behavior.

FORENSIC PSYCHIATRISTS

Forensic psychiatrists are medical doctors, with training in the medical sciences as well as the behavioral sciences. Their training prepares them for much the same type of work as the forensic psychologist.

CRIMINOLOGISTS

This group is slightly different from the rest, as these are often academics (many with some law enforcement background) who tend to study known offender populations. Anyone can claim to be a criminologist, and anyone can claim expertise in studying criminal populations. Criminologists are not necessarily trained in psychology, and they are not necessarily trained in forensic science or even death investigation techniques.

They may, however, be trained to do research. Research results in empirical data, which results in statistics, which are the grist for inductive offender profiles.

DETECTIVES AND INVESTIGATORS

This category includes law-enforcement officers and private-sector criminal profilers around the world who train themselves in a hodge-podge of techniques by attending an assortment of courses and seminars, by reading a variety of books and research, and by accumulating investigative experience. Some have formal educational backgrounds. Some do not.

The lesson here is not that everyone involved in the criminal-profiling community is equally unqualified. Only that a lot of them are. It all really depends upon the type of profiling that they claim to be doing. The real question for those seeking to evaluate whether or not a criminal profiler is qualified, is whether or not their training, education, and experience are commensurate to the types of analysis and interpretation they are engaged in.

OBJECTIVITY

One of the largest issues that any forensic examiner faces is the question of objectivity. The objective forensic examiner's role is that of a neutral, disinterested participant, never degenerating into that of an advocate. As forensic investigators of fact, criminal profilers are no different from other forensic examiners and are bound by the same ethical standards.

In cases where the offender is unknown, it is less difficult to navigate objectivity than in cases where a suspect or a defendant is involved. To better maintain objectivity, a profiler should not conduct suspect interviews, and further should not have contact with case related defendants, at any time prior to the development of the final profile. This guideline helps to prevent the profiler from "tailoring" their conclusions to include or exclude a particular type of individual based on contact with a suspect or defendant. Adherence to this guideline keeps the final profile a product of crime scene behavior and victimological assessments deducted purely from forensic evidence and witness testimony, and truly enables a more objective rendering (Turvey 1997).

As Burgess *et al.*(1988) explicitly state in their treatise on the subject of sexual homicide, regarding case material submissions by requesting agencies:

> Information the profiler does not want included in the case materials is that dealing with possible suspects. Such information may subconsciously prejudice the profiler and cause him or her to prepare a profile matching the suspect.

This author would go even further by stating that the influences of suspect or defendant information on subsequent criminal profiles can be conscious as well as unconscious.

This is an ethical issue that each profiler must confront, but that can be avoided by adherence to the above guideline. However, a reality of the nature of profiling is that pure objectivity is an ideal and not always attainable. So whether a criminal profiler is retained by the prosecution, the defense, or another interested party, the value of their interpretations or opinions should ultimately be judged solely by how well they account for the facts of the case and nothing more.

GUILT

The U.S. courts have spoken very plainly and very competently on the issue of guilt in reference to inductive profiling evidence and syndromes:

> Evidence which only describes the characteristics of a typical offender has no relevance in determining whether the defendant committed the crime in question, and the only inference which can be drawn from such evidence, namely that the defendant who matches the profile must be guilty, is an impermissible one. (State v. Clements, Kansas 1989)

Deductive criminal profiling will not implicate a specific individual in a specific crime. It can be used, however, to suggest a specific type of individual, with specific psychological and emotional characteristics (i.e. motives and needs). But it describes only the characteristics evident in the behavior of the crime at hand, as well as the circumstances of that behavior. It does not concern itself with the characteristics of typical offenders.

BENEFITS

The criminal-profiling process offers many benefits to the trial attorney. In the guilt phase of a trial this can mean recognizing evidence, adding to the reconstructive effort, and providing insight into the overall picture of an offense. In the penalty phase, the benefits can be found in how the criminal-profiling process addresses special mitigating or aggravating behavioral issues.

Whether engaged during the guilt phase or the penalty phase, the criminal-profiling process is designed to address those issues of behavioral evidence that the court is often interested in. It goes beyond a simple reading of the facts that establish the crime and helps inform an understanding of motive, intent, and circumstance, placing offender behavior into context.

RECOGNIZING EVIDENCE

As discussed, the most effective criminal profilers tend to be those who have first been trained as competent forensic investigators, with an appreciation for the value of forensic evidence, and the ability to perform at least some level of wound pattern analysis (see Chapter 8). In as much as this is true, a criminal profiler should first go through the process of analyzing the physical evidence in the case presented to them, in an effort to determine the actual nature of the interaction between the victim and the offender from all available documented sources. This includes first responder's reports, investigators' reports, autopsy reports, results of sexual-assault examination, witness interviews, victim statements (when available), and all available photos and videos.

The result of an equivocal forensic analysis (see Chapter 6) is that the criminal profiler becomes better informed about the larger picture of the investigation, and better able to illuminate areas in the first stages of the investigation where weaknesses in evidence collection or recognition may have occurred. They may also uncover potential errors in forensic interpretation, and even complete omissions in evidence recognition.

This author has worked on several capital cases where crucial evidence was not recognized or collected by investigating detectives, coroners, and even highly-trained medical examiners. Yet the evidence was clearly visible in the crime scene and autopsy documentation, just waiting for someone to see it.

The type of physical evidence most commonly missed in the case experience of this author includes such highly probative evidence as:

- petechiae in the eyes and nasal mucosa;
- bloodstain patterns of varying nature and origin;
- human bitemark evidence misinterpreted as blunt force trauma;
- blunt force trauma misinterpreted as stab wounds;
- lacerations misinterpreted as stab wounds;

- deceased victims' gaping anal sphincters misinterpreted as anal rape;
- pattern injuries of varying origins unrecognized or uninterpreted.

The criminal profiler's role in instances where crucial physical evidence has been overlooked is not necessarily to interpret it. Unless the criminal profiler has the commensurate expertise, they should direct counsel to the appropriate forensic expert, i.e. if a potential human bitemark appears evident on a victim's arm, then the criminal profiler should recommend that counsel seek out a forensic odontologist.

MO BEHAVIOR, SIGNATURE BEHAVIOR AND MOTIVE

A common misconception on any side of the courtroom is that there is such a thing as a motiveless crime. As Geberth (1996) states in his definitive treatise on homicide investigation, "No one acts without motivation." What is also true, however, is that very often the specific motivation for a crime may only be known to the offender.

As previously mentioned, MO behaviors are those committed by the offender during the commission of the crime which are necessary to complete the crime. MO behaviors are unstable across offenses, and may alter as the offender gains confidence or experience. Signature behaviors are committed to serve the offender's fantasies, and psychological and/or emotional needs. Signature behaviors are thematic in nature, are suggestive of offender intent, and can be more stable over time. These concepts are thoroughly explored by Geberth (1996), and Chapters 13 and 14 of this work.

The criminal profiler identifies signature behaviors and MO behaviors, and interprets their meaning for the purpose of helping to link two separate offenses together as having been potentially committed by the same offender, or for the purpose of demonstrating how two crimes may be psychologically dissimilar (see Chapters 13 and 14).

STATE OF MIND

One of the major contributions of a criminal profiler to trial strategy can be the elucidation of an offender's state of mind before, during, and after the commission of the crime. The criminal profiler accomplishes this very effectively because the only source of information used is the offender's behavior and interactions with the victim. Where forensic psychologists and other assessors may use post-apprehension interviews, polygraph examinations, or personality measures which have been duped countless times by offenders over the years, the criminal profiler carefully examines what the offender did, and has little use for what the offender has to say about what they did (Turvey 1997).

Examples of the types of behaviors that can give insight into offender state of mind include, but are not limited to:

- The presence of violent, frenzied slashing injuries to the victim's person (indicating some level of rage and familiarity, or perhaps a need to depersonalize), in contrast to careful, methodical exploratory stab wounds (inflicted either to torture a conscious victim, or to satisfy the offender's curiosity with an unconscious victim).

- The nature of offender behavior towards a known victim prior to an attack in the light of victimology (hostility, indifference, pleasantness, impending divorce or separation, etc.).

- The presence of remorse after a crime has been committed, evidenced by undoing behavior (symbolic undoing of a crime). This can include washing or bathing the victim, placing a pillow under the victim's head, covering the victim with a blanket, sitting the victim upright in a vehicle, or otherwise returning the victim to a natural-looking state.

MALICE AFORETHOUGHT

Another contribution of a criminal profiler to trial strategy can be the elucidation of whether or not an offender demonstrates *malice aforethought.*

For example, the California codes, Penal code section 188 states that:

Such malice may be express or implied. It is express when there is manifested a deliberate intention unlawfully to take away the life of a fellow creature. It is implied, when no considerable provocation appears, or when the **circumstances** attending the killing show an abandoned and malignant heart.

When it is shown that the killing resulted from the intentional doing of an act with express or implied malice as defined above, no other mental state need be shown to establish the mental state of malice aforethought. Neither an awareness of the obligation to act within the general body of laws regulating society nor acting despite such awareness is included within the definition of malice.

This is related to the motivational origins of force outlined in Chapter 8, as well as the concept of offender preplanning and intent (see Chapter 15). Examples of how behaviors may be suggestive of preplanning can include, but are certainly not limited to:

- bringing or possessing devices to an offense to facilitate a victim's torture;
- bringing a blindfold or tape to cover the victim's eyes;
- possessing surveillance material (photos, videos, etc.) of past and potential future victims;
- possessing fantasy material relating to the type of behavior engaged in during an offense.

TORURE

In many states in the U.S., evidence of torture is considered a special circumstance. Forensic psychologists, psychiatrists, and criminal profilers may be called to address this issue at trial. For example, the California codes, Penal code Section 190.2 states that special circumstances of torture exist when:

> The murder was especially heinous, atrocious, or cruel, manifesting exceptional depravity. As used in this section, the phrase "especially heinous, atrocious, or cruel, manifesting exceptional depravity" means a conscienceless or pitiless crime that is unnecessarily torturous to the victim.

> The murder was intentional and involved the infliction of torture.

This author has noticed a desire on the part of prosecution experts to not only establish that torture occurred in certain cases, but that it was sadistic as well. This may be because it is a diagnosable condition and therefore familiar territory for the expert. Or it may be because it represents a more heinous type of crime.

In any case, torture can be defined as the infliction of severe physical pain as a means of punishment, coercion, or offender gratification. This requires intent on the part of the offender to cause victim pain for those purposes, and a living, conscious victim to experience the pain.

Sadism, however, is the torture of a victim for offender sexual gratification. To establish sadism in a criminal offense, three things are required (see also Chapter 17):

- a conscious victim;
- evidence of torture;
- evidence of offender gratification from victim suffering.

In this author's experience, the most commonly misinterpreted or ignored element in cases of alleged sadism is addressing whether it can be determined if the injuries suggestive of torture occurred before or after the victim's death. It seems basic. For sadism to be evident, the victim must be alive, conscious, and suffering. But as forensic psychologists, forensic psychiatrists, law-enforcement profilers, and criminologists (who may be called to speak on this issue) do not often tender themselves to reconstructive efforts, mistakes regarding this issue are not uncommon.

REFERENCES

Burgess, A., Douglas, J. and Ressler, R. (eds) (1988) *Sexual Homicide: Patterns and Motives*, New York: Lexington Books.

Edwards, C. (1998) "Behavior and the Law Reconsidered: Psychological Syndromes and Profiles," *Journal of Forensic Sciences*, 43 (1): 141–50.

Fitzgerald, H. and Marcus, N. (1998) "Witness claimed false degrees," *Sun-Sentinel Company and South Florida Interactive, Inc.*, January 16.

Geberth, V. (1996) *Practical Homicide Investigation*, 2nd edn, New York: CRC Press.

Horvath, F. and Meesig, R. (1996) "The Criminal Investigation Process and the Role of Forensic Evidence: A Review of Empirical Findings," *Journal of Forensic Sciences*, November, 41 (6): 963–9.

State v. Clements (1989) 770 P.2d 447, 448, Kansas.

Turvey, B. (1997) "The Role of Criminal Profiling in the Development of Trial Strategy," *Knowledge Solutions Library*, October 30.

CHAPTER 20

ETHICS AND THE CRIMINAL PROFILER

Brent E. Turvey, M.S.

We have to condemn publicly the very idea that some people have the right to repress others. In keeping silent about evil, in burying it so deep within us that no sign of it appears on the surface, we are implanting it, and it will rise up a thousand-fold in the future.

To stand up for truth is nothing. For truth you have to sit in jail.

(Alexsandr Solzhenitsyn, *The Gulag Archipelago*)

This chapter is an attempt to begin an honest dialogue about ethical dilemmas specific to the criminal-profiling community, and set out some standards for consideration among those who do the work. This is straight talk on serious issues without hedging.

The term *ethics*, as we will use it, is meant to refer to rules or standards that have been established to govern the conduct of the members of a profession. The problem here is that criminal profilers, to date, have not professionalized (see the author's Preface). Subsequently, one could make a very effective argument for the position that criminal profilers are allowed the luxury of giving expert opinions without having to worry about being held responsible for them.

As an example, the author is aware of numerous colleagues who hide behind the phrase: "Profilers don't solve crimes, detectives do." Now this is a true statement and should be kept close to the breast when the time comes for recognition. Detectives are the ones who solve crimes and profilers tend to act in an advisory capacity. But that does not absolve criminal profilers of the responsibility to question the facts of a case, to make investigatively relevant suggestions, to fully explain the limitations of their profiles, to be forthcoming regarding the basis of their opinions, and to conduct themselves in an ethical manner.

The author finds himself alarmed by continuous examples of reckless, unethical behavior in the criminal-profiling community. Many do not seem to be in touch with, or concerned by, the real-world consequences of their unethical behavior. In fact, many seem dangerously preoccupied with recognition (and that has come to mean *media* attention) for "coining" dubious terms (renaming the obvious, or renaming someone else's ideas) and publishing dubious work (research born from newspaper clippings and rehashed cases).

Responsibility is crucial where ethics are concerned. Keep in mind that a profiling method may be incompetent and a profiling result may be incorrect. But only the behavior of the criminal profiler can be referred to as unethical (i.e. a profiler that continues to use a method, which they know to be incompetent). If criminal profilers perceive no duty to actually assist an investigation, and see themselves only as academics with a higher scientific or academic goal in mind, then this absolves them of any ethical responsibility to a case. That means having no moral obligation to opinions rendered in a given case.

How dare we.

INVESTIGATIVE VS. CLINICAL GOALS

Whether used in unsolved investigations or during preparation for trial, behavioral-evidence analysis techniques are designed to serve investigative and reconstructive goals, not clinical ones.

The clinician's first duty is to the diagnosis of a client for the purposes of treatment. In other words, their first responsibility would be to an offender's mental health and well being.

> The diagnostic task is to determine what is wrong with the offender, what has led him to commit his sexual offense, and what can be done to remedy this situation. (Groth 1979)

Many treatment models support the belief that to treat an offender effectively, a clinician must empathize with them as a person. Of course the danger here is that in their zeal to treat, and to establish these empathic connections, clinicians run the risk of "credulously accepting the offender's rationalizations" for their crimes, and perhaps even supplying them with new ones (Marshall *et al.* 1990).

In any case, these treatment issues are of no concern to the criminal profiler. The criminal profiler's goals are investigative, and by that it is meant that they are interested only in the objective investigation of fact. They are not interested in an offender's well being or mental health, but rather are interested in protecting society, and future victims, by virtue of serving justice.

This is a potential ethical conflict, then, for clinicians who wish to become involved in criminal profiling during the investigative phase of a case. They must be willing to set aside their treatment-oriented goals, and their tools for promoting a strong positive regard for the offender, and work to serve justice. They must set aside their traditional roles as healers and advocates, and work to help capture those who might otherwise be clients. This is by no means an impossible conflict to resolve. However it is one that must be addressed up front, and in a straightforward manner to prevent the dangers previously mentioned from affecting the achievement of investigative goals.

This also sheds light on a potential ethical conflict for criminal profilers who would seek to use tools and methods that are specifically designed for offender treatment as part of the criminal-profiling process. The first problem of course is that criminal profilers may not be trained to use or understand diagnostic and treatment tools, psychology being perhaps well outside their education and experience. The second problem is that, as previously discussed, many diagnostic and treatment tools such as Freudian theories, rigid offender classifications, and the identification of personality syndromes (average offender types) are not designed for investigative purposes. They are designed for the diagnosis and treatment of personality disorders. And, finally, these tools and methods often require clinical interviews with the offender (which are not available during the investigative phase – nor are offender interviews or contact of any kind advised for the criminal profiler in the trial phase, for the sake of maintaining objectivity).

Whether or not criminal profilers can work around or within this particular ethical conundrum is still a matter of debate.

VOYEURISM AND PROFILING

A *voyeur* is one who receives sexual gratification from viewing erotic scenes and behavior. Just as there is a voyeuristic appeal to certain types of therapy that can attract a certain type of person into the work, the same can be said of criminal profiling.

Over the years, the number of students displaying excitement and fervent anticipation of graphic or explicit case materials has constantly dismayed this author. In order to combat this phenomenon, and to properly educate students as to the requisite respect that must be given all victims, the author has developed the following strategies.

THE SPEECH

Before the author distributes any new case material, or shows explicit material of any kind, students are educated as to the human price that has been paid for the lessons that they will learn. For any of us to learn these kinds of lessons, someone must pay the price with their dignity, with their body, and sometimes with their life. We have a responsibility to respect that sacrifice, to learn from it, and not to trivialize it. This is done didactically, by telling students to treat the material and the victim with respect in all exchanges and discussions. But more importantly this is done by example.

THE EMPATHY EXERCISE

Students are given or shown case materials. Then they are asked to write a letter from the victim to a parent, spouse, or loved one of their choice explaining the events that took place before and during the attack in detail (up to the point of death, when necessary). Almost invariably students choose loved ones who represent people from their own lives, and wind up projecting a great deal of their own issues into the letter. But the point of the exercise is for students to begin seeing victims as people, and that the lesson will carry over to other cases. Obviously the exercise could get in the way of any future objectivity regarding the case at hand, but objectivity without some concern for victim pain and suffering is an inhuman quality that this author does not wish to see encouraged in students.

THE MEDIA AND ENTERTAINMENT INDUSTRY: A CONFLICT OF INTEREST

Because of the high amount of emotional and sexual voyeurism inherent in the criminal profiling process, it has an equally high entertainment value whether true or fictionalized. This attracts not only a large number of consumers to profiling related media, but arguably a high number of students to college courses on the subject as well.

In any case, criminal profilers are constantly being asked to contribute to, consult on, or opine for media-related projects on real or fictional offenders and offenses.

NEWS AGENCIES

Very often news agencies will contact criminal profilers and ask them to opine on a case that has captured the attention of the public for whatever reason. The first consideration that a profiler should make is whether or not they are qualified to speak about a particular case. The second consideration is whether or not there is enough publicly available information to form any kind of relevant opinion. And the third is whether or not the public dissemination of their opinion will be of harm or advantage to the case[1].

It is not the policy of this author to give opinions on a case without a great deal of specific case information, which the media typically does not have. In most cases, the author will only discuss general profiling techniques and how they may be generally applied to a certain type of investigation.

[1] In Chapter 5, I give an example of a threshold assessment that I constructed for a news agency. This is the exception that proves the rule, if anything. It is not generally my policy to provide insights and opinions on an open case without invitation. But I was told everything that law enforcement knew at the time.

And I also knew that they were getting an FBI-trained profiler's help. I felt that his insights would be non-specific to the case. I also took into consideration the public safety issue.

If the circumstances were right, I would do it again. But it's not standard practice.

A very real danger comes when a criminal profiler begins to perceive media attention as a form of professional validation. Their inflated ego can become so used to reading its own name in print that it becomes lonely for itself when not seen in the paper or heard on the news. They may begin to do things specifically to attract media attention, or they may begin to solicit the attention of the media directly. In either case, this type of behavior inevitably undermines one's public and professional credibility.

BOOKS, FILMS AND TV

It is commonplace for film and television studios to call on the expertise of those with specialized knowledge to consult on projects that deal with technical subject matter, or where an element of realism is crucial to the effectiveness of a project.

One example includes the author Thomas Harris who was allowed the incredible, unprecedented privilege of consulting with the FBI's then Behavioral Sciences Unit (BSU) for character and plot development relating to his acclaimed written work of fiction, *Red Dragon*, and the sequel, *The Silence of the Lambs*. In 1986 the De Laurentiis Entertainment Group released the feature film *Manhunter*, based on *Red Dragon*[2]. And in 1991, Orion Pictures released the Academy-Award-winning, *The Silence of the Lambs*.

Bringing these works of written fiction to film elevated the members of the FBI's then Behavioral Sciences Unit to superstar status. Arguably, this hurt the image of the BSU more than it helped it.

The precedent set by the success of *The Silence of the Lambs*, and other films, as well as the popularity of the published memoirs of several former FBI profilers has opened the door for criminal profilers to be invited by the entertainment industry to act as creative consultants on other film and television projects dealing with the subject. Many of these programs promote the myth that criminal profiling involves psychic or paranormal ability. Given the bulk of the published literature in the field, it is evident that most profilers do not agree with this position. The ethical dilemma for the criminal profiler, then, is whether or not a creative consultant position on a fictional project that promotes the use of the supernatural as an aid to criminal profiling represents a public endorsement of misinformation about the field.

However, both programs openly endorse the idea that criminal profiling involves the utilization of psychic or paranormal ability. Given their published work on criminal profiling, it is clear that neither Hazelwood nor Ressler agree that this is the case. The ethical dilemma for the criminal profiler, then, is whether or not a creative consultant position on a fictional program that promotes the use of the supernatural as an aid to criminal profiling, represents a public endorsement of it, and by extension promotes misinformation.

[2] I really did enjoy the film Manhunter, and recommend its use as a training film. It effectively combines the psychological aspects of profiling with the requisite deliberation and attention to the physical evidence.

That film was made more than a decade ago and showed the use of forensic techniques that are still not widely practiced or available to many law enforcement agencies.

TRUE CRIME

The true-crime market is in the business of dramatizing, over-vilifying, packaging, and selling the acts of violent, predatory offenders to the public. As we have already discussed, criminal profilers have made successful publishing forays into the realm of true crime through published memoirs. An ethical concern arises, however, when criminal profilers seek endorsement from those whose business is *selling* cases rather than solving them.

This speaks to the old saying that one person cannot effectively serve two masters. One cannot effectively service the objective investigation of fact, while financially attached to the dramatization of that fact for public consumption.

WHEN PROFILING HARMS

Dr Paul Wilson, a professor and criminologist at Bond University in the Gold Coast, Australia, articulated the issue of ethics as it relates to criminal profiling very well indeed:

> There should be an onus on experts to point to the limitations of profiling...

> ...profiling is no more unethical than any other investigative technique. It is how profiling (or any other technique) is used in any given case, which is important... (Kocsis *et al.* 1998)

Essentially, there are numerous ways that profiling can cause harm, not limited to:

1 Delaying the apprehension of an offender by providing false leads.
2 Delaying the apprehension of an offender by pointing to false suspects.
3 Delaying the apprehension of an offender by excluding viable suspects.
4 Harming the personal life of a citizen by an implication of guilt based solely on the characteristics in the profile.

The first three represent the fruits of incompetent methods of profiling. Only the fourth represents a breach of ethics by virtue of misuse. However, an argument for unethical behavior is warranted if a criminal profiler continues to advocate and use methods, without proper warning to the end user, which are known to result in the first three.

There are numerous examples of the unethical uses of criminal profiles. Keep in mind what is meant by unethical use. And also keep in mind that what is unethical is not necessarily criminal.

Take the following cases.

Example: T. Cullen Davis

Near midnight on August 2, 1976, a man dressed in black entered a mansion owned by oil tycoon T. Cullen Davis and shot four people: Priscilla Davis (his ex-wife), Stan Farr (her boyfriend), Gus Gavrel (her acquaintance), and 12-year-old Andrea Wilborn (Cullen Davis' stepdaughter). Both Stan Farr and Andrea Wilborn were killed during this attack.

Mr Davis was quickly identified as a suspect with a strong motive. First of all, Priscilla Davis had received more than $3,000,000 from her ex-husband in their divorce settlement. Moreover, on the day of the shooting the divorce court had doubled the support payments she would receive from him to $5,000 per month. He was charged, taken to trial, and acquitted.

Having survived the attack, and despite the acquittal in criminal court, Priscilla Davis decided to sue her ex-husband for the wrongful death of Andrea Wilborn.

Former FBI profiler Russell Vorpagel was called to testify:

> Russell Vorpagel, an expert in psychological profiles of crime suspects, portrayed Davis as a "cold, cruel, callused" man who forms 'no emotional attachments to others.'…

> Vorpagel, who said he developed his expertise in compiling psychological profiles during his 22 years with the FBI, said he reviewed testimony from Davis' criminal trials, police reports, crime-scene photographs and witness statements to formulate a psychological sketch of the mansion gunman.

> He said the killer was likely motivated by anger and revenge and took sufficient ammunition to the scene to kill several people…

> "I saw vengeance, anger, and that anger was exhibited in the excessive shooting of one of the individuals," Vorpagel said referring to the four shots fired into Farr's torso and neck. "He knew he'd need more than one gun-full."…

> Vorpagel said he later compared his profile of the killer to two psychological evaluations of Davis that were made in the months following the killings in 1976. The evaluations "fit the psychological profile to a T," he said.

> Vorpagel said Davis comes across as "cold, cruel, callous, egotistical, as a man who is a male chauvinist, who feels like women are greedy." (*The Dallas Morning News* 1987)

While we can appreciate the apparent competency of Vorpagel's insights into the general motivational aspects of the offense as suggested by the physical and behavioral evidence, he goes too far. As suggested already by this author, and by numerous others, criminal profiles are not to be used to suggest guilt. They certainly are not meant to be "fitted" to individual people. The above statement by Vorpagel implies to the court that the clinical psychological evaluations of Mr Davis and his psychological profile are identical. And as we have discussed, this level of absolute certainty regarding the comparison of shared psychological characteristics is not possible (see Chapter 14).

Example: Richard Jewell

On July 27, 1996, a backpack with a bomb in it was placed next to the AT&T Global Village stage in Centennial Park, in Atlanta, Georgia. Centennial Park was an open facility, crowded with people at the time, housing sponsors' tents for the 1996 summer Olympic games. The device, a pipe bomb, exploded at 1:20 a.m., killing Alice Hawthorne of Albany, Georgia, and injuring 111 others. A Turkish cameraman also died of a heart attack as a result of the blast.

Richard Jewell, a security guard working in the park, had just alerted police to the suspicious knapsack and was helping to evacuate people from the area moments before it exploded. (CNN 1996)

> The portly 34-year-old security guard, with a soft Southern drawl and a passion for police work, was hailed for his bravery and professionalism after he found a bomb underneath a bench in Atlanta's Centennial Olympic Park.
>
> He helped clear people from the area before the bomb went off early on July 27, 1996, quick action that likely saved lives. But despite what he did, Jewell never claimed the mantle of hero for himself. He was, he insisted, just doing his job.
>
> But within days, the story of the Olympic Park bombing seemed to take an unbelievable, melodramatic turn: The FBI suspected that Jewell had planted the bomb himself.
>
> The tidal wave that overwhelmed Jewell began on the afternoon of July 30 when the Atlanta Journal-Constitution, citing unidentified law enforcement sources, published a special edition saying the FBI considered him a suspect. (CNN 1997a)

A zealous, inexperienced FBI agent leaked information to the press that a psychological profile had identified Jewell, a private security guard at the time, as the likely perpetrator. The press published that Richard Jewell was indeed the FBI's prime suspect, saying that he matched an FBI profile that described the bomber as a former policeman who longed for heroism.

> In their quest for potential clues, agents removed everything from firearms to dryer lint from the apartment in Atlanta that he shares with his mother, Barbara, 60. In its original request for a search warrant, the FBI cited evidence that Jewell "had no girlfriend… lives and breathes police stories," and "was exposed to explosives and bomb instruction and lectures on two separate occasions." In short, the one-time police officer and campus security officer fit what some agents felt was the profile of a law enforcement wannabe who might plant a bomb and then "discover" it to win acclaim. (Hewitt 1996)

This was combined with the reports of other items taken from Jewell's home during the service of search warrants, such as a collection of newspaper clippings describing Jewell as a hero. These elements just added fuel to the media fire.

When Jewell was brought in for questioning by the FBI, he was lied to. He was told that the questioning was not formal, nor was their interest in him as a suspect genuine. They led him to believe that they were using him as part of a training video for federal agents. An appeal, no doubt, to their perception of his need for attention.

However, when this all came to light, and the search warrants failed to produce physical evidence of any kind, the FBI ultimately capitulated. Jewell was issued a notification that he was no longer a suspect:

The letter that finally arrived from US Attorney Kent B. Alexander, the prosecutor investigating the Atlanta bombing, fell far short of an apology, but it did free Jewell from the fear that he would be arrested at any moment. Jewell, the letter stated, was "not considered a target" of the investigation. "Barring any newly discovered evidence," it continued, "this status will not change."

That language does not foreclose a future investigation of Jewell, and some FBI agents still wonder if he was somehow involved. But absolutely no evidence has been found to link him to the bombing. The search of his mother's house yielded nothing. It would be impossible to make a bomb as crude as the one at Centennial Olympic Park without handling the powder, but no trace of explosives was discovered anywhere on Jewell, in his truck or at his home, even by the vaunted devices used by the FBI that can detect one part per trillion. "They knew within days of going through his apartment that he didn't do it, but they continued to accuse him," says G. Watson Bryant Jr, one of Jewell's attorneys. "Their conduct is just despicable." (Collins 1996)

And the special agent who had leaked the information to the press regarding the psychological profile was reprimanded:

FBI agents in Atlanta rallied in support of a fellow colleague Thursday after he returned to work following a five-day suspension without pay for his role in interviewing Olympic bombing suspect Richard Jewell.

Several dozen people applauded as agent Don Johnson entered Atlanta FBI headquarters. Asked if Johnson was a political scapegoat, agent Harry Grogan said, "Yes, I do."

The FBI suspended Johnson last week and censured Atlanta special-agent-in-charge Woody Johnson and Kansas City special-agent-in-charge David Tubbs for their roles in the Jewell investigation.

Jewell was never charged in the deadly 1996 bombing at Olympic Centennial Park, and the FBI eventually cleared him of suspicion. (CNN 1997b)

This case involved not only the unethical use of a criminal profile to point out a specific individual as guilty for a particular crime by the FBI, but by the media as well. Fortunately, the absolute lack of any hard physical evidence linking Jewell to the crime whatsoever kept this case from finding its way into the criminal courts. And Jewell's financial settlements with media organizations for what amounts to public character assassination kept it out of the civil courts.

Example: Colin Stagg
In July of 1992, 23-year-old Rachel Nickell, her two-year-old son, Alex, and their dog went for a walk on Wimbledon Common in London, England. She was stabbed 49 times, right in front of her son. It was the country's most publicized crime of that year. Law enforcement accepted the help of psychologist Paul Britton, who prepared a psychological profile that reportedly described a man

named Colin Stagg with a great deal of accuracy. However, law enforcement lacked any evidence of the man actually committing any kind of crime. They decided, with Britton's help, to have a female officer engage in suggestive correspondence with him (Kocsis *et al.* 1998):

> Through an attractive blond undercover policewoman, the psychologist initiated an eight months' liaison with the 31-year-old Stagg in which she shared violent sexual fantasies, confessed to the ritual sexual murder of a baby and a young woman, and egged him on to match her stories; even telling him that she wished he were Nickell's murderer because, "That's the kind of man I want."

> Stagg never claimed credit for the killing, but from 700 pages of letters and transcribed telephone conversations and public meetings, the psychologist [Paul Britton] concluded that Stagg's fantasies, modeled upon information fed to him by those familiar with the details of the crime, revealed unique knowledge of the crime scene which could only be known by the murderer. Dragged before a judge in open court at the Old Bailey, defense quickly pointed out that Stagg hadn't even made good guesses – he didn't know the location of the crime and had wrongly asserted that the victim had been raped...

> Clearing the accused and acknowledging the understandable pressure on the police, the judge was nevertheless forced to conclude that the operation betrayed "not merely an excess of zeal, but a blatant attempt to incriminate a suspect by positive and deceptive conduct of the grossest kind." (Edwards 1998)

This case involved a psychologist who stepped beyond their expertise into the interpretation of crime-scene behavior, who ignored inconsistencies in the suspect's stories, and who ultimately set out to prove their theory regarding the case despite the established facts, by attempting to entrap an innocent man.

Ultimately, Colin Stagg was not the only victim of this profiling farce. On June 12 of 1998 it was announced that:

> A woman detective at the center of a controversial undercover operation into the murder of model Rachel Nickell has taken early retirement.

> The 33-year-old officer – who has been known only by her cover name of Lizzie James – has left the Metropolitan Police on health grounds following her "traumatic" role in the investigation of Miss Nickell's death...

> Conversations and correspondence between Lizzie and Mr Stagg formed the basis of the prosecution case when he went on trial at the Old Bailey...

> Lizzie, who has served 13 years in the Metropolitan Police, including time with Scotland Yard's SO10 covert operations squad, continued to work following the Nickell investigation...

> Fellow officers have claimed she never recovered from the trauma she suffered during her harrowing work on the Nickell inquiry, which was ultimately perceived as a failure. (BBC News 1998)

ETHICAL GUIDELINES FOR THE CRIMINAL PROFILER

The author strongly recommends that criminal profilers adhere to the following ethical guidelines to check and govern the potential abuses of criminal profiles. These may seem basic or obvious to some. However, given what has taken place in the criminal-profiling community in the past, these guidelines are sorely needed.

Criminal profilers must:

1 Conduct all research using the appropriate control groups for comparison when appropriate.

2 Not utilize the work or ideas of others without appropriate citation or reference.

3 Treat all information from an agency or client with the confidentiality required.

4 Render opinions and conclusions strictly in accordance with the evidence in the case.

5 Not allow any preconceived ideas or biases regarding potential suspects or offenders to influence the final profile in any way.

6 Testify in a clear, honest, straightforward manner and refuse to extend beyond their field of competence, phrasing any testimony in such a manner so that results and opinions are not misinterpreted.

7 Not use a profile for the purposes of suggesting the guilt of a particular individual for a particular crime.

8 Not exaggerate, embellish, or otherwise misrepresent qualifications when testifying, or at any other time, in any form.

9 Make efforts to inform the court of the nature and implications of pertinent evidence if reasonably assured that this information will not be disclosed in court.

10 Maintain an attitude of independence and impartiality in order to ensure an unbiased analysis and interpretation of the evidence.

11 Maintain the quality and standards of the professional community by reporting all unethical conduct that is observed to the appropriate authorities or professional organizations.

REFERENCES

BBC News (1998) "Rachel Nickell detective quits at 33," June 12.

CNN (1996) "Olympic bomb chronology," October 26.

CNN (1997a) "Richard Jewell faces cloudy future," July 7.

CNN (1997b) "FBI peers applaud suspended agent in Jewell case," May 29.

Collins, J. (1996) "The Strange Saga of Richard Jewell," *Time*, November 11.

Edwards, C. (1998) "Behavior and the Law Reconsidered: Psychological Syndromes and Profiles," *Journal of Forensic Sciences*, 43 (1): 141–50.

Groth, A. N. (1979) *Men Who Rape: The Psychology of the Offender*, New York: Plenum Press.

Hewitt, B. (1996) "Justice Delayed," *People*, November 11.

Kocsis, R., Lincoln, R. and Wilson, P. (1998) "Validity, Utility and Ethics of Profiling for Serial Violent and Sexual Offenders," *Psychiatry, Psychology and Law*, 6 1–11.

Marshall, W. L., Laws, D. and Barbaree, H. (1990) *Handbook of Sexual Assault: Issues, Theories, and Treatment of the Offender*, New York: Plenum Press.

The Dallas Morning News (1987) "Ex-FBI Agent Testifies Davis Fits Mental Profile of Slayer," June 6.

CHAPTER 21

DEDUCTIVE PROFILING – A CLINICAL PERSPECTIVE FROM THE UK

Dr Diana Tamlyn, M.B. B.S., M.R.C.Psych., Forensic Psychiatrist

Forensic psychologists and psychiatrists are often called upon by either defense or prosecution in criminal proceedings, to provide reports for the court and to act as expert witnesses. The roles of the two disciplines overlap considerably, although the academic background and training differs. An important difference is that the latter will commonly focus on the presence or absence of mental disorder, with attention to the implications for "disposal" under the provisions of the Mental Health Act 1983. The psychologist has at his or her disposal, skills and assessment techniques which allow for detailed psychometric testing, and can quantify intelligence and personality traits in comparison with statistical norms. Ideally a psychologist and psychiatrist will complement each other when collaborating on a case.

Criminal proceedings in the Magistrate's Court and Crown Court involve three stages, referred to as pretrial, trial, and sentencing. During the first stage, the role of the clinician is commonly to assist the court in determining the "fitness to plead" and capacity to stand trial of a defendant. This concept was recognized as early as the fourteenth century (Walker 1968) and by the nineteenth century the criteria by which defendants were found unfit became determined by case law. The current accepted criteria for fitness to plead and to stand trial are as follows:

- Able to understand the indictment and plead appropriately.
- Instruct legal advisers.
- Understand that a juror can be challenged.
- Comprehend the details of the evidence.
- Follow the court proceedings.

Issues in which the clinician might be involved here are, for example, the intellectual capacity of the defendant, when the court would appropriately be advised by a psychologist, or the effect of current mental illness, when psychiatric expertise is pertinent.

During the trial stage, the clinician expert witness in a criminal case, whether called by the defense or the prosecution, will normally be expected to have examined the defendant and prepared a comprehensive report on the defendant's personal history, including an assessment of personality and psychosexual development (if relevant), history of mental illness, and history of offending. The factors contributing to the offense will be addressed, as will the defendant's attitude to the offense and the victim(s). Ideally, this information will assist in helping the jury to understand better the offender and the context of his behavior. Recommendations based on the assessment will include competency to stand trial, issues of "diminished responsibility," and advice regarding sentencing, which in the case of the psychiatrist will include medical disposals under the Mental Health Act. The defense of diminished responsibility was introduced in England and Wales under Section 2 of the Homicide Act 1957, and involves cases where there are mitigating circumstances which reduce the charge of murder to manslaughter. Section 2(1) of the Homicide Act states:

> Where a person kills or is party to the killing of another, he shall not be convicted of murder if he was suffering from such abnormality of mind (whether arising from a condition of arrested or retarded development of mind or any inherent causes or induced by disease or injury) as substantially impaired his mental responsibility for his acts and omissions in doing or being a party to the killing.

Having reached a better understanding of the defendant, the clinician should in the case of violent offences, sexual offences, or arson, be in a position to offer advice regarding the likelihood of further offences of this nature and risk to the public, with appropriate guidance as to how the risk might be reduced. The question of guilt or innocence is of course for the jury to decide, and comments regarding sentencing should always be couched in terms of "respectful advice."

At the sentencing stage, the clinician may assist the court with an evaluation of the defendant's capacity to benefit from custody and rehabilitation, with advice about his mental health including risk of self harm or suicide, and the need for treatment. A consultant psychiatrist may arrange medical supervision of the defendant either as a condition of a community disposal, such as a probation order, or by hospital admission to an appropriate establishment under a Court Order for Treatment.

THE CLINICIAN-PROFILER IN THE UK

When the clinician is involved in the investigative phase of profiling a case, there is no opportunity to conduct direct examination or assessment. In the past, criminal profilers have relied on indirect methods, typically involving intuition, psychodynamic ideas, forms of behavioral analysis, and statistical inference (Gudjonsson and Copson 1997). Whilst offender profiling is best viewed as an investigative tool in police investigations, expert evidence with regard to profiling has in recent years been brought before the courts both in the United States and the UK. Ormerod (1996) discusses the evidential implications of offender profiling and makes comparisons between the English and American courts. Admissibility of profiling evidence in criminal trials is related to the relevance and reliability of the evidence. With regard to relevance, profiling can only give an indication of the type of person who might have committed an offense, rather than indicating any one individual, who happens to fit the profile. Since offender profiling relies on the expert's opinion, there are no empirical findings to support the reliability of his or her evidence. Both lawyers and profilers would say that profiling is too inexact a science to figure in the decision between guilt or innocence.

Gary Copson of the Metropolitan Police reported in his study of offender profiling (1995) that, out of 184 commissions by detectives of operational profiling advice, there were 90 instances of profiling in cases which went to court. Of these, there were only six reports that profiling had been an issue during proceedings, and only two of the profilers being required to give evidence. These were the Torney case and the Stagg case.

In the Torney case (1996) in Northern Ireland, a psychiatrist and a psychologist gave evidence in the Crown Court in the case of a police officer who was charged with the murder of his wife, son, and daughter. The defendant alleged that his 13-year-old son had "gone berserk" and shot to death his mother and sister, before turning the gun on himself. Professor Gisli Gudjonsson, forensic psychologist, examined all the available evidence, including crime-scene photographs, and testified that the murders of the mother and daughter were not consistent with an act that had resulted from loss of temper of a person who has "gone berserk." The murders appeared to have been carefully and efficiently executed by someone who was familiar with firearms and confident in their use. Profiling evidence suggested that it was more probable than not that the defendant rather than the son had committed the murders. The defendant was convicted of the murders (Gudjonsson and Haward 1998).

Colin Stagg was tried and acquitted in October 1994 of the murder of Rachel Nickell on Wimbledon Common on July 15, 1992. Clinical psychologist Paul Britton produced a profile of the murderer, who he diagnosed as a psychopath with deviant sexual fantasies. Following Stagg's release from custody after interrogation in September 1992, the police with Mr Britton's cooperation, commenced a "covert operation" in January 1993. An undercover policewoman befriended Stagg with the brief of eliciting a confession, or to elicit sexual fantasies consistent with the profile of the murderer. After several months, Stagg disclosed deviant fantasies and responses, which Mr Britton argued were "indistinguishable from that expected from the murderer." The crown argued that Mr Britton as a profiler should be accepted in court as an expert witness. The defense argued that the psychologist's opinion was inadmissible in proof of identity. Gudjonsson, in his reports commissioned by the defense, found that there was no evidence to support the contention that Colin Stagg was a sexually deviant psychopath, and that his fantasies were the product of a process of influence exerted during the covert operation. The adjudged unfairness of the undercover operation led to the dismissal of the case. The Honorable Mr Justice Ognall's ruling in the case encompassed some discussion of profiling, and while it was made clear that there were great and potentially insurmountable difficulties in introducing profiling as evidence in the British courts, nothing was said to undermine its use as a basis for investigative decision making (Ognall 1994).

PROFILING METHODOLOGY

The majority of forensic clinicians in the UK are employed by either the universities or the National Health Service. They are dependent on the goodwill of their employers in taking on profiling work at the potential expense of their contractual duties. Many work with the police in their spare time, and the majority are unpaid.

On this informal basis, the scene is set for misunderstandings on the part of the profiler about the requirements and expectations of the police, and misunderstandings of the meaning of operational profiling advice offered (often verbal rather than written) (Copson 1995).

The methodology employed by clinicians as profilers is by no means uniform. Many psychiatrists (including this author) will concentrate on behavioral analysis of crime scenes and available information on the victim and witness accounts to provide insights into the characteristics of the offender. This approach has its roots in the earliest methods of the FBI's Behavioral Sciences Unit, and has evolved to what we will refer to as "deductive profiling" for the purpose of this review. Deductive criminal profiling has been described as "a set of offender characteristics that are reasoned from the convergence of physical and behavioral evidence patterns within a crime or a series of related crimes" (Turvey: in press). The FBI has long since changed, and currently employs a profiling method based more on intuition and investigative experience than behavior-evidence analysis, or statistical inference. This methodology is largely inductive. Another inductive profiling model was developed by Professor David Canter, formerly of the University of Surrey, with the assistance of Rupert Heritage, of Surrey Police. This model is based on statistical analysis and use of probabilities derived from an empirical base. One such system, the Informed Offender Profiling System (IOPS), developed at the Centre for Investigative Psychology, University of Liverpool, compares new crimes with a database of existing crimes to produce a predictive profile of the offender's likely characteristics. Canter has recently described a "geographical investigative support tool *Dragnet*," based on the discovery of "powerful consistencies in the geographical locations of serial offender's crimes" (Canter 1998).

There remains disagreement amongst British profilers about the respective merits of deductive behavioral analysis versus inductive statistical prediction. Recent work by Gary Copson (Copson *et al.*: in press) and others has attempted an analysis of the process of both profiling methods, demonstrating by stepwise progression how deductive behavioral inference is developed and applied to offender profiling.

ETHICS OF PROFILING

A register of accredited profilers has been established via the National Crime Faculty at Bramshill in the UK. Profilers are encouraged to submit CVs to the Behavioral Sciences sub-committee of ACPO (Association of Chief Police Officers), whereupon they are invited to interview. Those clinicians who have relevant experience in profiling cases are accredited, and their involvement in conferences to facilitate exchange of information and peer review is encouraged. In its early stages, it is envisaged that the work of the National Crime Faculty in this area will lead to improved quality of profiling work by clinicians and the setting of recognized standards. The Faculty acts as a source of information and advice for regional police forces, who are able to access a central database. Currently, police forces throughout the UK vary in the extent of use of the facility, which is reflected in the considerable variation of opinion between forces and individual SIOs (Senior Investigating Officers) on the role and value of the profiler.

Typically, forensic clinicians establish a relationship with the police through their clinical work. Forensic psychiatrists are routinely involved in the assessment of mentally disordered offenders after arrest, and may be called upon to offer advice about fitness for interview, management in police custody, or hospital transfer. Many regions in the UK operate a "Public Protection Policy" – a system of assessment of violent offenders in the community, during which a team including senior police, probation officers, and a psychiatrist will review potential risk of violence to the public and the means of reducing that risk. Such interdisciplinary work for the clinician is particularly rewarding, since it provides the opportunity to develop better mutual understanding of the approach and difficulties of others working towards the same end. It is a natural progression for a forensic clinician known to the police to be asked to advise over the phone, for example on the question of the possibility of a mentally disordered offender known to the clinician having been involved in another offense. The clinician may be invited to step outside his or her clinical domain in order to comment on the reliability of witnesses during an investigation, and it is a short step from here to the engagement of the clinician as a profiler during a homicide investigation. At what stage does the clinician become a profiler? In this author's opinion, what is more relevant is that it is established at the outset in which capacity he or she will operate and the contractual basis for the work.

Ethical considerations arise when the clinician is asked to contribute towards an investigation involving a patient under his care. Forensic psychologists and psychiatrists in the UK are bound by the code of conduct determined by their professional bodies; the BPS (British Psychological Society) and the GMC (General Medical Council). Essentially, the clinician should take all steps to maintain the confidentiality of information obtained through professional practice. There are some exceptions to the rule of professional secrecy:

- Information may be disclosed to a third party with the patient or his legal adviser's consent.

- In circumstances where it is undesirable on medical grounds to seek the patient's consent but is in the patient's interests to disclose information.

- The clinician has a duty to disclose information when there is a perceived risk to society, for example a patient with advanced dementia refuses to comply with his doctor's advice to stop driving.

- Disclosure may be justified on the grounds that it is in the public interest, which in certain circumstances, such as the investigation by the police of a grave or very serious crime, might override the doctor's duty to maintain his patient's confidence.

Having made the decision to breach confidentiality by disclosing information to the police, the clinician must be prepared subsequently to justify his actions. This is a particularly sensitive issue for forensic psychiatrists, for whom the very nature of their work involves assessment of risk to the public, which potentially puts them at risk of being subject to disciplinary proceedings. It is important to note that no privilege attaches to communications between doctors and their patients in the UK in the way that privilege attaches to communications between solicitors and their clients. A doctor can, therefore, be directed by the court to disclose information (Walton 1990).

The forensic clinician assisting in an investigation should at all times maintain professional standards. As a profiler engaged by an investigating team, he or she will ideally:

- Clarify the nature of his role, having reached an understanding of the expectations of the commissioning team.
- Establish the basis of the work including issues of payment, time available, and access to information and personnel.
- Treat the other members of the team with courtesy and respect.
- Behave at all times with integrity and truthfulness.
- When offering advice, do this in writing if possible, making clear the grounds for the conclusions reached and the limitations of the advice. If time or information has been limited, and the profiler has some doubts about the value of the conclusions, then he or she should make this plain to the investigating team.
- Interrogation strategies, when offered, should be founded on a proper understanding of the legal and ethical framework within which police interviews with suspects should be conducted (Police and Criminal Evidence Act 1985).

DANGEROUSNESS

In the course of an investigation and occasionally during the trial, the forensic clinician may be asked or may offer advice on the dangerousness of an offender. A careful behavioral analysis of all available evidence may lead the clinician to form conclusions about the habits, fantasies, personality traits, and mental state of the offender from which inferences can be drawn about the likelihood of further violent offences, the nature and (occasionally) identity of potential victims, and likely high-risk situations for the victims and the offender. Such information may be invaluable to the investigating team not only as an aid to the investigation but in terms of protecting the public and reducing the risk of further successful offending.

TEAMWORK AND COLLABORATION

Collaborative research between clinicians and police can facilitate inter-disciplinary understanding of profiling and investigative issues, whilst contributing to the central database. This author has recently become involved in research commissioned by the Home Office aimed at developing a profile of offenders involved in so-called "distraction burglaries." These offenses, involving the use of bogus identities to gain entry into the homes of vulnerable victims, mainly elderly people, are extremely common. Although they cause distress, such crimes rarely result in violence. The murder of an elderly woman in West Yorkshire in 1996 was believed to have occurred in the course of a distraction burglary, and although the offender has not yet been apprehended, questions arose from the investigation regarding the possibility of narrowing the field of suspects and protecting the potential victims of these offences. From interviews by the SIO and clinician profilers, of prolific distraction burglars who have become informants, is emerging a picture of the "typical bogus burglar," usually from traveler or "gypsy" background, who takes pride in his expertise and avoids violence, and the atypical offender, less likely to be of gypsy origins, who differs in his behavior, personality traits, and habits. During the course of the research a strategy is emerging, informed by the offenders themselves, which will assist in the protection of vulnerable elderly people in this region and others.

At this stage in the development of profiling in Britain, approaches to profiling are so idiosyncratic as to be indistinguishable from the identity of the profiler. It appears that advice from inductive statistical profilers is less well appreciated by investigators than advice from deductive behaviorally oriented profilers (Copson 1995). In this author's experience, a thorough deductive approach combined with a willingness to learn from the experience of the other members of the investigating team is rewarded with the cooperation and respect of the team. Profiling work, although often a taxing commitment on the part of the clinician, is potentially an informative and enriching experience.

REFERENCES

Canter, D. (1998) "New Developments in Investigative Psychology," *The Fifth International Investigative Psychology Conference*, September 14–16.

Copson, G. (1995) *Coals to Newcastle? Police Use of Offender Profiling*, London: Home Office Police Dept.

Copson, G., Badcock, R., Boon, J. and Britton, P. (in press) "Articulating a systematic approach to clinical crime profiling," *Criminal Behaviour and Mental Health*.

Gudjonsson, G. H. and Copson, G. (1997) "The role of the expert in criminal investigations," in J. L. Jackson and D. A. Bekerian (eds), *Offender Profiling, Theory, Research and Practice*, Chichester: John Wiley & Sons.

Gudjonsson, G. H. and Haward, L. R. C. (1998) *Forensic Psychology. A Guide to Practice*, London and New York: Routledge.

Ognall, Justice (1994) Judgement in the trial of Colin Stagg: Central Criminal Court, 14 September.

Ormerod, D. C. (1996) "The evidential implications of psychological profiling,"
   Criminal Law Review: 863–77.

Turvey, B. (in press) "Criminal Profiling," *Encyclopedia of Forensic Science*, London:
   Academic Press.

Walker, N. (1968) *Crime and Insanity in England: Historical Perspectives*, Edinburgh:
   Edinburgh University Press.

Walton, J. (1990) "The General Medical Council of the United Kingdom and professional
   conduct," in R. Bluglass and P. Bowden (eds), *Principles and Practice of Forensic
   Psychiatry*, Leeds: Churchill Livingstone.

CHAPTER 22

ALTERNATIVE METHODS OF OFFENDER PROFILING

Brent E. Turvey, M.S.

Do not put your faith in what statistics say until you have carefully considered what they do not say.

(William W. Watt, quoted in *Peter's Quotations* 1989)

Recall from Chapter 1 that the process of inferring distinctive personality characteristics of individuals responsible for committing criminal acts has commonly been referred to as *criminal profiling*. Aside from the deductive method of criminal profiling, referred to as behavioral evidence analysis, there are also inductive alternatives (described generally in Chapter 2). The focus of this chapter will be some of the specific alternative methods of inferring specific or general offender characteristics.

SCIENTIFICATION

Many of the methods that we will be covering in this chapter suffer from what this author will refer to ironically as *scientification*. The term scientification will be used to describe the bolstering of any method or theory, by a group or individual, via technological affect or professional affect, for the purposes of making the method or theory appear more credible. Those who feel the need to engage in scientification suffer from what we will refer to as "Pay no attention to the little man behind the curtain" syndrome[1].

This includes the repeated, unqualified use of the term "scientific" to describe a device, method, or process. This also includes the use of technology, such as machines or computers, to record or collate information that must still be interpreted by an analyst. The key feature here is that the machine or computer does not give a conclusion, but rather requires interpretations that may vary widely depending upon the experience and skill of the analyst or examiner (who may or may not employ the scientific method – see Chapter 3).

Getting a PhD, putting on a lab coat, saying words like "multivariate," and using technology, does not a scientist make. Furthermore, science is not just

[1] For those who do not know, this is a reference to the film The Wizard of Oz. The main character Dorothy and her companions went on a quest, seeking out the wisdom of the renowned Wizard. When they finally arrived in Oz, the Wizard tried to frighten them away with a terrifying, thunderous façade.

The Wizard, in fact, had no knowledge or wisdom to give, and had built a reputation based on fear and ignorance. He was merely a small man running the impressive but ultimately empty façade from behind a curtain just off the stage.

When he was accidentally observed, the "Wizard" had the façade command: "Pay no attention to the little man behind the curtain!"

in the collection or gathering of competent, objective data. It is found in the method that one uses to analyze, test, and interpret that data.

THE POLYGRAPH

Polygraphy is perhaps one of the most clever attempts at scientification yet. It puts itself forward as a case solver, a truth finder, and a scientific instrument that is used in accordance with a scientific theory. But then, when push comes to shove, most polygraphers will admit the non-scientific nature of the tool and the process involved in interpreting suspect deception (see Figure 22.1).

Figure 22.1

Polygraph room in a police station. Notice how the examinee is facing away from the instrument so that they (theoretically) cannot see it respond to their biological indicators. Notice how it is also too close to the polygraph for that to make any difference (you can still hear the needles moving across the paper).

A polygraph, or "lie detector," as it is inappropriately referred to, measures the biological indicators of breathing, blood pressure, pulse rate, upper body movement, and galvanic skin response (the amount of moisture secreted by the skin). It is used during suspect interrogation and is based on the theory that when a person is being deceptive, their body will respond or react (out of the fear of detection).

Five very basic problems with this theory keep this instrument, and the subsequent polygraph examiner, from being universally reliable:

- What the polygraph examiner actually claims to be able to interpret from the polygraph readout is fear, and fear is not the same as deception. Even if this claim were true, it is accepted that there are other emotions which, on a polygraph readout, can appear much the same.

- While the theory that fear is reflected by biological indicators may hold true for some individuals, the precise nature of that reaction has yet to be firmly established or agreed upon. As this is true, it has not been established that the polygraph detects any of those biological indicators that might be associated with fear or any other emotion.

- The device itself only measures what the body is doing, as listed out above. There is no established polygraph "profile" of a deceptive reaction, or a lie (there could not be, because everyone reacts differently to different stimuli and thus would have varying constellations of biological indicators for any one emotion, if there were any indicators at all). Therefore the polygraph requires a subjective, non-scientific interpretation of the read-out by the polygraph examiner. So if a person lies or is deceptive and they still pass a polygraph test, they have not beaten the box. They have beaten the polygraph examiner.

- The psychopathic individual can easily defeat this device, or rather the examiner, as they have no remorse. Thus there may be no biological response or reaction to the examiner's questions, and no variation in biological sign for the instrument to read.

- Even a normal person of sufficient will can convince themselves of certain truths, and thus give no biological indicator of a "variation from the baseline" which suggests deception for certain crucial questions.

While it is true that the polygraph measures objective biological indicators, it is not true that polygraph examiners can equate those indicators directly with deception or any other human emotion or response. Additionally, just about any theory may claim to be scientifically derived. This is meaningless without the correct qualification. What the process needs is a strict adherence to the scientific method (detailed in Chapter 3), as well as the willingness to be honest about the nature and quality of final results, and how they are obtained[2].

It should be mentioned at this point that the author is not dismissing the use of polygraphy, or merely the threat of polygraphy, as a valid investigative tool. The results of polygraphy, however, are not evidence of guilt, or even criminal activity, no matter how certain the examiner is of their interpretation. We would be wise to remember this.

[2] Polygraph examiners tend to be as arrogant as criminal profilers. This is because they get to be right a lot. And that happens because very few of them deal with non-criminal, non-deceptive suspects on a regular basis.

By that I mean to say that they don't often have a lot of experience working with innocent people.

STATEMENT ANALYSIS

Statement Analysis is a method for examining written words independent of case facts, exclusively for the purposes of detecting deception (Adams 1996).

> Developed in the early 1980s and known variously as 'content analysis,' 'statement analysis' or 'linguistic forensic analysis,' the technique is widely used to ferret out signs of truth or deception in patterns of words. (*Washington Post* 1998)

Some methods of statement analysis, such as that outlined by Stan Walters, are quite rigorous, readily accepting evident limitations and following strict guidelines for use. For example, Walters (1996) suggests that it will not be reliable when the subject writing the statement is mentally deficient, psychotic, mentally disturbed, suffering from a brain disease, or under the effects of drugs or alcohol. This of course requires extensive background information on a subject and competent writing samples. This method, then, cannot reliably be used to examine the opportunistically acquired statements of unknown offenders.

Other methods of statement analysis, however, involve treating any written statement as an individual crime scene with its own merits and inferences. They regard statement analysis as a scientific process that gives the analyst unique, universal insight, and the ability to almost instantly solve cases[3]:

> SCAN (Scientific Content Analysis) will solve every case for you quickly and easily. You only need the subject's own words, given of his/her own free will...
>
> SCAN will show you:
>
> - whether the subject is truthful or deceptive
> - what information the subject is concealing
> - whether or not the subject was involved in the crime (*LSI SCAN* 1998)

When used without the benefit of a full criminal profile, or without knowledge of the other facts of the case, the implementation of statement analysis violates one of the very basic tenets of behavioral-evidence analysis. That is, it takes a single manifestation of offender behavior (the written or verbal statement), and attempts to infer its meaning separate from the context that it was produced in. This deprives the analyst of the ability to understand the full meaning of the statement to the offender or suspect, and requires that the analyst project an interpretation of the meaning in from one of two sources:

1 The analyst's own personal experiences, which may or may not be commensurate to the type of criminal activity involved in the case.

2 Correlational studies carried out on the statement habits of similar offenders.

Further still, there are statement analysts who claim to be able to generate criminal profiles from statements alone, who refer to themselves as criminal profilers or behavioral profilers. This is well beyond the scope of this very limited tool.

> Statement analysis is an aid that can be used to obtain a confession; it is not an end in itself... (Adams 1996)

And of course, content analysis has its limits. It can detect whether someone is using

[3] *LSI SCAN also claims to require full, competent, and untainted statement samples before the technique can be used. However, their website is replete with examples of full examinations performed on materials acquired from the media. The author finds this practice disingenuous.*

cautious, hedged language or words that imply a greater intimacy with another than the speaker is willing to admit, but it cannot determine the precise intent behind such language. It can only point out promising lines of inquiry for investigators. (*Washington Post* 1998)

While the author does recognize the importance of written or verbal behavior as one of the components that needs attention, it is not the only component. Moreover, that type of behavior certainly should not be interpreted outside of, or independent from, the other facts of a case.

HANDWRITING ANALYSIS

Handwriting analysis, or *graphology*, is the inference of a person's personality characteristics based solely on the style and manner in which they write. This is not to be confused with *handwriting identification*, a sub-discipline of *questioned document examination* (QDE), which is used to identify the authorship of a document by observing the distinguishing, individual features of the handwriting. Sadly, many graphologists have bootstrapped themselves as experts into the field of handwriting identification by playing on the ignorance of those who employ them.

As with statement analysis, when used without the benefit of a full criminal profile, or without knowledge of the other facts of the case, the implementation of handwriting analysis violates one of the very basic tenets of behavioral-evidence analysis. That is, it takes a single manifestation of offender behavior (the written document), and attempts to infer its meaning out of the context that it was produced in. This deprives the analyst of the ability to understand the full meaning of the statement to the offender or suspect, and requires that the analyst project an interpretation of the meaning in from one of two sources:

1 The analyst's own personal experiences, which may or may not be commensurate to the type of criminal activity involved in the case.

2 Correlational studies carried out on the statement habits of similar offenders.

The author does not endorse or recommend the use of handwriting analysis for any part of investigative strategy. This author further suggests that a complete analysis be made of any document found in connection with a crime scene by a qualified questioned-document examiner. This should be done in order to ensure that the maximum amount of physical evidence is elicited from it, and that distracting theories regarding the writing characteristics of typical offenders do not misdirect the investigation of a case.

GEOGRAPHIC PROFILING AND CRIMINAL GEOGRAPHIC TARGETING (CGT)

In 1995, Detective Inspector Kim Rossmo, who is in charge of the Vancouver Police Department's Geographic Profiling Section, wrote his doctoral dissertation on the geographic profiling of serial murderers (Rossmo 1995). In essence, Rossmo's work suggests that a geographical analysis should include a reconstruction of (Holmes 1996):

- crime location type;
- arterial roads and highways;
- physical and psychological boundaries;
- land use;
- neighborhood demographics;
- routine activities of victims;
- displacement.

CGT is a computer program developed by Rossmo that assesses the spatial characteristics of an offender's crimes. It is used to produce a topographic map that assigns probabilities to different areas for the location of the offender's residence or, anchor point within the community (Holmes 1996).

> Geographical profiling software takes the locations of a series of connected rapes, murders, arsons or other serial crimes that are likely to be committed by a single offender, and then uses those locations to figure out likely locations where the offender might live. (Wheelwright 1997)

In the experience of this author, the method used by Rossmo contains the following shortcomings, making its use in serial cases just as enlightening as deploying stickpins on a large area map (which is a pretty good idea, in point of fact):

- This method breaks the same tenet of behavioral-evidence analysis as the others mentioned above: it takes a single manifestation of offender behavior (offense location selection) and attempts to infer its meaning out of the overall behavioral and emotional context that it was produced in.

- This method is actually employed without the benefit of a psychological profile. Though Rossmo states that he requires a psychological profile for a competent geographical analysis, he has been known to proceed without one or to construct his own.

- The result of ignoring overall behavioral context and not utilizing fully drawn psychological profiles is that geographic profiling cannot, and does not, distinguish between two or more offenders operating in the same area.

- This method assumes that all cases that are submitted have been positively linked by law enforcement. It does not check the veracity of this or any other information provided by law enforcement.

- This method assumes that offenders most often live near or within easy reach of their offense area.
- Rossmo's dissertation very competently outlines the weaknesses and the shortcomings of the published research on serial murder. Then, his dissertation goes on to base theories regarding geographic profiling, and the CGT software, on those admittedly flawed studies (Rossmo 1997).
- The technology used in CGT is impressive, but amounts only to so much *scientification*. Inferences regarding offender anchor points and spatial behavior must still be drawn by the analyst.

Fortunately, Rossmo himself does not openly advocate the use of geographic profiling as an investigative silver bullet, and openly encourages the use of other techniques for prioritizing leads and focusing investigations.

> Profiles never solve a crime, they are only meant to be one more tool in an investigator's toolkit…They focus an investigation and serve as an information management strategy because these cases usually suffer from information overload. (Wheelwright 1997)

This author recognizes the value of analyzing offender geographic behavior as a part of the criminal-profiling process, and sees hope for the future that methods like this will be useful for its analysis. However, it is the opinion of this author that the current technology, and method, are too poorly formed and too encumbered by assumptions to be investigatively useful at this time.

INVESTIGATIVE PSYCHOLOGY AND SMALLEST SPACE ANALYSIS (SSA)

Investigative psychology is the name for the theory-based criminology program at the University of Liverpool in England.

> Investigative psychology introduces a more scientific and systematic basis to previously subjective approaches to police investigations. This behavioural science contribution is best thought of as working at various levels, from that of the crime itself, through the gathering of information and on to the actions of police officers working to identify the criminal. (University of Liverpool 1998)

The goals of investigative psychology are, as one might suspect, purported to be investigative in nature:

Major Contributions of Investigative Psychology:

- Linking a number of offences to a single offender
- Inferring offender's characteristics from crime scene actions and other information
- Guidance on investigative interviewing
- Support to detective decision making (*ibid.*)

In 1990, David Canter and Rupert Heritage published their treatise on Smallest Space Analysis (SSA). It asserts that there are essentially five modes of offender interaction with a victim: Intimacy, Sexuality, Impersonal, Violence, and Criminality. Offender behaviors have been classified, based on inductive offender studies, into one of those categories. The following is adapted from Canter and Heritage (1990):

INTIMACY BEHAVIOR

- victim's reaction influences/deters the offender;
- offender requires the victim to participate verbally during the assault;
- offender requires the victim to participate physically during the assault;
- approach is one of a confidence trick;
- offender is inquisitive about the victim;
- offender compliments the victim;
- offender apologizes to the victim.

SEXUAL BEHAVIOR

- vaginal intercourse;
- fellatio initially;
- fellatio as part of the attack sequence;
- cunnilingus;
- initial anal intercourse;
- anal intercourse as part of the offence sequence.

VIOLENCE BEHAVIOR

- violence used as a means of controlling the victim;
- violence used, but not as a means of control;
- aggressive verbal behavior;
- insulting language.

IMPERSONAL BEHAVIOR

- 'blitz' attack;
- impersonal language;
- no response to victim reaction;
- surprise attack;
- tearing of victim clothing;
- victim's clothing disturbed by offender.

CRIMINAL BEHAVIOR

- use of bindings;
- use of gagging;
- stealing from the victim;
- use of some form of a disguise;
- blindfolding the victim;
- demanding goods;
- controlling the victim with a weapon.

As it is designed, the SSA places each behavior into the same category no matter what context it occurs in. For example intercourse of any kind will always go into the intimacy category. And use of bindings will always go into the criminal category. This inductive behavioral typology has the following very important shortcomings:

- The author's interpretation breaks two basic tenets of behavioral evidence analysis: it takes a single offender behavior, and attempts to infer its meaning out of the context that it was produced in. Then it pre-interprets a given offender's behavior based on the inductively derived meaning of offender behavior in unrelated cases, and ignores the reality that the nature of human behavior is multi-determined.
- Like Rossmo's method, this method assumes that all cases that are submitted have been positively linked by law enforcement. It does not check the veracity of this or any other information provided by law enforcement.

This method is put forth as being the basis for a "development of a scientific base for offender profiling to be written by Professor Canter…" (Canter and Heritage 1990), yet it shows a limited basis in the scientific method and in the use of physical evidence. The n is low (27). Professor Canter shows little original insight here, only the reorganization and limiting of Groth's rapist typologies (see Chapter 15). And he further seems to equate science with the use of broad statistical generalizations from poorly rendered data.

Professor Canter has for some time publicly criticized the current methodology of the FBI for being non-scientific. However, this author is uncertain as to how SSA is more scientific than the FBI's current inductive (experiential and statistical) approach. But this author is at a loss as to how SSA is investigatively relevant for use in the analysis of individual unsolved cases given the amount of analyst projection involved, and the clear disinterest in establishing the motivations for the behaviors of individual offenders.

USING ALTERNATIVE METHODS

The author is very concerned about the current reliability of many alternative methods of criminal profiling largely because, as discussed, most isolate behavior and try to interpret it out of the context of a dynamic offense or event. This is almost as concerning as some of the blatantly outrageous claims of those who are attempting to market their techniques. Investigatively speaking, they should be used with great caution, and with great respect for their limitations. When seeking to utilize any of these methods in an investigative effort, investigators should be sure to enlist only the services of competent professionals who are willing to engage in frank discussions about the limitations of their method.

REFERENCES

Adams, S. (1996) "Statement Analysis: What Do Suspect's Words Really Reveal?" *FBI Law Enforcement Bulletin*, October.

Baeza, J. (1998) *Personal communication with the author*, September 22.

Canter, D. and Heritage, R. (1990) "A Multivariate Model of Sexual Offence Behavior: Developments in 'Offender Profiling,'" *The Journal of Forensic Psychiatry*, 1 (2): 185–212.

Holmes, R. (1996) *Profiling Violent Crimes*, 2nd edn, Thousand Oaks: Sage Publications.

LSI SCAN (1998) "Scan Gets The Truth," Http://www.lsiscan.com/brochure.htm, September 3.

Rossmo, D. K. (1995) *Geographic Profiling: Target Patterns of Serial Murderers*, Dissertation, Simon Frasier University.

University of Liverpool (1998) "Centre for Investigative Psychology", website: http://www.liv.ac.uk/InvestigativePsychology, July.

Walters, S. (1996) *Principles of Kinesic Interview and Interrogation*, Boca Raton: CRC Press.

Washington Post (1998) "Follow the Wording," April 26 : C01.

Wheelwright, G. (1997) "Closing the Net on Serial Crimes," *Canada Computer Paper, Inc.*, August.

CHAPTER 23

USE OF FIRE AND EXPLOSIVES

Brent E. Turvey, M.S.

> Cruelty has a Human Heart
> And Jealousy a Human Face:
> Terror, the Human Form Divine
> And Secrecy, the Human Dress...
>
> (William Blake, *A Divine Image*)

One of the most important behavioral-evidence analysis concepts to understand is the nature of the relationship between a person's behavior and their motives or needs. Human behaviors are a manifestation of need. They are the expression of want. And they can be windows to *intent*[1].

Take the behaviors of fire setting and explosives use. They can be analyzed just like any other offender behavior. They can occur in a variety of contexts, and satisfy or be motivated by multiple offender needs. They are not limited to use in a particular kind of criminal offense or against any particular type of victim. Their use in a particular offense is constrained only by offender motive, offender intent, offender skill level, and the availability of materials.

> [1] Keep in mind that the term *motive* refers to the offender's material, psychological, or emotional needs.
>
> The term *intent* is more concrete. It refers to the planned or expected results or purpose of an offender's actions or behaviors.

DEFINITIONS

The term *arson* is a penal classification. Like the term rape or homicide, it is used to refer to a certain constellation of criminal behaviors. The type of behavior generally described by the term "arson" is the intentional setting of a fire with the intent to damage or defraud (DeHaan 1997). There are of course non-criminal motives for starting fires. To keep in the habit of staying away from subjective penal classifications that imply guilt, the author will use the neutral behavioral descriptor *fire setting* throughout the chapter.

The term *bomb* refers to an explosive that is detonated by impact, proximity, timing, or other predetermined means. An *explosive* is any material that can undergo a sudden conversion of a physical form to a gas with a release of energy. Explosives are used to create *explosions*, which are defined generally as the sudden conversion of potential energy (chemical or mechanical) into kinetic energy with the production of heat, gases, and mechanical pressure (*ibid.*). The manufacture of explosives into a bomb for use in a criminal offense is also offender behavior.

The focus of this chapter will be the use of fire and/or explosives in criminal offenses, and the necessary considerations for behavioral evidence analysis.

It should be noted that the reconstruction and interpretation of offender behavior, when fire setting and explosives are involved, may appear particularly difficult. This is because fire, explosions, and/or suppression efforts may destroy some or most of the recognizable physical evidence relating to the offense. What should be understood by the criminal profiler, however, is that this does not mean that there is no evidence, or that cases involving arson or explosives are difficult to solve.

> Whenever a rash of arson fires makes the local news, a uniformed official under the glare of news cameras will often trot out the usual list of excuses about why arson fires are so difficult...
>
> The real problem occurs when present or prospective fire/arson investigators accept this bleak outlook as though it were fact... It has been our experience that most arson fires are not only possible to solve, in many cases, average arson fires are very easy to solve. (Corry and Vottero 1997)

But it is only easy when the investigation involves a considerable pooling of skills and resources. Teamwork between the arson investigator, the laboratory criminalist, and the criminal profiler is mandatory for the successful reconstruction of offender behaviors and subsequent motivations in these cases.

For specific texts devoted in part or in whole to the concepts and procedures involved in the investigation of fire setting and explosives use, the author strongly recommends that readers reference the following textbooks:

- DeHaan, J. (1997) *Kirk's Fire Investigation*, 4th edn, Upper Saddle River: Prentice Hall, Inc.
- NFPA (1998) "NFPA 921: Guide for Fire and Explosion Investigations, 1998 Edition," *Technical Committee on Fire Investigations*, Quincy: National Fire Protection Association.
- Saferstein, R. (1998) *Criminalistics: An Introduction to Forensic Science*, 6th edn, Upper Saddle River: Prentice Hall, Inc.

FIRE AND EXPLOSIVES USE AS *FORCE*

The use of fire and explosives are an extension of an offender's will to use force. They are agents of an offender's will. They injure or damage intended targets and victims, and leave behind visible, recognizable patterns that can be interpreted by the nature and the extent of the resulting human damage, structural damage, and environmental damage.

As extensions of an offender's will to use force, fire and explosives can be weapons that are used for the same motives as other types of force, from defensive to lethal (see Chapter 8). In order to interpret their motivational origins, like any other behavior, close attention needs to be paid to their context in terms of victimology and crime-scene characteristics.

> Motives, devices, intents, and targets for arson fires are all interrelated to some degree… the discovery of one can be used to suggest or deduce the others. (DeHaan 1997)

VICTIMOLOGY

One of the most important things to establish is who or what the intended target or victim was. Who or what was meant to receive the force that was unleashed by the offender in the form of fire or explosives, and who or what was meant to suffer as a result. And by extension who or what was not.

The targets of fire setting and explosives use can include not only individual people, but groups, property, and symbols as well. In this context, a *target* is defined as the object of an attack from the offender's point of view. This is separate from the concept of the victim. The *intended victim* is the term for the person, group, or institution that was meant to suffer loss, harm, injury, or death. The intended victim and the target may be one and the same. There may also be more than one intended victim.

Because of the unpredictable, uncontrollable, and often imprecise nature of fire and explosives use, there may also be *collateral victims.* This term refers to victims that an offender causes to suffer loss, harm, injury, or death (usually by virtue of proximity), in the pursuit of another victim. "Once set, the fire is no longer responsive to the desires or dictates of the firesetter." (Geller 1992).

INDIVIDUALS

This refers to those who have been targeted for emotional, psychological, or precautionary reasons, as well as those who are collateral victims. Victims that have been targeted may also be symbolic. In this context, a *symbol* is any person who represents something else such as an idea, a belief, a group, or even another person.

Examples include, but are by no means limited to:

- parents;
- spouses;
- ex-spouses;
- children;
- a child who finds a device intended for a particular individual, group, or property;
- homeless individuals sleeping in or near targeted property;
- supervisors;

- the President of the United States;

- strangers who look like the offender's ex-wife or mother;

- the CEO of a company that is perceived to be destroying the environment;

- the Pope;

- the leader of the American Civil Liberties Union;

- victims of homicide;

- victims of rape-homicide.

GROUPS

A *group* can mean any collection of people unified by shared characteristics such as sex, race, color, religion, beliefs, activities, or achievement. It also includes groups that are symbolic. In this context, a *symbol* can be any group that represents something else such as an idea, or a belief.

Examples include, but are by no means limited to:

- United States citizens;

- Catholics;

- Jews;

- African Americans;

- women;

- the homeless;

- government employees;

- school teachers;

- co-workers;

- classmates.

PROPERTY

The term *property* refers to structures, vehicles, or other material items. It includes those items that have material or evidentiary value, as well as symbols and collateral items (items that are unintentionally damaged or destroyed by virtue of proximity). In this context, a *symbol* can be any item that represents something else such as an idea, a belief, a group, or a person.

Examples include, but are by no means limited to:

- old buildings that are heavily insured;

- neighboring buildings and vehicles;

- car used in a robbery;

- boat used in a homicide;

- the other boats in the marina;

- abortion clinics;

- victim clothing from a rape-homicide;
- pictures of the victim and the offender together;
- personal belongings;
- military installations;
- foreign embassies;
- federal buildings;
- the White House;
- schools;
- churches;
- the Statue of Liberty;
- the Eiffel Tower;
- the United Nations building;
- the Empire State building.

CRIME-SCENE CHARACTERISTICS

The same general crime-scene characteristics detailed in Chapter 11 are appropriate, with minor adjustments, for the analysis of cases involving fire setting and the use of explosives.

The following additional characteristics, however, must be determined as they related to any manufacture or deployment of incendiary or explosive materials or devices.

METHOD

It must be determined what type of involvement caused the damage at the scene: fire, explosion, or both (definitions given above).

ACCELERANTS AND/OR EXPLOSIVE MATERIAL

An *accelerant* is any fuel (solid, liquid, or gas) that is used to initiate or increase the intensity or speed of the spread of fire. Once it has been established that an accelerant was used, it must further be determined whether or not the accelerant is native or foreign to the environment. The type of accelerant that the offender utilizes is dictated by experience, availability, motive, and intent (DeHaan 1997).

Some common accelerants include:

- gasoline;
- kerosene;
- lighter fluid;
- potable liquors;
- newspaper;

- accumulated trash;
- rags;
- clothing.

Regarding a professional "torch," however, DeHaan points out that they often follow two guidelines in terms of materials use:

> (1) the simpler the better, and (2) use fuels available at the scene. Both guidelines minimize the materials that must be brought to the scene by the arsonist, and the fewer the number of times the individual is seen in the area (especially carrying containers or odd packages) the less the chances of being spotted by a witness. (*ibid.*)

The nature of explosive materials involved in an offense can range from the use of crude, home-made concoctions (gasoline in a sealed container), to the use of commercially available explosive material (dynamite), and to the use of special, non-commercial explosives (Military C-4). Like accelerants, the type of explosive materials that an offender utilizes is also dictated by experience, availability, motive, and intent.

POINT OF ORIGIN

The *point of origin* is a term used to refer to the specific location at which a fire is ignited (DeHaan 1997), or the specific location where a device is placed and subsequently detonated. Do not discount the possibility of multiple points of origin until all of the facts of the case are in.

The point of origin is highly suggestive of the offender's intended target, and their intended victim.

METHOD OF INITIATION

The way that an offender chooses to start, or delay, the burning of accelerant or the detonation of a device is dependent upon the types of fuels or explosives used, the amount of delay time that is desired, and the mobility of the target.

Methods of initiation for fires, adapted from DeHaan, include but are not limited to:

- open flames (matches, lighters, and so on);
- fuses (any length of readily combustible material);
- smoldering materials;
- cigarettes;
- electrical arcs;
- glowing wires;
- chemical reaction (commercial or improvised);
- black powder and flashpowder.

Methods of initiation for explosive devices, adapted from NFPA 921 (NFPA 1998), include but are not limited to:

- blasting caps;
- hot surfaces;
- electrical arcs;
- static electricity;
- open flame;
- sparks;
- chemical reaction (commercial or improvised).

NATURE AND INTENT

When considering the nature and intent of any fire or explosive used by an offender, it will be helpful to determine intentional vs. actual damage. This means learning as much about the environmental structure and fuels in the point of origin as possible. This should be compared with the amount of accelerant or explosive used, and the amount of damage incurred by the target[2]. The more fuels or explosives used by the offender, the more damage they intended to inflict upon their target.

> Under ideal theoretical conditions the shape of the blast front from an explosion is spherical. It expands evenly in all directions from the epicenter. In the real world, the confinement or obstruction of the blast pressure wave changes and modifies the direction, shape, and force of the front itself. (NFPA 1998)

[2] As suggested earlier, a skillful offender may use or take advantage of materials from the environment. Therefore, a low amount of fuels or explosives used by an offender does not exclude the possibility of the intent to inflict high amounts of damage.

Another important element to bear in mind when considering the nature and intent of any fire or explosive used by an offender is the targeting. By that we mean to ask of the evidence regarding devices, initiation, and origin, just what the fire or explosive was intended to inflict damage upon. Was it intended to harm, damage, kill or destroy a narrow target selection, or a broad target selection? *Narrow targeting* refers to any fire or explosive that is designed to inflict specific, focused, calculated amounts of damage to a specific target. *Broad targeting* refers to any fire or an explosive that is designed to inflict damage in a wide-reaching fashion. In cases involving broad targeting, there may be an intended target near the point of origin, but it may also be designed to reach beyond that primary target for other victims in the environment.

OFFENDER SKILL

Manufacture, point of origin, method of initiation, and nature of the fire or explosion should all be taken into account when assessing the offender's skill level. The key questions include:

- How competent was the intended design and/or manufacture of the burn or the blast to achieving the offender's objective?
- How competently was the burn or blast delivered to the point of origin and initiated?
- Did the burn or blast achieve the offender's objective?

MOTIVATIONAL ASPECTS OF FIRE SETTING AND EXPLOSIVES USE

There is a tendency on the part of those who study arsonists and bombers to develop tidy inductive offender typologies from which to infer typical offender characteristics once an offender has been classified. As already discussed in Chapter 15 of this work, these are not the methods or intentions of behavioral evidence analysis.

For example, the FBI's National Center for the Analysis of Violent Crime has suggested that there are six major motivations for arsonists which consistently appear and have proven to be helpful in identifying offender characteristics. They are (Burgess *et al.* 1997):

1   revenge;
2   excitement;
3   vandalism;
4   profit;
5   crime concealment;
6   extremist.

In point of fact, this is actually just another re-creation of the Groth rapist typology (Groth 1979) with some non-sexual motivations (point 4 and point 5) and a non-motive (point 3) thrown in. The NCAVC "revenge" motivation and the "extremist" motivations listed above both correspond with Groth's *anger* motivated offender (the extremist motivation, as defined, could also correspond with *reassurance* or *assertive* motivations). The NCAVC "excitement" motivation corresponds with Groth's *power* motivated offender (or with *reassurance, assertive* or *sadistic* motivations – as defined this is not a very exclusive category because there are so many different kinds of offender "excitement").

Furthermore, "vandalism" is not an offender motive. It is a penal classification, or, as we have discussed, a constellation of behaviors. While reflective of motive, such as assertive-oriented needs, reassurance-oriented needs, or revenge-oriented needs, it is not a motive in its own right. It would require further behavioral analysis before we could start understanding why the offender was doing it.

APPLYING THE BEHAVIOR-MOTIVATIONAL TYPOLOGY

As already stated numerous times, the author does not support the inductive use of motivational typologies, but does support their deductive use.

The author further suggests that the typology detailed in Chapter 15 of this work is more than adequate to the task of classifying the behaviors associated with fire setting and explosives use, with the single addition of *precautionary-oriented* behaviors to be covered in the next section.

Please keep in mind that the behavior-motivational typology is meant to be a guide to help criminal profilers classify behavior, in context, in relationship to the offender need that it serves. It is not intended for use as a diagnostic tool, where offenders are crammed into one typology or another and labeled. And there are no bright yellow lines between them.

Also keep in mind the need to investigate obvious connections, as stated by Corry and Vottero (1997):

> Most adults set fires for revenge, spite, to hide another crime, or for fraud. Many juveniles set fires during vandalism, for revenge, or to achieve some other "logical" criminal purpose. In many cases there is some type of direct connection between the arsonist and the structure [or item, or victim] that he sets on fire.

PRECAUTIONARY-ORIENTED FIRE SETTING AND/OR EXPLOSIVES USE

This motivational aspect is a more inclusive category than the FBI's crime-concealment motivation given previously[3].

Recall from Chapter 11 that a *precautionary act* is any behavior committed by an offender before, during, or after an offense that is consciously intended to confuse, hamper, or defeat investigative or forensic efforts for the purposes of concealing their identity, their connection to the crime, or the crime itself.

Precautionary-oriented fire setting and/or explosives use refers to the use of fire or explosives as a precautionary act. That is, when they are used to conceal, damage or destroy any items of evidentiary value. That includes the partial or complete immolation of a crime scene, and/or the victim.

It should be noted that these types of precautionary acts are not always very thorough. Items intended for destruction should always be thoroughly examined by forensic scientists to exploit them for their full evidentiary potential, no matter how little may be left in terms of debris.

Examples include, but are not limited to:

CONCEAL, DAMAGE, OR DESTROY THE CRIME SCENE

- setting a fire in an apartment after robbing it;
- burning a shed to destroy blood evidence left behind from an abduction-homicide;

[3] *The crime-concealment motivation is perhaps the most useful part of the FBI's arsonist motivational classification system, yet it does have one shortcoming. It describes crime concealment as associated with penal classifications, and not how it disrupts the relationship of evidence transfer between the crime scene, the victim, and the offender (Burgess et al. 1997). This is not useful from a behavioral analysis point of view, though it is likely useful for offender classification.*

■ blowing up a residence with the victim inside, using the gas main, to conceal a homicide.

CONCEAL, DAMAGE, OR DESTROY THE VICTIM

■ burning a victim's body in the woods after a rape-homicide;

■ blowing a victim's body up with explosives and hiding the pieces in different locations to conceal a homicide;

■ placing a victim's body in the trunk of a vehicle and burning the vehicle to conceal a homicide.

CONCEAL, DAMAGE, OR DESTROY EVIDENTIARY MATERIAL LINKING OFFENDER TO THE VICTIM

■ setting a victim's pubic area on fire to conceal evidence of sexual assault or rape;

■ burning bloody victim clothing;

■ burning bloody offender clothing;

■ burning records, deeds, titles, and policies.

CONCEAL, DAMAGE, OR DESTROY PERSONAL ITEMS LINKING OFFENDER TO THE VICTIM

■ burning pictures, videotape, computer hard-drives, or other types or locations containing physical documentation of the victim and the offender together;

■ burning gifts given to the victim by the offender;

■ burning gifts given to the offender by the victim.

CASE EXAMPLES

The following case examples are provided to give readers an applied sense of the variety of criminal offenses involving the use of fire and explosives, as well as the motivational possibilities. Readers are once again reminded that these are behaviors, not motives, and are expressive of offender needs. Approaching offender fire and explosives use from this perspective should provide for a more penetrating understanding of an offender in a given case.

Burglary–Arson: Precautionary Aspect
This case involves a serial burglar who operated in the San Francisco, California South Bay Area during 1998. It includes the use of fire as a precautionary act.

Santa Clara County authorities are searching for a serial arsonist who they say has burglarized and then torched at least a dozen apartment units over the past eight months...

Although no one has been hurt in any of the fires, police and fire officials fear that the next time someone will be injured or killed.

"These are high-density apartment buildings," said San Jose police officer John Carrillo. "Most of these apartments share common walls and floors. A fire could spread rapidly to other units and trap someone inside."

...police and fire agencies from the Peninsula, South Bay and Fremont have formed a task force. The group is working with the FBI and the state fire marshal's office on developing a profile of the arsonist.

"We don't know why he goes from city to city," said Mountain View police Sergeant Rich Alias, who added that at this point officials don't know if the burglar is setting fires to cover his tracks. "He may just be a firebug who derives pleasure from this sort of thing," he said.

Police say the arsonist breaks into apartments in multiunit buildings during daylight hours. The person usually gets in by forcing open a window or the front door, Pipkin said. On one occasion the thief used a crowbar to break in, he said. Then the person grabs personal possessions such as cash and jewelry before setting the place a blaze. (*San Francisco Chronicle* 1998a)

When Patrick Salinas was finally apprehended in connection with the arson-burglaries, it was found that he had a long history of criminal behavior going back to 1993.

Sunnyvale police... arrested a man they believe is the South Bay serial arson-burglar who stole from apartments and set them on fire, most likely to cover his tracks.

Patrick Salinas, 31, an unemployed computer technician, was booked into Santa Clara County Jail in San Jose Wednesday on 14 counts of burglary and 12 counts of arson...

Salinas... was charged earlier this year with residential burglary in Milpitas, and was convicted in 1993 of attempted extortion, court records show.

According to police, a search of the home where Salinas lived with his parents yielded a stereo, camera, computer equipment, a VCR, hand tools and jewelry among other items that police suspect were stolen during the burglaries...

The string of incidents dates back to last September and occurred in Palo Alto, Mountain View, Sunnyvale, Santa Clara, San Jose and Milpitas.

Most involved a burglar who broke into large apartment buildings, stole valuables and started a fire before leaving. No one was injured because firefighters put out flames before they spread...

A young woman who emerged from the Salinas' home and identified herself as his girlfriend said only: "He's not the type of person who would do something like this. It's not in his character." (*San Francisco Chronicle* 1998b)

Robbery–Arson: Retaliatory Aspect

This case in Washington D.C., just before Christmas in December of 1997, is a good example of a robbery involving fire setting for non-precautionary motives. The nature of this use of force could best be described as punishment oriented.

A 71-year-old woman was doused with a flammable liquid in her Southeast Washington apartment and set afire late Sunday after she rebuffed a female robber who demanded money and food stamps, D.C. police said. The elderly victim was severely injured, and the resulting blaze gutted three attached apartment houses, leaving at least nine adults and five children homeless.

The robber got away with $30…

The robbery began about 10 p.m. when a woman – described by police as in her late twenties, about 5 feet 8 inches tall and about 200 pounds – demanded money and food stamps from Hudson in her second-floor apartment, according to investigators…

Police said the alleged assailant, who was still being sought last night, is an acquaintance of Hudson's son and is familiar to many residents in the area, which has been infested with illegal drugs for years. Police said that at some point Sunday night, Hudson's son had left his mother's apartment, leaving her alone with the woman now suspected of robbing her.

When Hudson refused the demand for money and food stamps, police said, the woman doused her with an unidentified flammable liquid, set fire to a rolled-up newspaper and touched the torch to Hudson's body, setting her ablaze. The fire quickly spread through Hudson's apartment and the three other units in the brick building, then spread to two attached brick buildings, each with four apartments.

Sometime later, upon extinguishing the fire, police said in a statement, firefighters found Hudson in an upstairs bedroom. (*The Washington Post Company* 1997)

Arson–Vandalism: Retaliatory Aspect

This case in Ledger, Montana, in 1998, is a good example of arson used to terrorize a group of individuals because of the prosperity that results from their religious and cultural values. They are called Hutterites. The Hutterites originated in Eastern Europe in 1528 and are named after an early leader, Jacob Hutter (who was, ironically, burned at the stake in 1536). Even more ironically, the Hutterites immigrated to North America in the late 1800s to escape religious persecution.

Hutterites live communally and dress plainly, however they embrace any technology that helps them farm better. Their farms tend to be large, efficient, and prosperous. Often they are more prosperous than their neighbors. (Associated Press 1998)

Arsonists and vandals are preying on an Amish-like religious sect known as Hutterites, but their neighbors haven't evinced much sympathy for the victims. They mutter darkly about the Hutterites, not their tormentors.

Wheat prices are low, the rumblings go. We don't need competition from people who are buying up our farms to expand, who don't pay their fair share of taxes, don't save to send their kids to college, don't even buy televisions and air conditioners, for goodness' sake.

"I think they use their religion as a front to hide their grand plan, which is to control a good share of agriculture," said one non-Hutterite farmer, who spoke on condition of anonymity.

On March 8, an arsonist set fire to a shed full of lumber to be used for housing and other buildings for the fledgling colony. The blaze caused more than $100,000 in damage. The arson followed a rash of vandalism, including damage to vehicles and grain bins.

Undersheriff Dave Robins said investigators have a suspect, but there have been no arrests. The FBI is investigating it as a hate crime. But Robins isn't ready to label it religious bigotry.

"To me it looks more like jealousy," he said. "Not that they hate the people for what they stand for, just that they're making a go of property and land that others aren't able to."

Christine Kaufmann, co-director of the Montana Human Rights Network, and Mark Nagasawa of the Montana Association of Churches said the absence of community outrage is troubling.

"I expected people to jump up on this and go, 'I can't believe this is happening,'" said Nagasawa, whose efforts at organizing a community meeting got a lukewarm response. But, "there's been a lot of resentment building up over the years," he added. (*ibid.*)

Arson–Stalking: Retaliatory Aspect
This case involves a man named Rene Matias who was fired from Air Logistics Corporation of Pasadena, California in 1995. It is alleged that he stalked a group of senior company managers, sent fake bombs to them, and burned one of their vehicles. In this case, fire is used both in a retaliatory and reassurance-oriented way, arguably.

Matias... had been stalking his former bosses... In August, prosecutors said, his alleged victims obtained a temporary restraining order against him.

Matias faces two counts of sending false bombs, stemming from incidents on May 16, 1996, and July 16 this year. He also is charged with 13 counts of stalking, and one count of arson in the burning of a car a manager owned, authorities said. (*Los Angeles Times* 1997)

Abduction–Rape–Arson–Homicide: Precautionary Aspect
This case took place in May of 1998, in Auckland, New Zealand. It involves the abduction, rape, robbery, and murder of a woman in her vehicle. The fire-setting behavior likely was meant to conceal or hamper the investigation of all of the criminal activity in the case by the destruction of physical evidence. The homicidal intent of the fire setting is also likely precautionary, as it prevents a living witness to those crimes.

... The tests show Claire was lying in a significant amount of petrol, that she was probably doused in it, and that it was found elsewhere around the car.

Medical tests showed the victim was alive when the fire was lit, although probably unconscious.

The dead woman's estranged husband, Peter Hills, said he was stunned when told how his wife died. He had been considering approaching her about a reconciliation before the murder.

Pouring petrol on her like that is nothing short of animalistic. That's barbarism as far as I'm concerned, the devout Jehovah's Witness said…

Police are investigating the possibility Ms Hills, who worked at McDonald's at Auckland International Airport, was intercepted on her way to work, raped, and robbed before being set alight.

Mr Hills said he believed his wife might have been car-jacked, probably by more than one person. (*The Christchurch Press* 1998)

Bombings in China: Explosives used for Retaliatory Motives
This segment details a litany of retaliatory oriented bombings in China during 1998. It is important to note because these same types of crimes have very pronounced Western equivalents.

A disgruntled school teacher set off a bomb at a citation ceremony for outstanding instructors in China's southwestern Yunnan province in April, killing himself and five other teachers...

The April 3 [1998] attack also wounded 41 teachers, the Communist Party boss of Micheng town in Midu County and a town vice-mayor, a county police official said by telephone.

The dead and wounded were among about 120 people at the ceremony. The rest escaped unhurt.

The blast was the latest in a string of explosions which have struck a blow at law and order in China at a time of rising social tension linked to wrenching industrial transformation and slowing economic growth.

Kuang Yingxue, 38, a teacher at Micheng's Number Three Primary School, had been recommended to receive an award for outstanding teachers but was frustrated after he was passed over for citation, the official said.

Kuang was killed on the spot in the blast, but it was unclear if it was a suicide attack or an accidental explosion. It was also unclear where or how Kuang learned to make a bomb and obtained the 1–1.5 kg (2.2–3.3 lb) of explosives he used…

On the same day in the same province, Zhu Zenghua, 48, an electrician, killed himself and wounded the director and deputy director of Luxi county's radio and television bureau in a bomb attack at the director's office…

Bureau director Shi Haibin and his deputy, Zhu Jiarong, were still in hospital, police said.

The electrician had explosives strapped to his body…

Police declined to say what the electrician's motive was. Hong Kong's Chinese-language *Ming Pao* newspaper said he had financial problems and felt helpless because his superiors would not come to his aid…

…in May, a businesswoman in the industrial city of Wuhan hired two farmers to plant a fatal time bomb in the car of a banker with whom she had a financial dispute.

The banker was killed in the blast. The businesswoman and the peasants were arrested.

Wuhan was rocked by a much deadlier blast in February, when an explosion aboard a bus killed 16 people. Police blamed the explosion on a revenge attack by a jilted farmer.

In January, a farmer who had lost a leg in a train accident killed himself and three others and wounded five in a bomb attack on the Ministry of Railways in Beijing.

Other deadly explosions in China have been linked to diverse factors including Muslim separatism in northwestern China, by organized crime and property disputes. (Reuters 1998)

REFERENCES

Associated Press (1998) "Burning Jealousy?" May 9.

Burgess, A., Burgess, A., Douglas, J. and Ressler, R. (1997) *Crime Classification Manual*, San Francisco: Jossey-Bass, Inc.

Corry, R. and Vottero, B. (1997) "A New Approach to Fire and Arson Investigation," *Fire Investigation Guideline*, Massachusetts State Fire Marshall.

DeHaan, J. (1997) *Kirk's Fire Investigation*, 4th edn, Upper Saddle River: Prentice Hall, Inc.

Geller, J. (1992) "Arson in Review: From Profit to Pathology," *Psychiatr Clin North Am*, September, 15 (3): 623–45.

Groth, A. N. (1979) *Men Who Rape: The Psychology of the Offender*, New York: Plenum Press.

Los Angeles Times (1997) "Former Air Logistics Employee Charged in Stalking of Managers," December 27.

NFPA (1998) "NFPA 921: Guide for Fire and Explosion Investigations, 1998 Edition," *Technical Committee on Fire Investigations*, Quincy: National Fire Protection Association.

Reuters (1998) "School Teacher Detonates Bomb, Kills Six," June 23.

San Francisco Chronicle (1998a) "Firebug Thief Eludes Police in 6 Cities: At least 12 break-ins, blazes since September," Friday, May 29: A1.

San Francisco Chronicle (1998b) "Serial Arson Suspect Arrested: Sunnyvale man faces 14 counts of burglary," Friday, August 7: A20.

The Christchurch Press (1998) "Tests show victim alive when car set on fire, police say," May 25.

The Washington Post Company (1997) "For $30, Robber Burns 71-Year-Old," December 23: A01.

CHAPTER 24

SERIAL RAPE AND SERIAL HOMICIDE

Brent E. Turvey, M.S.

What is it, what nameless, inscrutable, unearthly thing is it; what cozening, hidden lord and master, and cruel, remorseless emperor commands me; that against all natural lovings and longings, I so keep pushing...

Is it that by its indefiniteness it shadows forth the heartless voids and immensities of the universe, and thus stabs us from behind with the thought of annihilation... Wonder ye then at the fiery hunt?

(Herman Melville, *Moby Dick*)

It is very troubling, our transcultural human fascination with violent, predatory serial crime. Books on the subject written by detached academics abound. Articles and pieces detailing rape and murder flood the news. The popular media dramatizes it to excite our senses (and we pay them handsomely for it).

It is as though we harvest nihilistic and existential pleasure or excitement from knowing, and romanticizing the fact, that such humans exist. Humans that exercise what the cynics among us have finally come to regard as some sort of socially unjust lottery that is at once horrific, but then also tolerated and encouraged by the values that we espouse. The psychopathic values of unbridled materialism, and objectification, where others have little value outside of the pleasure that they can bring us.

We objectify each other, we minimize each other's pain by focusing on our own, we belittle others to make ourselves feel more powerful, we marginalize the needs of others, we teach social and cultural isolationism by example, and we have a pathological fear of intimacy that keeps us emotionally alienated.

All of this, and yet we have the astounding ability to pretend that this is not the case, that these are not our values, and that we are not excited by these things that come from the suffering of others. All of this, and yet we have the gall to ask where those predators come from. What creates them? What makes them?

The answer, undeniably, is that they are we. We are they. It is the organic consequence of our arrogance, our denial, and our lack of intimacy. We are cultures close to converging on the point where Holden Caulfields (the name of the main character from *The Catcher in the Rye*, by J.D. Salinger) are the rule, rather than the exception.

TERMS AND DEFINITIONS

Because of the legal consequences of offender behavior, and perhaps even as a result of the law-enforcement divisions which separate investigative focus, the crime of serial rape and the crime of serial homicide have been rendered unrelated. This is a mistake that we will undo right now.

The motivations for offender homicidal behavior and offender rape or sexual assault related behaviors are the same. The only exception to this likeness is that, as with fire setting or explosives use, the act of homicide can be motivated by precautionary needs. Investigators and profilers alike would be well to keep in mind two very important things that place serial rape and serial homicide behavior on the same level of priority:

1   The act of homicide is not a motive. It is a behavior that expresses an offender need. A related series of homicides can easily contain sexual aspects, and motives that are expressed by sexualized behavior for which homicide is ultimately a precautionary act. A series of homicides may also contain living victims that successfully evaded capture, that escaped captivity, or that were released by the offender.

2   The act of rape is not a motive. It is a behavior that can express other offender needs beyond those of pure sexual gratification. Any series of related rapes may also include victims who were killed, either accidentally or intentionally, by the offender. Rape or sexual assault cases who involve offenders using any amount of force can easily become homicides given the right set of circumstances.

The rest of this chapter, then, will be devoted to strategies for investigating serial rape and serial homicide, with an eye to the reality that both behaviors can occur within the same series.

SERIAL CRIME

The term serial killer was first coined by Robert K. Ressler to describe offenders who are obsessed with fantasies that go unfulfilled; pressing them onward to the next offense (Ressler 1992). It was used as a red flag. This is because the economy of law enforcement is such that decisions are made on a daily basis to determine how their scarce resources may be allocated against their current caseload. The term "serial killer" was developed to put associated cases at the top of that resource-allocation pile.

Here is a short list of similar terms that have been used as meaning the same thing, but in fact may not:

- serial killings;
- serial murders
- serial homicides.

Due to the variety of individuals who undertake the investigation and research of the above types of cases, there are no general or standardized definitions for these terms. And these terms are used interchangeably throughout the published literature. This is not a problem as long as we define our terms when we use them.

This author prefers the term *serial homicide*, or *serial murder*, because these terms most accurately relate the behavior of legal interest, while being the least sensationalistic. In that spirit, we will use definitions of terms that are investigatively useful for suggesting the allocation of resources, but which are so broad as to be useless for academic research purposes. These are not exclusive descriptors, and are meant to describe the type of *case* as opposed to describing the type of *offender*.

- *Serial homicide/murder*: two or more related cases involving homicide behavior.
- *Serial arson*: two or more related cases involving fire setting behavior.
- *Serial bombing*: two or more related cases involving the use of explosives.
- *Serial rape*: two or more related cases involving rape or a sexual assault behavior.

This author does not get into the semantics of "spree" vs. "mass" vs. whatever offenses. These terms do nothing to aid the investigative effort, are very subjectively interpreted, and are just as useless for research purposes by virtue of being too inclusive.

RESPECTING THE VICTIM

In cases where living victims are involved, there is the potential for *re-victimizing* them. This is the term that is used to describe the habitual disrespect shown for victims by virtue of:

- Unnecessary, duplicated efforts to interview and re-interview victims by the many agencies involved in the investigation of sex crimes in our benevolent criminal-justice systems. Everyone wants their chance to get the victim's story first-hand. Quite frankly, this sporadic and intensely painful mechanism for eliciting facts from the victim can become a redundant, and therefore unnecessary and abusive, process.
- Apathy or cynicism on the part of any of the above towards the victim's pain or suffering.

There is no better way to foster resentment in a victim of a sex crime than by treating them as though they are not important, or by not listening to them.

Each should be treated with respect, should be treated with dignity, and should be given the time that they need before they can be fully cooperative.

It is therefore the recommendation of this author that each victim be assigned a single detective, or partnered detectives, who will be their consistent point of contact and two-way conduit for information. It is the further recommendation of the author that all living victims in serial crimes be administered the *behavioral-oriented interview*.

THE BEHAVIORAL-ORIENTED INTERVIEW

Where words are scarce,
they are seldom spent in vain,
For they breathe truth that breathe their words in pain.

(Shakespeare, *King Richard II, Act 2, Scene 1*)

Robert Hazelwood has very competently developed a set of questions designed to elicit the behavioral aspects of the victim–offender interaction from the victims of sex crimes. This interview strategy assists not only in corroborating the facts of a case, but it can give the criminal profiler the information needed for case linkage, motive assessment, and the development of investigatively relevant strategy.

The experience of this author suggests that investigators who utilize this format, in combination with an "in your own words describe the attack" format, get the most useful investigative information from their victims. But it really does take a gentle hand and a desire to find the facts. That means being objective to the established facts of the case and assuming nothing.

Taken from *Practical Aspects of Rape Investigation* (Burgess and Hazelwood 1995):

1 Describe the manner in which the offender approached and gained control over you.

2 How did he maintain control of you and the situation?

3 Specifically describe the physical force he used and when during the attack it occurred.

4 Did you resist either physically, verbally, or passively? If so, describe each instance you can recall.

5 What was his reaction to your resistance?

6 Did he at any time experience a sexual dysfunction? If so, describe what type, whether he was later able to function sexually, and any particular act or behavior he performed or demanded that you perform to overcome the dysfunction.

7 Describe all sexual acts forced upon you or performed by the offender on himself and the sequence in which they occurred, including repetitions.

8 As precisely as possible, try to remember what he said to you, his tone of voice, and his attitude at the time he spoke.

9 Did he demand that you answer questions, repeat phrases, or respond verbally in any manner whatsoever? Try to recall specifically what he demanded you to say.

10 When, if ever, did his attitude appear to change? In what manner did it change, and what occurred immediately before the change?

11 What actions did he take to ensure that you would not be able to identify him? Did he take any precautions to ensure the police would not be able to associate him with the crime?

12 Did he take anything when he left? Have you carefully inventoried your personal belongings (undergarments, photographs, etc.) since the assault?

13 Did you receive any calls or notes from unidentified people before or since the assault? Have you had any experience to indicate that he specifically targeted you for the assault?

14 How do you believe people who associate with the rapist on a daily basis would describe him as a person?

The reason that this interview strategy is so helpful is that it can illuminate the nature and extent of specific behaviors that an offender engaged in. Consistent use of this technique makes it easier to elicit and document offender offense behavior, and link similar offenses over time. In serial cases this is especially important.

Whether detectives are investigating a single offense, or a series of related rapes and/or sexual assaults, they should employ the 14-question behavioral-oriented interview. That way it will be easier to come back and evaluate cases that may have appeared unrelated to other attacks at the time that they were committed. This will save countless hours, while encouraging the habit of using the interview strategy.

If detectives come across a case that they believe is part of a series of related sex crimes, where no behaviorally oriented interview has been done, the interview strategy can be retroactively applied, even many years after the original offense. This would not be redundant, but it could be traumatic for the victim. Investigators need to be sensitive when re-interviewing victims of unsolved sex crimes after the passage of time. Some appreciate that the crime is still of interest to investigators, and others may have been mistreated by investigators in the past and may be very agitated.

In any case, victim cooperation is vital from the moment a complaint is filed until after an offender has been sentenced and used up their appeals. Detectives must establish a good, trusting, two-way relationship with their victims. If an investigator cannot do this, lacks the personality or temperament, or feels that it is an imposition, then the author suggests that they find another line of work.

STRATEGIES FOR EVALUATION OF SERIAL BEHAVIOR

In order to help develop competent investigative strategies for the successful identification and apprehension of serial offenders, as well as for the development of competent insight into offender motive and intent, the author recommends that the following behavioral considerations be examined.

VICTIM SELECTION

As discussed in Chapter 9, if we can understand how and why a serial offender selects a particular victim, then we may also be able to establish the relational links between the victim and that offender. Additionally, if we can come to understand an offender's overall strategy for the selection of their victims, then we have a better chance of predicting the type of victim that they may select in the future.

When determining how an offender may have selected a particular victim, the profiler must ask of the behavioral evidence certain basic questions in order to begin eliminating the possibilities.

1 Was the victim *opportunistic* or *targeted?*
2 If the victim was targeted, what appears to be the offender's selection criteria?
  - Location type (indoor, outdoor, apartment complex, parking lot, woods, supermarket, etc.).
  - Occupation (prostitute, homeless, exotic dancer, student, banker, teacher, etc.).
  - Vulnerability (intoxicated, tired, distracted, etc.).
  - Physical characteristics (height, weight, hair style/color, clothing, etc.).
  - Activity (jogging, hiking, driving, shopping, sleeping, internet, etc.).
3 If the victim appears to have been targeted, what presurveillance behaviors would be required by the offender, given the activity of the victim? What activities do investigators and patrol need to be on the lookout for to spot an offender that may be engaged in presurveillance relating to the series of crimes at hand?
4 If the victim could not have been targeted or pre-surveilled, then did the offender have to step outside of their daily, non-criminal routine to acquire them, or was the offender likely trolling for potential victims?
5 If the offender was not actively trolling, and the victim could not have been preselected or pre-surveilled, then the offender likely acquired the victim during their daily routine of activity. This suggests that a reconstruction of the victim's lifestyle, habits, and routines may give direct insight into the lifestyle, habits, and routines of the offender.

OFFENDER DEPARTURE STRATEGY

How an offender chooses to leave behind *living victims,* after an attack is concluded, gives insight into the motive and intent of their offense behavior (and their skill level). It may also reveal information regarding where the offender intends to go after the offense, their personal schedule, how much time they need to get away, and how concerned they are that the victim might recognize them at a later date. These are of course just some of the strategies involved, and will be used in combination with each other depending upon the offender and the circumstances of the attack.

- Leaves the victim conscious.
- Leaves the victim unconscious (nature of the force involved?).
- Leaves the victim clothed.
- Leaves the victim partially clothed, or nude (was clothing discarded at the scene, near the scene, or taken from the scene?).
- No restraints on the victim.
- Restrains the victim physically (type of controlling force used?).
- Victim is able, mobile.
- Disables the victim physically, making them immobile or in need of medical attention (nature of the force involved?).
- Leaves the victim at or near the point of contact.
- Leaves the victim at a location far away from the point of contact.
- Takes the victim to a remote location to drop them off after an attack.
- Takes the victim to wherever they wish to go (work, home, friend's house).
- Physical threat: "Don't follow me or I'll kill you!" "Don't call the police or I'll find you and cut your throat!".
- Implied threat: "Don't follow me or else!" "Don't tell anyone or you'll be sorry!".
- Verbal command: "Don't follow me!" "Count to 500 and then leave.".
- Rationalization: "You shouldn't have been walking out here alone." "I could have done a lot worse to you." "You deserved it.".
- Apology: "I'm sorry." "This isn't me." "I didn't mean to hurt you.".

DISPOSAL SITE ASPECTS

How an offender chooses to leave behind *deceased victims* in the disposal site also gives insight into the motive and intent of their offense behavior (and their skill level). Criminal profilers must try to establish the relation of the victim's body to the disposal site, and the evidence that is in it. The following is a list of disposal site aspects that are useful in the process of answering the following questions:

1 Whether or not an offender intended for the victim's body to be found.
2 Where an offender intends for the victim's body to be found.
3 When an offender intends for the victim's body to be found.
4 Whom an offender intends to find the victim's body.

CONVENIENCE ASPECT

This refers to a disposal site that an offender chooses by virtue of the fact that it is available, or less difficult than another location. This may result when an offender is constrained by time, or by the inability to move a victim's body either physically, or without being observed or detected.

REMORSE ASPECT

This refers to a disposal site where there is evidence that the offender felt some regret over the victim's death. This can be seen in behaviors that attempt to "undo" the homicide, including washing the blood off a victim, dressing them in clean clothes, and placing them in a natural state such as sleeping, sitting in a chair, or in the seat of a vehicle.

PRESELECTED ASPECT

This refers to a disposal site that an offender chooses prior to actually committing an offense, by virtue of it being particularly suitable for the activities with which they wish to engage the victim. In outdoor cases, it may be a small clearing just out of sight and earshot from a well-trodden path, or an indoor location that the offender must transport the victim to.

PRECAUTIONARY ASPECT

This refers to a disposal site where an offender has gone to some effort to destroy evidence or otherwise hamper the investigative effort. This can be in the form of mutilating the body to prevent identification, disposing of it in water to wash away evidence, disposing of it in a remote or hard to reach location, or burying it very deep to forestall or prevent its recovery.

STAGED ASPECT

This refers to a disposal site that an offender has contrived for the purposes of purposefully misleading the investigation. This may be in the form of a murderer placing a gun in the hand of a shooting victim, or in the form of making a ligature strangulation appear as a suicide by hanging.

ARRANGED ASPECT

This refers to a disposal site where an offender has arranged the body and the items within the scene in such a manner as to serve ritual or fantasy purposes. This can be found when victim's bodies are displayed post-mortem in a very public location, when victims are placed in humiliating sexual positions after death, and when the position of the body serves the purposes of a particular offender ritual. The question in cases where the body or the scene has been arranged by the offender is: Who is meant to see the arrangement – the offender, law enforcement, or others who would happen upon the scene?

SOLVING CASES

In most texts on the subject of serial murder or rape investigation, little or no attention is given to how unsolved cases are solved. Keppel (1989) actually comes the closest when he suggests the following:

> ...the successful completion of a serial homicide investigation is dependant upon a combination of so-called solvability factors. These are:
>
> 1 The quality of police interviews with eyewitnesses.
> 2 The circumstances which led to the initial stop of the murderer.
> 3 The circumstances which established the probable cause to search and seize the physical evidence from the person and/or the property of the murderer; specifically, the solvability factors in each case.
> 4 The quality of the investigations at the crime scene(s).
> 5 The quality of the scientific analysis of the physical evidence seized from the murderer and/or his property and its comparison to physical evidence from the victims and the homicide scenes.

This is not a list of how cases are solved but rather a list of elements that the successful apprehension and prosecution of serial offenders depends upon. In as much as this is true, it emphasizes quality and thoroughness, and is therefore quite robust.

But it does not quite give us what we need. What we need is a list of mechanisms by which serial investigations are most often solved. That is to say, a list of the most common ways that suspects are initially identified by law enforcement.

As we have discussed, criminal profilers and criminal profiles do not solve cases, typically. In the investigative phase, they inform investigative processes that lead detectives to good suspects. Good suspects most commonly come to light in a serial investigation via the following mechanisms:

1 A confession.
2 Another offender turning in the serial offender.
3 The coming forward of an offender's spouse, family members, friends, co-workers, or neighbors to report evidence of aberrant, suspicious, or criminal activity.
4 The identification of an offender by a witness to the crime.
5 The identification of an offender by a victim who has eluded or evaded an attack.
6 The identification of an offender by a victim who has suffered an attack but was subsequently released by the offender.
7 The identification of an offender by a victim who has suffered an attack but subsequently escaped from captivity.

8 The routine stop of an offender for a minor violation (expired vehicle tags, traffic violation, parking violation, and so on).

9 The arrest of an offender for an offense unrelated to violent, predatory activity (burglary, purse snatching, indecent exposure, assault, and so on), and subsequent linkage to physical evidence on file associated with unsolved crimes such as fingerprints, photo ID, or DNA.

10 The linkage of a known offender to a series of offenses by the use of databased information or evidence such as gun registrations, driver's licenses, fingerprints, or DNA.

11 Good detective work, which includes following up on all tips, investigating all leads to their conclusion, sharing information and collaborating with other law-enforcement agencies, and working the physical evidence until it is an exhausted possibility.

The full utilization and exploitation of these mechanisms requires an alert, educated, and responsive law-enforcement community. The deductive criminal-profiling process, applied as investigative philosophy, prepares detectives to be just that.

USING THE MEDIA

As suggested in the previous section, the public availability of discriminating information regarding an unsolved serial case be a useful tool for getting witnesses, family members, and previous victims to come forward with vital information regarding the identity of suspects. This makes the media an investigative lifeline to the community. If we want the community to work with us on these cases, we have to give them enough information to work with.

The criminal profile can be a constructive part of this effort.

But as we all know, the media is a double-edged sword. Detectives are charged with the task of giving enough information to the public so that they can be an effective extension of the investigation. However they have the equally important responsibility of holding enough specific details back to:

■ prevent the offender from understanding the full nature of investigative efforts and significantly altering his MO, depriving the investigators of the ability to link cases;

■ screen copycats and those who would give false confessions.

Detectives should also monitor the media coverage of a given serial case very closely and keep track of which case details are made public and when. Subsequently the dissemination of this information should be tracked with known offender behavior to monitor for any changes in the offender MO, no matter how subtle or discrete. If the offender is paying attention to news coverage, and either learning or reacting to it, detectives will want to be the first to know.

CASE EXAMPLES

The following case examples are provided to give readers an applied sense of the international variety of serial rape and homicide offenses, as well as the motivational possibilities. Readers are once again reminded that rape and homicide are behaviors, not motives, and are expressive of offender needs. Approaching them from this perspective should provide for a more penetrating understanding of an offender in a given case.

Florence, Italy: Pietro Pacciani
In 1994, this farmhand was convicted of the murders of seven couples and sentenced to life in prison. From 1974 to 1985, it is alleged that he selected couples who were sitting in their vehicles or camping in the Tuscan countryside. It is also alleged that he sexually assaulted them, murdered them, and in some cases engaged in post-mortem mutilation, including the partial removal of breasts and genitals. His conviction was overturned in 1996 and he was to receive a new trial. However, he died at the age of 72 of a heart attack in his Florence home during February of 1998, seven months before his new trial could begin (*Sydney Morning Herald* 1998).

Wenatchee, Washington: Richard Thomas Andrews
Between 1992 and 1995, this 60-year-old resident of Wenatchee, Washington confessed to fire-bombing abortion clinics, targeting facilities in Kalispell, Missoula and Helena, Montana; Boise, Idaho; Jackson, Wyoming; and Redding and Chico, California. An anti-abortion activist since the late 1980s, he had been arrested four times previously during demonstrations as part of Operation Rescue, the national anti-abortion movement (*San Francisco Chronicle* 1998).

In April of 1997, police officers in Vancouver, Washington conducting a routine traffic stop found arson gear in Andrews' car. Inside the vehicle, they discovered a police scanner set to emergency frequencies in the cities where the bombed clinics had been located, a stocking mask, rubber gloves, five plastic containers of gasoline, and flares used as triggering devices. Officers also found some maps showing the cities where bombings had occurred. Andrews was apparently on his way to set another fire when he was arrested (*ibid.*).

Austin, Texas: Christopher Ted Dye
In 1996, this habitual Methamphetamine user, burglar, and auto mechanic confessed to 15 sexual assaults that had begun in 1993. He was initially linked to the crimes by the unique verbal behavior that he used with each victim, a search through suspects collected over the course of three years, and the similarity of his criminal-file photo to the composite sketch of the serial-rape suspect.

Dye was reportedly using drugs when he engaged in his rape behavior. All of the sexual assaults that he is suspected of committing happened between 1 a.m. and sunrise. In most of the 15 cases, the victims were attacked after he entered through an unlocked door or window. He also introduced himself to his victims, using his first name. He would then threaten them with a knife before tying them up, assaulting them, and often robbing them. One victim testified at his trial about being awoken by a stranger with a knife that bound her, cut off her clothes, raped her, then casually sifted through her belongings (*Austin American-Statesman* 1997).

The bulk of the credit for breaking this case went to Patrol Officer Joann Gerbrands, who was assigned to research information that had been gathered on about 100 suspects to see if any could be eliminated as possibilities. She examined criminal records, driver's license and utility records, and collated mugshots. She then noticed that Dye had been convicted of burglaries in the same blocks as the sexual assaults. She further checked his photo and physical description, and noticed that they were similar to suspect descriptions given by the victims. Dye was put under surveillance, then subsequently arrested. The resolution of this case falls under the heading of good detective work (*Austin American-Statesman* 1996).

Van Nuys, California: Jose Luis Zarate
In a three-week period around Christmas 1996, 28-year-old Jose Zarate abducted, raped, and robbed four women at gunpoint, all Latinos in their early 30s. One was attacked while walking to work, another was attacked getting into her car to drive to work, one was forced off the road at gunpoint, and the last was attacked while she washed clothing at a coin laundry. He stole credit cards and other personal belongings from his victims.

In January of 1997, police asked the victims to spend a day with a sketch artist so a composite could be released to the public. Investigators also released the tag number of the stolen Dodge Neon he was driving. On January 9, two days after they issued the news release, an anonymous caller led police to Zarate who was living in a San Francisco motel (*Los Angeles Times* 1998).

Gauteng, South Africa: David Mmbengwa
Between 1996 and 1998, this 34-year-old employee of the Northern Province Agricultural Department in Giyani attacked a still unknown number of couples parked on "lovers lanes," resulting in at least eight deaths. Believing he was on a divine mission from God, and carrying a bible with passages regarding sexual behavior underlined, he would target the male side of the vehicle. According to the survivors, five women, he did not say anything or make any contact before approaching the vehicle and opening fire. One of the male victims was shot 14 times. At least three of his victims were policemen and their girlfriends (*Gauteng Sunday Times* 1998).

Tehran, Iran: Ali Reza Khoshruy Kuran Kordiyeh
In August of 1997, this 28-year-old man from Tehran, Iran was publicly executed for the kidnap, rape, and murder of nine girls and women between the ages of 10 and 47 years, including a mother and daughter. He posed as a freelance taxi driver and selected his victims from those who sought his services. When he was through with them, he would burn their bodies so that they could not be identified. His known victims were all killed in the course of four months (CNN 1997).

Cairo, Egypt: Aida Nur el-Din
In August of 1997, this 42-year-old female nurse confessed to killing 18 patients because they were disturbing her work. She murdered them by injecting them with drugs stolen from the hospital dispensary. She confessed, and was being led by police to the prosecutor's office, when she made a suicide attempt by jumping from a third story window (*Miami Herald* 1997).

REFERENCES

Austin American-Statesman (1996), "Police: Dye took drugs, then raped," September 3.

Austin American-Statesman (1997) "Dye gets request for life sentence," September 12.

Burgess, A. and Hazelwood, R. (eds) (1995), *Practical Aspects of Rape Investigation*, 2nd edn, Boca Raton: CRC Press.

CNN (1997) "Iranian Murderer Publicly Whipped and Hanged," August 13.

Gauteng Sunday Times (1998) "Accused killer 'believed he was on divine mission'," July 19.

Keppel, R. (1989) *Serial Murder: Future Implications for Police Investigators*, Cincinnati: Anderson Publishing Co.

Los Angeles Times (1998) "Rapist Sentenced to 157 Years to Life," March 28.

Miami Herald (1997) "Nurse confesses to killing 18 patients," August 17.

Ressler, R. (1992) *Whoever Fights Monsters*, New York: St. Martin's Press.

San Francisco Chronicle (1998) "Anti-Abortion Activist Pleads Guilty in Clinic Fires 4 states hit in 3-year arson spree," February 11.

Sydney Morning Herald (1998) "Accused serial killer dies of heart attack," February 23.

CHAPTER 25

CYBERPATTERNS: CRIMINAL BEHAVIOR ON THE INTERNET

Eoghan Casey, M.A.

INTERNET ACTIVITY AS BEHAVIOR

William Gibson coined the phrase "cyberspace" in his novel *Neuromancer* (Gibson 1984), to describe a global computer network similar to, but far more advanced than, the Internet. As suggested by the title, the tone of *Neuromancer* is sinister and the general message is that technology is dangerous, even deadly. Today, the term cyberspace has become synonymous with the Internet, and many people try to create the illusion that old and ordinary concepts are fresh, mysterious, and somewhat dangerous by appending the word *cyber* to them. The truth is that the same criminal motivations and behaviors have been around for centuries, regardless of new terms like *cybercrime, cybertrails, cyberstalkers*, etc. that we use to describe them. Computer and Internet crime is nothing more than the same old criminal behavior with a high-tech *modus operandi*.

> The Net is not populated by a new set of people. Everyone using the Net is deeply entrenched in the land-based world, and sharing heritage of thousands of years of land-based cultural and social development. We bring history with us when we go on-line. Whether we view our heritage as an asset or as wasteful baggage, groups of people instinctively erect their acculturated understandings all around them in the Net. As a result, legal scenarios on-line will look very, very familiar to those of us who have spent any time in the physical world (Rose 1994).

This is not to say that the Internet is a trivial matter to criminals or investigators. The Internet facilitates a wide range of criminal activity and can be very useful as an investigative tool. Individuals use the Internet to purchase goods, meet and communicate with others, exchange information, and much more. Consequently, the Internet contains a vast amount of information about people. As well as containing some addresses, phone numbers, social-security numbers, and credit-card numbers, the Internet records many of our actions and words. An individual's thoughts, choices, interests and desires can be inferred from his/her actions and words. Thus, by recording individuals' actions and words, the Internet has become an archive of individuals' behaviors. Marketers, stalkers, investigators, criminal profilers, and anyone else who wants to learn more about an individual, will find this behavioral archive to be very useful.

Marketers have been cashing in on the behavioral archive aspect of the Internet for some time now. For example, when a customer purchases a book from Amazon.com, the online book and music store at http://www.amazon.com, other books that might interest the customer are recommended. These recommendations are, in part, based on other customers' preferences and decisions, making initial generalizations and thus taking an inductive approach. Amazon.com and other sites also keep track of their customers on an individual basis by making a note of each choice that an individual makes, creating a raw record of behavior. Ideally, marketers are trying to create a personalized profile of each customer using a rough combination of inductive and deductive inferences about behavior, and though they probably do not use the techniques espoused in this book, they obviously do well enough to justify the extra effort of creating such profiles. This might seem like a mammoth task, but computers make this type of information storage, retrieval, and manipulation quite manageable.

Investigators, including criminal profilers, can take advantage of the behavioral-archive aspect of the Internet in a slightly more advanced but less automated way, using information gathered during the deductive profiling process to direct and focus searches. An investigator, equipped with information about victimology, MO and signature, can search for connected evidence and similar cases. Some rudimentary but helpful profiling tools already exist, such as the one provided by Dejanews, the Usenet archive at http://www.dejanews.com. This tool simply lists all messages posted by a specified individual thus giving an investigator information about the individual's behavior. However, this tool uses a simple algorithm and will not find messages posted by the same individual under another name or e-mail address. While there are many other clever programs that can make an investigator's work easier, they are all limited in some way. Investigators and profilers should use convenience programs with full awareness that they cannot substitute for solid investigative and profiling work.

The fact that the Internet contains so much personal information about individuals makes it a very attractive tool for criminals as well. Most criminals require information about their targets and the more detailed and personal the information is the better. Stalkers, for example, use the Internet to gather information about their victims, monitor their victims' activities, and communicate with their victims. There have also been several recent homicide and rape cases in which offenders have communicated with their victims using the Internet. Why and how the Internet was used can tell a profiler a great deal about both the offender and victim. Additionally, by recording the interactions between offenders and victims, the Internet gives investigators a rare insight into offender–victim interaction. In the past, few crimes enabled investigators to witness offender–victim interaction first-hand. Depending on second-hand accounts, especially interviews with offenders, is a poor substitute for full recordings of conversations and exchanges. Having access to an offender's interactions with a victim will enhance the profile at hand and can improve an investigator's general understanding of offender–victim interaction.

One of the main limitations of the Internet as a behavioral archive is that it only has the latest version of information. Thus, if a Web page is changed or someone retracts a Usenet post, the old information is usually lost. This limitation of Internet archives could change in the near future. Alexa Internet (http://www.alexa.com) is archiving and cataloging information on the Web and in Usenet to create a repository that contains past as well as current information. However, until such comprehensive archives are well established, the only reliable way to observe an individual's Internet behavior change over time is to monitor that individual continuously. Another implication of the Internet's transience is that it cannot be assumed that evidence will remain on the Internet for any duration, so it should be collected as quickly as possible.

It is important to note that there are activities on the Internet that are not automatically archived. Though transient, these activities contain a wealth of behavioral information about the individuals who are involved. For instance, the Internet supports live interaction, enabling individuals to converse with each other and exchange information in real-time. Though it takes more effort to be in the right place at the right time, witnessing live interactions can greatly benefit an investigation or profile. With training and practice investigators and criminal profilers can fully realize the potential of the Internet as a source of archived and live behavioral evidence.

INTERNET SERVICES

A basic knowledge of the Internet and criminal activity on the Internet is a prerequisite to understanding how criminal profiling applies to the Internet and how investigators and profilers can use the Internet as a source of evidence. Though there are thousands of programs that allow people to navigate the Internet in many different ways, the process of understanding the Internet can be simplified by considering its four main services:

- Electronic mail (e-mail);

- Newsgroups;
- Synchronous Chat;
- World Wide Web (the Web or WWW).

It is worth noting that the following summary of Internet services does not include Bulletin Board Systems (BBS). (For an extended discussion of investigating BBS, read *Investigating Computer Crime* by Clark and Diliberto (1996).) Nor does it include value-added networks like America Online. (Value-added networks offer their customers a range of services including access to the Internet. The line between value-added networks and Internet Service Providers (ISPs) is becoming less distinct over time. Therefore, value-added networks do not warrant a separate discussion.) Both have many capabilities that are similar to those of the Internet but they are not Internet services.

E-MAIL

E-mail, as the name suggests, is a service that enables people to send electronic messages to each other. Provided a message is correctly addressed, it will be delivered through cables and computers to the addressee's personal electronic mailbox. Every e-mail message has a header that contains information about its origin and receipt. It is often possible to track e-mail back to its source and potentially identify the sender using the information in e-mail headers. Even if a header is forged it can contain information that identifies the sender. For example, though this header was forged to misdirect prying individuals, it still contains information about the sender, ec30@is4.nyu.edu.

> Received: from NYU.EDU by is4.nyu.edu; (5.65v3.2/1.1.8.2/26Mar96-0600PM) id AA08502; Sun, 6 Jul 1997 21:22:35 -0400
>
> Received: from comet.connix.com by cmcl2.NYU.EDU (5.61/1.34) id AA14047; Sun, 6 Jul 97 21:22:33 -0400
>
> Received: from tara.eire.gov (ec30@IS4.NYU.EDU [128.122.253.137]) by comet.connix.com (8.8.5/8.8.5) with SMTP id VAA01050 for <eoghan.casey@nyu.edu>; Sun, 6 Jul 1997 21:21:05 -0400 (EDT)
>
> Date: Sun, 6 Jul 1997 21:21:05 -0400 (EDT)
>
> Message-Id: <199707070121.VAA01050@comet.connix.com>
>
> From: fionn@eire.gov
>
> To: achilles@thessaly.gov
>
> Subject: Arrangements for Thursday's battle: spears or swords

It takes training and practice to learn how to identify the sender of an e-mail message and there is no single reliable method. However, learning how to read e-mail headers and becoming fluent with the tools used to track e-mail will enable investigators and profilers to adapt their approach to each message that they encounter. Useful tracking tools include finger, ph, whois and traceroute. It is also helpful to have a solid understanding of Telnet and the Standard Mail Transfer Protocol (SMTP).

Despite the identifying information that e-mail contains, it is one of the most important vehicles for criminal activity. E-mail offers a high level of privacy, especially when encryption is used, making it difficult to determine if e-mail is being used to commit or facilitate a crime. Though an e-mail message can be intercepted at many points along its journey or collected from an individual's computer, personal e-mail is usually protected by strict privacy laws, making it more difficult to obtain than other forms of evidence. Even if investigators can obtain incriminating e-mail, it can be difficult to prove that a specific individual sent a specific message.

NEWSGROUPS

Newsgroups are the online equivalent of public bulletin boards, enabling asynchronous communication that often resembles a discussion. Anyone with Internet access can post a message on these bulletin boards and come back later to see if anyone has replied. Most newsgroups are part of a free, global system called the User's Network (Usenet) that began in 1979. As was mentioned before, individuals' thoughts, choices, interests and desires can be inferred from their words and actions on the Internet and this is especially true of Usenet. For example:

Subject: >>>>Wanna Buy My Worn...Pantyhose...and Panties????
From: nancyc544@aol.com (NancyC544)
Date: 1996/05/15
Message-ID: 4nduca$2j4@newsbf02.news.aol.com
Newsgroups: alt.pantyhose
organization: America Online, Inc. (1-800-827-6364)
reply-to: nancyc544@aol.com (NancyC544)
sender: root@newsbf02.news.aol.com
Hi! My name is Nancy. I am 25, have Blonde hair, green eyes am 5'6 and weigh 121. Is anyone out there interested in buying my worn...pantyhose...or....panties? This is not a joke or a wacky internet scam. I am very serious about this. I live in the U.S. but I can ship them anywhere in the world. If you are serious you can e-mail me at: nancyc544@aol.com

There are archives, like Dejanews (http://www.dejanews.com), which contain millions of messages from tens of thousands of newsgroups. These archives are invaluable tools for criminal profilers because they contain a vast amount of detailed information about individuals and their interactions. However, these archives are not comprehensive and should not be depended on completely when dealing with Usenet. Few archives include message attachments and anyone can specify that they do not want their postings to be archived. Any newsgroup posting with "x-no-archive: yes" as its first line will be ignored by archiving software. Also, there are newsgroups that are not a part of Usenet and are not archived. Therefore, it is important for investigators and profilers to become involved in the actual newsgroups rather than depend on the archives.

Like e-mail, newsgroup messages have headers containing information about the sender and the journey that the message took. However, the format of the headers in newsgroups is slightly different from e-mail. As with e-mail, the sender can modify the header to make it more difficult to identify him/her. With training and practice investigators and profilers can learn to extract a great deal of information from newsgroups.

SYNCHRONOUS CHAT NETWORKS

By connecting to a synchronous chat network, individuals can interact in real-time using text, audio, video and more. Most synchronous chat networks comprise chat rooms, sometimes called *channels*, where people with similar interests gather.

Channel	Users	Topic
#0!!!!!pre-teens	12	Children Pics! Children Pics! Children Pics! Children Pi
#00teenpics	9	Type !jarm for a fserver with no ratios!! Unlimited
#gayteenboyz	7	Join the LUV channel. Theres NOBODY i LUV more than JEREI
#gayteeninages	6	FSERVES HOT Pix, Avis, Stories NO KIDDIE PORN!!!
#klang-teens	5	|!8*'~'`~'*8!||!8*'~'`~'*8!| cum in and cum here !! |!8*
#Malaysian-Teens	2	
#teens	41	Go to www.manifest1.com/indigo98/ to get Indigo '98 ▌- ▌
#teens_and_stuff	3	COME ON IN!!!!NO RULES!
#teensex	23	anything but a topic with omens name in it
#teenside	2	I did and i had a great time!!!!!!!
#teenskaters	5	Teenskaters - the broken finger support group

Figure 25.1

A listing of several channels on IRC

Internet Relay Chat (IRC) and I Seek You (ICQ) are currently the most widely used synchronous chat networks (in April 1998, ICQ had ten million users) (see Figure 25.1). America Online has a substantial chat network but this is separate from the Internet and is only available to its subscribers. There are also several chat networks that allow individuals to create three-dimensional representations of themselves and wander through a three-dimensional environment, meeting and chatting with others. Some of these aspiring virtual reality networks even allow users to add to the environment much like the older, text-based Multi User Domains (MUDs).

On IRC, ICQ and many other chat networks such as AOL's, investigators can find some basic information about an individual using tracking tools and techniques. However, many chat networks enable people to create their own private areas and some chat programs allow users to initiate a direct connection with each other, bypassing the chat network altogether. Therefore, much of the information on chat networks is transient and sometimes difficult to find. To access this information, investigators and profilers must develop a solid understanding of the Internet, the chat network being used, and the search features built into the chat network.

The privacy, immediacy, and impermanence of synchronous chat networks make them particularly conducive to criminal activity; predators can obtain victims immediately without leaving a trace of evidence. This, in turn, makes synchronous chat networks a valuable investigative tool. Investigators and profilers can learn a surprising amount from the activities in the multitudes of online chat rooms.

THE WEB

The Web first became publicly available in 1991 and has become so popular that it is often mistakenly referred to as the Internet. This mistake is not surprising since many older Internet services including e-mail, Usenet, and synchronous chat networks, are now accessible through the Web. The popularity and rapid growth of the Web is mainly due to its commercial potential. Using the Web, organizations and individuals alike make information and commodities available to anyone in the world. As always, criminals go where the money is, and as the Web becomes more widely used to make monetary transactions, the associated criminal activities grow. Some criminals use the Web to disseminate information to, and communicate with, fellow criminals. For example, there are an increasing number of recipes for illegal substances on the Web. Also, the Web contains a large amount of information about criminal activity including fraud, abuse and homicide.

Because the Web contains so much loosely ordered information, searching for something in particular can be like looking for a needle in a haystack. This is why it is crucial to learn how to effectively search the Web. Search engines, like AltaVista (http://altavista.digital.com) and Hotbot (http://www.hotbot.com) are the most useful tools for finding information on the Web (see Figure 25.2). Though search engines are not especially difficult to use, there is some skill involved. Each search engine has different contents, archiving methods, and search features. Getting to know which search engines are best for which types of searches will greatly improve a profiler's ability to search the Web. There are many other search tools and topic specific databases on the Web that can be useful in certain cases.

It is prudent to use a specific search method when searching for information on the Web. For example, one approach is to start by searching broadly to get an overview and a sense of the common terminology and slang. Gradually narrow the search to get a more refined sense of the most pertinent words and phrases. Next, make another broad search using the highly pertinent words and phrases. Continue this process until leads are exhausted. Another approach is to initially make several broad searches, noting possible leads.

Figure 25.2

Searching the Web for unsolved homicides using Altavista

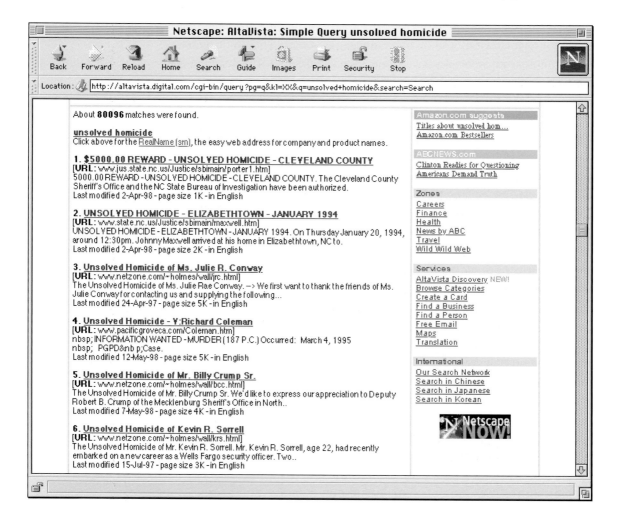

After completing the broad search, follow each lead independently. The approach chosen depends on what is being searched for. Be assured that training and practice will greatly improve search results.

CYBERCRIME: CRIME AND THE INTERNET

The Internet can play a role in any type of crime including homicide, rape, abduction, child abuse, solicitation of minors, child pornography, stalking, harassment, fraud, theft, drug trafficking, computer intrusions, espionage, and terrorism. However, there are two basic ways that the Internet can be a part of a crime or criminal investigation. We either become aware of a crime via the Internet and our investigation leads to further evidence in the physical world, or we become aware of a crime in the physical world and our investigation leads to further evidence on the Internet (see Figure 25.3).

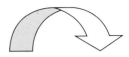

Physical world   Internet

Figure 25.3
Physical world/Internet interaction

PHYSICAL WORLD → INTERNET

On April 22, 1996 in Greenfield, California a woman contacted the local police and reported that her six-year-old daughter had been molested during a slumber party by Ronald Riva, the father of the host. Additionally, a 10-year-old girl at the party reported that Riva and his friend, Melton Myers used a computer to record her as she posed for them. Riva and Myers led investigators into an international ring of child abusers and pornographers that convened in an Internet chat room called the Orchid Club. Sixteen men from Finland, Canada, Australia, and the United States were charged. One log of an Orchid Club chat session indicated that Riva and Myers were describing their actions to other members of the club as they abused the 10-year-old girl.

Their investigation into the Orchid Club led law enforcement to a larger group of child pornographers and pedophiles called the Wonderland Club. After more than two years of following leads, police in fourteen countries arrested over 200 members of Wonderland, in the largest coordinated effort to crack down on child exploitation and abuse to date. Evidence gathered during this latest effort suggests that there are members of the Wonderland Club in more than 40 countries, so the investigation is by no means over.

INTERNET → PHYSICAL WORLD

In February 1998 a man posted pictures on Usenet of himself having sex with his 10-year-old daughter. The FBI contacted the man's Internet service provider, obtained his name and address in San Diego, and arrested him.

CASE EXAMPLES AND DISCUSSIONS

The following is a demonstrative sampling of the varied ways in which the Internet has been involved in crimes and is not intended to be an exhaustive classification of Internet crime.

HOMICIDE

The Internet has facilitated homicides, has been used to track down suspected murders, and has been used to collect additional evidence in homicide cases. In one case, a man is accused of mailing a pipe bomb that killed 17-year-old Christopher Marquis after their Internet business transaction went awry. In another case, police used a suspected murderer's e-mail messages to track him down to a computer in a public library.

As another example, in October 1997 a Maryland woman named Sharon Lopatka traveled to North Carolina to meet her killer; Robert Glass. Lopatka's husband informed police that she was missing and provided them with e-mail messages between his wife and Glass. There were hundreds of messages between Lopatka and Glass about their torture and death fantasies. The contents of the e-mail led investigators to Glass, and to Lopatka's shallow grave near Glass' trailer. Lopatka's hands and feet had been tied and she had been strangled. Glass' attorney claims that Glass killed Lopatka accidentally during sex.

In another homicide case, involving arson, the Internet played several roles in the investigation. On March 22, 1998 in his e-mail based support group, Larry Froistad made the following confession about killing his five-year-old daughter, Amanda three years before:

> My God, there's something I haven't mentioned, but it's a very important part of the equation. The people I'm mourning the loss of, I've ejected from my life. Kitty had to endure my going to jail twice and being embarrassed in front of her parents. Amanda I murdered because her mother stood between us... I let her watch the videos she loved all evening, and when she was asleep I got wickedly drunk, set our house on fire, went to bed, listened to her scream twice, climbed out the window and set about putting on a show of shock, surprise and grief to remove culpability from myself. Dammit, part of that show was climbing in her window and grabbing her pajamas, then hearing her breathe and dropping her where she was so she could die and rid me of her mother's interferences.

Froistad, a 29-year-old computer programmer, was arrested and extradited from California to North Dakota. He apparently confessed again while in police custody. However, upon mature reflection, Froistad pleaded innocent to the charge of murder, a charge that can lead to life imprisonment but not execution since North Dakota does not have a death penalty. His lawyers have argued that someone else could have sent the e-mail messages and that he was mentally ill. While investigating Froistad's other Internet activities, the FBI found that he had traded child pornography and admitted to sexually abusing his daughter. This additional evidence could change the charge to sexual exploitation of a minor ending in the victim's death – a charge that could lead to a death sentence.

RAPE

There have been several cases in which online associations have led to rape. In one case the offender obtained the victim's phone number and address and raped her in her home. In most cases however, the victim was lured into a meeting and was subsequently raped by the offender.

Oliver Jovanovic, a graduate student at Colombia University, was charged with kidnapping and sexually abusing, on November 22, 1996, a female student that he befriended over the Internet. There are many e-mail messages that indicate that Jovanovic and the victim communicated with one another. These e-mail messages are a rich source of verbal behavior evidence. Though Jovanovic and his family still protest his innocence, he was accused of arranging a meeting with the victim through e-mail, inviting her back to his apartment to watch videos, tying her legs to a chair, gagging her, biting her, burning her with candle wax, sodomizing her with a baton, and threatening to dismember her.

CHILD SOLICITATION, ABUSE AND PORNOGRAPHY

It is no secret that there are national and international pedophile rings that operate independently of the Internet and it should be no surprise that these rings use the Internet. None the less, the amount of evidence of child abuse on the Internet has astonished the most veteran crime fighters, as has the number of pedophile rings using the Internet.

Of course, not all pedophiles operate in groups. There are many individuals who solicit minors using the Internet. In one case involving a minor (April 1997), 13-year-old Jessica Woehl was found with Keir Devon Fiore, a 22-year-old man whom she had met in an online chat room, three weeks after she went missing. Fiore, who persuaded Woehl to run away with him, was charged with crossing state lines to engage in sex with a minor. In another case, Richard Romero was charge with kidnapping a 13-year-old boy with the intent to engage in sexual activity. Romero befriended the boy on the Internet, initially posing as a young boy himself. Romero persuaded the boy to meet him at a Chicago hotel and travel with him to St. Petersburg. After the boy's mother alerted police of her son's absence, a taxi driver reported driving Romero and the boy to a bus station and investigators were able to arrest Romero before he and the boy reached their destination. The FBI found child pornography on

Romero's computer and evidence to suggest that Romero frequently befriended young boys on the Internet.

CYBERSTALKING AND HARASSMENT

Cyberstalking works in much the same way as stalking in the physical world. In fact, many offenders combine their online activities with more traditional forms of stalking and harassment such as telephoning the victim and going to the victim's home. Stalking is often accompanied by harassment. Harassment consists of persistently irritating or tormenting another person. The motive is often revenge for perceived wrongs or can simply be to terrorize a person in an effort to feel powerful. Harassment ranges from one angry e-mail message to persistent terrorism and threats. Harassment sometimes escalates and has led to homicides and other very tangible, physical-world crimes. Some harassers put personal information about their victims on the Internet, encouraging others to contact the victim.

FRAUD AND THEFT

Fraud is loosely defined as deception deliberately practiced in order to secure unfair or unlawful gain. The motive of fraud and theft is almost always profit. The anonymity and large number of "marks" on the Internet make it an attractive place for con artists because there is a low risk of being caught and a high potential gain. Theft of computer components, data, credit card numbers, and other valuable information is also profit motivated.

COMPUTER INTRUSIONS, ESPIONAGE, AND TERRORISM

Many organizations, including government agencies, use the Internet to communicate and do business with others. Thus, individuals who can intrude upon these computer transactions can obtain money, confidential information, or can interfere with the organization's operations. For example, a man from Sweden disabled a 911 emergency call system in Florida for an hour, crippling the networks responsible for speedy responses by police, fire and ambulances. The man did all of this from his computer in Sweden. The United States government has recognized the potential threat that computer intrusion poses and has declared that it is a national security risk. Though there have not yet been any serious incidents, the concern is that spies and terrorists will try to obtain confidential information or disrupt important systems like power stations and satellite networks.

FOLLOWING THE CYBERTRAIL

In the Wild West of North America, posses of deputized citizens led by sheriffs and marshals followed the trails and physical signs of passing left behind by outlaws. Modern investigators have come to understand and follow a criminal's paper trail, in the form of invoices, policies, and records that each leaves behind as evidence of their passing. With the advent and popularity of the Internet, investigators have a new trail to follow. Let us jump on the cyberbandwagon and call it the *cybertrail*. Think of the cybertrail as an additional source of evidence – *digital evidence*. (For the purposes of this discussion, let us define digital evidence as any and all information in binary form (made of 1s and 0s) that can establish that a crime has been committed or can provide a link between a crime and its victim or a crime and its perpetrator.) The cybertrail can include but is not limited to Web pages, Usenet messages, e-mail, digitized still images, digitized video, digitized audio, digital logs of synchronous chat sessions, files stored on a personal computer, and computer logs from an Internet Service Provider (ISP).

The cybertrail is an additional source of evidence. It is both an extension of crime scenes in the real world, and a digital crime scene in itself. If a crime occurs in the physical world and there is a computer with Internet access at the crime scene, search the computer and Internet for related digital evidence. Similarly, if a crime is first witnessed or recorded on the Internet, collect all relevant digital evidence on the Internet and, if possible, determine the physical locations of the primary computers involved and treat those locations as crime scenes (obtain search warrants, gather physical and digital evidence, etc.). In some cases it might not be obvious that the cybertrail holds key evidence. If investigators and profilers neglect to follow the cybertrail, they not only risk losing valuable evidence; they also risk being held liable for their negligence.

Even if investigators and profilers are not responsible for collecting evidence from the Internet in a given case, they should have a basic understanding of what digital evidence can exist so that they will be attuned to the possibility that it is missing. For example, in the case of a cyberstalker, e-mail sent to the victim often holds the key to the stalker's identity. The stalker's computer will usually contain relevant digital evidence. If the stalker's computer does not contain any related evidence, perhaps it was deleted. Fortunately, in many cases, deleted digital evidence can be recovered. However, if an investigator or criminal profiler does not know this, evidence that is key to developing a profile could be lost.

Guidelines for following the cybertrail are provided here to give a general idea of what is involved when searching for digital evidence related to a given crime. These guidelines are not intended to be comprehensive procedures and cannot substitute for thorough training.

DOCUMENT THE SEARCH

> Continuity of possession, or chain of custody, must be established whenever evidence is presented in court as an exhibit. Adherence to standard procedures in recording the location evidence, marking it for identification, and properly completing evidence submission forms for laboratory analysis are the best guarantee that the evidence will withstand inquiries of what happened to it from the time of its finding to its presentation in court (Saferstein 1998).

When collecting digital evidence, it is crucial to defend it against the most common criticisms that it will receive: is it reliable and was it obtained legally? Many individuals consider digital evidence to be less reliable than physical evidence because it can be changed in such a way that the change is undetectable. Also, because digital evidence is relatively new, few investigators are fully aware of all of the legal issues surrounding digital evidence. When in doubt about any stage of following the cybertrail, consult with experts and err on the side of caution. "Make sure your legal advisor is available to help with the legal challenges you will face and that your management understands what you are doing and supports the endeavour" (Clark and Diliberto 1996).

- Maintain a chronological list of dates, times, programs and services used, and actions taken during search.

- Collect and protect digital evidence according to standard procedures. Consider photographing, videotaping, capturing, and printing the evidence using screen captures or automatic logging utilities. This process of collecting the same evidence in multiple ways will enable cross comparison. If anyone wants to verify that one form of evidence has not been altered (the log file for example) they can look at the other forms (like the video).

- Make a note of important information and possible leads – it is easy to forget where the needle was in the haystack.

- Keep a list of possible aliases. Many people have (or have had) multiple Internet accounts and Internet aliases, especially individuals who want to protect their true identity.

- Keep a list of possible Internet acquaintances. If a search fails to turn up anything on one individual, following the activities of acquaintances can lead to relevant information.

- When searching for information about an offender, note any indications of employment, skill level, education, hobbies, personal interests, relationship status, unusual or repeated verbal behaviors, level of planning and forethought, precautionary acts and any other potentially individuating information. Also, note potential MO and signature behaviors.

- When searching for information about a victim, note any information that is relevant to victimology.

SEARCH THE WEB

■ Use search engines, directories, utilities, and other methods for finding information on the Web. Search for real names, nicknames, e-mail addresses and segments of e-mail addresses. Some people protect themselves by using computer-smart nicknames such as En0chIan instead of Enochian. The zero instead of an "o" and the pipe (I) instead of an "i" confound search algorithms. In such cases, clever searches are required and information about victimology, MO, and signature become particularly important. Also, if the offender has a distinctive user name, search for variations of that name (e.g. cobra12; Cobra_12).

■ Look for Web sites/pages, FTP sites, Web-based discussion groups, and mailing-list archives that might attract the offender or victim. Use what is known about victimology, MO, and signature to focus such searches.

■ Look for mention of private Web sites, FTP sites, discussion groups, newsgroups, mailing lists, BBS, and chat channels.

■ Search for possible Internet acquaintances.

SEARCH NEWSGROUPS

■ Search Usenet archives for real names, nicknames, e-mail addresses and segments of e-mail addresses. Search for computer-smart nicknames and simple variations of e-mail addresses and nicknames.

■ Monitor areas that would attract the offender, as determined in the threshold assessment. For example, if the offender has a torture fantasy, look in newsgroups that feed into the torture fantasies. As another example, if the offender targets young victims, look in newsgroups that attract youth.

■ Participate in discussions when necessary to learn more about possible suspects.

■ Try to establish and/or verify the identity of possible suspects. This can involve examining message headers, performing another search of the Web, and looking into synchronous chat activities. Use what is known about victimology, MO, and signature to direct and focus these searches. Consider contacting the suspect's ISP with a court order to obtain identifying information.

SEARCH SYNCHRONOUS CHAT NETWORKS

■ Larger chat networks have limited search utilities. Search for real names, nicknames, full e-mail addresses and segments of e-mail addresses. Whenever possible search for unusual interests, and use what is known about victimology, MO, and signature.

■ Monitor areas that would attract the offender, as determined in the threshold assessment. Attempt to blend in. Even consider playing a role that will attract the offender but avoid doing anything that could be construed as entrapment.

■ Thoroughly document all activities and interactions that occur, especially when conversing directly with possible suspects. The easiest way to do this is using the automatic logging features available in many chat programs. However, consider videotaping and taking screen captures during important sessions.

- Try to establish and/or verify the identity of possible suspects using non-intrusive methods. This can include a Web and Usenet search and the use of utilities like dnslookup, traceroute, whois, and finger. A more intrusive way of establishing the identity of a suspect is to contact his/her ISP with a court order.

SEARCH PERSONAL COMPUTERS FOR INTERNET ACTIVITY

Collecting evidence from a personal computer is not a trivial matter, either technically or legally. Investigators should not attempt to search or seize a personal computer without proper authorization and training.

- Examine the area surrounding the computer for Internet account information like passwords, e-mail addresses, bills from an ISP, dial-up phone numbers, etc.

- Examine the area surrounding the computer for storage media such as magnetic tapes, floppy discs, compact disks, etc. These storage media can contain Internet applications and information that can shed light on how the owner uses the Internet. Keep in mind that books can indicate how the owner uses the Internet and that videocassette recorders can be attached to computers to digitize video and store video clips on cassettes.

- Make a note of all Internet related programs on the computer. Applications that are used most regularly should be noted since they can provide the strongest indications of the skill level and activities of the user.

- Examine all applications for Internet account information like passwords, e-mail addresses, billing information, dial-up phone numbers. Also look for information about Internet acquaintances such as e-mail addresses, user names, etc.

- Examine the Web browser's bookmarks, cache and history. Also look through cookies for information about which sites were accessed.

- Look for newsgroup activity (e.g. which newsgroups had been subscribed to, any messages that were saved).

- Look for synchronous chat programs and any associated information (e.g. log files, user names, default server).

- Search for files that are commonly transmitted using the Internet such as executable programs and digitized photographs/video clips.

- If there is an indication that relevant information is being stored on other computer systems, those computer systems should be searched. Again, investigators should not attempt such a search without proper authorization and training.

THOROUGHLY EXAMINE E-MAIL

E-mail is usually stored on an individual's computer or on an e-mail server. In either case, retrieving e-mail can be an involved process, both technically and legally. Therefore, investigators should not attempt to retrieve e-mail without proper authorization and training.

- Determine if any part of the e-mail header is forged. If the header was modified, try to determine if the modification was MO or signature oriented. Was it necessary to commit the crime or not?

- Attempt to identify the source of the e-mail message using the information in the header.
- Examine the contents of messages for information about the offender including MO and/or signature behaviors.
- Examine the contents of messages for information about the victim.

CRIMINAL PROFILING AND THE INTERNET

It should be clear at this point that the cybertrail is a useful source of evidence when developing a criminal profile. It might be less clear, however, how criminal profiling can help investigators follow the cybertrail (see Figure 25.4).

Because the Internet is so vast and allows various levels of anonymity, it can be very difficult to find the perpetrator(s) of, and digital evidence relating to, a specific crime. Deductive criminal profiling is an ideal tool in this situation since its primary purpose is to assist in the process of moving from a universal set to a unique set of related suspect behaviors and characteristics. For instance, a profile can help investigators understand an offender's behavior and can give them a better sense of where he will go and what he will do to fulfill his motives and fantasies. In other words, a profile can help narrow a search. The type of focus that a criminal profile can provide is useful in any investigation but it is invaluable when the Internet is involved.

Profiling   Cybertrail

Figure 25.4
Profiling/cybertrail interaction

Also, criminal profiling can be useful for developing investigative strategies. If investigators get an opportunity to interact with a suspect in an Internet chat room, these strategies can be very helpful. For example, one investigative strategy might be to pose as a young girl. Provided investigators make no attempt to entrap a suspect, such encounters with suspects can be very helpful to a case, generating new leads in an investigation and/or providing new inputs for a profile. As new inputs are found on the cybertrail, they should be used to refine a profile and as the profile is refined, more refined searches of the cybertrail should be made. After all, criminal profiling is a dynamic process and not a static result.

Past efforts to apply criminal profiling to crimes involving computer networks have taken a heavily inductive approach and therefore have given quite static results. For example, the Computer Crime Adversarial Matrix (Icove *et al.* 1995), first developed for the FBI, is the result of applying inductive criminal profiling to a selection of computer crimes including fraud, espionage, computer intrusion, data theft, and vandalism. The matrix uses past cases to draw generalizations about computer crackers (groups and individuals), computer criminals (espionage and fraud/abuse) and vandals (strangers and users). The generalizations are grouped into four categories of characteristics: organizational, operational, behavioral and resource.

ORGANIZATIONAL CHARACTERISTICS			
CATEGORIES OF OFFENDERS	ORGANIZATION	RECRUITMENT/ATTRACTION	INTERNATIONAL CONNECTIONS
CRACKERS			
Groups	Unstructured organization with counterculture orientation.	Peer group attraction.	Interact and correspond with other groups around the world.
Individuals	None; these people are true loners.	Attracted by intellectual challenge.	Subscribe to cracker journals and may interact on cracker bulletin boards.
CRIMINALS			
Espionage	Supported by hostile intelligence services.	In most cases, money; some cases of ideological attraction; attention.	Use computer networks to break into target computers around the world.
Fraud/Abuse	May operate as small organized crime group or as a loner.	Money; power.	Use wire services to transfer money internationally.
VANDALS			
Strangers	Loner or small group. May be quite young.	Revenge; intellectual challenge; money.	Use of computer networks and phone systems to break into target computers.
Users	Often employee or former employee.	Revenge; power; intellectual challenge; disgruntlement.	None

Figure 25.5

Computer Crime Adversarial Matrix.

Reprinted with permission from Icove et al. (1995) Computer Crime, © 1995 O'Reilly & Associates, Inc. *For orders and information call 800-998-9938.*

OPERATIONAL CHARACTERISTICS			
CATEGORIES OF OFFENDERS	PLANNING	LEVEL OF EXPERTISE	TACTICS/METHODS USED
CRACKERS			
Groups	May involve detailed planning.	High	Enter target computer via computer networks. Exchange information with other crackers and groups.
Individuals	Study networks before attempts are made.	Medium to high. Experience gained through social networks.	Use networks but more likely to use trial and error online than to do careful research and planning. Use BBS's to share accounts on other systems.
CRIMINALS			
Espionage	Same characteristics as crackers.	High	May contract with crackers to conduct information and data collection.
Fraud/Abuse	Careful planning prior to crime.	Medium to high, although is typically more experienced at fraud than at computer programming.	May use more traditional intrusion methods such as wiretapping and trap doors. Will break into systems using basic methods.
VANDALS			
Strangers	Not much planning. More crime of opportunity.	Varies	Looks around until able to gain access to system.
Users	May involve detailed planning and execution.	Varies. May have high level of expertise.	Trap doors and Trojan horse programs. Data modification.

BEHAVIORAL CHARACTERISTICS			
CATEGORIES OF OFFENDERS	MOTIVATION	PERSONAL CHARACTERISTICS	POTENTIAL WEAKNESSES
CRACKERS			
Groups	Intellectual challenge; peer group fun; in support of a cause.	Highly intelligent individuals. Counterculture orientation.	Do not consider offenses crimes. Talk freely about actions.
Individuals	Intellectual challenge; problem solving;	Moderately to highly intelligent.	May keep notes and other documentation of actions.
CRIMINALS			
Espionage	Money and a chance to attack the system.	May be crackers operating in groups or as individuals.	Becomes greedy for more information and then becomes careless.
Fraud/Abuse	Money or other personal gain; power.	Same personal characteristics as other fraud offenders.	Becomes greedy and makes mistakes.
VANDALS			
Strangers	Intellectual challenge; money;	Same characteristics as crackers.	May become too brazen and make mistakes.
Users	Revenge against organization; problem solving; money.	Usually has some computer expertise.	May leave audit trail in computer logs.

RESOURCE CHARACTERISTICS			
CATEGORIES OF OFFENDERS	TRAINING SKILLS	MINIMUM EQUIPMENT NEEDED	SUPPORT STRUCTURE
CRACKERS			
Groups	High level of informal training.	Basic computer equipment with modem.	Peer group support.
Individuals	Expertise gained through experience.	Basic computer equipment with modem.	BBS; information exchanges.
CRIMINALS			
Espionage	Various levels of expertise.	Basic computer equipment with modem. In some cases, uses more sophisticated devices.	Support may come from sponsoring intelligence agency.
Fraud/Abuse	Some programming experience.	Computer with modem or access to target computer.	Peer group; possible organized crime enterprise.
VANDALS			
Strangers	Range from basic to highly skilled.	Basic computer equipment with modem.	Peer group support.
Users	Some computer expertise. Knowledge of programming ranges from basic to advanced.	Access to targeted computer.	None

This tool provides some insight into the general culture of certain criminal groups. However, the motives and behaviors detailed in this matrix are not clearly based in psychological research and a distinction is not made between MO and signature. Also, this matrix is inordinately self-referential and has the weaknesses of any inductive criminal-profiling result, dealing only in generalities. Generalities are of very limited use when trying to investigate a specific and unique crime. For example, in the case of espionage, the matrix indicates that the criminal is supported by hostile intelligence services, has a high level of computer expertise, uses computer networks to break into target computers around the world after careful planning, is motivated by profit or ideology, and might be a computer cracker or a group of computer crackers (two other offender categories in the matrix). So, a spy has no less than half of the characteristics mentioned in the matrix, including "Do not consider offenses crimes. Talk freely about actions." A very unusual criminal profile emerges – a spy who talks freely about his/her actions.

In all fairness, the matrix comes with the warning that it is meant to be used as an investigative tool, not as a definitive descriptive or predictive weapon and the "spy who talks freely" example is an obvious abuse of the matrix. However, this example does demonstrate the inherent problems in inductive criminal-profiling tools. Making generalizations about human behavior is a difficult business, often leading to unreliable results. Since investigators usually require specifics rather than generalizations, criminal profiles should contain specific conclusions, substantiated by evidence. Any generalization should be made with great care and extensive research or it is likely to be a hindrance in an investigation rather than help. The limitations of the Computer Crime Adversarial Matrix are to be expected at the early stages of development. The data that was used to develop the matrix could potentially be used to create some powerful motivational typologies with the help of psychologists, experienced investigators, and profilers.

So, past efforts to apply inductive criminal profiling to crimes involving networks have not been wildly successful. More success can be achieved using the deductive process described in this book because the resulting profiles are more thorough and contain specific conclusions, substantiated by evidence, that are related to the crime(s) at hand. The specific conclusions in a deductive profile are much more useful in an investigation, than the more general conclusions provided by inductive profiles that have been created using tools such as the Computer Crime Adversarial Matrix.

The deductive criminal-profiling process does not change simply because the Internet is involved. Many of the questions that a deductive criminal profiler would ask about physical world crimes can be adapted to apply to the cybertrail:

- Who frequently uses the Internet programs and services?
- Why did the offender choose those specific services or programs?
- When were the victim and/or offender using the Internet?
- Was there any ritual aspect to the crime?

Also, timelines of events surrounding a crime can be constructed to include all relevant Internet activities, digital crime scenes can be reconstructed and profiled, and offender profiles can incorporate information obtained from the cybertrail. In some cases, such as computer intrusion, determining what was changed, added, or taken will say a great deal about the offender.

The following sections describe in more detail some of the ways that the Internet can play a role in the deductive criminal-profiling process. For the sake of brevity, not all of the phases of the deductive profiling process are detailed here. However, since the deductive profiling process and the format of the final profile do not change when the Internet is involved, readers will have little difficulty applying the concepts in this chapter to all of the phases.

THRESHOLD ASSESSMENT

An important step in the deductive criminal-profiling process is to develop a threshold assessment. A threshold assessment generally comprises known patterns of behavior, established victimology, potential motives, and a few potential characteristics of the offender. A demonstrative case example is provided here.

A former bus driver, age 31, was arrested and accused of possessing sexually explicit photos of himself with a child. His computer and many photographs, magazines, and videos were seized. Searching the Internet showed that his nickname and e-mail user name was Zest. His Web page was simple but telling, depicting him topless in Arizona at age 23. He had also posted several messages to newsgroups offering to scan risqué photographs. The following is a representative post:

```
Subject:    *a_Will scan your Pic's
From:       Zest zest@oneworld.owt.com
Date:       1996/09/29
Message-ID:  324F1FAF.33B@oneworld.owt.com
Newsgroups: alt.sex.pedophilia.boys, alt.sex.pedophilia.girls,
alt.sex.pedophilia.pictures, alt.sex.pedophilia.swaps, alt.sex.phone, alt.sex.pictures,
alt.sex.pictures.d, alt.sex.pictures.female, alt.sex.pictures.male,
alt.sex.pictures.misc, alt.sex.plushies,alt.sex.pre-teens,alt.sex.prevost,
alt.sex.prevost.derbecker, alt.sex.prevost-derbecker,alt.sex.prom,
alt.sex.prostitution, alt.sex.raj.NOT, alt.sex.reptiles, alt.sex.safe, alt.sex.senator-
exon, alt.sex.services, alt.sex.sgml, alt.sex.sheep,
```

alt.sex.sheep.baaa.baaa.baaa.moo, alt.sex.skydiving.bondage, alt.sex.sm

Need a picture scanned? Nobady local to do it? Or the content is risky? I'm your man, I will scan your pic's for you. One dollar ($1) per pic, and postage, is all that it will cost you. I will save in formats of your choice. GIF, BMP, PCX, TGA, JPG, and TIFF. I'm also able to enlarge your original photo. All pictures are kept confidential.

Interested??? E-Mail me at the address below. I will reply to setup arranangements with you.

zest@owt.com

A sample threshold assessment based on the suspect's physical-world activities, Web page, and Usenet posts is provided here:

The Web page is likely a lure. The page depicts Leon half-naked and smiling in a remote outdoor location almost ten years ago. This suggests his youthful view of himself, as does his nickname of choice, "Zest." The Web page also refers to time spent in Arizona. Leon is a traveler. Look into trips he took by examining food, lodging and gas receipts, credit card records, and ATM transactions. Pull all of his phone records to find out who he was calling and when. Find out about his time in Arizona to determine if other victims exist. Check his criminal history there, and anywhere else that he lived. Also check his parent's house/properties for hidden items, as well as checking for storage facilities.

This is likely not a one-time occurrence. All of these elements indicate a long history of pedophilic fantasy and victim acquisition. That he is a bus driver is not coincidence. Being a bus driver gives him access to a victim population out of his own neighborhood/community. For him, the Internet appears to be a tool not necessarily for acquiring victims, but rather for soliciting sexually explicit images from private parties. He needs this material to feed his very strong pedophilic fantasies between "relationships" with young males. And it is not posed material, but privately created material. He specifically asks for risqué materials and suggestively illegal material in his advertisements to Usenet. These would have been sent directly to his account, as advertised, and his Internet Service Provider (ISP) would be the best source of information regarding messages he received (his incoming and outgoing e-mail might be stored on his ISP's system or even archived by his ISP).

Leon needs his real-life victims to be within travelling distance so that he can develop personal, emotional relationships with them. The Internet is only his means for fantasy development, enhancement, and transitory sustenance. The newsgroups he posted to tell us about the type of pornography he was hoping to acquire from private parties. These posts would not encourage potential victims to inquire, but rather are meant to get people to send him their private illegal pedophilic photos. In as much as this is true, this would also help him network with others who share his interests. There might have been a profit motivation at work here so that he could get into a network where he could sell the pornography that he created, and/or fantasy motive that would allow him to "trade in" to a group of pedophiles who share pornography.

Also, Leon believes that he is genuinely in consensual relationships with these children. He sees nothing about his behavior as criminal or exploitative. He believes that he is merely seizing the day, and that what he is doing benefits the children he exploits. His motive is not to physically harm his victims but to be loved and admired by them. He confuses his own identity with theirs, to an extent, projecting a childlike effect to them. An interview strategy that exploits these factors by being sympathetic to them will be successful in getting the most information from this suspect.

In summary, look for more victims in other locations, look for more evidence in other storage locations. Check for secret compartments under his house, under his parent's house, in attics and look for digital storage devices, negatives, proof sheets, and videos. Check local rental places and see if he rents video equipment.

VICTIMOLOGY

> The victim is the last person to witness the crime. If alive, the victim can tell a great deal about the crime. If the victim is deceased, however, the crime scene must tell the story. In either instance, the profiler should be as interested in the activities of the victim as in any element of the submitted packet of information accompanying the request for a profile. (Holmes 1996)

Victimology, including risk assessment, is key to understanding why the offender chose a specific victim and what risks the offender was willing to take to acquire that victim. Also, with known offenders, victimology can be significant to understanding motive and planning behavior. As a rule, victimology should include a thorough search of the cybertrail. It might not be obvious that a victim used the Internet and if a thorough Internet search is not performed, information that could drastically change victimology might be missed. Consider Sharon Lopatka, the woman who traveled from Maryland to North Carolina to meet her killer. Friends described Lopatka as a normal woman who loved children and animals. Lopatka's activities on the Internet give a very different impression, however. Lopatka was evidently interested in sex involving pain and torture. Victimology that did not include her Internet activities would have been incomplete, lacking the most relevant aspects of her character and would probably describe her as a low-risk victim when in fact she was quite a high-risk victim.

Remember that a major part of victimology is to look for possible links between the victim and offender. Consider the possibility that the offender communicated with the victim using the Internet, used the same Internet services as the victim, was from the same geographic location and/or had a similar schedule as the victim. Anything that has caused the offender to cross paths with the victim prior to a criminal investigation is significant. Determine if the victim has Web pages, posts to Usenet regularly, uses chat networks, and so on. Try to determine the what, why, where, how, and when of the victim's Internet activities by asking questions like:

- What did the victim do on the Internet?

- What did the victim get from the Internet that was not accessible otherwise?

- How did the victim access the Internet, e.g. their own account, parents' account, friend's account or stolen account?

- From where did the victim access the Internet, e.g. at home, work, a café or bar?

- Why did the victim pick that location to access the Internet, e.g. privacy, business, or to meet people face to face?

- What Internet services did the victim use and why?

- Did the victim try to make money on the Internet?

- Did the victim exhibit any behavior that sheds light on the victim's mental state, sexuality, lifestyle, intelligence, or self-image? For example, was the victim involved in abuse recovery newsgroups or mailing lists? If so, why?

- Are there discernable patterns in the victim's Internet activities that suggest habits or schedules?

Also, when reconstructing the period before the crime, include any Internet activity. If the victim did not use the Internet during that time, determine if that is unusual or significant. Whenever possible, individuals with whom the victim interacted on the Internet should be interviewed. Finally, try to make a risk assessment to get a better understanding of why the offender chose a specific victim and what risks the offender was willing to take to acquire that victim.

Risk assessment on the Internet works in the same way as in the physical world as the comparisons in Table 25.1 demonstrate.

Table 25.1

Risk assessment in the physical world and on the Internet.

RISK	PHYSICAL WORLD	INTERNET
High-risk Victim	Unattended child who talks with strangers walking home from school.	Unattended child in an Internet chat room who talks with strangers.
High Offender Victim	Offender who acquires victims in an area that is surveyed using security cameras.	Offender who acquires victims in an area of the Internet that is monitored or recorded.
Low-risk Victim	Individual who avoids going into certain areas unaccompanied and does not give personal information to strangers.	Individual who avoids using areas of the Internet unaccompanied and does not give personal information to strangers.
Low Offender Risk	Offender who wears a mask and performs covering behavior to avoid detection.	Offender who uses anonymity provided by the Internet and performs covering behavior to avoid detection.

In crimes where computers are the targets, criminal profilers should still try to develop victimology. In such cases the victim is the computer, except when the computer was targeted because of its owner. Though a computer is not a person, the underlying question is the same – why did the offender choose the target computer and what was the risk the offender was willing to take?

Gather information about the computer including the make and model, the operating system, where it was located, what it contained, who had access to it, what other computers it regularly connected to and how difficult it was to break into. Determine whether there were any previous unsuccessful attempts to access the computer.

MO AND SIGNATURE

Modus operandi (MO) are those behaviors that were central to commit a given crime. Signature behaviors are those behaviors that are more personal to the offender. Table 25.2 contains some MO and signature behaviors related to the main steps that must be taken to commit a crime using the Internet. Asterisks denote behaviors that are potentially both MO and signature oriented.

ACTIVITY	MO BEHAVIORS	SIGNATURE BEHAVIORS
ISP Selection	Selecting an ISP based on its location, ease of access while travelling, familiarity and/or tolerance of potentially illegal activity.	*Selecting an ISP to target a specific type of victim.
User name selection	Selecting a user name that will make it easier to acquire intended victims.	Selecting a user name that is personally significant to the offender.
Internet service selection	Selecting a service to target a specific type of victim or to commit a specific type of crime.	*Selecting a service that gives the offender high visibility and thus attracts attention.
Software selection	Selecting an application because of its unique capabilities. *Creating own applications with unique capabilities.	Selecting an application because it helps the offender feel powerful or reassured.
Acquiring victims	Playing a role to win the confidence of a specific type of victim.	*Type of victim selected.
General activities	Taking elaborate steps to hide true identity. Creating an Internet persona using Web pages, Usenet postings, etc.	Seeking reassurance or being verbally abusive. Keeping trophies. *Using a set sequence of actions. *Forging e-mail to impersonate others.

Table 25.2

MO and signature behaviors related to the main steps in committing crime using the Internet

For a more in-depth example of the difference between MO and signature, consider one of the most infamous computer crackers in the US, Kevin Mitnick. Mitnick had a very advanced MO that made it very difficult to track him down. Apparently, he would break into telephone networks, create a clever dial loop to hide his whereabouts, and would then use a cellular phone to dial into a large Internet Service Provider. He would then use advanced techniques to break into computers and steal software, credit cards and data. A team consisting of computer expert Tsutomu Shimomura and the FBI finally tracked Mitnick down using cellular-frequency direction-finding antennae. Though Mitnick's main motivation seemed to be profit, he exhibited some other behaviors that were clearly not necessary to commit crimes, i.e. signature behaviors. For example, after Mitnick broke into Shimomura's computer and stole advanced computer software, he left taunting and sometimes threatening voice messages for Shimomura. The motivation underlying these messages was most likely a combination of power reassurance and anger retaliation.

Deductive criminal profiling is a particularly useful tool in cases involving computer crackers. Computer crackers, sometimes mistakenly called hackers, are individuals who use computer networks to commit a range of crimes including intrusion and theft. Though computer crackers are careful to hide their identities, they often have quite distinct MO and signature behaviors. Crackers often have preferred hunting grounds like a specific operating system that they are familiar with or computers that contain a particular type of information. Crackers usually have a clear motivation such as profit, retaliation, power reassurance and/or power assertion. The skill level and experience of a cracker is usually evident in the methods and programs that are used to break into a system. For instance, a cracker who uses readily available software and chooses weak targets for little gain is generally less skilled and experienced than a cracker who writes customized programs to target strong installations. A cracker's signature can include but is not limited to vandalism, threats, verbal behavior, types of covering behavior, and sequence of actions. What a cracker takes or leaves behind can also be used to fill out a profile.

MO and signature can be very useful when scouring the Internet for information regarding a case. MO and signature can help investigators/ profilers decide what to look for and where to look. Remember that the Internet has many areas that are quite private and might never show up in a routine search. Sometimes an offender's MO or signature will indicate that he uses one or another of these out-of-the-way places. Using verbal behavior to link cases is particularly important on the Internet because in many cases it is all you have. For example, cases involving offenders who change their online identities or operate anonymously can still be linked using things that the offender says and things that the offender wants the victim to say. Another important consideration when trying to link cases is the area in which the events occur. Many offenders favor a particular part of the Internet or a specific type of communication enabled by the Internet. For instance, if an unknown offender commits a crime using a specific Internet chat network, profilers/investigators should monitor that area and areas like it for individuals who exhibit similar behaviors as the offender.

MOTIVATIONAL TYPOLOGIES

As signature behaviors are identified, a general pattern will emerge that is called the signature aspect. Signature aspect is closely related to offenders' fantasies and motives and can tell a profiler a great deal about an offender. Some general motivational typologies were developed to help serial rape investigators identify and comprehend common signature aspects. Though developed for rape crimes, these typologies can also shed light on other types of crime, including those involving the Internet (see Table 25.3).

TYPOLOGY	SCENARIO INVOLVING THE INTERNET
Power Reassurance	Posting child pornography on Usenet and openly claiming to be so smart that law enforcement cannot catch him.
Power Assertive	Cracker breaking into well-protected computer system and confidently completing mission without looking for reassurance from others or exhibiting anger.
Anger Retaliation	Using Internet services to harass and threaten victim because of perceived wrongs. Harassment can involve stalking or physical encounters.
Sadistic	Acquiring victims in a sadomasochistic online discussion group and arranging to meet. Face to face meeting leads to torture, rape and/or homicide.
Opportunistic	Finding confidential information during normal Internet activities and using it to commit a crime such as blackmail or espionage.
Profit	Putting thousands of stolen credit card numbers onto a CD and selling them.

Table 25.3

General motivational typologies.

It is important to remember that these typologies are not mutually exclusive. For instance, Mitnick could have been motivated by a mixture of anger-retaliation and power-reassurance when he broke into Shimomura's computer.

Other typologies exist, such as those for pedophiles and stalkers that can also shed light on the motivations and behaviors of an offender. However, there is one significant caveat to using motivational typologies. These typologies describe general patterns that were observed in past cases. Keep in mind that everyone is different, that times change, and that an offender might not fit easily into one or any of the typologies that have been developed. Do not think of the typologies as an oracle of human behavior but rather as a tool to help recognize patterns in signature behaviors and help develop a better understanding of signature aspect.

THE IMPORTANCE OF TRAINING

This chapter has outlined how deductive criminal profiling applies to the Internet and how investigators and profilers can use the Internet as a source of evidence. However, there are many details that have been excluded for the sake of brevity. For example, this chapter does not discuss the technicalities of how the Internet works, how to collect digital evidence on the Internet, or how the law applies to the Internet. Also, this chapter does not go into the legal and technical complexities of collecting digital evidence from a personal computer.

Many investigators believe that they can learn about computers, computer networks, and the Internet on their own. However, this casual approach will rarely enable investigators to reach a level of expertise that is comparable to that of criminals. Criminals are using the Internet to share information in an unprecedented manner. This collaboration, combined with the rapid development of the Internet, is making it increasingly difficult for law enforcement to keep up. As law enforcement becomes more adept at apprehending and prosecuting criminals for crimes committed in one area of the Internet, criminals are moving to, and even creating, other areas to avoid capture. As a result, the Internet is primarily the criminals' domain, leading many people to compare it to the Wild West.

In short, investigators and profilers need formal training and need to collaborate like never before. It is not enough to know how to use search engines or Usenet. Even if investigators and profilers are aware of all of a victim's Internet activities, they need to be familiar with the Internet to interpret the significance of the activities. For example, if a victim uses synchronous chat networks, it is not safe to assume that he/she is an advanced Internet user. The type of chat network is significant as are the victim's other activities. To realize the full potential of the Internet, investigators and profilers must learn about all aspects of the Internet including its technical nuances, nooks and crannies, different subcultures, and pertinent laws in their region of the world.

Fortunately, training opportunities that deal specifically with crime on the Internet are beginning to emerge. However, no single course can deal with all of the relevant topics thoroughly, so profilers and investigators should seek specialized training to learn more about digital evidence, computer networks (including the Internet), and the law as it applies to computers and computer networks. Table 25.4 summarizes the types of training that are offered by several organizations, including the author's own (Knowledge Solutions).

Table 25.4

Types of training offered by organizations

ORGANIZATION (URL)	TRAINING
Knowledge Solutions LLC (http://www.corpus-delicti.com)	Internet crime, criminal profiling, digital evidence collection, crime on computer networks.
SEARCH (http://www.search.org)	Investigating computer and Internet crime, seizing and examining microcomputers, and detecting network intrusions.
NTI (http://www.secure-data.com)	Computer evidence and security training.

Unfortunately, few computer crime-training programs cover computer networks adequately. Learning about crime on the Internet is an excellent start but as computer networks become ubiquitous, knowledge of how networks function will become increasingly important. In a world where just about everything is networked (e.g. governments, businesses, homes, airplanes, cars, televisions, and personal organizers) collecting digital evidence is becoming more complex and requires knowledge of computer networks.

Keep in mind that the benefits of Internet training extend beyond the Internet to the physical world. For instance, investigators can learn more about the criminal activity in their jurisdiction by getting to know their local online communities; the people in the area who use the Internet. If investigators find that a member of the community is distributing child pornography over the Internet, they could charge him immediately or could use the opportunity to determine if he is involved with other members of the community, and if he is committing more serious crimes. In this way, the Internet can be used as a looking glass into everyday crime. Also keep in mind that training is necessary, but not sufficient. If profilers and investigators have any hopes of keeping up with technology and criminal activity, they must work together to keep up with changes in technology and criminal activity, sharing information and expertise. Needless to say, a strategic use of computer networks will greatly facilitate such collaboration.

REFERENCES

Clark, F. and Diliberto, K. (1996) *Investigating Computer Crime*, Boca Raton, FL.: CRC Press.

Gibson, W. (1984) *Neuromancer*, London: Victor Gollancz Limited.

Holmes, R. (1996) *Profiling Violent Crimes: An Investigative Tool*, 2nd edn, Thousand Oaks: Sage Publications.

Icove, D., Seger, K. and VonStorch, W. (1995) *Computer Crime: A Crimefighter's Handbook*, Sebastopol, CA: O'Reilly & Associates.

Rose, L. (1994) *Netlaw: Your Rights in the Online World*, New York: Osborne McGraw-Hill.

Saferstein, R. (1998) *Criminalistics: An Introduction to Forensic Science*, 6th edn, Upper Saddle River, NJ:Prentice Hall.

WHITECHAPEL: THE RIPPER MURDERS

Brent E. Turvey, M.S.

Between August 6 and November 9, in 1888, a frightful series of crimes sent terror through the British public. On the night of August 6 the body of a thirty-five year old streetwalker named Martha Turner [Tabram] was found in Whitechapel. Her throat had been cut. On August 31 another prostitute, Mary Ann Nicholls, was murdered. Four more murders took place in rapid succession: Annie Chapman on September 8, Elizabeth Stride and Catherine Eddowes on September 30, and Mary Jane Kelly on November 9. All of the victims were streetwalkers whose throats had been cut, in several cases with such terrible force that the heads were nearly severed from their bodies. But as if this were not enough, in at least five cases the murderer had cut entire organs out of the bodies of the women – in a manner which suggested that he had some training in surgery. The Murders all took place at night between 11pm and 4am in the London Districts of Whitechapel, Spitalsfield, and Stepney... 'Jack the Ripper' became a synonym for terror... After the death of Mary Kelly, the murders ceased as suddenly as they had begun – and remain unsolved.

(Jurgen Thorwald (1964) *The Century of the Detective*, New York; Harcourt Brace & World, Inc.)

There have been many speculations regarding the precise identity of "Jack the Ripper," the person who is believed to have killed some eight women in London's East End between August 6 and February 13, 1891. In fact, this author would argue that the very reason most historians, or academics, have put pen to paper on the subject is for the sole purpose of implicating a particular individual (or two) by virtue of a personally held belief or theory regarding the case.

Even we profilers have "gone on the game." Despite the fact that very few actual photos exist, despite the fact that most of the physical evidence was lost, destroyed, or uncollected, we still put our opinions forward. Most of us, fortunately, do not seek to implicate particular individuals, but there does seem to be disinterest in coming up with ideas that go outside popularly accepted suspect theories.

John Douglas' rendering, for example, is a boilerplate of *organized* and *disorganized* traits, with laundry-list characteristics taken from the criteria for personality disorders, like Anti-Social Personality Disorder (Douglas places Jack in the organized category for seemingly arbitrary reasons, but in reality Jack is a mix – like most offenders).

> Douglas opines that the Ripper was raised in a family with a domineering mother, probably fond of drink and the company of different men, and a weak and/or absent father... He became socially detached and developed a 'diminished emotional response towards people in general'. His anger was internalized. But, in his younger years, his pent-up destructive emotions were expressed by lighting fires and torturing animals... As an adult the Ripper was an asocial loner. At work he was seen as quiet, shy and obedient, and his dress was neat and orderly. He would look for employment in positions in which he could work alone and experience vicariously his destructive fantasies, perhaps as a butcher or hospital or mortuary attendant. He was not adept at meeting people socially and his sexual relationships were mostly with prostitutes. He may have contracted a venereal disease. If so it would have fueled his hatred and disgust of women. He is unlikely to have been married. He carried a knife to protect himself against possible attack. 'This paranoid type of thinking would in part be justified by his poor self image.' He lived or worked in the Whitechapel area and his first homicide would have been near his home or place of work [That was redundant].
>
> (Philip Sugden (1995) *The Complete History of Jack the Ripper*, New York: Carroll & Graf Pubs. Inc.)

Douglas seems to have fallen a bit prey to what this author regards as the most confining assumption of all Ripper dogma. The Golden Calf of *Ripperology*, as it were – that the police surgeons were universally correct when they continuously asserted that the offender must have possessed professional surgical skills. It is the opinion of this author that the injuries described by those surgeons do not evidence professional skill at all, but rather familiarity and practice (there is a difference). But we will get to that later.

The author must agree with Douglas, however, on at least two central motivational issues: anger, and the need for reassurance. There is a lot of passive anger evidenced in these crimes, and other behaviors speak to a lot of inadequacy on the part of the offender.

Let us review the details then, keeping in mind that this piece is not intended to be a profile, or even a threshold assessment. Rather, this author is interested in eliciting general motivational aspects from the established behavior for historical purposes. These police, medical, and witness accounts have been compiled from the efforts put forth by the authors of the following works, with much gratitude:

- Sugden, P. (1995) *The Complete History of Jack the Ripper*, New York: Carroll and Graf Publishers, Inc.

■ Tulley, J. (1997) *Prisoner 1167: The Madman Who was Jack the Ripper*, New York: Carroll and Graf Publishers, Inc.

MARTHA TABRAM

On August 6, 1888, the body of Martha Tabram, a 39-year-old prostitute, was discovered on the first landing of the George Yard Buildings by a man leaving his room for work at 4:45 a.m. She was reportedly lying on her back in a pool of blood. According to the first responder who testified at an inquest two days later, "The clothes were turned up as far as the centre of the body, leaving the lower part of the body exposed; the legs were open, and altogether her position was such as to suggest in my mind that recent intimacy had taken place."

She had been stabbed at least 39 times, and, according to the police surgeon, had been dead at least three hours. Additionally, there was hemorrhaging beneath the scalp, and, according to Dr Timothy Killeen who performed the first examination of the body:

> …the left lung was perforated in five places, and the right lung in two places… The heart… was penetrated in one place… the liver was healthy but penetrated in five places, the spleen was perfectly healthy, and was penetrated in two places… the stomach was perfectly healthy, but was penetrated in six places… The lower portion of the body was penetrated in one place, the wound [incision] being three inches in length and one in depth… Death was due to hemorrhage and loss of blood.

However, Dr Killeen found no evidence of recent sexual activity, and no evidence of a struggle.

There is rage expressed in this crime, distinguishing it from the others. The offender may have known this victim as an acquaintance, or have had dealings with her in the past. In any case, the offender perceived (that perception being actual or symbolic) that this individual had wronged him somehow, and this was her punishment.

The author links this victim to the Ripper murders for the following reasons:

- ■ Method of approach/attack was generally similar (no evidence of a struggle).
- ■ Time of the attack was generally similar to the Ripper cases.
- ■ Victimology was generally similar to the Ripper cases.
- ■ Nature and extent of the injuries were of the same constellation as those in the Ripper cases.
- ■ The method of disposal was similar to the Ripper cases.
- ■ No other offenses with remotely similar MO and signature behavior (arranging of body after death with genitals exposed) were being committed at the time in that area.

MARY ANN NICHOLS

On August 31, 1888, the body of Mary Ann Nichols, a 42-year-old prostitute, was discovered at 3:40 a.m. lying on the pavement along Buck's Row in Whitechapel, by two men on their way to work. She was lying on her back, and her skirts were drawn up to her stomach. They briefly inspected her and felt that she was drunk, asleep, or dead and went on their way. One of them did agree to find a constable if the opportunity should arise.

At about 3:45 a.m., a constable on his beat happened upon the scene. He observed that the victim's hands were not clenched, her legs were slightly apart, and that her eyes were wide open. He also noted that there was blood coming out of wounds on her neck. When a police surgeon was called to the scene, he observed that her body and legs were still warm, and believed that she had only been dead for about a half an hour.

Upon examination of her body by Dr Rees Ralph Llewellyn, it was learned that the victim's abdomen had been cut open up to the breastbone, exposing her intestines, and her throat had been cut. Inspector John Spratling of the Metropolitan Police was assigned to the case, and he made this summary of the doctor's findings:

> …her throat had been cut from left to right, two distinct cuts being on the left side, the windpipe, gullet, and spinal cord being cut through; a bruise apparently of a thumb being on right lower jaw, also on left cheek; the abdomen had been cut open from centre of bottom of ribs along the right side, under pelvis to left of the stomach, there the wound was jagged; the omentum or coating of the stomach, was also cut in several places, and two small stabs on private parts; [all] apparently done with a strong bladed knife; death being almost instantaneous.

ANNIE CHAPMAN

On September 7, 1888, some local workmen discovered the body of Annie Chapman, a 47-year-old prostitute, on No. 29 Hanbury Street. Inspector Joseph Chandler, who responded to the scene, gave the following in his account:

> I at once proceeded to No. 29 Hanbury Street and in the back yard found a woman lying on her back, dead, left arm resting on left breast, legs drawn up, abducted, small intestines and flap of the abdomen lying on the right side, right above the shoulder, attached by a cord with the rest of the intestine inside the body; two flaps of skin from the lower part of the abdomen lying in a large quantity of blood above the left shoulder; throat cut deeply from left and back in a jagged manner right around the throat.

Dr George Philips, who performed an examination of the body at the scene, noted:

> The small intestines and other portions were lying on the right side of the body on the ground above the right shoulder, but attached. There was a large quantity of blood,

with a part of the stomach above the left shoulder… The throat was dissevered deeply.
I noticed that the incision of the skin was jagged, and reached right round the neck.

At the scene, he also noted that there were no obvious signs of struggle – but that the victim's personal items had been "arranged" in the scene. Near her feet were found a small piece of coarse muslin, a small toothed comb, and a pocket comb in a paper case. There were also two new farthings, some other assorted coins, and two brass rings.

He also stated that, based on bruises to the victim's chin and other associated injuries:

I am of the opinion that the person who cut the deceased's throat took hold of her by the chin, and then commenced the incision from left to right… My impression is that she was partially strangled.

Additionally, it was noted that certain body parts were missing, including the navel, the womb, the upper part of the vagina, and the greater part of the bladder.

This victim also evidenced professional skill to Dr Phillips, by virtue of how organs were removed without disturbing other organs or with a single, deliberate stroke of the knife. In fact, it was Dr Philips who put forth the opinion that:

The whole inference seems to me that the operation was performed to enable the perpetrator to obtain possession of these parts of the body.

The author agrees with this latter opinion, noting the lack of anger in the infliction of injuries, and the deliberation with which everything seems to have been carried out. The offense does contain reassurance-oriented elements of experimentation. However other signature behaviors include the deliberate post-mortem display of the victim, the arrangement of her organs, and the arrangement of her belongings at her feet. This begins to suggest the following offender needs:

- to further humiliate the victim upon her discovery;
- to shock and horrify those who make the discovery;
- to terrorize the inhabitants of the area;
- to demonstrate his unequivocal power.

Again, this does concur with John Douglas' assertion that the offender has an inadequate sense of himself that needs reassuring through the fear of the police and the public.

However, it should be cautioned that deliberation and clean cutting (any sharp instrument can make a cut that looks clean and deliberate) do not a professional surgeon make. Rather this suggests experience, or practice. In agreement with Douglas, this author would suggest that this offender had likely committed this type of crime before, perhaps in another city, region, or country.

CONTACT

The Mile End Vigilance Committee was formed on September 10, in response to the death of Annie Chapman. It was felt by many that the police were inadequate to the task of solving the crimes, and the public outcry was great. But the Committee, 16 members in all, was not designed to be antagonistic towards the police, nor were they overzealous or out of control. They limited their activities to gathering money for a reward for information leading to the Ripper's identity, and to reporting suspicious behavior in the neighborhood to officers on patrol.

On September 28, 1888, the Central News Agency received a letter addressed to "The Boss, Central News Office, London City," which they did not disclose until after the morning of September 30. It was written in red ink, and was the first letter signed "Jack the Ripper":

25 Sept: 1888

Dear Boss

I keep on hearing the police have caught me but they wont fix me just yet. I have laughed when they look so clever and talk about being on the right track. That joke about Leather Apron gave me real fits. I am down on whores and I shant quit ripping them till I do get buckled. Grand work the last job was. I gave the lady [Annie Chapman] no time to squeal. How can they catch me now. I love my work and want to start again. You will soon hear of me and my funny little games. I saved some of the proper red stuff in a ginger beer bottle over the last job to write with but it went thick like glue and I cant use it. Red ink is fit enough, I hope ha. ha. The next job I do I shall clip the lady's ears off and send to the police officers just for jolly wouldnt you. Keep this letter back till I do a bit more work, then give it out straight. My knife's so nice and sharp I want to get to work right away if I get a chance. Good luck. Yours truly, Jack the Ripper Dont mind me giving the trade name.

wasnt good enough to post this before I got all the red ink off my hands curse it. No luck yet. They say I'm a doctor now ha ha"

LIZ STRIDE AND KATE EDDOWES

On Sunday morning, September 30, 1888, two more victims fell.

The first was Elizabeth Stride, a 45-year-old prostitute who was found by a hawker in an alley at about 1:20 a.m.

Dr Phillips gave the following description of her neck injuries to an inquest on October 3:

> Cut on neck; taking it for the left to the right there is a clean cut incision 6 inches in length, incision commencing two and a half inches in a straight line below the angle of the jaw... The carotid artery on the left side, and the other vessels contained in the sheath were all cut through save the posterior portion of the carotid to about a line of 1–12th of an inch in extent, which prevented the separation of the upper and lower portion of the artery... It is evident that the hemorrhage which probably will be found to be the cause of death, was caused through the partial severance of the left carotid artery.

He further agreed that there were no signs of gagging, and no marks on the head or neck that suggested strangulation. There was no abdominal mutilation or injury whatsoever.

This case, if any, is the least likely to be included as part of the Ripper crimes. But the bottom line is that we do not have enough information to know for sure whether or not this is an interrupted event (depriving the offense of signature activity) – and the victimology, timing, and MO are consistent. The strongest argument for inclusion comes from the second letter signed "Jack the Ripper" that was sent to the news agency. It references the first letter, and references two victims, the first being described as an interrupted, incomplete event.

The second victim was Catherine "Kate" Eddowes, a 43-year-old prostitute found 45 minutes later in Mitre Square by a police constable who patrolled the area.

Not only was this victim's throat cut, but her abdomen was also mutilated extensively, with a great jagged incision running from the pubic region to the breastbone. The offender had also removed her left kidney and part of her womb, taking them from the scene.

This was also the first time that the offender mutilated his victim's face, making numerous cuts to her lips, nose, jaw, and cheeks. This clear expression of anger may not suggest a familiarity with this victim, but rather that this victim was probably used as a vehicle for the offender's frustration at failing to achieve his objective, and being interrupted, earlier in the evening.

After this second killing, the offender washed his hands in a nearby public sink, and wrote on a doorway the following message: "The Juwes are not the men to be blamed for nothing."

Just a few hours later, before a public announcement regarding the offenses had been made, a letter was sent to the police referring to both killings. It read:

> I wasnt codding, dear old Boss, when I gave you the tip. Youll hear about Saucy Jackys work tomorrow double event this time number one squealed a bit couldnt finish straight off. Had not time to get ears for police thanks for keeping last letter back till I got to work again. Jack the Ripper.

Two days after the attack, the offender sent a cardboard box to George Lusk, the Chairman of the Whitechapel Vigilance Committee. It contained a kidney taken from Kate Eddowes. It also contained a note, which read:

> From hell Mr Lusk Sor I have sent you half the kidne I took from one woman prasarved it for you tother piece I fried and ate it was very nise I may send you the bloody knif that took it out if you only wate a whil longer signed Catch me when you can Mister Lusk.

MARY KELLY

On November 9, 1888, a landlord peering through a window discovered the body of Mary Kelly, a pregnant, 25-year-old prostitute, in her room on Miller's Court. He knocked first, but then found a broken window and looked in. Police had to break down the door with a pick-axe as it had been blocked by a heavy chest of drawers.

Dr Thomas Bond's notes of the scene include the following:

> The body was lying naked in the middle of the bed, the shoulders flat, but the axis of the body inclined to the left side of the bed... The legs were wide apart, the left thigh at right angles with the trunk and the right forming an obtuse angle with the pubes.

> The whole surface of the abdomen and thighs were removed and the abdominal cavity emptied of its viscera. The breasts were cut off, the arms mutilated by several jagged wounds and the face and neck were severed all around down to the bone. The viscera were found in various parts of the viz: the uterus and kidneys with one breast under the head, the other breast by the right foot, the liver between the feet, the intestines by the right side of the body.

> The flaps removed from the abdomen and thighs were on a table.

Also of note was that her breasts had been removed by more or less circular incisions, her arms and forearms showed extensive cuts and lacerations, and that her heart was missing.

This is, by some, felt to be the final victim of Jack the Ripper. This author disagrees with that opinion.

This manifestation of offender behavior represents an escalation. Not only was the offender confident enough to go into the victim's room before initiating the attack, he also let his victim defend herself. He forced himself to earn his victim, to struggle for her. And when she was sufficiently disabled, he indulged in the full range of his signature behaviors and took his time without fear of interruption.

It is unlikely that he would stop after having experienced what was possibly his most successful, most satisfying event.

ALICE MCKENZIE

After two months without an attack, the belief was that the Ripper had simply vanished never to return. In agreement with this perception, the law enforcement presence in the East End was reduced significantly.

However, six months later, another body was discovered in Whitechapel. On Wednesday, July 17, 1889, at about 12:50 a.m., a constable on his beat found the body of Alice McKenzie, a 40-year-old prostitute. She was observed to be on the pavement between a brewer's dray and a scavengers wagon, which were chained together. Her clothing (skirts) was pulled up just under her chin, with her mutilated abdomen and genitals exposed, and she had bled from her neck.

There were two jagged cuts beginning on the left side of her throat, four inches long each. There was also an incision, which started seven inches below the right nipple. It was seven inches long and curved, being deepest at its origin and becoming superficial near the end. There was no evidence of a violent struggle, however, there were injuries to the back of her head. It was determined that she died from blood loss as a result of her neck wounds.

Dr Thomas Bond felt that this was the work of the Ripper. Dr George Philips did not, based on his opinion that a different type of weapon was used and that the offender seemed to demonstrate less overall skill in the infliction of wounds. This author is inclined to agree this case should be linked with the Ripper murders for the following reasons:

- Method of approach/attack was generally similar (no evidence of a struggle).
- Time of the attack was generally similar to the Ripper cases.
- Victimology was generally similar to the Ripper cases.
- Nature and extent of the injuries were of the same constellation as those in the Ripper cases.
- The method of disposal was similar to the Ripper cases.
- No other offenses with remotely similar MO and signature behavior (peri-mortem mutilation, arranging of body after death with genitals exposed) were being committed at the time in that area.

The differences in skill level and weapon use observed by Dr Philips can be explained simply by the passage of time. Having said that, however, this author is willing to entertain the possibility of a copycat. It is a slim possibility that all of the above could have been inspired by the original six Ripper murders, and successfully mimicked, given the high amount of information made publicly available about the case at the time. But the behaviors are far too discrete and suggestive of a particular type of offender need, to eliminate the Ripper as a possibility without the corroboration of hard physical evidence. This case cannot be excluded from the Ripper series. Nor should investigators treat it as separate.

FRANCES COLES

After three more months without an attack, the belief was, again, that the Ripper had simply vanished, never to return. In agreement with this perception, again, the law enforcement presence in the East End, which had been temporarily elevated, was reduced significantly.

But a year and a half later, a body was discovered in Swallow Gardens. On Friday, February 13, 1891, at about 2:15 a.m., a constable on his beat heard footsteps running away behind him, and investigated to find Frances Cole, a 26-year-old prostitute, bleeding to death in the street. He touched her face, and it was warm, and one of her eyes flickered. By the time he was able to get help, she had died. She suffered two cuts in the throat, and had not been mutilated in any other way. However, there were injuries to the back of the head and beneath her chin. This suggested that the offender had held her to the ground, exposing her neck with his hand on her chin, and administering the cuts.

Again, Dr Philips felt that this attack lacked the skill of the others, and certainly lacked the feature of abdominal mutilation. This case was ruled out of the Ripper series and other suspects were investigated.

It is not investigatively advised to fully eliminate the possibility of linkage between any two cases that share general similarities, without conclusive physical evidence. Therefore, this author is not yet willing to exclude the Frances Coles case from the Ripper series, for the following reasons:

- Any deterioration of the offender's skill level can, again, be explained by time; the lack of practice.
- The neck injuries are of a similar nature as those in the Ripper cases.
- Time of the attack was generally similar to the Ripper cases.
- Victimology was generally similar to the Ripper cases.
- The method of disposal was similar to the Ripper cases.
- No other offenses with remotely similar MO were being committed at the time in that area.
- The attack was very likely interrupted, meaning that the offender did not have the opportunity to engage in the full range of signature behaviors (several other offenses appear to have an interrupted aspect).
- The location selection did suggest that the offender was going to want the victim's body to be found when he was through, as with the other Ripper cases.

AUTHOR'S OPINION

This author is not going to try to "solve the case" of Jack the Ripper, as so many have already attempted to do, based on the woefully inadequate historical documentation available. Rather, this author would like to give investigatively relevant suggestions as if this were a cold case. It is hoped that in these suggestions (based on the reliably documented historical evidence that does exist) we can learn something about investigating these types of serial crimes in our own time.

In the spirit of cold-case assessment, we should view these crimes as though the last one happened yesterday. If possible, this author would make the following comments and suggestions to those investigating the case. This offender has a limited and underdeveloped understanding of female sexuality. He has strong sexual desires, but fears his own humiliation in expressing them physically. This may be the result of, or have evolved to cause, physical sexual dysfunction.

RETALIATORY ASPECT

In the case of the first victim (Tabram), who we include because of the strong evidence of connective MO and signature behaviors (victim sexual humiliation via post-mortem display), it is possible that she and the offender were on their way to a room to engage in sex acts. It is further possible that the offender, either because of his sexual dysfunction or because of a disparaging remark that she may have made regarding his sexual dysfunction (or some other aspect of his sexual prowess), became angry and violent. This may have resulted in a sudden, brutal attack on the victim that evidences a great deal of rage. Nothing was apparently taken from this scene, and the only gain realized by the offender was through the expression of his rage, and through the post-mortem arranging of the victim's body into a humiliating position.

This is the only Ripper attack with any rage in it. The MO in subsequent attacks is designed by the offender to avoid *any* interaction with a living, conscious victim in order to circumvent the possibility of offender sexual humiliation. Victims after Tabram are attacked in a blitz fashion, with no chance to defend themselves, most often from behind, and are then mutilated peri-mortem and post-mortem barring offense interruption by law enforcement or witnesses.

It is likely that the offender is a well-blended background fixture of these locations; the type of person people look right past in order to observe those who appear suspicious. He is not likely to be nervous, but rather meek and with-drawn. If stopped by law enforcement, he is likely to be acquiescent and compliant.

REASSURANCE ASPECT

In regards to investigative strategy, it is also advised that the prostitutes who work in the areas where victims have been targeted be administered the behavioral-oriented interview. Given his ability to approach his victims in such a manner as to not draw attention or encounter resistance, it is very likely that he pre-selects his target area by soliciting local prostitutes for their services before and after an attack.

He targets prostitutes because:

- they sell the very thing (physical sex) that he does not fully understand, that he feels has control over him, and that humiliates him;
- by selling it, they reinforce his belief that females are dirty and that sex is a corrupting influence.

Prostitutes will describe this offender with phrases like:

- "He's harmless."
- "He wouldn't hurt a fly."
- "He's a real gentleman."
- "He's very shy."
- "He's not the sort who could hurt anyone."

Prostitutes should be advised that the offender will likely be the type of customer who:

- Is quiet and nervous in sexual contexts.
- Likes to watch sexual activity rather than engage in it; may request a show of some kind.
- Is uncomfortable being naked; may not even take off his clothes.
- Refuses to kiss.
- May fondle her, or insert fingers or devices into her orifices, but that is the limit of direct sexual contact.
- Will not, at any time, show his penis or engage in any form of penile intercourse.

OCCUPATION

It is not likely that this offender was in law enforcement at the time of the attacks, as the prostitutes would have begun to recognize him over time. Given his need to involve the news media, and his deprecating attitude and comments towards law enforcement, it is more likely that he was either:

- discharged from government, police, or military work of some kind in the past (one to three years prior to the first victim), possibly as the consequence of violent behavior; or
- an ex-con with a grudge against law enforcement for what he perceives as injustice.

In either case, his involvement of the news media in the case suggests a very public humiliation of some kind in the past that he wants rectified. This author therefore makes four suggestions:

- A search through employee records for those who were recently fired from government jobs for attitude problems, problems with authority, or violent behavior.

- A search through local police and military records for those who have been discharged for attitude problems, problems with authority, or violent behavior.

- A search through local newspaper archives dating back 5–10 years before the crimes for those who suffered humiliation in print, being accused of crimes, or having been discharged from employment (especially the front page or the editorials).

- A list of all criminals released 6–8 months prior to the attack on Tabram.

- A search through criminal records for local area offenses against woman such as battery, assault, theft, and even domestic disputes (the offender likely has a history of violent behavior towards women).

NEED TO AFFECT OR WITNESS THE INVESTIGATION AND EXPERIENCE REACTIONS

Law enforcement should also be advised that this offender might try to interject himself into the investigation in order to manipulate and hamper investigative efforts. He has likely already done so after previous attacks by coming forth as a witness, and by frequenting pubs or other establishments where law enforcement habituate. All witnesses should be screened as potential suspects, with special attention paid to accounts that appear to demonstrate uncanny insight into the crime, that appear to be hyperbole, or that show contempt for the victim.

Along the same lines, all crowds around future crime-scenes should be photographed, and all persons accounted for by direct law-enforcement interview. His letters refer to overhearing the police conjecture. He enjoys this as well as the public's reaction to the crimes and he may want to experience both firsthand.

OFFENDER MOTIVE

As already suggested by the author, there are three very strong reassurance-oriented needs suggested by this offender's behavior, and a very specific fantasy.

1 Power over the victim's sexuality by humiliating them with post-mortem mutilation and displaying of their bodies. This behavior is also experimental in nature, as opposed to ritualistic (he does different things with the organs from each body – not the same exact thing every time).

2 The need to instill fear, terror, or shock in the public and law enforcement, thereby demonstrating his power and superiority to law enforcement.

3 The need to have his actions seen or heard about by others; the need to have his victims found and his "work" on display.

Obviously we cannot go back and reinvestigate these crimes for any purpose other than our historical curiosity. The offender can no longer be alive, and therefore does not exist to be apprehended. However, we can learn from the investigative mistakes of the past and apply what we learn to current and future investigations.

EVALUATING INDUCTIVE PROFILES – THE JONBENET RAMSEY CASE

Brent E. Turvey, M.S.

The purpose of this appendix is to offer a critique of both the competence and the investigative relevance of the inductively rendered criminal profile that was commissioned by the Ramsey family. This requires some review of the publicly known facts of this case. Please note, however, that the purpose of this appendix is not to offer a deductive criminal profile, as this author does not have sufficient information to do so.

The information in this appendix has been referenced from Bosworth, C. and Wecht, C. (1998) *Who Killed JonBenet Ramsey?*, New York: Onyx Books.

On December 26, 1996, at 6 a.m., Boulder Police officers received a report that six-year-old JonBenet Ramsey had been kidnapped from her home in the 700 block of 15th Street, near the University of Colorado campus. She was the 1996 Little Miss Colorado, and the daughter of Access Graphics president John Ramsey, 53, and Patricia Ramsey, 39.

Patricia Ramsey had called 911 at 5:52 a.m. on Thursday, after finding JonBenet missing from her bed, and discovering a handwritten ransom note on their stairs demanding $118,000. Around the same time, the Ramseys also called Fleet White, and his wife Priscilla, who was an oil-company executive and a friend of the family who lived nearby. They also called their friends John and Barbara Fernie, as well as their priest, Reverend Rol Hoverstock, who joined them at the house before detectives arrived at 8:10 a.m.

Her body was found in the basement of their home at 1:23 p.m. by her father, John, who was searching the house top to bottom one last time. He was in the basement with Fleet White when he disappeared into one of the basement's many rooms, one that was intended to be a future wine cellar. Mr White had reportedly searched that room earlier, but found nothing. Upon finding JonBenet's blanket-wrapped body, John Ramsey pulled off the duct tape that covered her mouth, carried the body upstairs, and laid it on the living room floor near the front door.

According to the autopsy report performed on December 27, 1996, but not released by the Office of the Boulder County Coroner until August 13, 1997, the cause of death was "asphyxia by strangulation associated with cranio-cerebral trauma."

An excerpt from that autopsy report gives us the following details:

> The body of this six-year-old female was first seen by me after I was called to an address identified as 755 – 15th street in Boulder, Colorado, on 12/26/96. I arrived at the scene approximately 8 PM on 12/26 and entered the house where the decedent's body was located at approximately 8:20PM. I initially viewed the body in the living room of the house. The decedent was laying on her back on the floor, covered by a blanket and a Colorado Avalanche sweatshirt. On removing these two items from the top of the body the decedent was found to be lying on her back with her arms extended up over her head. The head was turned to the right. A brief examination of the body disclosed a ligature around the neck and a ligature around the right wrist. Also noted was a small area of abrasion or contusion below the right ear on the lateral aspect of the right cheek. A prominent dried abrasion was present on the lower left neck. After examining the body, I left the residence at approximately 8:30PM.

> EXTERNAL EXAM
> The decedent is clothed in a long sleeved whit knit collarless shirt, the mid anterior chest area of which contains an embroidered silver star decorated with silver sequins. Tied loosely around the right wrist, overlying the sleeve of the shirt is a white cord. At the knot there is one tail end which measures 5.5 inches in length with a frayed end. The other tail of the knot measures 15.5 inches in length and ends in a double loop knot. This end of the cord is also frayed. There are no defects noted in the shirt but the upper anterior right sleeve contains a dried brown-tan stain measuring 2.5x1.5 inches, consistent with mucous from the nose or mouth. There are long white underwear with an elastic waist band containing a red and blue stripe. The long underwear are urine stained anteriorly over the crotch area and anterior legs. No defects are identified. Beneath the long underwear are white panties with printed rose buds and the words "Wednesday" on the elastic waist band. The underwear is urine stained and in the inner aspect of the crotch are several red areas of staining measuring up to 0.5 inch maximum dimension.

> EXTERNAL EVIDENCE OF INJURY
> Located just below the right ear at the right angle of the mandible, 1.5 inches below the right external auditory canal is a ⅜ x ¼ inch area of rust colored abrasion.
> In the lateral aspect of the left lower eyelid on the inner conjunctival surface is a 1mm in maximum dimension petechial hemorrhage. Very fine, less than 1mm petechial hemorrhages are present on the skin of the upper eyelids bilaterally as well as on the lateral left cheek. On everting the left upper eyelid there are much smaller, less than 1mm petechial hemorrhages located on the conjunctival surface. Possible petechial hemorrhages located on the conjunctival surfaces of the right upper and lower eyelids, but livor mortis on this side of the face makes definite identification difficult.

Wrapped around the neck with a double knot in the midline of the posterior neck is a length of white cord similar to that described as being tied around the right wrist. This ligature cord is cut on the right side of the neck and removed. A single black ink mark is placed on the left side of the cut and a double black ink mark on the right side of the cut. The posterior knot is left intact. Extending from the knot on the posterior aspect of the neck are two tails of the knot, one measuring 4 inches in length and having a frayed end, and the other measuring 17 inches in length with the end tied in multiple loops around a length of around tan-brown wooden stick which measures 4.5 inches in length. This wooden stick is irregularly broken at both ends and there are several colors of paint and apparent glistening varnish on the surface. Printed in gold letters on one end of the wooden stick is the word "Korea". The tail end of another word extends from beneath the loops of the cord tied around the stick and is not able to be interpreted. Blonde hair is entwined in the knot on the posterior aspect of the neck as well as in the cord wrapped around the wooden stick. It appears to be made of a white synthetic material. Also secured around the neck is a gold chain with a single charm in the form of a cross.

A deep ligature furrow encircles the entire neck. The width of the furrow varies from one-eighth of an inch to five/sixteenths of an inch and is horizontal in orientation, with little upward deviation. The skin of the anterior neck above and below the ligature furrow contains areas of petechial hemorrhage and abrasion encompassing an area measuring approximately 3x2 inches. The ligature furrow crosses the anterior midline of the neck just below the laryngeal prominence, approximately at the level of the cricoid cartilage. It is almost completely horizontal with slight upward deviation from the horizontal towards the back of the neck. The midline of the furrow mark on the anterior neck is 8 inches below the top of the head. The midline of the furrow mark on the posterior neck is 6.75 inches below the top of the head.

The area of abrasion and petechial hemorrhage of the skin of the anterior neck includes on the lower left neck, just to the left of the midline, a roughly triangular, parchment-like rust colored abrasion which measures 1.5 inches in length with a maximum width of 0.75 inches. This roughly triangular shaped abrasion is obliquely oriented with the apex superior and lateral. The remainder of the abrasions and petechial hemorrhages of the skin above and below the anterior projection of the ligature furrow are non-patterned, purple to rust colored, and present in the midline, right, and left areas of the anterior neck. The skin just above the ligature furrow along the right side of the neck contains petechial hemorrhage composed of multiple confluent very small petechial hemorrhages as well as several larger petechial hemorrhages measuring up to one-sixteenth and one-eighth of an inch in maximum dimension. Similar smaller petechial hemorrhages are present on the skin below the ligature furrow on the left lateral aspect of the neck. Located on the right side of the chin is a three-sixteenths by one-eighth of an inch area of superficial abrasion. On the posterior aspect of the right shoulder is a poorly demarcated, very superficial focus of abrasion/contusion which is pale purple in color and measures up to three-quarters by one-half inch in maximum dimension. Several linear aggregates of petechial hemorrhages are present in the anterior left shoulder just above deltopectoral groove. These measure up to one inch in length by one-sixteenth to one-eighth of an inch in width. On the left lateral aspect of the lower back, approximately sixteen and one-quarter inches and seventeen and one-half inches below the level of the top of the head are two dried rust colored to slightly purple abrasions. The more superior of the two measures one-eighth by one-sixteenth of an inch and the more inferior measures three-sixteenths by one-eighth of an inch. There is no surrounding contusion identified. On the posterior aspect of the left lower leg, almost in the midline, approximately 4 inches above the level of the heel are two small scratch-like abrasions which are dried and rust colored. They measure one-sixteenth by less than one-sixteenth of an inch and one-eighth by less than one-sixteenth of an inch respectively.

On the anterior aspect of the perineum, along the edges of closure of the labia majora, is a small amount of dried blood. A similar small amount of dried and semifluid blood is present on the skin of the fourchette and in the vestibule. Inside the vestibule of the vagina and along the distal vaginal wall is reddish hyperemia. This hyperemia is circumferential and perhaps more noticeable on the right side and posteriorly. The hyperemia also appears to extend just inside the vaginal orifice. A 1 cm red-purple area of abrasion is located on the right posterolateral area of the 1x1 cm hymenal orifice. The hymen itself is represented by a rim of mucosal tissue extending clockwise between the 2 and 10:00 positions. The area of abrasion is present at approximately the 7:00 position and appears to involve the hymen and distal right lateral vaginal wall and possibly the area anterior to the hymen. On the right labia majora is a very faint area of violet discoloration measuring approximately one inch by three-eighths of an inch. Incision into the underlying subcutaneous tissue discloses no hemorrhage. A minimal amount of semiliquid thin watery red fluid is present in the vaginal vault. No recent or remote anal or other perineal trauma is identified...

Vaginal Mucosa: All of the sections contain vascular congestion and focal interstitial chronic inflammation. The smallest piece of tissue, from the 7:00 position of the vaginal wall/hymen, contains epithelial erosion with underlying capillary congestion. A small number of red blood cells is present on the eroded surface, as is birefringent foreign material. Acute inflammatory infiltrate is not seen.

Suspicion soon fell on John Ramsey and his wife, both publicly and from within the formal investigation being conducted by the Boulder Police Department.

In the middle of January 1997, retired FBI agent and former Behavioral Sciences Unit Chief, John Douglas, agreed to profile the case for the Ramsey family. At the end of January, Douglas went on *Dateline NBC* and stated to the world that he knew in his heart, based on a 4½ hour interview with both parents, that John and Patsy Ramsey were not involved in the murder of their daughter. He further stated: "If they are responsible for the killing, they are tremendous liars."

He then prepared and released this profile of the murderer of JonBenet Ramsey to the public (referenced from Robinson, M. (1997) "Ramseys update own probe," *Denver Post*, January 24:

The family's profile of the killer says:

■ JonBenet's killer may have been suffering from stress in the weeks and months preceding the crime.

- A triggering event, such as a job crisis or crisis in a personal relationship may have caused the suspect to vent anger, perhaps at a female close to him, or perhaps at John Ramsey.

- The killer is someone who may have previously been in the Ramsey home.

- Since the murder, the killer may have intently read news reports and listened to talk radio shows dealing with the murder.

- He (the profile consistently describes the suspect as a male) may have increased consumption of alcohol or drugs.

- He may have turned to religion.

- He may be rigid, nervous and preoccupied.

- He may have tried to appear very cooperative with the authorities if he was contacted during the course of the police investigation.

- He may have quickly constructed an alibi for his whereabouts the night JonBenet was killed and may have repeated it several times to key individuals around him.

The following will be a cogent criticism of the methodology and usefulness of this profile.

First, Douglas was not given access to the police reports, the physical evidence, the crime-scene photos, the autopsy report, or the autopsy photos. The basis for any insight into offender behavior with the victim was elicited from the 4½–hour interview conducted by Douglas with the parents, and their recollection. This breaks many of the rules of criminal profiling, which include his own, regarding the need for reliance on physical evidence and access to adequate inputs:

> Any forensic pathologist, as well as most good detectives, will tell you that the single most important piece of evidence in any murder investigation is the victim's body.

(John Douglas, *Mindhunter*)

Second, Douglas broke an inviolate rule of suspect interview strategy. He interviewed the parents together, as opposed to separately. As any interviewer will explain, it is important to interview suspects separately, not jointly, for any evaluations, and subsequent profiling work, to be valid. Conducting independent interviews of suspects allows the investigator to compare responses for inconsistencies and determine the veracity of each suspect's responses. Douglas did not do this.

And finally, Douglas went on national television and endorsed the innocence of his client based upon this poorly rendered, almost boilerplate profile. This breaks the most important ethical rule of criminal profiling, which is that criminal profiles alone should not be used to address the issue of guilt. And even if they were, what Douglas feels in his heart about a case is not relevant. What is important is what the facts of the case suggest, behaviorally. As Douglas did not have the facts of the case at his disposal, it is the opinion of this author that he had no business rendering any opinions on the case whatsoever.

AUTHOR'S OPINION

There is much information that is still unknown about this case. It would therefore be irresponsible for this author to engage in unhelpful speculation. However there are some aspects to the case that are fairly well established, which Douglas' profiling effort failed to account for in any way (other than by being so general as to not exclude anyone). Based on the autopsy report alone, the crime scene in the basement appears to have been staged, and the victim has clearly suffered a sexual assault (with physical indications of at least a recent history of sexual molestation). Also, based on the Ramsey residence and the known victimology, there was a high amount of offender risk.

Follow the logic:

- There is petechial hemorrhaging above the ligature furrow on the neck, face, and in the eyes. This is the result of sudden trauma, in this case brought on by the ligature. The heart must be pumping and the veins filled with blood for this to occur. She was therefore alive when she was being strangled.
- There are abrasions associated with the ligature furrow, above it and below it. This means that she was most likely conscious while she was being strangled, and moving around, needing to be restrained by use of controlling force.
- The blow to the victim's head cracked her skull and caused massive trauma and hemorrhaging; it would have rendered her almost instantly unconscious.
- If the blow to the head would have rendered her unconscious, and there is evidence suggesting that she was alive and conscious when she was being strangled, then the blow to the head came after the strangulation activity with the ligature.

STAGING ASPECT

There is only evidence of one blow to the victim's head, which does not by itself suggest anger or punishment. If the victim was unconscious, then it would not serve corrective or coercive ends either. If it was delivered post-mortem, it could serve no other purpose to the offender other than as an attempt to misdirect the investigation. This is accomplished by distracting investigators from the ligature as a cause of death, and from the evidence of sexual activity, with another fatal injury (barring the possibility that the head injury was somehow inflicted accidentally).

WRIST LIGATURES

The ligature around the victim's wrists appears to be the same material and dimensions as a shoelace, and was placed over the victim's sleeves. This suggests that the victim was wearing the garment during the activity that led to her death, and that the offender did not want to leave behind marks on the victim's wrists. This infers not only that the offender intended for the victim to survive and be seen by others, but that the offender had previous experience with this type of activity (either with this victim or with other victims). The offender knew that wrist ligatures could leave visible marks and that placing material between the ligature and the victim's skin would prevent that from happening.

SEXUAL ASSAULT

According to the section of the autopsy report that is referenced above, there are bloodstains on the victim's underwear and there are associated injuries to the victim's vaginal area, some of which are described as "chronic." This represents very clear evidence of not only recent sexual assault, but of sexual assault several days prior to the victim's death. A very extensive investigation into the victim's medical history would seem to be requisite here, but the clear inference is that she was being sexually molested even prior to the day that she was reported missing.

HIGH OFFENDER RISK

A great deal more needs to be understood regarding victimology in this case for the development of investigative leads. However we can establish that the victim represented a very high risk to any offender who was not native to her everyday environment. She was only six years old, had a fixed schedule, and was under almost constant supervision. Therefore she would be missed immediately if abducted, and she would be difficult for a stranger to gain access to, especially in her home (the security alarm was off, but unless the offender had prior knowledge of this they would have assumed it was on).

Hopefully, the above considerations illuminate the need for profiling, only after one has an appreciation for the behavioral context of an event from the physical evidence. Without the right inputs, crucial information can be ignored, overlooked, or dismissed, and behaviors subsequently can be interpreted out of context. If the purpose of a criminal profile is truly to be an investigative aid, then it should at least seek to work with the facts that the investigation has established.

EVALUATING INDUCTIVE PROFILES – THE SOFIA SILVA CASE, THE KRISTIN AND KATI LISK CASE

Brent E. Turvey, M.S.

The purpose of this appendix is to give some of the publicly known facts regarding these linked cases, and a critique of the investigative relevance of the inductively rendered profile that was subsequently prepared for public distribution by the FBI. Please note, however, that the purpose of this appendix is not to offer a deductive profile of these cases, as this author does not have sufficient information to do so.

The following information is taken from the extensive news archives of *The Free Lance-Star*, in Fredericksburg, Virginia, which has made information regarding these cases publicly available on their website (http://www.flstarweb.com).

On September 9, 1996, in Oak Grove Terrace, Virginia, 16-year-old Sofia Silva arrived home from Courtland High School at around 3:15 p.m. According to her 21-year-old sister, who was at home at the time, Sofia spoke with a friend on the phone and then took a 30-minute nap. When she woke at 4:30 p.m., she took her homework and a grape soda out onto the porch.

At about 5 p.m., Sofia's sister came out onto the porch looking for her, having been on the phone for 30 minutes in her bedroom. She did not see Sofia anywhere, but noticed her half-finished can of grape soda and homework on the front step.

Sofia's backpack was still in her bedroom. Inside of it were her house keys, her makeup, and her wallet. She was not known to be dating, and did not own a car. When Sofia's mother got home from work, she checked with neighbors and Sofia's friends, but was unable to find her. At 9:30 p.m., she reported her daughter missing to the Spotsylvania County Sheriff's Office.

On October 14, five weeks later, Sofia's body was found partially submerged in water in the Sealston area of King George County off State Route 3, a remote area not far from Fredericksburg, some 20 miles away from her home. It was found by workers in the process of breaking up a beaver dam that was causing water to back up on property owned by Dominion Growers, a nearby nursery. Her body was wrapped in a light green moving blanket, tied with a rope.

The body had been in the water for some time. It was so badly decomposed that it was difficult to positively identify except through dental records. Also, precise cause of death could not be determined, though the Medical Examiner felt that it was strangulation, asphyxiation, or stabbing. Sofia's body was found dressed in the blue-jean shorts and long sleeved, white ribbed, sweater that she had been last seen in. She was even wearing the same jewelry she had on that day. However, her shoes, socks, bra, and underwear were not recovered from the disposal site.

The FBI developed a quick profile, giving it to law enforcement for use in the development of suspects. It included such things as radical changes in behavior, relocation of residence shortly after the date of the victim's disappearance, and driving around in areas where children could be found.

In December of 1996, the Spotsylvania SO began to focus on 44-year-old Karl Michael Roush in earnest as a primary suspect. He was an itinerant house painter who rented a basement just a few houses away from Silva at the time of her disappearance. His former landlord told police that he fit the profile of their suspect:

- Roush's behavior had changed after September 9, from drinking beer to drinking whiskey.
- Roush moved out of the basement he was living in two weeks after September 9.
- Roush was known to sit in his van and watch neighborhood children.

Police obtained warrants to collect fiber evidence from Roush's van and former residence in the basement. They even interviewed his ex-wife, looking for leads or connections.

On January 8, 1997, Robin G. McLaughlin, a forensic scientist in the state's Division of Forensic Science's crime lab, reported that four of the fibers found in Roush's van *matched* fibers that were found on Sofia Silva's body. Roush was indicted by a grand jury shortly thereafter, and law enforcement closed the case.

However, though the fiber evidence was said to *match* (and fiber evidence is *class evidence*, it never "matches," it is only "consistent with"), and though the suspect fit the profile, there was still an inconsistency. DNA taken from Sofia's vaginal area was not consistent with Roush as a donor, if there were only one offender.

It was not until June 9, 1997, when an FBI analysis of the fibers was completed, and results were compared to those from Virginia DFS, that an evidentiary revelation occurred. The FBI's criminalists determined that the four fibers recovered from Roush's van *did not* match fibers recovered from the body of Sofia Silva. On June 9, FBI lab personnel met with personnel from Virginia DFS and they concurred. The forensic scientist at Virginia DFS had made an error in her analysis and interpretation. The head of the Virginia DFS at the time, Paul B. Ferrara, came forward and immediately apologized to the public and to law enforcement. Robin G. McLaughlin, the forensic scientist who made the error, was ultimately forced to resign. And every case that she had worked on for over 12 years, some 1,200 involvements, was placed under review.

To add forensic insult to forensic injury, during the inquiry McLaughlin's supervisor argued that he had not reviewed her work on the case. He argued that he had no responsibility to quality control the work of those under his supervision. That supervisor was demoted.

On June 16, 1997, a judge ordered the state to drop charges against Roush for the abduction, rape, and murder of Sofia Silva. And law enforcement reopened the investigation into the Silva case. But it was already too late.

On May 1, 1997, Kristin Lisk, age 15, and her sister, Kati, age 12, of Spotsylvania, Virginia both disappeared after getting off separate school buses at their home. Kristin attended Spotsylvania High School, and Kati attended Spotsylvania Middle School. They lived 10 miles from Sofia Silva's home in Oak Grove Terrace.

Their school bags and personal belongings were at home, suggesting that they had each arrived there. But when their concerned father got home at 4 p.m. to determine why they weren't answering the phone, they were nowhere to be found. One book bag was found inside of the house, and another was in the front yard with a math book just a few feet away from it.

Both of their bodies were found five days later, on May 6, in the South Anna River, in Hanover County, 40 miles from their home. Neither was wrapped in a blanket, and both were wearing underwear, but Kristin's bra was not recovered. The medical examiner reported that both girls died from asphyxiation, and did not report any other discrete injuries or signs of violence.

The next day, and for the next few weeks, the Spotsylvania County Sheriff's Office continually assured the public and everyone concerned that there was no connection between the murder of Sofia Silva, and the murders of Kristin and Kati Lisk.

The belief that Karl Roush was responsible for the Sofia Silva murder was what led authorities to disregard any possible links between that case and the Lisk case. Their logic was that Roush had been in jail at the time of the Lisk killings. And if he was in jail, then he wasn't out killing anyone, so the cases were necessarily unrelated.

However, on June 9 of 1997, the same day that the errors regarding the fiber evidence analysis were revealed, Spotsylvania County Sheriff's Office admitted for the first time that the same person could have killed all three girls. They pointed to several similarities, namely:

- Age group: Sofia 16; Kristin 15; Kati 12.
- Build: All victims were slim with dark hair.
- Location: Victims lived within ten miles of each other.
- Abduction MO: All victims disappeared after school, taken or lured from their homes at approximately the same time, during daylight in similar residential areas.
- Clothing: All three victims were found clothed, but Kristin and Sofia were missing undergarments.
- Disposal behavior: All three victims were disposed of in water 20+ miles from their home.
- Disposal site only: In both cases, the locations where the victims were found were disposal sites only. They were not the primary scenes.
- ?Signature?: Sofia's pubic area had been shaved, and Kristin's was reportedly partially shaved. Some feel this is a signature behavior. However, the regular grooming habits of these girls, and their sexual habits, have not been established to sufficiently rule out the possibility that the victims shaved themselves for other reasons. Without this victimological information, one is left assuming that the shaving behavior must be attributable to the offender, and this may not be the case.

On July 31, 1997, an FBI lab report formally concluded, based on fiber evidence and DNA traces found on the bodies of all three victims, that a single offender was responsible and that the cases were related.

An FBI profile of the offender responsible for the Lisk murders was released to the media shortly after the bodies of both victims were found. It was published in *The Free Lance-Star* on May 8, 1997. As the Sofia Silva case has been linked with their deaths, the following may be considered the FBI's profile of the serial murderer in this case:

FBI PROFILE OF GIRLS' KILLER

Investigators released a list of characteristics they believe the girls' killer may have had before the crime, and changes in behavior he may show now.

They caution that no one change means someone committed a crime.

Before the crime:

- The person may have experienced some stressful event in his personal life.
- This could have been a problem at school with teachers, at work with managers or co-workers, at home with parents, spouse, or girlfriend, or with law enforcement.
- He would have displayed a preoccupation with adolescent girls but an awkwardness or lack of success in establishing relationships with them.
- He would spend time driving in areas young girls could be found and be seen staring at them to the point of the girls becoming uncomfortable.

- He may have displayed an avid interest in TV shows, movies or magazines featuring young girls, especially in athletic roles.

After the crime:

- Changes in the consumption of alcohol, drugs or cigarettes. Avoidance of family, friends and associates; absence from school, work or appointments.

- Unplanned disruption of daily activities. May attempt to leave the area for plausible reason such as a work-related trip, or to visit a distant relative or friend, etc.

- Highly nervous, irritable, short-tempered disposition. Disruption of normal sleeping patterns. Changes in physical appearance, such as hair coloring or new cut, removal or growth of facial hair. Lack of pride in appearance.

- Unexplained injuries, such as scratches or bruises.

- Uncharacteristic turn to or away from religious activity.

- Physical sickness.

- Intense interest in status of the investigation through discussion, media monitoring, etc.

- Changes to his vehicle. May clean or change appearance of vehicle (paint, removal of accessories). May hide, sell or dispose of it.

This author has not been involved in this case in any fashion. This author has not reviewed the crime-scene photos, autopsy photos, or visited the crime scenes. Therefore this author is not qualified to question the veracity of the conclusions presented.

However, it should be noted that the profile itself is clearly inductive, telling us about the likely behaviors of average offenders, and not about the motivations, needs, or behavioral patterns of the offender at hand. In fact, the characteristics mentioned are so general as to describe a great many people. It is, in effect, a boilerplate that closely resembles the one given by John Douglas in the JonBenet Ramsey case (see Appendix IIa).

Furthermore, it gives little investigative direction, and very limited insight into the physical evidence (which is understandable to some extent), victimology (victim risk or victim selection would have been a helpful start), or crime-scene characteristics of the cases. And it ultimately tells us nothing about the offender's motivations, essentially leaving out one of the most helpful parts of any criminal profile: why the offender chose the behaviors that he did.

Readers are left with the task of deciding for themselves, given what they have learned from this text, whether or not this profile is truly investigatively relevant. It is the author's opinion that these inductive profiles, and others like it, are not investigatively relevant, and that more robust and relevant forms of analysis should be employed.

BEHAVIORAL-EVIDENCE ANALYSIS – STEVE E. BRANCH, CHRIS M. BYERS, JAMES M. MOORE

Brent E. Turvey, M.S.

This report was prepared for the client as an investigative document. Its primary purpose is to provide the client with investigative direction, and subsequently illuminate the need for further examination of evidence by other appropriate forensic experts in order to fully appreciate available evidentiary potentials. It was not prepared for the purposes of implicating a specific individual or individuals.

HOMICIDE OF JAMES M. MOORE

8 YO white male;
Investigated by Arkansas State Crime Laboratory, Medical Examiner Division & City of West Memphis Police Department, West Memphis Arkansas
M.E. Case No. ME-329-93

HOMICIDE OF STEVE E. BRANCH

8 YO white male;
Investigated by Arkansas State Crime Laboratory, Medical Examiner Division & City of West Memphis Police Department, West Memphis Arkansas
M.E. Case No. ME-330-93

HOMICIDE OF CHRIS M. BYERS

8 YO white male;
Investigated by Arkansas State Crime Laboratory, Medical Examiner Division & City of West Memphis Police Department, West Memphis Arkansas
M.E. Case No. ME-331-93

LOCATION

On May 6, 1993, all three victims were found, bound wrist to ankle with shoe laces, in the water of a drainage ditch, in a heavily wooded area called the Robin Hood hills, behind the Blue Beacon Truck Wash in West Memphis, Arkansas.

EXAMINATIONS PERFORMED

An equivocal forensic examination of all available crime-scene and autopsy photos, crime-scene video, investigator's reports, witness statements, family statements, autopsy reports and numerous other sources to be listed as referenced in the endnote section of this report. The purpose of this preliminary examination was to competently assess the nature of the interactions between the victims and their environments as it contributed to their deaths as indicated by available forensic evidence, and the documentation regarding that evidence.

FORENSIC ANALYSIS

ESTABLISHED TIMELINE OF EVENTS

According to statements made by Mark Byers to Det. Brian Ridge of the West Memphis PD during a formal police interview dated 5-19-93:

From **9:00AM to 2:45PM** on 5-5-93, Mark Byers was at a clinic in Memphis having tests performed on him for his health condition.

According to parents of the three victims, **Weaver Elementary let out around 3:00PM**. All three victims, attendants of Weaver Elementary, would have left school at that time.

According to the Offense Incident Report on file with the West Memphis Police Department, Pamela Hobbs (the mother of Steve E. Branch), reported her son **missing at 3:30PM on 5-5-93**. She stated that her son left home after arriving there from school, and she hadn't seen him since. **This report was filed at 9:25PM**.

The following details are taken directly from statements made by Mark Byers to Det. Brian Ridge of the West Memphis PD during a formal police interview dated 5-19-93:

Mark Byers arrived home at **3:10PM**. Chris Byers was not waiting outside the home as he was expected to do (Chris Byers did not have a key to the family home, and was supposed to wait for Mark Byers or Ryan Byers, his brother, to let him in). Ryan Byers arrived home at **3:30-3:35PM. At 3:50PM**, Mark Byers drove Ryan Byers to the courthouse for a **4:00PM** appointment where Ryan was a witness at a trial. Mark Byers left Ryan Byers at the courthouse, to pick-up his wife Melissa Byers from work. Mark instructed Ryan to get a ride home with Chad Bell and his mother if court got out before he returned. At **5:20PM**, Mark Byers and Melissa Byers arrived at their home and found signs that Chris had been there but had been unable to get into the home through an open window. The front door was locked.

Mark Byers left the home to pick up Ryan at the courthouse, and on the way found Chris Byers playing on his skateboard. Mark Byers drove Chris home and gave him "two or three licks," described as a spanking with his belt in front of Melissa Byers. This was punishment for Chris not waiting outside the family home until Mark or Ryan arrived home to let him in. Ryan had a key, but Mark Byers explained that Chris was too young to have a key.

Mark Byers then left the Byers home to pick up Ryan, and instructed Chris to clean up the area around the carport until he returned.

According to the Offense Incident Report on file with the West Memphis Police Department, Mark Byers reported his step-son, Chris Byers, **missing as of 5:30PM on 5-5-93**. In the report, Mark Byers states that Chris Byers was last seen cleaning the yard at that time. **This report was filed at 8:10PM.**

According to the Offense Incident Report on file with the West Memphis Police Department, Diana Moore reported her son, Michael Moore, **missing as of 6:00PM on 5-5-93**. She states in this report that she observed her son riding bicycles with his friends Steve Branch and Chris Byers at this time. She further states that she lost sight of them, and sent her daughter to find them. The daughter was unable to locate the boys. **This report was filed at 9:24PM.**

The following details are taken directly from statements made by Mark Byers to Det. Brian Ridge of the West Memphis PD during a formal police interview dated 5-19-93:

At 6:30PM, Mark Byers arrived home with his son Ryan from the courthouse. Chris was not outside the house, and he was not found inside the house. Melissa Byers was, at that time, on the phone with her boss.

From 6:30-7:30PM, Mark, Melissa, and Ryan Byers drove around the neighborhood and surrounding areas looking for their missing son. There is an indication that they wanted to find him and then proceed to dinner at a local restaurant. During this time, they came across a black police officer on patrol, informed him of their missing son, and Mark Byers claims that the patrolman advised them to wait to make an official report to police until 8:00PM. Mark Byers explained to the officer, at this point, that he was very concerned because his son had never disappeared like this before.

(*Note*: This is in direct conflict with statements made by Melissa Byers in an interview with Det. Allen of the West Memphis PD dated 5-25-93. She states in this interview that Chris had on several occasions disappeared for several hours at a time, and that she believed that Chris lied to her about going to the Robin Hood area at least once.)

At approximately 8:00PM, Officer Regina Weeks of the West Memphis PD arrived at the Byers residence in response to a phone call from Mark Byers that his son Christopher was missing.

At approximately 8:15PM, Diana Moore shows up in the Byers' neighborhood looking for her son James M. Moore. She makes contact with the Byers, and Mark Byers explains that this is the first time he was informed that Chris was with other children. Diana Moore explains that she saw Steve Branch on his bike, James Moore on his bike, and Chris Byers on the back of Steve Branch's bike.

At approximately 8:30PM, Diana Moore, Mark Byers, Melissa Byers, and Ryan Byers begin a search of the last known location of the boys near the Robin Hood area. It was dark by this time, according to Mark Byers.

At this time, Mark Byers leaves the search party alone and returns to his home to change his clothing. The search party included, but was not limited to Ryan Byers, Ritchie Masters, Brett Smith, and Brett Smith's sister. Mark Byers was wearing shorts and flip-flops, and changes into boots and coveralls.

After changing his clothes, he returned to the search area and met up with Officer Moore of the West Memphis PD. Together they searched the woods until **10:30 or 11:00PM**.

At this time, Mark Byers returned home and called the Sheriff to request a search and rescue team. He was advised to call Denver Reed, the leader of the Crittenden County search and rescue team, in the morning.

Mark Byers states that, after this phone conversation, he drove out to the Blue Beacon Truck Wash with his son Ryan. There he told everyone inside what he was doing, informed them of the missing children, and then drove his vehicle around back. He and Ryan stood outside shouting towards the woods for the children, and honking the car horn. They continued this for some time.

After this, Mark Byers and Ryan Byers drove back to the Byers' home and met up with Melissa Byers, Terry Hobbs (Steve Branch's grandfather) and Diana Moore. They talked for a while, then decided to make another pass through the woods in a search effort.

Between **1:30-2:30AM** on 5-6-97, Sgt. Ball of the West Memphis PD drove by the Byers residence, and spoke with Mark and Melissa Byers. He advised them that a search was ongoing, and that officers in the area were looking for the children.

Shortly after this, Mark Byers' friend Tony Hudson arrived at the Byers residence. He and Mark Byers went to the Mid-continent building, which had been blown over, and was being rebuilt. They felt that the boys might be playing over there. At that location, they noticed a black van which was locked, and which appeared to belong to the people performing repairs on the building. They searched this location from between **2:00AM to 3:00AM**. According to Byers, the children were not found at this location.

At that point, Mark Byers decided to wait for daylight before engaging in further search efforts.

At daybreak, Terry Hobbs, Diana Moore and others arrived at the Byers residence to resume search efforts. The search of the Robin Hood area lasted until **about 8:00AM**.

At **6:30AM**, Mark Byers had called Denver Reed and arranged to meet him at the search area with the search and rescue team at approximately 8:30AM–9:00AM. **Between 8:30AM and 9:00AM** on 5-6-93, Mark Byers and Denver Reed met, and the search of the Robin Hood area began again.

According to the handwritten, unsigned, un-initialed six-page investigative report labeled "Crime Scene Notes" dated 5-6-93, the first body of one of the missing boys was located on Thursday, May 6, 1993 **at 1:45PM**, by Sgt. Mike Allen. A location is not given. However it is implied that the body was found in a creek. The first body was pulled from the creek by police officers at **2:45PM**. Det. Ridge located the second body in the creek at **2:56PM**, approximately 25ft South of the first body. **At 2:59PM**, the third and final body is located in the creek 5ft South of the second body.

According to an undated report drafted by Kent Hale, the Crittenden County Coroner, Mr Hale was contacted by the West Memphis PD on May 6, 1993 at **3:20PM**. He was advised that they had found the bodies of three boys in the woods near the Blue Beacon Truck Wash. Upon his arrival at the scene, all of the bodies had been removed from the creek, which was actually a drainage ditch, by officers on the scene.

Per his official reports, all dated 5-6-93, Kent Hale pronounced all three boys dead at the scene as follows:

- Steve E. Branch   5-6-93, 3:58PM
- Chris M. Byers   5-6-93, 4:02PM
- James M. Moore   5-6-93, 4:02PM

AUTOPSY REPORT – JAMES M. MOORE

The following forensic information is taken directly from the official autopsy report filed by Dr Frank J. Peretti of the Arkansas State Crime Lab, Medical Examiner Division, dated 5-7-93, Case No. ME-329-93 and/or from The official coroner's report filed by Kent Hale, Crittenden County Coroner, dated 5-6-97.

The purpose of this section is not to present an all inclusive, detailed account and explanation of every piece of information in these reports, but rather to explore these reports, with the corresponding photos, for consistency, possible omissions, and to review injuries or patterns that this examiner deemed to be significant to the case.

The victim, James M. Moore was a white male, eight years of age, born July 27th, 1984, who died of multiple traumatic injuries to the head, torso, and extremities with drowning. He was found in a drainage ditch, drowned in 2½ ft of water, near the bodies of two other 8-year-old male victims. He was found completely nude, with his wrists bound to his ankles by shoelaces.

TIME OF DEATH ESTIMATES

The Coroner's report completed by Mr Kent Hale states that lividity (the red discoloration in the skin caused by the pooling and settling of the blood within the blood vessels) was present. It also states that the lividity blanched with pressure. Lividity begins about 30 minutes after death has occurred. After four or five hours, dependent on environmental conditions, lividity fixes and will not blanche. It takes about eight to ten hours for lividity to become fixed. This could place the time of death (which can only be given as a range) of James Moore at sometime after daybreak on May 6, 1993. However it is only one biological indicator, and no one indicator should be used to determine the time of death.

The Coroner's report completed by Mr Kent Hale further states that Rigor Mortis (the chemical process of the exhaustion of ATP in muscle tissue, which begins after death, that results in the stiffening or contracting of muscles in the body) was present, but that it was difficult to assess due to the way the victim was bound. As a general biological guideline, Rigor Mortis begins about two to four hours after death. And full Rigor Mortis is complete about eight to 12 hours after death. Cold slows Rigor Mortis down, and heat speeds the process up.

When Dr Peretti conducted his autopsy of James M. Moore, on May 7th, 1993, he stated that "Rigor was present and fixed to an equal degree in all extremities." The time that the autopsy was conducted is not noted on the report, therefore is difficult to gauge how far the body was into rigor. However, Dr Peretti was confident that Rigor was evenly present throughout the extremities, and that he made no mention of any dissolution. As a general guideline, Rigor reaches full even distribution within 12 to 24 hours after death. Also as a general guideline, Rigor begins to disappear within 12 hours after that, at which time decomposition begins. Again, by itself, the use of Rigor Mortis to determine a time of death, or a time range of death, is not advised. Several biological indicators should be used.

As the above suggests, a time of death of any kind is very difficult to estimate given the differences in metabolic processes between individuals, given varying individual anatomy, and given varying environmental factors. The presentation and stages of Rigor Mortis and/or Livor Mortis (lividity) used to make such estimations are not absolute, and should be treated as guidelines, not hard and fast biological principals to be blanketly generalized from case to case.

WOUND PATTERN ANALYSIS

This victim received more traumatic head injuries than any of the other victims in this case. Dr Peretti states that defense wounds were present on the victim's hands. These wounds were very few, indicating that the victim was incapacitated quickly after the attack began. So the nature of these head injuries, and the limited defensive type wounds, combine to indicate sudden, forceful, and repeated blows that resulted in abraded contusions, multiple lacerations, and multiple skull fractures.

There is an unexplained directional pattern abrasion just below the victim's right anterior shoulder area.

This unexplained injury does not correspond with any of the physical evidence collected at the location that victim was discovered. It is furthermore inconsistent with any of the naturally occurring elements that exist in that environment. The best conclusion that this examiner can reach is that this pattern abrasion was created by forceful, directional contact with something that was not found at that crime scene, whether it be a weapon, a surface or something else capable of creating that pattern.

The shoelace ligatures used to restrain this victim did not leave deep furrows, and also did not leave abrasions. This indicates that the victim was not struggling while the ligatures were in place. This indicates further that the victim was very much unconscious when the ligatures were affixed to his wrists and ankles.

We know that the victim drowned, that is to say that hemorrhagic edema fluid was present in the victim's lungs, indicating that the victim was breathing when he was placed into the 2½ ft of water in the drainage ditch at Robin Hood Hills.

Together, these facts suggest that the purpose of the ligatures in this victim's case was to keep the victim from moving around or being able to swim should he regain consciousness once he had been thrown into the water. It is this examiners opinion that the assailant in this case demonstrated all manner of awareness and cognizance at this location. The assailant knew that this victim was not dead when they threw this victim into the water, and that the ligatures would assist to complete the act of deliberate homicide should the victim become conscious.

SEXUAL ASSAULT/RAPE INDICATORS

The victim in this case does not show any signs consistent with sexual assault or rape. As Dr Peretti's examination concluded, no sperm were present in any of the orifices, no injuries were detected on or at the victim's genitals and an examination of the victim's anus revealed no injuries in the mucosal surfaces, which are very tender and sensitive.

Mr Hale in his Coroner's report states that the victim may have been sexually assaulted. That is not a helpful statement. What may have occurred is not at issue. It is more accurate to state, after a full examination, that there is no evidence of sexual assault. It is further important to note that sperm evidence, along with many other types of physical transfer evidence, would have been washed away when the victim was placed in the water. So a determination of whether or not a rape or sexual assault occurred is not always possible under these conditions.

It is also important to note that though the victim's anus was dilated, this by itself does not indicate or suggest anal penetration. The anus is a sphincter; a muscle which is tight and closed in most living individuals, and always open and dilated in deceased individuals. When someone dies their anus relaxes and dilates. The presence of a dilated anus taken to indicate sexual assault or rape is a very common misinterpretation made by untrained individuals when examining those who have met with violent death.

LACK OF INJURIES

When compared to the other two victims in this case, who were found at the same location, bound nude with shoelace ligatures in the same fashion, the most striking discrepancy is the lack of injuries suffered by this victim. In the crime-scene and autopsy photos made available to this examiner, there were no readily discernable bitemarks visible, the genitals have not been visibly disturbed or molested, and there are no discernable stab wounds. This lack of attention is very telling, and will be discussed in the Offender Characteristics section of this report.

There is again a lack of evidence to support any sort of strangulation. Dr Peretti states that his examination of the neck of this victim revealed no injuries, and the photos that this examiner has seen support that conclusion.

There is also, again, a lack of mosquito bites to this victim, which, as mentioned earlier, suggests that he received his injuries elsewhere first. This because the injuries took time to inflict, time during which many mosquito bites would have been received, even after death.

RECOMMENDATIONS

It is apparent from the physical evidence in this case that James M. Moore was attacked with sudden, violent force from which he defended himself in only a limited fashion. It cannot be known whether or not this was done before or after his clothes were removed. After the attack, he was unconscious, as it was at this point that he was bound with the shoelace ligatures.

It is this examiner's recommendation that the clothes of James M. Moore, recovered from the drainage ditch, be reanalyzed by experts to determine if bloodstain patterns are evident. If present, they may tell us the nature and angle of blows delivered; if blood is not present, then this could help establish whether or not the victim was wearing clothes when he was attacked.

Furthermore, the piece of cloth (pictured clutched in the victim's hand at the right), found in this victim's hand at the scene, should be re-examined. This is a very critical piece of physical evidence that has not been fully examined by qualified individuals to determine its full evidentiary value in this case. The cloth is a potential link from this victim directly to a suspect. Where this victim tore this piece of cloth from is a question that begs answering. And given that it could be physically matched back to the material of origin, this makes its evidentiary value all the greater.

AUTOPSY REPORT – STEVE E. BRANCH

The following forensic information is taken directly from the official autopsy report filed by Dr Frank J. Peretti of the Arkansas State Crime Lab, Medical Examiner Division, dated 5-7-93, Case No. ME-330-93 and/or from The official coroner's report filed by Kent Hale, Crittenden County Coroner, dated 5-6-97.

The purpose of this section is not to present an all inclusive, detailed account and explanation of every piece of information in these reports, but rather to explore these reports, with the corresponding photos, for consistency, possible omissions, and to review injuries or patterns that this examiner deemed to be significant to the case.

The victim, Steve E. Branch, was a white male, eight years of age, born November 26, 1984, who died of multiple traumatic injuries to the head, torso, and extremities with drowning. He was found in a drainage ditch, drowned in 2½ ft of water, near the bodies of two other eight-year-old male victims. He was found completely nude, with his wrists bound to his ankles by shoelaces.

TIME OF DEATH ESTIMATES

The Coroner's report completed by Mr Kent Hale states that lividity (the red discoloration in the skin caused by the pooling and settling of the blood within the blood vessels) was present. It also states that the lividity blanched with pressure. Lividity begins about thirty minutes after death has occurred. After four or five hours, dependent on environmental conditions, lividity fixes and will not blanche. It takes about 8 to 10 hours for lividity to become fixed. This could place the time of death (which can only be given as a range) of Steve Branch at sometime after daybreak on May 6, 1993. However it is only one biological indicator, and no one indicator should be used to determine the time of death.

The Coroner's report, completed by Mr Kent Hale, further states that Rigor Mortis (the chemical process of the exhaustion of ATP in muscle tissue, which begins after death, that results in the stiffening or contracting of muscles in the body) was present, but that it was difficult to assess due to the way the victim was bound. As a general biological guideline, Rigor Mortis begins about two to four hours after death. And full Rigor Mortis is complete about eight to 12 hours after death. Cold slows Rigor Mortis down, and heat speeds the process up.

When Dr Peretti conducted his autopsy of Steve E. Branch, on May 7, 1993, he stated that "Rigor was present and fixed to an equal degree in all extremities." The time that the autopsy was conducted is not noted on the report, therefore is difficult to gauge how far the body was into rigor. However, Dr Peretti was confident that Rigor was evenly present throughout the extremities, and that he made no mention of any dissolution. As a general guideline, Rigor reaches full even distribution within 12 to 24 hours after death. Also as a general guideline, Rigor begins to disappear within 12 hours after that, at which time decomposition begins. Again, by itself, the use of Rigor Mortis to determine a time of death, or a time range of death, is not advised. Several biological indicators should be used.

As the above suggests, a time of death of any kind is very difficult to estimate given the differences in metabolic processes between individuals, given varying individual anatomy, and given varying environmental factors. The presentation and stages of Rigor Mortis and/or Livor Mortis (lividity) used to make such estimations are not absolute, and should be treated as guidelines, not hard and fast biological principals to be blanketly generalized from case to case.

WOUND PATTERN ANALYSIS

There are numerous violent, traumatic injuries to this victim's face and head, as well as numerous superficial scratches, abrasions, and contusions noted throughout the rest of his body. Dr Peretti, however, does not note the presence of extensive defensive wounds.

This indicates a violent, overpowering attack on this victim that he was unable to put up resistance against. The constellation of wounds are very similar to those inflicted on James Moore, however they are much more intense and include the victim's face.

This level of attention paid to the victim's face, in terms of depersonalization and rage, is indicative of familiarity and that will be explored later on in this report.

Furthermore, there is the existence of patterned injuries all over this victim's face that could be bitemarks. Since the ME may have missed this crucial evidence, other areas of his body may show bitemark evidence as well. The autopsy photos of this victim supplied to this examiner were not of sufficient quality to make an absolute determination of any kind, and would require a thorough examination by a qualified forensic odontologist for an informed, conclusive analysis.

Bitemark evidence is very important in any criminal case because it demonstrates behavior and lends itself to individuation. It can reveal to an examiner who committed the act, because bitemarks can be as unique as fingerprints. And, once established, it also reveals the act itself; biting.

Another unidentified pattern compression abrasion can be found on the back of Steve Branch's head. The source of this injury caused a 3½ inch fracture at the base of the skull with multiple extension fractures that terminate in the foramen magnum (that's the hole at the base of the skull where the spinal cord connects to the brain). Upon close examination, this pattern injury is consistent with compression made from footwear. Again, without better photos supplied to the examiner showing a variety of angles, it's very difficult to make a positive identification of any kind. But the pattern is consistent with a footwear impression, and would require a footwear impression expert to analyze and make an informed, competent determination.

The shoelace ligatures used to restrain this victim did leave deep furrows, and also did leave patterned abrasions on both the wrists and ankles. This indicates that the victim was struggling while the ligatures were in place. This indicates further that the victim was very much conscious before or after the ligatures were affixed to his wrists and ankles.

We know that the victim drowned, that is to say that hemorrhagic edema fluid was present in the victim's lungs, as well as in the victim's mouth, indicating that the victim was breathing when he was placed into the 2½ ft of water in the drainage ditch at Robin Hood Hills.

Together, these facts, again, suggest that the purpose of the ligatures in this victim's case was to keep the victim from moving around or being able to swim should he regain consciousness once he had been thrown into the water. It is this examiner's opinion that the assailant in this case demonstrated all manner of awareness and cognizance at this location. The assailant knew that this victim was not dead when they threw this victim into the water, and that the ligatures would assist to complete the act of deliberate homicide should the victim become conscious.

SEXUAL ASSAULT/RAPE INDICATORS
As Dr Peretti's examination concluded, no sperm were present in any of the

orifices, no injuries were detected on or at the victim's genitals and an examination of the victim's anus revealed no injuries in the mucosal surfaces, which are very tender and sensitive.

Mr Hale in his Coroner's report states that the victim may have been sexually assaulted. That is not a helpful statement. What may have occurred is not at issue. It is more accurate to state, after a full examination, that there is no evidence of sexual assault. It further important to note that sperm evidence, along with many other types of physical transfer evidence, would have been washed away when the victim was placed in the water. So a determination of whether or not a rape or sexual assault occurred is not always possible under these conditions.

It is also important to note that though the victim's anus was dilated, this by itself does not indicate or suggest anal penetration. The anus is a sphincter; a muscle which is tight and closed in most living individuals, and always open and dilated in deceased individuals. When someone dies their anus relaxes and dilates. The presence of a dilated anus taken to indicate sexual assault or rape is a very common misinterpretation made by untrained individuals when examining those who have met with violent death.

LACK OF INJURIES

There is again a lack of evidence to support any sort of strangulation. Dr Peretti states that his examination of the neck of this victim revealed no injuries, and the photos that this examiner has seen support that conclusion.

There is also, again, a lack of mosquito bites to this victim, which, as mentioned earlier, suggests that he received his injuries elsewhere first. This because the injuries took time to inflict, time during which many mosquito bites would have been received, even after death.

RECOMMENDATIONS

It is apparent from the physical evidence in this case that Steve E. Branch was attacked with sudden, violent force from which he defended himself in only a limited fashion. It appears as thought this attack took place, at least in part, while his cloths were off and while he was restrained by the shoelace ligatures.

It is this examiner's recommendation that both a forensic odontologist and a footwear impression analyst review the aforementioned photos for evidentiary saliency. Without such experts it will be difficult to accurately assess the validity of the related evidence as indicated by the autopsy photos. The photos indicate pattern evidence that is consistent with bitemark and footwear impression evidence, but without an expert's eye and experience the usefulness of that evidence will be limited.

AUTOPSY REPORT – CHRIS M. BYERS

The following forensic information is taken directly from the official autopsy report filed by Dr Frank J. Peretti of the Arkansas State Crime Lab, Medical Examiner Division, dated 5-7-93, Case No. ME-331-93 and/or from The official coroner's report filed by Kent Hale, Crittenden County Coroner, dated 5-6-97.

The purpose of this section is not to present an all inclusive, detailed account and explanation of every piece of information in these reports, but rather to explore these reports, with the corresponding photos, for consistency, possible omissions, and to review injuries or patterns that this examiner deemed to be significant to the case.

The victim, Chris M. Byers, was a white male, eight years of age, born June 23, 1984, who died of multiple traumatic injuries to the head, as well as the violent removal of his penis, the scrotal sac, and the testes, and associated cuts and stab wounds to the genital area.

This victim was found in a drainage ditch, in 2½ ft of water, near the bodies of two other eight-year-old male victims. He was found completely nude, with his wrists bound to his ankles by shoelaces.

It should be noted that this victim's injuries were the most extensive, most violent, and most overtly sexual of all the victims in this case. The nature and extent of this victim's wounds indicate that the assailant spent the most time with this victim. Additionally, this victim's toxicology report revealed non-therapeutic levels of carbamazepine in the blood. All of these differences are very important, and will be explored in the later sections of this report.

TIME OF DEATH ESTIMATES

The Coroner's report completed by Mr Kent Hale states that lividity (the red discoloration in the skin caused by the pooling and settling of the blood within the blood vessels) was present. It also states that the lividity blanched with pressure. Lividity begins about 30 minutes after death has occurred. After four or five hours, dependent on environmental conditions, lividity fixes and will not blanche. It takes about eight to ten hours for lividity to become fixed. This could place the time of death (which can only be given as a range) of Chris Byers at sometime after daybreak on May 6, 1993. However it is only one biological indicator, and no one indicator should be used to determine the time of death.

The Coroner's report, completed by Mr Kent Hale, further states that Rigor Mortis (the chemical process of the exhaustion of ATP in muscle tissue, which begins after death, that results in the stiffening or contracting of muscles in the body) was present, but that it was difficult to assess due to the way the victim was bound. As a general biological guideline, Rigor Mortis begins about two to four hours after death. And full Rigor Mortis is complete about eight to 12 hours after death. Cold slows Rigor Mortis down, and heat speeds the process up.

When Dr Peretti conducted his autopsy of Chris M. Byers, on May 7, 1993, he stated that "Rigor was present and fixed to an equal degree in all extremities." The time that the autopsy was conducted is not noted on the report, therefore is difficult to gauge how far the body was into rigor. However, Dr Peretti was confident that Rigor was evenly present throughout the extremities, and that he made no mention of any dissolution. As a general guideline, Rigor reaches full even distribution within 12 to 24 hours after death. Also as a general guideline, Rigor begins to disappear within 12 hours after that, at which time decomposition begins. Again, by itself, the use of Rigor Mortis to determine a time of death, or a time range of death, is not advised. Several biological indicators should be used.

As the above suggests, a time of death of any kind is very difficult to estimate given the differences in metabolic processes between individuals, given varying individual anatomy, and given varying environmental factors. The presentation and stages of Rigor Mortis and/or Livor Mortis (lividity) used to make such estimations are not absolute, and should be treated as guidelines, not hard and fast biological principals to be blanketly generalized from case to case.

WOUND PATTERN ANALYSIS

There are numerous violent, traumatic injuries to this victim's head, specifically to the base of the skull. There was also evidence of the violent emasculation of the victim's sex organs, extensive lacerations and bruising to the victim's buttocks, as well as numerous superficial scratches, abrasions, and contusions noted throughout the rest of his body. Dr Peretti also noted that there were numerous healed injuries of varying nature on this victim. Dr Peretti, however, did not note the presence of defensive wounds.

Again, this indicates a violent, overpowering attack on this victim that he was unable to put up resistance against. The general constellation of wounds to this victim is more advanced, more extensive, more overtly sexually oriented and includes the use of a knife.

This knife was used not only to inflict multiple stabbing and cutting injuries to the victim's inner thighs and genital area, it was used in the emasculation process. There is, unmentioned in either the ME's or Coroner's reports, what appears to be a clear impression of the knife handle on the right side of the large gaping defect left behind after the removal of the victim's penis, scrotal sac, and testes. This impression was created when the knife was thrust full length into the victim by the assailant, during the process of emasculation. This indicates forceful, violent thrusts. The nature of this emasculation, as indicated by these wounds, is neither skilled nor practiced. It was a rageful, careless, but purposeful act carried out in anger. It is the opinion of this examiner that this injury would have resulted in massive, uncontrollable blood-loss, from which the victim could not have survived without immediate medical attention.

It should also be pointed out that the nature of the stab wounds inflicted on the victim's genital area, separate from those received during the emasculation process, show marked irregular configuration and pulling of the skin. This indicates that either the knife was being twisted as the assailant stabbed the victim, or that the victim was moving as the blade was withdrawn.

As stated by Mark Byers, the step-father of Chris Byers, to Det. Brian Ridge of the West Memphis PD during a formal police interview dated 5-19-93, Mark Byers gave Chris "two or three licks," described as a spanking with his belt in front of Melissa Byers shortly before his disappearance. There are only three sets of injuries in Chris Byers' buttock area noted by Dr Peretti in the official autopsy report that would seem to be the result of this spanking. Dr Peretti does not venture to explain which of those three sets of injuries are the result of the spanking delivered by Mark Byers.

The first set of injuries is described as faint contusions on the surface of the right buttocks (not pictured). These injuries could be consistent with the parental whipping given to Chris Byers by Mark Byers.

The second set of injuries is described as five superficial cutting wounds on the left buttock (pictured on the left in this photo at the right). It should be noted that these injuries are actually lacerations, as indicated by the bridging between the open tissue, and the irregular edges. Both indicators are apparent upon close examination of the photographs. It is the opinion of this examiner that this set of injuries is most consistent with the parental whipping given to Chris Byers by Mark Byers. It is further the opinion of this examiner that after having received this set of injuries, which tore open the skin and would have resulted in some severe bleeding, the victim would have been unable to walk or ride a bicycle without incredible pain and discomfort.

The third set of injuries is the multiple linear superficial interrupted cuts on the right buttock region (pictured in the photo above on the right). These injuries are not consistent with having been made by a belt as they are cuts. The edges are not irregular, and the cuts are interrupted, again indicating movement by the victim or the assailant during the attack.

Furthermore, there is the existence of bruised ovoid compression injuries all over this victim's inner thigh that could be suction type bitemarks. Since the ME may have missed this crucial evidence, other areas of his body may show bitemark evidence as well. The autopsy photos of this victim supplied to this examiner were not of sufficient quality to make an absolute determination of any kind, and would require a thorough examination by a qualified forensic odontologist for an informed, conclusive analysis.

Bitemark evidence is very important in any criminal case because it demonstrates behavior and lends itself to individuation. It can reveal to an examiner who committed the act, because bitemarks can be as unique as fingerprints and positively identify a suspect. And, once established, it also reveals the act itself; biting.

The shoelace ligatures used to restrain this victim did leave deep furrows, and also did leave patterned abrasions on both the wrists and ankles. This indicates that the victim was struggling while the ligatures were in place. This indicates further that the victim was very much conscious before or after the ligatures were affixed to his wrists and ankles.

We know that this victim did not drown, that is to say that no hemorrhagic edema fluid was present in the victim's lungs, or well in the victim's mouth. This indicates that the victim was already dead when he was placed into the 2½ ft of water in the drainage ditch at Robin Hood Hills. This is, again, very different from the other two victims in this case.

On a final note, Mr. Hale states in his supplemental report on Chris Byers that there is a stab wound on his head. This is actually incorrect, and rectified by Dr Peretti who states in his autopsy report of Chris Byers that the same injury is a 1¼–inch laceration to the left parietal scalp.

SEXUAL ASSAULT/RAPE INDICATORS

As Dr Peretti's examination concluded, no sperm were present in any of the orifices. There were also no apparent injuries to the anus. However the victim was brutally emasculated, and shows some evidence of bitemark injury on the inside of his thighs. This victim was sexually assaulted, and the attack on this victim was highly sexual in its nature.

There are, however, no clear indications of rape (that is, forceful penetration). It is also important to note that though the victim's anus was dilated, this by itself does not indicate or suggest anal penetration. The anus is a sphincter; a muscle which is tight and closed in most living individuals, and always open and dilated in deceased individuals. When someone dies their anus relaxes and dilates. The presence of a dilated anus taken to indicate sexual assault or rape is a very common misinterpretation made by untrained individuals when examining those who have met with violent death.

LACK OF INJURIES

There is again a lack of evidence to support any sort of strangulation. Dr Peretti states that his examination of the neck of this victim revealed no injuries, and the photos that this examiner has seen support that conclusion.

There is also, again, a lack of mosquito bites to this victim, which, as mentioned earlier, suggests that he received his injuries elsewhere first. This because the injuries took time to inflict, time during which many mosquito bites would have been received, even after death.

Additionally, unlike Steve Branch, there is no overkill present in this victim's face. That is to say that this is another of the marked differences between the killings of Steve Branch and Chris Byers which is very important to note, and which will be explored more thoroughly in this report.

RECOMMENDATIONS

It is apparent from the physical evidence in this case that Chris M. Byers was attacked with sudden, violent force from which he defended himself in only a limited fashion. It appears as though this attack took place, at least in part, while his cloths were off and while the shoelace ligatures restrained him. He was sexually assaulted (an assault of a sexual nature, to areas of the body considered to be sexual, that does not include sexual penetration), and associated stab wounds indicate that he may have been conscious during several phases of the attack.

There is also evidence to suggest previous, but recent, physical abuse of Chris Byers. Given the use of corporal punishment by the father, Mark Byers, and given the healed injuries noted by Dr Peretti, and the extent of the injuries to Chris Byers' buttocks, this possibility should be thoroughly investigated.

It is this examiner's recommendation that a forensic odontologist review the aforementioned photos for evidentiary saliency. Without such experts it will be difficult to accurately assess the validity of the related evidence as indicated by the autopsy photos. The photos indicate pattern evidence that is consistent with bitemark evidence, but without an expert's eye and experience the usefulness of that evidence will be limited.

It is also the recommendation of this examiner that an expert in child abuse injuries be asked to review the photographs of the injuries to this victim and make a comment.

VICTIMOLOGY

JAMES MICHAEL MOORE

The information available to this examiner regarding this particular victim was very limited. It is the opinion of this examiner that a full background investigation should be made of this victim, as well as establishing friends, enemies, regular activities, and that at least a full reconstruction be done of his last 24 hours before he was determined to be missing. It is also the opinion of this examiner that an investigation into the medical records and school records of this child is requisite.

BACKGROUND

The victim, eight-year-old James M. Moore, was born on 7-27-84. At the time of the attack that resulted in his death, he lived on 1398 E. Barton in West Memphis, Arkansas with his mother, Diana Moore. His family is in the lower socioeconomic class.

He attended Weaver Elementary School, and was an avid Boy Scout. In fact he was wearing his Boy Scout shirt and cap at the time of his disappearance, both of which were recovered at the scene with his body.

PHYSICAL TRAITS

The victim is described by his mother, in the missing person's report filed with West Memphis PD on 5-5-93, as: 4 ft. tall, 60 lbs., with brown hair and blue eyes.

CLOTHING

On the evening of his disappearance, according to his mother, the victim was wearing blue pants, a blue Boy Scouts of America shirt, an orange and blue Boy Scouts hat, and tennis shoes.

RISK ASSESSMENT

This victim normally lived **a low–medium risk lifestyle**. He had a structured schedule involving school and extracurricular activities with friends and family. He was expected to be home for dinner, and his mother appeared to be aware of his whereabouts, generally. That is to say, he is normally at low-medium risk of being the victim of this type of crime because of his activities and lifestyle.

On the night of the victim's disappearance, he was not under the direct care of a parent or guardian. And he was engaging in activities away from his neighborhood and the protective eyes of the community. This put him at **medium risk** of being the victim of this type of crime.

However, he still would have been an extremely **high-risk victim** from the viewpoint of the assailant responsible for this crime for the following reasons:

1 The victim was in a group, not alone: the assailant would have had to successfully con or incapacitate all of the victims at once to prevent them from getting away. This is possible, but requires ability, strength and competence on the part of the offender.

2 The victim and his friends were young: young children are very carefully attended to, in general, and are expected places, and will almost always be missed within a short period of time.

STEVE EDWARD BRANCH

The information available to this examiner regarding this particular victim was very limited. It is the opinion of this examiner that a full background investigation should be made of this victim, as well as establishing friends, enemies, regular activities, and that at least a full reconstruction be done of his last 24 hours before he was determined to be missing. It is also the opinion of this examiner that an investigation into the medical records and school records of this child is requisite.

BACKGROUND

The victim, eight-year-old Steve E. Branch, was born on 11-26-84. At the time of the attack that resulted in his death, he lived on 1601 E. McAuley in West Memphis, Arkansas with his mother, Pamela Marie Hobbs. According to the Missing Person's Report filed by Pam Hobbs, at the time of his disappearance the family did not have a telephone at their residence. The Hobbs family is in the lower socioeconomic class.

Steve Branch attended Weaver Elementary School, and was an avid Boy Scout, according to statements made by Mark Byers.

PHYSICAL TRAITS

The victim is described by his mother, in the Missing Person's Report filed with West Memphis PD on 5-5-93, as: 4'2" tall, 60 lbs., blonde hair and blue eyes.

CLOTHING

On the evening of his disappearance, according to his mother, the victim was wearing blue jeans and a white T-shirt. He was also riding a 20" black colored "Renegade" bicycle.

PERSONALITY/MEDICAL HISTORY

N/A

RISK ASSESSMENT

This victim normally lived **a low–medium risk lifestyle**. He had a semi-structured schedule involving school and extracurricular activities with friends and family. He was expected to be home for dinner, and his mother appeared to be aware of his whereabouts, generally. That is to say, he is normally at low–medium risk of being the victim of this type of crime because of his activities and lifestyle.

On the night of this victim's disappearance, he was not under the direct care of a parent or guardian. And he was engaging in activities away from his neighborhood and the protective eyes of his parents and the community. This put him at **medium risk** of being the victim of this type of crime.

However, he still would have been an extremely **high-risk victim** from the viewpoint of the assailant responsible for this crime for the following reasons:

1. The victim was in a group, not alone: the assailant would have had to successfully con or incapacitate all of the victims at once to prevent them from getting away. This is possible, but requires ability, strength and competence on the part of the offender.

2. The victim and his friends were young: young children are very carefully attended to, in general, and are expected places, and will almost always be missed within a short period time.

CHRISTOPHER MARK BYERS

BACKGROUND

The victim, eight-year-old Christopher Mark Byers, was born on 6-23-84. At the time of the attack that resulted in his death, he lived on 1400 E. Barton in West Memphis, Arkansas with his mother, Melissa Byers, his step-father, John Mark Byers, and his half brother, 13-year-old Ryan Byers, who has dyslexia.

Chris was born Christopher Lee Murray. According to reports written by Pediatric Neurology, P.A., where Chris was a patient, Chris' biological father had "multiple sociopathies" and was believed to be a paranoid schizophrenic. His biological father was also very aggressive, had a history of difficulty with the law as well as a history of substance abuse.

According to a police interview with Det. Allen dated 5-25-93, Melissa Byers states that John Mark Byers adopted Chris "two or three years ago" at which time Chris' name was changed to Christopher Mark Byers. (Pediatric Neurology, P.A. lists the patient as Chris Murray throughout 1993, but as Chris Byers during 1990).

At the time of Chris Byers' death, the Byers family lived primarily from the disability pay received by Mark Byers, who claims to have been diagnosed with a brain tumor which he further claims results in black-outs and slurred speech. Mark Byers was also trained as a jeweler, regularly attended swap meets, and claimed to be taking the prescription drug Tegretol for his seizures (trade name for Carbamazepine). At this time, Mark Byers was also a drug informant for the West Memphis PD, and enjoyed their confidence and trust, being on a first name basis with most of the detectives investigating this case.

Chris Byers attended Weaver Elementary School, and was not an avid Boy Scout, according to statements made by Mark Byers, but did attend one or two meetings and expressed a desire to become more involved.

PHYSICAL TRAITS

Chris Byers is described by his stepfather, in the missing person's report filed with West Memphis PD on 5-5-93, as: 4'4" tall, 50 lbs., light brown hair and brown eyes.

CLOTHING

On the evening of his disappearance, according to Mark Byers, the victim was wearing blue jeans, dark shoes, and a white long sleeve shirt. He was also riding a 20" black colored "Renegade" bicycle.

INTELLIGENCE/SCHOLASTIC ACHIEVEMENT

The following information is according to a medical report filed by Donald J. Eastmead, MD of Pediatric Neurology, P.A. in Memphis, Tennessee on 1/14/93:

> Chris has been tested and appears to be at normal levels, and has a purported "C" average, but attends special-education classes.

PERSONALITY/MEDICAL HISTORY

The following information is according to a medical report filed by Donald J. Eastmead, MD of Pediatric Neurology, P.A. in Memphis, Tennessee on 1/14/93:

> Chris is seen with his mother and stepfather (six years) for extreme impulsivity, destructiveness, opposition, defiance, hyperactivity, extremely low frustration tolerance and refusal to follow commands...there have been episodes of fire starting and anger outbursts with fighting towards the other children. The other children and their parents refuse to let their children play with Chris.

On page two of that report, Dr Eastmead gives three diagnosis' of Chris condition: Encephalopathy demonstrated by Attention-Deficit Hyerpactivity Disorder; Intermittent Explosive Behavior; and Conduct Disorder (it should be noted that the onset of conduct disorder before the age of 15 is one of the primary requirements of the Anti-social Personality Disorder).

Dr Eastmead also states:

> Chris is certainly a difficult child who may require in-hospital treatment to gain control of his behavior. I am increasing the medication and changing it to Dexidrine 5 to 10 mg morning and noon, 5 in the afternoon, as well as adding Tegretol (Carbamazepine) 50 to 100 mg t.i.d. Tofranil caused visual hallucinations, and this will not be tried.

It should also be noted that Chris had been prescribed a regular prescription of Ritalin since at least 4/21/92.

According to a missing persons report filed with the West Memphis PD on 5-5-93 by Mark Byers, Chris was on Ritalin at the time of his disappearance, but had not taken his medication that day.

According to an interview with Melissa Byers on 5-25-93 conducted by Det. Allen of the West Memphis PD, Melissa Byers claimed to be concerned that

Chris was being sexually abused. She reportedly spoke with the school guidance counselor regarding this issue, and confronted Chris about it directly. This in response to Chris' pattern of destructive, violent, and defiant behavior, including several incidents of fire setting.

RISK ASSESSMENT

This victim normally lived **a very high-risk lifestyle**. Not only was Chris a defiant child with tendencies towards violence and destructive anti-social behavior, but he was susceptible, needing the attention and approval from others that he was clearly not getting in his home environment. There are also some very clear indicators that lead this examiner to believe that Chris was being physically, if not sexually, abused. These indicators include Chris' Conduct Disorder, his ADD, and the healed injuries noted in the autopsy report.

It is also clear that despite Chris' pattern of behavior, Mark Byers and Melissa Byers put very little effort into regulating the behavior of Chris Byers. He certainly was not being monitored very closely on the day of his disappearance, despite statements by his parents that he was being punished for not waiting around outside his home until someone got home with a key to let him in. Chris Byers was an emotionally and physically vulnerable child who was constantly on medication, who desired the attention of others and who was constantly exhibiting defiant, violent, and impulsive behaviors. This was not a healthy child, living in a healthy home environment.

However, Chris still would have been a moderately **high-risk victim** from the viewpoint of any assailant responsible for this crime for the following reasons:

1 The victim was in a group, not alone: the assailant would have had to successfully con or incapacitate all of the victims at once to prevent them from getting away. This is possible, but requires ability, strength and competence on the part of the offender.

2 The victim and his friends were young: young children are very carefully attended to, in general, and are expected places, and will almost always be missed within a short period time.

CRIME-SCENE CHARACTERISTICS

SCENE TYPE

A primary crime scene is most often defined as the scene where the most interactions between the victim and the offender take place. The crime scene that these three victims were found at was a disposal site only. It was secondary to the primary crime scene. This is established by the following factors:

1   The nature and extent of the wounds inflicted upon these victims, especially the emasculation of Chris Byers, required light, required time, and required uninterrupted privacy. As it was dark in those woods, and as search parties were travelling in and out of the area all evening, this dictates a secluded structure of some kind away from the immediate area of attention.

2   The nature and extent of the wounds inflicted upon these victims, especially the emasculation of Chris Byers, would have resulted in a tremendous amount of blood loss. Very little blood was found at this scene on the banks of the drainage ditch.

3   The stabbing injuries and emasculation injuries inflicted upon Chris Byers alone, because Chris was conscious during at least part of the assault, would have resulted in a great deal of screaming. Of all the sounds reported that evening by searchers and local residents, screaming was not among them.

It is the opinion of this examiner, then, that this crime as it stands is at least three crime scenes short of being solved. That is to say that there are at least four crime scenes total involved in this crime:

1   The abduction site (presumably in or near the Robin Hood Hills area).

2   The attack site (a nearby structure or residence).

3   The dump site (the drainage ditch where the bodies were found).

4   The vehicle used to transport (a truck of some kind).

METHOD OF APPROACH

The three victims in this case were last seen together on two bicycles riding towards the Robin Hood Hills area. It is most likely that the assailant approached them while still together. This high likelihood and the sudden violent nature of the wounds, coupled with limited resistance on the part of the victims, is very suggestive.

These elements together suggest that someone that the victims knew and trusted approached them. They further suggest that once the confidence of the three victims was won, the assailant was able to take them to another location and gain control of them in some manner.

It is clear that the assailant was much larger and stronger than the victims, so physical intimidation and fear were factors. This would have been a factor in the initial approach. It is also clear that the assailant had a knife, but this would not have been displayed during the initial approach. The method of approach in this case was most likely a con of some kind to acquire trust, followed up at another location by a sudden, violent attack to gain control.

METHODS OF CONTROL

The assailant in this case controlled his assault on these three victims with very specific, deliberate methods.

First, he removed them to a location that he was familiar with, where he could feel dominant and establish his authority by his presence alone.

Second, he delivered sudden and violent traumatic blows to each of the victim's heads. The superficial blows could have been corrective in nature, that is to say, delivered with the intent to gain compliance. However it is clear that the main body of injuries were rageful in nature, being deep, forceful, and resulting in extensive damage.

Third, the assailant did bind each of the victims. Steve Branch and Chris Byers both show deep ligature furrows with ligature abrasions, indicating that they were alive and conscious while the bindings were in place. James Moore had no ligature abrasions, indicating he was unconscious while his bindings were in place. This indicates that the assailant did not feel the need to bind James Moore until much later in the offense. This indicates that either James Moore was completely compliant to the offender's commands, or that he was unconscious. Given the overall retaliatory nature of this attack, the level of excessive brutality, and the lack of emotional control demonstrated by the assailant in this case, it is the opinion of this examiner that James Moore was unconscious throughout most of this attack. He very likely received the first attack from the assailant, perhaps as an example to the other two victims.

Fourth, there is the indication that Carbamazepine (Tegretol) was used on Chris Byers, as it was found in non-therapeutic levels in his system according to the toxicology report. It needs to be established what that child was taking at the time, in what doses, and what should have been in his system. If this child received a non-therapeutic dose of Carbamazepine, this could indicate an attempt at a fourth method of control on the part of the assailant.

The assailant's *Methods of Approach* and his *Methods of Control* speak to an offender who knew these victims well, and who had given some limited thought as to how to carry off this crime before doing so. However the use of available materials in the commission of the crime (shoelaces for bindings, potentially Carbamazepine), the amount of physical evidence left behind on the bodies (despite the fact that it was originally overlooked), and the anger evident in these assaults speak to an offender who did not set out on that evening to commit the crimes committed.

AMOUNT OF FORCE

There was a high level of suddenly applied physical force used to gain these victims' initial compliance once they had been removed to the primary crime scene.

There was a brutal level of physical force used throughout the assault on the victims. The victims were all given violent, traumatic blows to the head; Steve Branch received massive gouging and/or bitemark injuries to his face;

and Chris Byers received multiple stab wounds to his groin, up to and including a violent, unskillful emasculation.

The offender's need for these excessive levels of force, victim damage, and specific sexual violence indicate an extremely reactive, angry, retaliatory offender. These kids were being punished for some real or perceived wrong.

The amount of force and the nature of the force that was used on these victims suggest also that this assailant would not have bargained with or listened to the pleas of these victims. The assailant was enraged, and concerned only with teaching these victims a lesson, from his point of view.

VICTIM RESISTANCE

The victims demonstrated only limited resistance to this attack. This is demonstrated by the very limited amount of defensive injury noted in the autopsy reports. This speaks to the sudden, unexpected application of force from an overwhelming assailant.

TYPE AND SEQUENCE OF SEXUAL ACTS

There is only physical evidence to suggest one overtly sexual act committed during the attacks on these three victims. That is the emasculation of Chris Byers. As will be explained, this is a sexual act with some sexual meaning to the offender. However it was more punishment oriented and should not be confused with something which would have necessarily sexually aroused the offender.

As explained in a prior section, the abrasions on Steve Branch's penis, which were likely self-inflicted, are not necessarily related to this particular attack. They do however, indicate a sexualized child which suggests a child who is being sexually abused.

PRECAUTIONARY ACTS

This case is replete with precautionary acts that were committed by the assailant. Precautionary acts are behaviors that the assailant purposefully engages in to protect his own identity, facilitate his escape from the scene, and destroy or deny the transfer of physical evidence (an uncomplex example would be a burglar who wears a mask and gloves; both are precautionary acts).

The following are examples of precautionary acts committed by the assailant. This is not meant to be an all-inclusive list, but rather to demonstrate the assailant's state of mind before, during and after the offense:

1 **Removal of the victims to a location that he controlled**: This act put the offender and the victims in an environment that the offender controlled. It facilitated an unseen, uninterrupted attack upon the victims, providing the assailant with the time to engage in those activities that he desired.

2 **Disposal of the bodies in the water**: This act very effectively washes all of the physical transfer evidence from the bodies of the victims. It also places the victims at a location separate from the assailant.

3 **Destruction of the victim's clothing and related evidence**: This act, carried out by dumping the victim's clothing in the water, used the water in the drainage to help wash away transfer evidence. It also serves the purpose of preventing investigators from finding the victim's clothing on the assailant should his residence or related location be searched.

Conclusions regarding these behaviors will be drawn in the Offender Characteristics section.

PURPOSE OF THE ASSAULT

It is the opinion of this examiner that the primary reason for these killings was punitive. The victims were being punished for some real or perceived wrong. The reasons for this opinion have been thoroughly established in other parts of this report.

It should be pointed out at this point that this examiner is under the opinion that James M. Moore was a collateral victim. That is to say that he was not an intended victim, and that he died because of his association with the other two victims at the time. The anger of the assailant in this case, manifested in victim damage and sexual mutilation, is directed primarily at Steve Branch and Chris Byers. This would indicate that the strongest personal associations with the assailant are with Chris and Steve.

NUMBER OF ASSAILANTS

It is the opinion of this examiner that the number of assailants in this case was most likely two. The presentation is more consistent with two offenders than with one, or three.

This is for the following reasons:

1 The number of victims abducted and killed would have been more easily accomplished with two assailants.

2 It would have been easier to inflict the range of injuries on the victims with two assailants, especially for the emasculation of Chris Byers.

3 The nature, quality and extent of the injuries to Chris Byers and Steve Branch are markedly different, and suggest two separate offenders with very different ways of expressing their rage.

- **Steve Branch** was bitten repeatedly about the face, with deep, tearing bites that left behind lacerations and poor detail. He suffered no stab wounds or cutting wounds. There is no sexual indication to the assault on his person, only punishment.

- **Chris Byers** suffered comparatively less injury to the face, receiving the greatest attention to his genitals, which were stabbed repeatedly and then ultimately removed. In addition, the bitemarks he appears to have suffered were of the "suck mark" type, which is more sexually oriented. There is, in fact, a sexual aspect in the attack to Chris Byers' genitals, which clearly points to an offender ashamed of his own sexuality, and perhaps confused and angered by his own sexual attraction to males. Part of why Chris is being punished is for his own sexuality, and the sexuality that his genitals represent to the assailant. The offender punished Chris and established, or re-established, sexual ownership of him through the emasculation. This is again most consistent with two separate offenders, because you would expect that the assailant would have emasculated both or neither given his propensity.

It is further the opinion of this examiner that the attack on Chris Byers was carried out by a male assailant. But that the attack carried out on Steve Branch could have been either a male or female assailant. The *battered child* nature of the bitemarks on Steve Branch, in the experience of this examiner, is more often associated with a female offender.

"SATANIC RITUAL" ASSESSMENT

This crime does not present at all as a satanic ritual, or cult related, homicide.

According to the *Crime Classification Manual* by Douglas *et al.*, a designation of **141: Cult Murder** has specific defining characteristics that are largely unseen in these particular homicides. They are as follows:

VICTIMOLOGY

Cult murders or satanic murders can be the result of randomly selected victims, but most often the victims are members of the group, or fringe members. Though it does generally involve multiple members.

CRIME-SCENE INDICATORS

The crime scene will generally contain items or imagery that are symbolic to the group or cult.

The disposal methods involving the bodies tend to be thorough burials in mass graves when the killing is meant to intimidate a small group of people. Little attempt will be made to conceal the body when the purpose of the killing is to intimidate a larger number of people, however the body will often be positioned symbolically in such cases.

There are, however, generally indications of multiple offenders, as in this case.

INVESTIGATIVE CONSIDERATIONS

The leaders of cults or such groups tend to have a masterful ability to attract and manipulate people, exploiting their vulnerability. The purpose for killing tends to be to eliminate troublemakers and/or tighten his control over the group.

"SERIAL KILLER" ASSESSMENT

VICTIMOLOGY

The victimology in this case does not lend itself to suggesting a serial offender. In fact, quite the opposite is true.

First, and most importantly, the victims would have represented a very high risk to any offender because there were three of them, and they were young children.

Three victims are a problem because if you grab one or two, the third could get away and later identify you. Serial offenders who grab kids off their bikes are going to take one, maybe two, victims at the most. But assaults or abductions of three victims or higher tend to occur when an offender breaks into a residence, or some other enclosed environment, with victims already inside. The offender would then be free to assault one victim at a time while able to control the others with bindings or a weapon of some kind.

Young children are a problem to serial offenders because they are missed very soon after they are acquired. So an offender grabbing a young child would most likely get as far away from the abduction site as possible before initiating any kind of activity such as an assault.

THE DISPOSAL SITE

The disposal site was a drainage ditch with 2½ ft of water located near a very busy Interstate, behind a very popular truck wash. The victim's clothing, the victim's bicycles, and the victim's bodies were disposed of there.

The disposal site itself is not visible from the Interstate, or even from the truck wash. In short, you'd have to be very familiar with the area to know that it was even there. You'd further have to be someone from the immediate area, which frequented that location recently, to know that there would be water available in which to dispose of the bodies. That drainage ditch can be dry, depending on a variety of factors.

Additionally, the assailant disposed of the clothes and the bicycles in that drainage ditch, suggesting that he needed to get rid of all of the related physical evidence. And the location itself is very near where the point of initial approach would have to be in this case. Both of those items point, again, to someone who is a local resident who knew the victims. They felt they would be searched because of their relationship to the victims so they dumped all of the physical evidence; in stranger crimes where sexual assault or ritual is the motivation the assailant might have kept the clothes to relive the experience later in fantasy.

But more importantly, the location of the dumpsite itself does not suggest a serial offender. As indicated, it's simply too close to the point of abduction.

If this assailant had been a stranger to the victims, then he would have grabbed them, and, knowing that others would be looking for the boys soon, he would have left the area immediately. Subsequently, the bodies would have been disposed of somewhere far away from West Memphis along down the Interstate, and a greater attempt would have been made to prevent the bodies from being discovered. All of this would have served to help a stranger or serial offender in his escape from the area, undetected.

Instead, the bodies were disposed of right where they were last seen, in the area where most of the people searching for them were looking. This suggests that the assailant wanted the bodies to be found quickly. No time was taken to conceal the bodies, because the offender did not have a great distance to go in order to be in his safe-zone. They were just dumped in the water, clothes, bicycles and all.

WOUND PATTERNS

The wound patterns inflicted on these victims are punishment oriented. That is to say that they were inflicted with the intention to punish these children for a real or perceived transgression. This is known because the wounds are violent, traumatic, and the product of rage. But in addition to that, the type of injuries inflicted, (i.e. the bitemarks and the evident anger), pointedly indicate a custodial type homicide.

Because this is so, and because of the other factors discussed, it further lessens the likelihood of a serial offender or stranger being involved in this case.

"BATTERED CHILD HOMICIDE" ASSESSMENT

In this examiner's opinion, this classification is the most consistent with the physical evidence, crime-scene and victimological presentation in this case.

According to *Practical Homicide Investigation* by Vern Geberth, 3rd edn, pp. 642–643, the interpretation of patterns of bitemark evidence breaks down, generally, as such:

- Homosexual homicides tend to involve bitemarks of the back, arms, shoulders, axillae (armpits, face, and scrotum of the victim).

- Heterosexual homicides usually involve bitemarks delivered by the assailant to the breast and thighs.

- Battered children most often have randomly placed bitemarks on the cheeks, back, and sides. However, bitemarks on battered children have also been found on the abdomen, scrotum, and buttocks. In child cases, biting seems to be done in a rapid, random, and enraged manner leaving tissue laceration, diffuse areas, and poor detail, as opposed to sexually associated bitemarks, usually inflicted in a slow and sadistic manner and resulting in excellent detail.

- Note: According to Dr Lowell Levine (as detailed in Practical Homicide

Investigation), there are two general but distinct types of bitemark patterns: (1) Those which are inflicted slowly, which leave a central ecchymotic area or "suck mark," and a radiating linear abrasion pattern surrounding the central area resembling a sunburst. The type is most often found in sexually oriented homicides; (2) Those which resemble a tooth-mark pattern. This is an attack or defensive bitemark and is seen most often in the battered-child type of homicide.

The bitemarks in this case appear to be, in the majority, of the nature and quality described above in the Battered Child Homicide.

Based on this evidence, and the location of the disposal site, and the victimology, and the other injuries inflicted on the victims, it is the opinion of this examiner that this case represents a battered child or child-custodial homicide. To a greater extent the parents, and to a lesser extent the guardians, relatives and anyone else who was allowed frequent, trusted access to these children should be thoroughly investigated as suspects in this case.

OFFENDER PERSONALITY CHARACTERISTICS

There are very likely two offenders involved in the deaths of these children. This section will focus on the characteristics of the primary, retaliatory offender.

As already stated, the purpose of this offense was to punish the victim and to establish or re-establish sexual ownership of the victim Chris Byers. He is likely very similar in relationships with women in the rest of his life. His own violent and selfish sexual behaviors are indicative of how he is perceived by those who know him. He is likely a very selfish and explosive individual with a potentially violent temper. He wants those around him to think that he does not care how others view him. He would be described by those who know him well as hostile, angry, and as someone who carries grudges. His sexual assault on the genitals of Chris Byers suggests that he projects a macho, heterosexual, in-control image to those around him despite deep homosexual urges.

This is an extremely egocentric individual who cannot take the criticism of others, or tolerate shortcomings of any kind. He would further be described as someone who requires instant gratification for his impulses, and who can react violently when those impulses are not satisfied.

He is glib and superficial, but also extremely manipulative. He must be dominant in all relationships with women. He can also become very possessive and irrationally jealous of those he feels are not spending enough time attending to his needs in his sexual relationships. His jealousy and possessiveness can and have manifested themselves in violent behavior acted out towards the females in his life.

ARREST HISTORY

The numerous precautionary actions taken by the offender, despite the fact the crime was not planned fully, demonstrate a level of knowledge and sophistication obtained through either repeated offenses, some level of exposure to law-enforcement training and techniques, or previous arrests for similar crimes. The offender shows some knowledge of forensic methods, and attempts to dupe those specific efforts.

This offender has very possibly spent some time in prison, and if not is committing other petty crimes to support himself. He will most likely have been arrested or detained for incidents involving drugs, violent behavior, and assaultive behavior.

MARITAL STATUS

The offender's behavior and attitude suggest someone who is capable only of short-term or sporadic on and off relationships with the females in his life. He very likely has been married more than once. His attitude towards women is very misogynistic, and his previous relationships with women would have involved a great deal of physical and/or emotional abuse.

If this offender was married at the time of the offense, and indicators are not clear on this issue, then his marriage would have been in crisis at the time of this offense. And his wife may very well have been the compliant partner in this crime.

RESIDENCE

The offender lives within a few miles of the disposal site. This is indicated by the very poor attempt at concealing the bodies when disposing of them, and the fact that they were disposed of where they would be quickly found, in the area being searched by so many people including law enforcement.

It is very likely, in fact, that the offender was part of the search effort for these children, and that he placed the bodies in a specific location with perhaps the intent of being the one to later find them in an attempt to shift the blame.

SKILL LEVEL

Given the demographic location of this offense, and the fact that the offender was likely a local resident with a great familiarity of the area and the habits of the people in the area, it is not likely that the offender is educated past the high-school level. He would have performed poorly in school due to his aggressive nature, intolerance for others, and his overall impatience. He does not demonstrate characteristics of education at the high school level, though he may have obtained a GED at some point.

However the offender demonstrates a wealth of applied criminal knowledge about investigative techniques and forensic methods. He is not the kind of offender to leave obvious physical evidence behind at a crime scene without making some attempt to obscure it. He demonstrates foresight in his disposal behavior, as well as a complete understanding of the criminal nature and quality of his acts, as clearly shown in his extensive regimen of precautionary behavior.

HOBBIES/PERSONAL INTERESTS

As indicated by his use of one or more knives in the commission of this crime, this offender has a very intense interest in knives and likely has an extensive collection of them in his home. It is also likely that the offender has the same type of interest in firearms, and in hunting.

He also very likely has a drinking problem, and/or a very bad drug habit which he must commit crimes to support.

EMPLOYMENT

It is very likely that this offender is unemployed. He lacks the skills, discipline, and patience to hold down a full time job. When employed, he is often late, absent, or fails to show up at all. His temper and disposition keep him from legitimate work, and likely his true source of income is the sale of drugs or other illegal activity.

TRANSPORTATION

If he does own a vehicle, it would be masculine, like a truck. This would also be consistent with the type of vehicle he would need to transport the victims to the disposal site. It would further be in strict keeping with his macho self-image of strength and control. The offender's own vehicle was likely used in this offense.

BEHAVIORAL EVIDENCE ANALYSIS – [15-YEAR-OLD WHITE FEMALE], [15-YEAR-OLD WHITE MALE], [13-YEAR-OLD BLACK MALE]

Brent E. Turvey, M.S.

IDENTITY OF VICTIMS AND LOCATION OF CRIME SCENES

The victims in this triple homicide case were three teenagers; one white female [15-year-old white female], one white male [15-year-old white male], and one black male [13-year-old black male]. All three were found at McGowan Creek Rd.# 16.2-17.2, MP0.6 in Springfield, Oregon. All three were found at this remote forest road landing in the Coburg Hills with multiple, fatal gunshot wounds to the head and/or upper body on 21 December 1995.

The victims in a related rape/abduction case, that occurred on 16 December 1995, were two teenagers; one white female [18-year-old white female] and one white male [18-year-old white male]. This attack occurred on a gravel road between East 37th and East 38th Avenue in Eugene, Oregon.

EXAMINATIONS PERFORMED

This examiner made an examination of much of the available material provided to the Law Offices of [Attorney-Client], as part of discovery, and most of the reports generated by defense experts, including, but not limited to: investigators reports and crime scene photos; autopsy reports and photos; witness interviews; victim interviews; suspect interviews; relevant criminal histories; related videotaped re-enactments; and Criminal Incident Reconstruction.

This examiner also visited the crime scenes, and related areas, during July of 1997.

VICTIMOLOGY: E. 38TH AVE. KIDNAP/RAPE

BACKGROUND

The victims were two teenagers: one white female [18-year-old white female], one white male [18-year-old white male]. [18-year-old white male] stated in his police interview that he and [18-year-old white female] had been dating for about two weeks. On the evening of 15 December 1995 he picked [18-year-old white female] up at around 9PM to go see the film "Father of the Bride II." After the film, they wanted to be alone, so at around 11PM they drove up to the gravel road between E. 37th and E. 38th and parked.

[18-year-old white male] further states that at about 12 Midnight a big vehicle drove by with two people in it. [18-year-old white female] states in her police interview that she and [18-year-old white male] were in the back seat of their vehicle (a 1983 Honda owned by [18-year-old white male]'s father) and were kissing at this point. The vehicle stopped, and a white male got out and approached them. He claimed to be a local resident, and asked them what they were doing.

According to [18-year-old white male], the man, described as a white male in his early 20s, 5'10" tall, with sandy brown hair, told them that they were trespassing. The man further stated, however, that since they were just parking they could remain where they were. [18-year-old white male] states in his police interview that the man presented himself as a nice guy, and that they only talked briefly before the man got back into his vehicle and left.

The co-defendant in the McGowan Creek Homicides, Jonathan Susbauer, admits that he was this individual. The victims both identified Jonathan Susbauer as this individual during a line-up.

According to [18-year-old white female], they were still in the back seat a short time later when the rapist, a white male, came up to their vehicle and confronted them. [18-year-old white male] states in his police interview that approximately 15 minutes had elapsed.

[18-year-old white male] stated that he got out of the vehicle, fully clothed, to speak with the rapist. He states that the rapist was wearing black, had his face covered, was waving around a machete, and was making noises that he described as being "like a ninja warrior." According to [18-year-old white female], the rapist hit the car window with the machete, and ordered her out of the vehicle.

According to statements made by the victims and co-defendant Susbauer, at least one person in addition to Susbauer was present during his initial encounter with the victims. However, there is no evidence that a second individual actively participated in the commission of this rape. This report will therefore be limited to the behavior of the rapist.

RELATIONSHIP STATUS

According to [18-year-old white male], he and [18-year-old white female] had been dating for approximately two weeks prior to this incident. It has not been established whether these two had spent time at this location prior to the date of the attack, or whether it was their first time.

EDUCATION AND RESIDENCE

Both victims were students at the time of the attack. Both victims lived with their parents at the time of the attack. Their car, the Honda, was registered to the father of [18-year-old white male].

CLOTHING

According to statements made by both victims, [18-year-old white male] was fully clothed at the time of the attack by the rapist. However, [18-year-old white female] had previously removed some of her clothing and was wearing only a shirt, underwear, and a bra when the rapist ordered her out of the car.

SUSPECT DESCRIPTION

Both victims describe the rapist as a white male in his 20s, wearing something dark over his head, and partially covering his face, (either a stocking cap or a dark hooded jacket with a scarf) dressed in black, and armed with a machete.

CRIME SCENE BEHAVIOR EVIDENCE ANALYSIS: E. 38TH AVE. KIDNAP/RAPE

LOCATION OF CRIME SCENE

[18-year-old white female] stated that on 16 December 1995, she and [18-year-old white male] parked on an unlit gravel road surrounded by wooded areas at approximately 11PM, between E. 38th Ave. and E. 37th Ave. in Eugene, Oregon. That location is physically isolated between two upper class residential communities. On one side (where they parked the Honda on the shoulder) there is a fenced off wooded area on a down-slope, and on the opposite side there is a shallow ditch and a steep face of hillside with more trees on an up-slope. The gravel road joins one residential community to the other.

METHOD OF APPROACH

[18-year-old white male] stated in interviews to police that a young white male in his 20s, approx. 5'10", with sandy brown hair, dressed in a plaid jacket, approached their vehicle posing as a local resident. The man openly approached them without outward signs of aggression. The man was also friendly to [18-year-old white male] during their conversation. It is the opinion of this examiner that the purpose of this approach was a con by the rapist, to make an assessment of the potential victims, and estimate their potential resistance to a kidnap/rape scenario.

This style of approach evidences an offender who is able to think on his feet, has a great desire to manipulate his victims' impressions of him, and is very comfortable deceiving people.

SCENE TYPE/LOCATION SELECTION

[18-year-old white male] told the police that he and [18-year-old white female] had parked at that location for at least one hour before they were approached, first by the man claiming to be a local resident. Shortly thereafter, and without any other vehicles passing by, the rapist appeared at the scene. The location does not reveal evidence that it is frequented by anyone or used for any particular purpose; the only signs of activity observed by this examiner were bags of trash and bottles dumped over a nearby slope into the woods. No evidence suggests that the rapist planned to encounter anyone, let alone the victims, or to rape anyone at that specific location, at that specific time. Given all of the circumstances, including the dark clothing which the rapist had in addition to his regular dress, it is probable that the rapist was travelling the back roads to this upper class residential area engaged in surveillance activities related to burglary and theft, and only by chance came upon the victims in their parked car.

METHODS OF CONTROL

The rapist's methods of control over both the crime scene and his victims include primarily, but are not limited to the following:

PRESENCE OF A WEAPON

According to the victims' statements, the rapist had a machete that he wielded throughout the attack. He held it to the female victim's neck, and also to her naked breasts when shouting verbal commands. He threatened to use it if his commands were not followed. The rapist used the machete to intimidate, coerce, and terrorize both victims.

VERBAL THREATS

According to statements made by the victims, more than once the rapist used profanity and threats of slicing the victims' throats and the female victim's breasts to maintain victim compliance. These threats and profanity and comments about the victim's virginity were likely intended to terrorize her, and her boyfriend, and achieve continued compliance, as well as a fear response.

LOCATION

It was very dark at the crime scene, due to the time of day and the trees that obscured any light from the surrounding neighborhoods. Additionally, it is probable that the rapist had used the access road in the past when pre-surveilling the area to burglarize residences. This gave him the advantage of familiarity at that crime scene.

VICTIM CLOTHING

According to the victims' statements, the rapist ordered both of them, under threat of harm with the machete, to remove all of their clothing. As seen in crime-scene photos, and more clearly demonstrated by a diagram of that crime scene drawn by police, the suspect discarded the victims' clothing into the woods, near the victims' vehicle, and further up the gravel road. In the dark, it would have been difficult for the victims to locate their clothing, even after the rapist left the scene. Unclothed and without shoes for foot protection, the victims were also less able to make a fast exit from the scene to seek aid or contact the police.

VICTIM SUBORDINATION

The rapist commanded the victims to get out of their vehicle and to get down on their knees with their hands behind their heads. This behavior is very similar to police commands during a felony car stop indicating the rapist's experience with this procedure.

VICTIMS' KEYS

According to the victims, the rapist took the car keys out of the ignition and threw them up the road. As shown in a diagram of the crime scene drawn by police, the keys landed approximately 100ft in the opposite direction than the parked vehicle's headlights were aiming. This would serve the purpose of preventing or significantly delaying the victims from driving off in their vehicle to seek aid.

VICTIMS' VEHICLE

According to the victims, the rapist used the machete to break the vehicle headlights. This action would prevent the victims from activating those headlights to locate their clothing and car keys.

AMOUNT OF FORCE AND VICTIM RESISTANCE

It should be noted that, according to the victims' statements, the victims followed the rapist's commands without deviation. They were totally compliant at all times and showed no physical or verbal resistance. The victims gave the rapist no opportunities to rationalize the use of physical force and inflict injuries. When the rapist wanted the victims to act, he would usually not physically force compliance, but rather verbally threaten in concert with the machete.

According to the victims' statements to police and hospital personnel, the rapist did not inflict physical injuries apart from his sexual assaults of [18-year-old white female]. Full frontal and rear photographs of [18-year-old white male] do not reveal any injuries. No significant injuries are noted to [18-year-old white female] in the Hospital's Sexual Assault Examination reports.

There was a *minimal level of physical force* evident in this offense. The rapist used only the level of force necessary to complete the attack.

However, according to [18-year-old white female], the rapist was intentionally profane. He commented on her virginity, which suggests that he inquired about that subject specifically, and he called her a bitch at least once. He also ran the machete along her neck and breasts as though he intended to injure them. As the victims at no time offered any resistance, and as the rapist used threats of mutilation and death, this demonstrates a *moderate level of verbal force.*

SEXUAL DYSFUNCTION

According to the victims' statements to the police, the rapist did not experience typical forms of sexual dysfunction, which include the more common premature ejaculation, retarded ejaculation, and the less common conditional ejaculation.

According to [18-year-old white female], however, the rapist was not successful in penetrating her vagina or her anus. Erectile insufficiency (the most common type of sexual dysfunction) on the part of the rapist is not specifically addressed in [18-year-old white female]'s statements to the police or hospital personnel. However the hospital reports state that these attempts were painful for [18-year-old white female], suggesting that the rapist's penis was erect. Additionally, the Lane County Sheriff Supplemental Report states that "...The man took his erect penis from his pants and attempted to rape her vaginally..."

Factors that could have contributed to the rapist's failure to penetrate the victim's vagina and anus, given the fact that he had achieved an erection, include her virginity, a lack of sufficient lubrication, and the size of the rapist's penis relative to the victim's vaginal and anal openings.

TYPE AND SEQUENCE OF SEXUAL ACTS

The exact sequence of these sexual acts has not been established. Victim statements, as recorded by the police, were not consistent or clear on what sexual acts occurred where. However, the type of sexual acts that occurred is more clearly established.

It appears that the first set of sexual acts may have occurred between the rapist and [18-year-old white female], on the hood of the car. At that time the rapist forced [18-year-old white male] to lay face down on the ground in front of the car, and at one point placed the machete to [18-year-old white male]'s neck and threatened to cut off his head. The rapist engaged in the following sexual behavior:

- kissing the victim throughout her body;
- fondling of victim's breasts.

It appears that the second set of sexual acts occurred when the rapist commanded [18-year-old white male] and [18-year-old white female] to perform sex acts while he watched. The rapist had inquired about [18-year-old white female]'s virginity, and upon discovering that she was a virgin, ordered [18-year-old white male] to take her virginity. The rapist ordered [18-year-old white male] to lay on top of [18-year-old white female] a few feet in front of their vehicle, which [18-year-old white male] did. The sexual assault examination reports that [18-year-old white female]'s hymen was unbroken at the time of examination, after the incident. The couple faked sexual intercourse for the benefit of the rapist for about 10 minutes, according to [18-year-old white male].

It appears that the third set of sexual acts occurred between the rapist and [18-year-old white female] on the trunk of the car. The rapist moved [18-year-old white male] to the rear of the car. The rapist then forced [18-year-old white female] onto the trunk of the car, and engaged in the following sexual behavior:

- attempted vaginal sex on the hood of the car;
- attempted anal sex on the hood of the car;
- attempted cunnilingus;
- digital penetration of vagina.

According to statements made by both victims to police interviewers, the fourth set of sexual acts occurred when the rapist ordered each victim to lay down on the ground. The rapist then placed a rock in-between the buttock cheeks of [18-year-old white female], and on the buttock cheeks of [18-year-old white male]. The rapist explained that he did this so that he would hear the rock fall if either of them got up before he was gone. However, this is an unlikely motive in the instance of [18-year-old white female] because a rock placed in-between the buttock cheeks is not likely to fall out if the victim does not want it to. This was most likely an act of sexual substitution, and meant to sexually degrade the victim further. Also, [18-year-old white male] would probably learn of this act of substitution later. This asserted the rapist's sexual control despite his failure to achieve penile penetration of [18-year-old white female], while ultimately sexually humiliating both victims.

VERBAL ACTIVITY

The rapist's verbal activity is revealing. In most instances, the victims did not relate the precise wording of the rapist's phrases, but the nature of the verbal activity is as follows:

- "Hey!" – first thing [18-year-old white male] hears.
- Makes ninja like noises – next thing [18-year-old white male] hears.
- Gruff speech; growls like the devil – next thing that [18-year-old white male] hears.
- Threatens [18-year-old white male].
- Orders [18-year-old white female] out of the vehicle.
- Promises not to rape [18-year-old white female] because he is not that kind of guy – prior to rape.
- Orders [18-year-old white male] and [18-year-old white female] to remove their clothing.
- Informs the victims that he has changed his mind about raping [18-year-old white female] – prior to rape.
- Threatens to cut off [18-year-old white male]'s head – after forcing him to lay down.
- Inquires about [18-year-old white female]'s virginity.
- Commands [18-year-old white male] to take [18-year-old white female]'s virginity.
- "You're trying to make this hard for me, bitch." – while he is attempting to vaginally penetrate [18-year-old white female].
- Told [18-year-old white male] that he was going to take his wallet, but leave behind his cards and license – after breaking out the headlights on the vehicle.
- States that he knows their names and where they live and that he will kill them if they report the incident – after going through [18-year-old white male]'s wallet.
- Told [18-year-old white female] that he was Satan – unknown if before or after rape.
- Told [18-year-old white female] that if she moved, he would kill her – after he placed the rock in-between her buttock cheeks, right before he left the scene.
- States that they should not leave and that he will come back in a few minutes to check on them – after forcing them to lay down with a rock between [18-year-old white female]'s buttock cheeks, and a rock on top of [18-year-old white male]'s buttock cheeks, as he was leaving the scene.

The verbal behavior reveals that this rapist wanted the victims to be frightened and in terror from the moment he appeared to them as "a rapist." He portrayed characters that in his own experience would command fear and respect while evoking terror; a ninja and Satan.

He commanded [18-year-old white female] to get out of the car. When he confronted this half-naked female, he likely became aroused. He wanted to control her sexually, and rape her. He ordered [18-year-old white male] to lie down on the ground, ordered [18-year-old white female] to get up on the hood of the car, and began assaulting her. But then his behavior changed. He experienced feelings of his own sexual inadequacy, as evidenced by his verbal behavior. He reacted to his feelings of insecurity by telling [18-year-old white female] that he was not a bad person and that he would not rape her. He inquired about her sexual experience, and upon learning that she was a virgin, gave her to [18-year-old white male] and ordered him to take her virginity. This behavior evidences that he does not perceive himself as a rapist, but rather as a participant in sexual activities that he orchestrates.

The rest of his verbal behavior would be characterized as command-oriented, hostile, threatening, and terroristic. This behavior serves the purpose of controlling the victims, while simultaneously serving the rapist's need to feel powerful and masculine.

PRECAUTIONARY ACTS

The following are examples of precautionary acts committed by this rapist:

1 Alteration of clothing: The rapist disguised his appearance by taking off or covering up his plaid jacket. He dressed in dark clothes, including a cap or hood, and a dark scarf obscuring part of his face.

2 Alteration of voice: The rapist growled and spoke "like the devil", causing fear in his victims but also obscuring his own voice.

3 Time of day: The time of day made the scene very dark, obscuring, at least somewhat, the rapist's facial features. This would make his willingness to seize this opportunity more likely.

4 Location selection: The location was determined by this rapist to be somewhat secluded and untravelled, and out of the visual range of any local residences. This would make his willingness to seize this opportunity to rape more likely.

5 Victim selection: The rapist selected complete strangers as his victims, decreasing the likelihood that the rapist could be connected to the crime at a later date.

6 Disposing of the victims' clothing: The rapist threw all of the victims' clothing into the darkness of the woods nearby. This could serve the purpose of delaying the victim's ability to get help or contact police.

7 Looked at [18-year-old white male]'s ID: The rapist examined the victim's identification to learn the victim's identities, and used a threat of future violence to further terrorize the victims. A secondary motive was to intimidate the victims from reporting the incident, or at least delay reporting.

ITEMS TAKEN

All of the victims' clothing was recovered from the surrounding area and collected as evidence, according to police logs. According to [18-year-old white male]'s statement, the rapist did search the interior of their vehicle, pulling items out of the glove box, but nothing appeared to be missing.

According to the victims, the only thing taken by this rapist from the scene was [18-year-old white male]'s wallet. The rapist emptied the contents of the wallet out on the ground next to the car, and took the wallet, as well as a small amount of money. This theft of the wallet serves as a trophy for the rapist.

PURPOSE OF THE ATTACK

This rapist utilized command-oriented behavior to both orchestrate and participate in a variety of sexual activities involving himself and the victims. The rape provided him with an experience of sexual control, including both domination and degradation of his victims. The victims complied with virtually no resistance to his commands, sexual and otherwise. The experience made him feel powerful. It was therefore sexually and emotionally reassuring. The behavior evidence leads to the conclusion that the primary motivation for this rape was the offender's need to feel powerful. That need arises from the rapist's fears of sexual inadequacy, as well as his sexual confusion.

A related motivation, evidenced by the rapist's verbal and sexual behavior with [18-year-old white female], is the offender's need for reassurance that he is not a rapist, but rather is an intensely desired masculine figure, who is virile, powerful, and good enough to have other men's women. This rapist probably perceives that his female victims eroticize and enjoy forcible sex, just as he does, to further fulfill his need for reassurance that he is not a rapist. This incident is classified as a *Power Rape* in terms of the motivational typology. The rapist used the assault to reassure himself of his masculinity by exercising his power over the victims by degrading them both physically and sexually. This type of rapist generally lacks the confidence to interact socially and sexually with women, and so he compensates, by engaging in power rape behavior.

This analysis will be continued in the Evaluation: Power Rapist Behaviors section of this report.

VICTIMOLOGY: MCGOWAN CREEK RAPE/HOMICIDES

BACKGROUND

The victims in this case were three teenagers: [15-year-old white female], [15-year-old white male], and [13-year-old black male].

A witness reports that these three victims were last seen getting into a suburban type vehicle with one driver and one passenger on Wednesday, December 20, 1995 at 11:30AM in downtown Springfield. This was approximately two blocks from the homes of [13-year-old black male] and [15-year-old white female]. Statements by Jonathan Wayne Susbauer establish that Susbauer was driving that vehicle, and that Conan Wayne Hale was the passenger.

According to police reports made by witness Michael Black, the boys were walking [15-year-old white female] home when Susbauer and Hale stopped to pick them up.

According to statements made by Susbauer, Susbauer and Hale were partners in criminal activities including, but not limited to, burglaries of vehicles and residences. They had returned from an overnight trip to Portland within a few hours of encountering the victims.

According to police interviews with family and friends, [15-year-old white female] and [15-year-old white male] were boyfriend and girlfriend at the time of their deaths. [15-year-old white female] also knew Hale and Susbauer, which probably contributed to the three accepting a ride from them. According to Susbauer's statements, he drove them for 25 minutes out of Springfield to a remote forest road, McGowan Creek Road, up in the Coburg Hills. He stopped in Springfield to buy beer on the way.

According to the toxicology reports, both [15-year-old white female] and [15-year-old white male] had consumed alcohol, and [15-year-old white male] had taken barbiturates.

At 2:46PM on December 21, 1995 (the next day), the police were notified that two civilians had found bodies at a landing at the end of a gravel forest road in the Coburg Hills. Those bodies are later identified as the three victims named above.

According to both the Criminal Incident Reconstruction and the medical examiner's reports, [15-year-old white male] suffered five gunshot wounds resulting in his death at the scene; [15-year-old white female] suffered two gunshot wounds resulting in her death at the scene; and [13-year-old black male] suffered two gunshot wounds. [13-year-old black male] lived for several days in the hospital before he died of his injuries, never regaining consciousness. A single .38 caliber revolver was used to inflict the injuries on all three victims.

The crime-scene photos show that [15-year-old white male] and [15-year-old white female] were found at the scene nude. Their bodies' appear posed in a sexual position, as though [15-year-old white female] were positioned to perform fellatio on [15-year-old white male]. The crime-scene photos and investigator's reports also show that [13-year-old black male] was lying near the couple. Still alive but unconscious, [13-year-old black male] was dressed in a female's rabbit fur coat (not associated with the victims), a white T-shirt of unknown origin, and [15-year-old white female]'s jeans over his own denim shorts. [13-year-old black male] was not wearing shoes or socks.

It is the opinion of this examiner, from an analysis of the crime-scene photos of [13-year-old black male], that he did not dress himself. This is consistent with the Criminal Incident Reconstruction.

VICTIM CHARACTERISTICS AND CLOTHING SUMMARY

[15-YEAR-OLD WHITE MALE]

[15-year-old white male] was a 15-year-old single white male, 6'1" tall with a slender build. He had reportedly dropped out of school, was unemployed and living sometimes at home with his father and sometimes on the streets. He was suspected in car burglaries and thefts. He was associated with juvenile gangs, had a temper, and reportedly used marijuana.

According to witness statements, he was last seen dressed in the following clothing(accuracy of witness descriptions unknown):

- tennis shoes – not recovered at the scene;
- green baggy pants – not recovered at the scene;
- long sleeved shirt – possibly recovered at the scene and blood stained;
- "Kurt Cobain" T-shirt – not recovered at the scene;
- yellow coat – not recovered at the scene, but unknown if he was wearing same;
- socks and underwear – not recovered at the scene, but unknown if he was wearing same.

[15-YEAR-OLD WHITE FEMALE]

[15-year-old white female] was a 15-year-old single white female, 5'3" tall with a chunky build. She had dropped out of school. She was unemployed, lived at home some of the time, but she was also a runaway. She was suspected of having been physically and sexually abused by her stepfather and reportedly was concerned about being pregnant when last seen on 12/20/95. She reportedly used marijuana and other drugs, but was not suspected of other criminal activities.

According to witness statements, she was last seen dressed in the following clothing(accuracy of witness descriptions unknown):

- combat style boots – recovered at the scene;
- purple socks – recovered at the scene;
- underwear with sperm (DNA match with stepfather) in crotch – recovered at the scene;
- bra – recovered at the scene;
- baggy blue jeans – worn by [13-year-old black male];
- flannel shirt – recovered at the scene;
- white T-shirt (may have been wearing) – only one found at the scene worn by [13-year-old black male];
- cowboy hat – not recovered at the scene.

[13-YEAR-OLD BLACK MALE]

[13-year-old black male] was a 13-year-old single black male. He was 5'11-½", with a slender build. He was a friend of [15-year-old white male] and [15-year-old white female]. He lived at home possibly with his aunt, had never been a runaway, and was not suspected of any criminal activities.

According to witness statements, he was last seen before the homicides dressed in the following clothing (accuracy of witness descriptions unknown):

- Nike high-tops – recovered at the scene, location unknown;
- black denim shorts – wearing beneath [15-year-old white female]'s jeans;
- baseball cap (Raiders logo) – recovered at scene;
- socks and underwear – not recovered (unknown if wearing);
- flannel shirt – not recovered (unknown if wearing);
- green coat – not recovered (unknown if wearing);
- [15-year-old white female]'s jeans – wearing when found at scene;
- white T-shirt – wearing beneath fur jacket when found at scene;
- rabbit fur jacket – wearing when found at scene (belongs to female victim from Eugene).

CRIME-SCENE BEHAVIOR EVIDENCE ANALYSIS: McGOWAN CREEK RAPE/HOMICIDES

Based on their statements to the police, Jonathan Susbauer and Conan Hale, both defendants in this triple homicide, do not dispute being present at the crime scene. Based upon the behavioral evidence analysis done by this examiner and upon the Criminal Incident Reconstruction done by Kay Sweeney, this examiner concludes that the rapist in this case was the person in control of the suspects' vehicle and in control of the firearm, and was the person who killed all three victims.

No behavioral evidence or any physical evidence establishes that both defendants engaged in the sexual assaults and shootings, or the peri-mortem and post-mortem activities with the victims, which occurred at McGowan Creek. The statements of the defendants are contradictory on this issue and thus cannot serve to support forensic conclusions. Therefore, this report will address the behavior of one person; the rapist/killer.

METHOD OF APPROACH

The offender acquired these victims by offering them a ride. The offender, who was known to at least one of the victims, approached them openly and acted in a friendly way towards them. He bought them beer and claimed to be driving them to a party. This examiner concludes that the purpose of this approach was a con by the offender who at the very least wanted to create an opportunity for sexual activities with these victims.

This style of approach evidences an offender who possesses strong manipulation and deception skills that they are very comfortable using, and who is capable of both thinking and acting quickly.

SCENE TYPE/LOCATION SELECTION

The McGowan Creek crime scene was both a primary scene and a disposal site: all available evidence establishes that the crimes against these victims occurred at the same location where their bodies were found.

Police reports, defense-witness interviews, and this examiner's observations of this area collectively disclose that the crime scene is at the dead end of a graveled logging road high up in the Coburg Hills. To reach this landing, one must travel up McGowan Creek Road, and then take several spur roads unmarked by road signs. This area is largely Bureau of Land Management (BLM) land, devoted to forestry and recreational uses; no residences or buildings were observed after passing the rifle range entrance of McGowan Creek Road. There is no artificial lighting for miles. The landing is not visible from the approaching road until the last few hundred feet. There are many such landings in these hills, and the crime scene as well as the other landings, serve as locations for target shooting, beer drinking, and partying. The area is well outside of town, and largely unpoliced. Discharging firearms in this area would be unlikely to attract interest. The crime scene contained numerous spent cartridge shells, a fire pit, trash and other evidence of being visited by persons unrelated to these homicides.

The following facts, taken as a whole, lead to the conclusion that the rapist knew this location well, and selected it as being suitable for offense behavior involving a firearm:

1 Its distance from the location where the rapist acquired the victims, and its distance from any residential area.

2 His ability to find that particular landing in the dark and after having consumed alcohol. It is also likely that he returned to that landing after a period of hours had passed, according to the Criminal Incident Reconstruction.

3 His willingness to discharge his weapon on as many as two different occasions during the night and morning hours, without evidence of behavior suggesting fear that the gunshots would attract attention.

4 His willingness to spend time with the victims after they were dead or dying, repositioning them and redressing [13-year-old black male], again without evidence of behavior suggesting fear that he might be caught in the act.

Because the rapist acquired these particular victims by chance, the evidence does not suggest that he had preselected this crime scene as the location to commit this specific criminal episode with these specific victims. However, the rapist probably had chosen this location well in advance of this particular incident as being suitable for committing this general type of interpersonal crime involving a firearm.

METHODS OF CONTROL

The methods of control used by the rapist include the use of a .38 caliber, six-shot revolver. He probably wielded this weapon throughout the attack. Other methods of control include, but are not limited to:

LOCATION SELECTION

It is a secluded, distant area with only one egress. It was very dark at the crime scene, with only the light from the suburban to see by. This in combination with the rapist's familiarity with the location gave him the advantage.

ORDERING VICTIMS TO DISROBE

Victims who are naked, and without foot protection in such terrain (gravel road up in the forest hills and in a Winter climate), are less able to make a competent escape.

VICTIM SUBORDINATION

The rapist commanded the naked victims to get down on their knees with their hands behind their heads. This behavior is similar to police commands given during a felony car stop, indicating the rapist's familiarity with this procedure.

Both defendants state that Hale hit [15-year-old white male] and [13-year-old black male] in the head with a baseball bat, rendering them semi-conscious. The available medical evidence does not exclude this from having occurred.

ALCOHOL

The rapist stopped for beer, and the toxicology reports make it probable that he shared the beer with the victims. [15-year-old white male] tested positive for ethyl alcohol and barbiturates; [15-year-old white female] tested positive for alcohol; [13-year-old black male]'s toxicology results were negative, but this result may occur because he was still alive and his metabolic processes were ongoing.

AMOUNT OF FORCE

There is a *brutal level of force* evident in this offense, characterized by the offender's use of the handgun. [15-year-old white female] and [13-year-old black male] were shot twice each. [15-year-old white male] was shot five times. The Criminal Incident Reconstruction diminishes likelihood that the number of shots to [15-year-old white male] indicates "overkill." According to the Criminal Incident Reconstruction, those five shots were inflicted on two separate occasions, and were required to kill [15-year-old white male] under those circumstances. According to the reconstruction, [15-year-old white male] was shot three times, [15-year-old white female] twice, and [13-year-old black male] once before being left for dead. When the rapist returned a period of hours later, [15-year-old white male] and [13-year-old black male] were still alive. He then shot [15-year-old white male] twice more, and [13-year-old black male] a second time.

VICTIM RESISTANCE

According to the Medical Examiner's autopsy report, there are no indications of defensive-type injuries on any of the victims. There is also no physical evidence or suspect statements suggesting the victims were bound as a form of restraint. It is possible that the rapist controlled the male victims by keeping the gun on the female during the sexual assaults, particularly since the victims were friends and would not want to risk further harm to [15-year-old white female]. It is also possible that Hale disabled the two males by hitting them with the bat; the female would still have to be under the control of the rapist, and the rapist would still have the gun.

Either of these possibilities would account for the lack of victim resistance evident in this crime scene.

TYPE AND SEQUENCE OF SEXUAL ACTS

This examiner relied upon statements made by Jonathan Susbauer, and physical evidence in the form of swabs taken from [15-year-old white female]'s sexual assault kit to determine the type and sequence of sexual acts. The first set of established sexual acts in this case include only Susbauer and [15-year-old white female]. The exact sequence of the following sexual acts cannot be established from these sources:

- kissed the victim up and down her body;
- touched her breasts;
- touched her bottom;
- performed cunnilingus or attempted cunnilingus on [15-year-old white female];

The second set of sexual acts is established by DNA test results finding semen in [15-year-old white female]'s oral, vaginal, and anal cavities. The sequence of these acts cannot be conclusively established.

- vaginal sex performed on [15-year-old white female];
- fellatio performed by [15-year-old white female];
- anal sex performed on [15-year-old white female]

According to the Criminal Incident Reconstruction, the positions of [15-year-old white male] and [15-year-old white female] at the time she was shot is consistent with performing sex acts on [15-year-old white male]. Therefore a third set of possible sexual acts in this case could have occurred when the rapist forced [15-year-old white male] and [15-year-old white female] to perform sex acts while he watched. However, [15-year-old white male] and [15-year-old white female]'s sexual assault kits do not establish that they engaged in sex, including fellatio. If the rapist was unable to achieve this desired result while [15-year-old white male] and [15-year-old white female] were alive, his motivation to observe them engage in sex could be gratified by post-mortem positioning of their bodies.

Anal swabs from the victim indicate the presence of sperm. The angle of the body after death makes it unlikely that sperm discharged down from the victim's vagina into her anus. This is a fourth set of possible sexual acts that may have occurred when the rapist returned to the crime scene and performed anal sex with the deceased body of [15-year-old white female]. The position of [15-year-old white female]'s body and the lack of trauma to her anus as reported by autopsy, support a conclusion that anal sex occurred post-mortem.

PRECAUTIONARY ACTS

The following are examples of precautionary acts committed by the rapist related to these homicides. This is not meant to be an all-inclusive list, but rather to give insight into the offender's state of mind before, during, and after the incident:

1 Removal of the victims to a remote location. This act put the rapist and the victims in an environment that he controlled. It facilitated unseen, uninterrupted, sexually oriented attacks upon the victims, providing the offender with the time to engage in those desired activities.

2 Removal of victim clothing. Unclothed victims would be more vulnerable and less likely to flee.

3 May have been wearing gloves during some parts of the incident. Gloves prevent the transfer of fingerprints, and keep unwanted transfer evidence from getting on one's hands.

4 Killed all of the victims involved. This act prevents victims from identifying the rapist at a later date.

5 Made an attempt to clean up the vehicle and dispose of it. A friend of the victims saw them enter the suburban; he declined a ride. The rapist knew it was possible that this witness could identify the suburban, and, if he was still driving it, could result in implicating him in the homicides. All items linked to Susbauer or Hale were removed from the suburban. Susbauer abandoned it at a parking lot at the University of Oregon. The keys were not recovered.

6 Disposed of gloves (unconfirmed). Susbauer reportedly had a pair of black

leather gloves that he constantly wore. These gloves were not recovered in Susbauer's room, or at the McGowan Creek Scene. Hale reportedly wore brown leather gloves. A pair of brown leather gloves was seized from Hale's bedroom.

The precautionary acts committed before, during, and after the crime are erratic, cursory, and occur in conjunction with other acts which could have led to the rapist's identification and arrest. Examples include:

- the rapist kept the gun;
- the rapist very likely left the crime scene and then returned after a period of hours and fired more shots, increasing the likelihood that someone would discover him at the scene;
- the rapist may have gone back and used the suburban at least once after cleaning it out and disposing of it, returning it a second time to the parking area next to the museum at the University of Oregon;
- the rapist did not hide the bodies very well or dispose of other evidence at the crime scene.

These acts evidence the impulsivity and egocentricity of this rapist. The rapist did as he pleased, satisfying his whims, and very likely did not initially believe that he would be caught or even connected to the homicides.

More conclusions regarding these behaviors will be drawn in the Offender Characteristics section.

ITEMS TAKEN

According to police evidence logs, the clothes reportedly belonging to [15-year-old white male] were not found at the scene. This most likely resulted from [15-year-old white male]'s clothes being placed into the suburban and then disposed of later.

PURPOSE OF THE ATTACK

This rapist utilized command-oriented behavior to both orchestrate and participate in a variety of sexual activities with at least [15-year-old white female], and perhaps including [15-year-old white male]. The crime-scene behavior evidences the rapist's need for the sexual control, domination, and degradation of his victims. The experience made him feel powerful. It was therefore sexually and emotionally reassuring. The behavioral evidence leads to the conclusion that the primary motivation for this rape was the rapist's need to feel powerful. That need arises from the rapist's fear of sexual inadequacy, as well as his sexual confusion, which is best evidenced by his activities with the victim's bodies.

A related motivation, evidenced by the first set of sexual activities (kissing and fondling), is the offender's need for reassurance that the victim is a willing participant and therefore that he is not actually a rapist. This rapist probably perceives his female victims as eroticizing and enjoying forcible sex, just as he does, to further fulfill his need for reassurance that he is desired as a sexual partner, and thus not a rapist.

This incident is classified as a *Power Rape* in terms of motivational typology. The rapist used the rape to reassure himself of his masculinity and his sexual normalcy by exercising power and control over his victims. This rapist lacks the confidence to interact socially and sexually with women, and so he compensates by engaging in power rape behavior.

This analysis will be continued in the Evaluation: Power Rapist Behaviors section of this report.

The rapist probably killed the victims as an ancillary act. He needed to eliminate witnesses to avoid being identified and arrested for rape. Based upon all of the behavioral evidence, this examiner concludes that this rapist would not necessarily kill victims who were strangers to him, and has likely engaged in similar sex crimes in the past. It is probable that this rapist did not plan to murder these victims from the outset, but rather, impulsively did so to satisfy his need to escape apprehension after raping [15-year-old white female].

POST-MORTEM DISPLAY OF THE VICTIMS

The repositioning of the bodies of the victims in this crime scene represents personation by the rapist. His motivation was most likely three-fold:

1 To get the victims out of immediate view from anyone who might come up the road and interrupt the rapist during his peri-mortem and post-mortem activities with the victims' bodies.

2 To service the probable post-mortem anal rape of [15-year-old white female].

3 To sexually humiliate and degrade the victims one final time, when others ultimately found their bodies.

CROSS DRESSING OF [13-YEAR-OLD BLACK MALE]

The cross-dressing of [13-year-old black male] while he was dying was most likely motivated by two needs of the rapist:

1 To satisfy the rapist's fetish while preserving his need to be perceived as normal. This rapist probably collects female garments and/or undergarments. Dressing in those garments is not something he would engage in openly during his regular relationships for fear of judgement (rejection and/or aversion) by others. He would likely only use female clothing in his private masturbatory behavior. The fact that he waited to dress [13-year-old black male] hours after inflicting the fatal head shot, and when all of the victims were either dead or near death, is behavioral evidence of the rapist's desire for secrecy regarding this fetish, and his own sexual confusion. He waited until he thought the victims were dead and most probably

returned to the scene alone to engage in this fetish that demonstrates his need to be perceived as "normal" by others.

2   To humiliate and degrade [13-year-old black male] when others ultimately discovered his body. The rapist has a desire to keep his fetish secret. So he projects the desire to engage in fetish behavior onto [13-year-old black male], making [13-year-old black male] bear that "abnormalcy." [13-year-old black male] represents the rapist; a person that watches normal couples that have normal sex, while personally in sexual confusion.

PURPOSE OF LEAVING THE CRIME SCENE AND THEN RETURNING

According to the autopsy reports and the Criminal Incident Reconstruction, the victims were most likely dead or dying when the offender repositioned them and engaged in the fetishistic behavior with [13-year-old black male]. Given that this rapist wants to be perceived as masculine, powerful, and normal by others, this examiner concludes that he would have engaged in this fetishistic behavior with [13-year-old black male] alone.

Furthermore, the autopsy reports, the anal swabs for semen, the Criminal Incident Reconstruction, the position of [15-year-old white female]'s body, and the angle at which [13-year-old black male] was shot are all consistent with the rapist having had anal intercourse with [15-year-old white female] after she was dead. This examiner concludes that the rapist probably would have engaged in post-mortem anal sex alone, rather than risk having others observe this and perceive him as less than masculine, powerful, and normal.

Thus, the rapist, motivated to fulfill these "abnormal" (from his perspective) sexual desires and presented with the opportunity, would be motivated to rid himself of any companion, and return to the scene alone.

EVALUATION: POWER RAPIST BEHAVIORS

The behavioral evidence analysis of the E. 38th Avenue Kidnap/Rape, and the McGowan Creek Rape/Homicides, leads to the conclusion that the same type of offender committed them.

VICTIM SELECTION IS OPPORTUNISTIC

The rapist prefers to attack male and female teenage couples. The offender chose them because of their availability in terms of time and place. He further chose them by their accessibility by cons available to him in his method of approach and his ultimate ability to control them. This examiner concludes that in both cases, E. 38th Ave. and McGowan Creek, the rapist happened upon the victims in the course of his regular, non-rape activities.

POWER AND CONTROL

At E. 38th Avenue, the rapist displayed a weapon and ordered the victims to submit. He ordered them to take all of their clothes off, ordered them onto their knees, he ordered them to perform sex acts together, while he watched, and he sexually assaulted the female in the presence of her male partner. Additionally, the majority of the verbal interactions were in the form of intimidating profanity, or commands.

At McGowan Creek, the rapist displayed a weapon and ordered the victims to submit by ordering them to take all of their clothes off, ordering them onto their knees, and by raping the female victim in the presence of her male partner. Some evidence suggests that he may also have ordered his victims to engage in sex acts while he watched. He also controlled their sexuality during acts of post-mortem repositioning by placing [15-year-old white female] and [15-year-old white male] in the positions of a sexual act, and probably by performing anal sex on [15-year-old white female] after she was dead, and by cross-dressing [13-year-old black male].

This examiner concludes that this rapist demonstrated a great need for power and sexual control over the victims at all times during the commission of both of these crimes.

LACK OF VICTIM INJURY DURING RAPE

At both E. 38th Ave. and McGowan Creek, the victims were not physically injured during sexual acts with the offender, apart from the sexual assault itself. This examiner concludes that this rapist demonstrates a desire not to physically injure his victims while he is engaging in sexual acts with them because he does not see these attacks as being a forced rape. He sees himself simply as a participant, and acts accordingly.

SEXUAL INADEQUACY

The offender engages in pseudo-foreplay with his female victims, kissing them, fondling them, and performing, or attempting to perform cunnilingus on them. These are very intimate forms of sexual expression, and used primarily in the exchange of mutual pleasure. He also watches, and then places the male victim in a position to watch, sex acts committed on the female victims. He does this to convince himself that he and the male victim are sexually sharing the female; if the male victim (a consensual sexual partner to the female) has sex with the female victim too, then there was no rape. He also does this to establish his sexual control, conquest and ownership of the female victim. Based on these behaviors this examiner concludes that this rapist has doubts about his sexuality, and about his masculinity. This rapist demonstrates feelings of sexual inadequacy in the form of the above reassurance oriented behaviors.

VERBAL ACTIVITY

Most of the rapist's verbal activity is assertive. He shouts commands, profanity, and verbal threats at his victims. This demonstrates his need to have power over his victims and achieve and maintain control.

The rapist comforts [18-year-old white female] by telling her that he is not a rapist, and makes personal inquiries about her virginity. This, like his pseudo-foreplay, demonstrates his need for reassurance.

MOTIVATION

The primary motive of this offender was to feel powerful and thereby reassure himself of his sexual normalcy, his adequacy, and his masculinity. The rape allows him to feel powerful, in control, and desired. He wants to be perceived as a man who is sexually virile, masculine, and capable of sexual conquest. That is his projection in rape and most non-rape scenarios in his life. His intended audience is not females, but other males as evidenced by his crime-scene behavior.

SIMILARITIES: THE E. 38TH AVENUE KIDNAP/RAPE AND THE MCGOWAN CREEK RAPE/HOMICIDES

The term "rapist" in this section is meant to refer to the individual who is responsible for the kidnap/rape at E. 38th Avenue, and who is also responsible for the rape and homicides at McGowan Creek.

The crime-scene behavior at E. 38th Avenue in Eugene and McGowan Creek in the Coburg Hills evidenced many specific similarities. The following is a list of the more significant behavioral similarities, however it is not meant to be an all-inclusive list.

OFFENDER CHARACTERISTICS

The term rapist in this section refers to the individual who is responsible for the kidnap/rape at E. 38th Avenue, and who is also responsible for the rape/homicides at McGowan Creek.

The following opinions concern the characteristics that the rapist evidenced through his crime-scene behavior. Examples of behaviors that evidence a particular characteristic are given. The examples are by no means the limit of such characteristic behavior. Furthermore this examiner concludes that the rapist would evidence these behavioral characteristics in the course of his criminal and non-criminal interactions, including interactions with his family, friends and partners in crime.

BEHAVIORAL CHARACTERISTICS

EVIDENCE OF EGOCENTRICITY

The offender needs to be seen while engaging in "normal" sex acts. This is a form of reassurance-oriented narcissism. He also demonstrates no regard for the rights and property of others. His behavior is oriented towards fulfilling his needs, regardless of the consequences of his behavior to others. He thinks himself superior to others, and tends to view others more as objects than fellow human beings with equivalent value.

He blamed the victim at E. 38th Avenue, stating "You're making this difficult for me, bitch," suggesting that his inability to penetrate her, and rape her, was her fault. His words suggest that she should have been helping him instead of being "difficult." He needs to externalize blame; to make his shortcomings or failures the fault of others. He ultimately shows no true regard for the consequences of his actions or the emotions of his victims. Even when he does verbally comfort his victims, engage in pseudo-unselfish sexual behavior (kissing and fondling), or lay down a jacket for his victims before he rapes them, he does this to satisfy his own need for reassurance.

The rapist left a great deal of physical evidence behind at McGowan Creek, and probably returned to use the suburban after he had disposed of it at the University of Oregon, despite that fact it had been recently used in the homicides. This evidences a great deal of egocentricity; the rapist acts like he will not be caught.

His motivations and behaviors are egocentric, in that he acts as if he is entitled to a sense of sexual and emotional reassurance from his victims about his own masculinity. He further acts as if law enforcement is not competent to the task of linking him to the crimes he has committed.

In non-rape environments, he would seek his own pleasure first, and act as though he was superior to others. He would probably plan to get rich quick through various criminal enterprises, evidencing a narcissistic, grandiose projection of his own intellect, skills, and ability. It would be important for him to associate himself with the symbols of wealth and power to others. He would do this either by grand exaggeration, deception, or theft.

EVIDENCE OF IMPULSIVITY

He does not spend much time weighing out his decisions at the crime scenes. He acts impulsively, evidenced by behaviors that achieve instant gratification for his egocentric motives rather than behaviors designed to ensure success in his criminal enterprises.

He also had a big truck and plenty of time at McGowan Creek, but did not transport the bodies of his victims away from that scene to a more remote location, evidencing the impulsivity of the killings by his subsequent failure to plan ahead for them.

Other examples of impulsivity include the selection of victims of opportunity at both E. 38th Avenue and McGowan Creek. Additionally, he was verbally abusive, using profanity, responding aggressively to his victims even when they demonstrated complete compliance to his commands.

In non-rape environments, he would be very much the same. He would think only of himself, and react quickly to the behavior of others. This could give him a reputation as someone with a short fuse. Being egocentric and grandiose, he would not handle criticism well. Perceived attacks on his intellect or abilities may trigger a quick, violent reaction.

EVIDENCE OF AN ABSENCE OF GUILT OR REMORSE

This rapist evidences no feelings for the pain and suffering that he inflicts on his victims. At E. 38th Avenue, the rapist becomes impatient with [18-year-old white female], blaming her for his inability to effectively rape her. He also forces [18-year-old white male] to participate in the sexual activity, to take her virginity. Both behaviors demonstrate the rapist's capacity to externalize the responsibility for the consequences of his criminal acts.

Upon his return trip to the McGowan Creek crime scene, he finds [15-year-old white male] and [13-year-old black male] still alive. He moves them over the edge of the landing. He may have put a sock in [15-year-old white male]'s mouth to muffle his moans. After dressing [13-year-old black male], who is dying from a head wound, in [15-year-old white female]'s clothing, he shoots him a final time. It is probable that he did not shoot [13-year-old black male] or [15-year-old white male] until he was ready to leave the crime scene. He evidences no concern for his victims' welfare outside of his own gratification, and he demonstrates no guilt or remorse when engaged in further activities at the scene during his return trip.

In non-rape environments, he would be much the same. His actions would serve his own gratification and not demonstrate concern or distress over the harm that his egocentric behavior causes others. Nothing would be his fault. Any negative situation that he was in, or anything bad that happened to himself or others as a result of his behavior, would be the fault of someone or something outside of himself.

EVIDENCE OF DECEITFULNESS AND MANIPULATION

At E. 38th Avenue he approached the victims with a con, pretending to be a property owner, when his true motive was to assess their ability to resist an attack and to make certain that they were not going to leave soon. He further deceived those victims by initially promising not to rape [18-year-old white female].

At McGowan Creek he approached his victims with a con, promising them a ride in his nice truck.

At both scenes these behaviors evidence an offender who is very comfortable deceiving others, and manipulating them to service his own needs.

In non-rape environments, he would be very much the same. He would be an accomplished liar, able to deceive professionals in mental health, law enforcement, and the legal community with great ease. He would have no regard for the truth or the facts outside of their usefulness to obtain his own ends. He would be very skillful at managing the impressions that others have of him.

EVIDENCE OF SEXUAL CONFUSION

This rapist confuses sexual control with emotional intimacy. He does not demonstrate an understanding of consensual human sexuality. This is evidenced by his need to force couples to have sex in front of him and by his own reassurance-oriented pseudo-foreplay with his victims.

In non-rape environments, he would be very much the same. He does not perceive the emotional difference between consensual sex, and his rape behavior at the crime scenes. He would be forceful and aggressive in his consensual sexual relationships. He would demonstrate a preference for anal sex with consensual partners, a desire to be watched while performing sex acts, a desire to watch others perform sex acts, as well as a need to hide his fetish.

In non-rape environments, he would have a great deal of difficulty meeting and socializing with females, and would evidence a need to ingratiate himself with other males by virtue of macho behaviors and affects.

TASK-FORCE MANAGEMENT

Det. John J. Baeza

A *task force* is a team of individuals assembled for the purposes of investigative information gathering, information organization, and information sharing in a major case or series of related cases. The primary goals of a task force include the streamlined development of investigative leads and strategy, the coordination of investigative efforts and resources, and the identification and investigation of suspects.

When the public and those outside of law enforcement hear the term "task force," many automatically think of a "lean, mean, investigative machine," that leaves no stone unturned, no lead unfollowed, and no possibility unchecked.

However, those of us who have participated on task forces know all too well how disorganized, political, and chaotic they can be. We hear the term "task force," and, sadly, we immediately envision bureaucratic or supervisory incompetence leading to a great deal of frustration for task force members.

This is hardly what we want, or need, but we must be honest with ourselves and identify these problems before we can engage effective solutions. A major case task force does not have to be a chaotic venture; but it often is. This brings us to the identification of the very first problem faced by those forming a major case task force: **no plan**!

Any agency's task-force protocols should be in place prior to the start of an investigation. This means starting today, while there is no investigative pressure bearing down on us, and establishing our own guidelines and protocols that will be there for us when we need them.

In that spirit, we offer the following guidelines and insights to aid investigators and supervisors when they undertake to plan for, or form, a major case task force. They are intended to provide a basic overview of some of the common problem areas related to task-force formation and operation. However, these guidelines are by no means an exhaustive list. In fact, it is hoped that others will find ways to improve upon the quality of these suggestions, and come up with their own innovative ideas that address their specific situation, and utilize their particular agency's resources and associations.

It is also intended that this will provoke others to think more critically about the organization and function of their existing task forces.

FORMATION OF A TASK FORCE

Task forces are formed for a variety of reasons. Typically, it is because a series of often-violent crimes is somehow linked, and the need for a task force becomes evident due to the large amount of information that needs to be investigated. These crimes can include sexual assaults, homicides, robberies, bombings, arsons, kidnappings, and the investigation of organized crime, just to name a few examples.

The litmus test for whether or not an agency needs to form a task force to address a crime or a series of related crimes consists of three basic qualifiers:

1 The case involves multiple victims or multiple jurisdictions.
2 The investigation of the case requires more resources than the investigating agency has on their own.
3 The case involves a serious, immediate threat to public safety.

The existence of any of these criteria may be sufficient for a department to form a task force. If more than two of the qualifiers exist in a given case, then task-force formation is almost mandatory.

Time is critical, once the need for the formation of a task force has been identified. Unfortunately, what happens all too often is that a task force is formed too late. The investigators then have to go back, sometimes years, and work on cases that have gone cold. Victims and witnesses may not be around for them to interview. Crucial evidence may be lost. All of this can be averted if a task force is formed as soon as possible after a series of crimes is linked.

When crimes are committed in different jurisdictions, the formation of a task force may be even more difficult. "Turf wars," rivalries, and egos may all contribute to losing precious investigative time. Even if one agency forms a task force, another agency that is involved may not cooperate or wish to share information. Decisions regarding who will lead the task force, how responsibilities will be delegated, and financial considerations, etc. need to be made as swiftly as possible.

The resolution requires teamwork, a plan for action, and setting aside all personal issues to encourage a streamlined, competent investigation.

HOW MANY INVESTIGATORS SHOULD BE ASSIGNED?

The answer to this question requires the consideration of many factors, the least of which should be the following:

- The amount of evidence and other case-related materials (reports, documentation, tips and leads) that need investigating.
- The number of cases being investigated.
- The resources, including manpower and budget, of the investigating agency (a department with 600 detectives can likely contribute less manpower than a department with 6,000).

WHO SHOULD BE ASSIGNED?

Supervisors need to look for investigators who are critical thinkers as well as hard workers. Investigators who work methodically and have an open mind can be a great asset to a task force.

Regarding experience – while having the appropriate level of experience can be an important consideration, it should not be the only requirement for assignment to a task force. An experienced investigator can still be a poor investigator. Experience means nothing if an investigator has performed poorly for 20 years.

If the case encompasses a crime, or a particular type of criminal behavior, that would ordinarily be investigated by a specialty unit (sex crime, robbery, homicide, bomb squad, juvenile crimes, etc.), then a representative from one of those units should be assigned to the task force. These investigators bring with them specialized insight and experience in their particular field.

When the crime is a sexual homicide, then homicide and sex-crime investigators should work side by side. Sex-crime investigators may not have much experience working homicides and dealing with crimes in which the victim is dead and, likewise, homicide detectives may not have much experience dealing with the dynamics of sexual assault and motives of sexual offenders. We get a more effective investigation when we pool individual talents.

LEAD INVESTIGATORS

There can be only one leader. Ideally, the lead investigator should have the most knowledge about the case, a strong background in working with the criminal behaviors involved in the case, and a good relationship with the victims or witnesses. A good relationship with a victim or witness can be invaluable when it comes time to show photos, conduct lineups, or go to trial. And there is no one better suited to advise the supervisor in charge of the case than the most knowledgeable investigator. The investigator who has this knowledge and relationship with the victim or witness does no good sitting on the sidelines.

TASK-FORCE MEETINGS

An initial task-force meeting should be held as soon as possible after all assigned detectives are gathered together. This meeting should be run by a supervisory officer who has full knowledge of all the details of the case up until this point. This supervisor can give an overview of the incident(s) and all investigative work done to date. Detectives who have completed some of the investigative duties can explain what has been done in the case to everyone in the task force; this brings everyone up to speed. The crime-scene photographs should be made available to all assigned detectives so they can familiarize themselves with the scene details. This is a crucial point because it gives all task-force members the knowledge they need when interviewing potential suspects and witnesses in the field. All assignments can be disseminated during this initial meeting (as well as at following meetings).

The initial meeting may be the most important gathering of assigned detectives. It is at this meeting that everyone is put on the same page as far as the investigation goes.

Follow-up meetings should be held at least twice daily. This allows detectives working different shifts to update each other on the progress of the investigation. When possible, each detective assigned should speak about what actions he or she has taken during the shift. The supervisor who conducts these meetings should discuss any questions or comments that the detectives have and clear up any misunderstandings or problems.

Charts and graphs can be used effectively to inform investigators about important information. A timeline of the victim's last 24 hours as well as victim and witness statements related to this 24-hour period should be charted and displayed for all assigned investigators. An evidence chart tracking all evidence related to the case can be very valuable to investigators. First, it gives everyone a clear picture of what was collected at the scene or scenes. Second, it helps investigators and supervisors keep track of all evidence and is especially useful at the time of trial. A chart showing a synopsis of each case being investigated should be displayed. This chart can include things such as day, date, time, and location of incident, as well as victim pedigree, offender description, weapon used, words spoken, sex acts committed, and a break-down of the details of the crime. These charts and graphs will help keep everyone involved informed and up-to-date. Information sharing is the main concern here.

All of the above actions promote information sharing and teamwork. The teamwork concept is a very important aspect regarding the success of a task force. Anything that derides teamwork, or bottlenecks information, should be avoided. For example, all too often a clique of investigators who know everything about the investigation will develop. They may withhold information, intentionally or not, leaving investigators on the outside who have scant information about the investigation. Utilizing the above methods can help eliminate these cliques by treating everyone involved as an important part of the team.

PITFALLS

This section will detail some of the major pitfalls in task-force management. This is by no means an all inclusive list, and is largely a product of the experiences of this detective:

1 Very often there are "*too many Chiefs and not enough Indians.*" These multiple "chiefs" may attempt to micromanage a task force or investigative effort. This is cited time and time again by investigators as the *number one pitfall* of a major case investigation.

2 *Supervisors with no organizational skills* who find themselves sinking rapidly amid a pile of information. Supervisors in charge of the task-force investigation must be well educated in the management of a major-case task force. Ideally, an experienced supervisor will head the task force from the start to eliminate any problems caused by information overload. An experienced supervisor, however, is not always the answer to the problem.

3 *Supervisor apathy.* The task force supervisor should maintain his own interest in the case and encourage his investigators to do the same. If the supervisor in charge has lost interest in the case, then ultimately, so will his subordinates. This can be avoided by holding regular meetings as well as simply talking with individual investigators about the case. Leadership, charisma, and the ability to instill investigators with the confidence that what they are doing is valued is key.

4 *The need for a quick fix.* Not all task forces result in immediate fixes. Sometimes these investigations can take months and even years. Investigative confidence can deteriorate. Task-force members and supervisors need to understand that most major cases are solved by a combination of luck and sound police work.

   For example: A composite sketch is prepared at the investigator's request. A citizen sees the composite printed in the newspaper, realizes it looks like an acquaintance and calls the information in to the hotline. A suspect is developed and arrested. All well and good.

   But what about the cases where nothing has worked? Sound police work has been employed but luck is not forthcoming. This is where the problems start. Some investigators, and supervisors, will now wait around for that lucky break. The investigation stalls and disinterest follows. Investigators assigned to prolonged investigations must realize that stubborn cases can be solved, even after many years. What it takes is endurance, constancy, deliberation, and hard work.

   What it may also take is willingness on the part of investigators to try innovative investigative tools and methods, such as those described later in this appendix.

TIPS AND LEADS

Here are some of the common tip and lead sources.

LAW ENFORCEMENT

Many times fellow law enforcement officers, both local and from outside agencies, will call in with information about prior cases, current cases, persons they have arrested in the past and so on.

THE PUBLIC

The nature and reliability of tips from the public vary widely. They can range from a caller who has seen a look-a-like of the suspect two years ago on a bus traveling downtown, to a caller who states that the suspect is her brother. Callers who state that the offender is their brother, sister, relative, or significant other should be given priority. Detectives need to use their judgement here and prioritize.

PSYCHICS

Quite often psychics will call to offer investigators assistance. Their motivations can vary from self-promotion to a heartfelt belief that they can help. Some will give specific information about the suspect's whereabouts, name, and past. Some will ask to visit the crime scene prior to providing information.

The use of a psychic to aid the investigation will most often lead to a wild goose chase and a waste of valuable investigative resources and time. If a psychic demonstrates knowledge of a case that was not obtained through the media or through casual conversation with investigators (watch out for this – they can be very tricky) then they should be investigated for relationships with potential suspects and as potential suspects themselves. All psychics should be viewed with suspicion by investigators.

THE MEDIA

This is another source of information where the motivations can vary from the quest for a good story to a real desire to assist the police. There are times when the media will provide "witnesses" for the police to interview as a smoke-screen to get inside details of the investigation. This does not happen often, but investigators should be aware that it occurs. Investigators usually know which reporters are honest and mean well, and information received from those individuals should be prioritized.

In any case, the task force should determine whether it wants to develop a healthy relationship with the media or no relationship at all. Sometimes the most effective task force is the one that is not made public. Task forces that are merely a public relations venture should not be ventured into at all.

The above is just an overview of the types of tips and leads that may be channeled into an investigation. Since it is not always possible to follow up on all tips and leads the moment they are received, investigators must be able to prioritize them and decide which can wait and which need to be investigated immediately. Developing competent mechanisms for prioritizing information is important, but do not forget that *all* tips and leads should be investigated to their conclusion.

Often, there is a desire to fit incoming tips and leads into case theories developed by investigators. This can cause tips and leads that do not fit those theories to be given less priority than others, or to be completely disregarded. Investigators must remain objective throughout the investigation and treat nothing as trivial.

PROCESSING TIPS AND LEADS

A vast amount of leads can come in at one time and the task force can be over-loaded with information. The ideal answer to this problem is a computerized case-management system that can process all tips and leads and cross reference other databases such as those that include motor vehicles witnessed in the area of the crime, persons stopped and questioned, criminal-record files, and so on. This can enable investigators to ascertain which suspects turn up on more than one database, and allow them to prioritize these suspects. The system can also allow tracking of tips and leads by keeping a record of which investigators are assigned, and what work has been done by them. There are several computer programs available that are custom-made to manage major case information.

While a computerized major-case-management system is a great asset to an investigation, there are other ways to manage information without one. Simple database programs are available that have the capability to search for entered information. The only drawback with such a system is that many times there is no cross-reference capability.

The reality of the situation is that many departments still handle incoming information without the aid of computer technology. Tips can be entered on tip/lead sheets and assigned unique identifying numbers (usually sequential) so that they can be logged and tracked. If this is the case, then one person, preferably a supervisor, should be in charge of all incoming tips and leads. This supervisor should have the responsibility for assigning the tips and leads and for making sure that all of these are followed up on and investigated fully. It is best to have every investigator informed of every tip and lead, but realistically this may not be possible. The supervisor in charge of tips and leads will have knowledge of all incoming tips and leads and can determine the priority of these prior to assigning them.

The task force should have a separate telephone line assigned solely for incoming tips. This telephone number can be distributed to the public through the media as well as informational posters and fliers. A member of the task force should be assigned to man this telephone at all times. If the telephone will be unmanned during the overnight then an answering machine should be in place to record any messages left during this period. If the hotline telephone number is changed for any reason then call forwarding from the old number should be arranged. Investigators assigned to this telephone should be advised to take the information first and then worry about the caller's name, address, and phone number. Callers may be leery about giving personal information and may hang up if this is the first thing they are asked. Pre-printed tip/lead forms should include space for all pertinent information about the incoming tip and the caller. This pre-printed form will ensure that investigators get all of the important information necessary.

THE MEDIA

Used properly, the media can assist the task force in getting important information to the public. This can include airing the case on a "most wanted" type show or featuring the case in the local newspaper. However, there should always be certain important facts withheld from the media. These include the fact that biological evidence containing DNA was recovered, signature elements of the offender, and the exact nature of items taken from the victim (as well as a host of other detailed facts). It is the duty of the task force supervisor to insure that these facts are withheld from the media. When these details leak out to the media, major problems should be expected. An offender may change his *modus operandi*, start using a condom if he was not using one before, cover his face, or destroy evidence such as souvenirs and trophies taken from the victims.

COMPOSITE SKETCHES

The use of composite sketches in major investigations has become commonplace. In most cases, if a victim or witness has observed the suspect, then a sketch is prepared. This happens even when the witness's recollection may be poor. A task force must use good judgement when deciding whether to have a sketch prepared, because a poor sketch can steer an investigation off course. There have been many cases where the composite sketch looked nothing like the offender. The public, investigators, and patrol officers usually put a lot of emphasis on the composite sketch of an offender. If the sketch looks nothing like the offender then all of them end up chasing a "red herring."

Sketch artists work in different ways. Some may show a victim photographs of faces and ask the victim to pick out facial features that are similar to the attacker. This method can severely distort and taint fragile recall. Others do not use photographs but use memory enhancement interviewing techniques.

It is best to use the services of a forensic artist who is schooled in memory, perception, and Post-Traumatic Stress Disorder (PTSD). These artists, sometimes called facial-identification specialists, do not use mug shots or facial catalogs, but instead rely on interviewing techniques that draw from the eye-witness's actual recall without implanting new information. Memory can be influenced and distorted very easily. For this reason, having the victim view numerous mug shots is discouraged by these artists. This may mean limiting victim viewing to six or twelve photographs and then only when a good suspect is developed. This may be difficult for many investigators who are hounded by supervisors to show as many photos as possible. It is may also be difficult because investigators and supervisors still do not understand the importance of what these forensic identification specialists are speaking about here. The "old school" still prevails when it comes to composite sketches and mug-shot viewing. We need to change this by educating investigators and supervisors.

CRIME-SCENE PERSONNEL

The task force must maintain a good working relationship with the crime-scene and crime-lab personnel. This provides the task force with two-way information roads regarding how available evidence is being documented, collected, tested, and the results of any analysis. The same should be true of the ME/Coroner's Office. To create these information roads, a member of both the ME/Coroner's office and the crime lab should be assigned to the case, and to the task force. That way one person in each agency can be relied upon by the task force to act as both an information conduit, and a diplomat.

PATROL OFFICERS

Patrol officers often play an important role in the apprehension of the suspects sought by a task force, by virtue of performing routine stops and being familiar with the MOs of criminals operating in the area. They work in the neighborhoods and on the streets where these crimes are committed. They know the people who live and work there. They also know the people who commit crimes there. Patrol officers often have a wealth of information to share and investigators would be wise to develop a working relationship with them.

At the very least, a representative of the task force should address the officers at roll call every day. The shift addressed will depend on the time the crimes are being committed. Keep the officers updated about the case and answer any questions they may have. Make them feel that they are part of the team. Advise them about what they should say and what they should not say to suspects. Give them the task force's telephone number in case they develop information that might relate to the case.

The task force may also wish to consider creating *Daily Confidential Bulletins* (DCBs) for patrol officers, with suspect information, relevant photos, and pertinent case developments. Basically, the DCB gives patrol officers something in-hand to reference when out on their patrol, making them a valuable part of the task force's arsenal.

THE DISTRICT ATTORNEY

The task force investigators must always keep in mind that a case is not over after an arrest is effected. Investigators are responsible for assisting in the prosecution of the offender.

Working closely with the District Attorney's office allows investigators easy access to legal advice to ensure that nothing the task force does jeopardizes the case at trial. This type of relationship with the District Attorney can act as a sort of early warning system. The District Attorney's office can also assist in the preparation of search warrants when the time comes. This suggestion in no way implies that the District Attorney's office will take over the investigation or direct it in any way. The District Attorney's role here is to assist with the investigation, not to usurp law enforcement's role as the lead agency.

It is not advised that the District Attorney's Office have hands-on control of the task force's day-to-day activities (to prevent micromanaging). It is recommended that their office assign someone to the task force as an advisor from the very beginning, to offer educated counsel, advice, and support when necessary.

THE COMMUNITY

Community groups may become more active when a major crime or crimes has been committed in their neighborhood. Most of these groups mean well, but if left undirected they can cause damage to an investigation. If these groups feel law enforcement is not responsive to their needs (whether this is real or imagined) then they may start using the media to attack law enforcement. This takes the focus off the offender and puts it on the task force.

This problem can be addressed by developing a relationship with these community groups. They should be contacted by the task force and reassured that a full-scale investigation is being conducted. These community groups, when given direction, can assist a task force immensely. They can distribute informational fliers and composite sketches, arrange to hold public meetings where the case is discussed, focus the media on the case, and offer a reward for the apprehension and conviction of the offender. Innovative investigators will think of many other ways to include these community groups in the investigation.

THE VICTIM

When task-force detectives are dispatched to a fresh crime scene in which there is a living victim, a task-force investigator (preferably the lead investigator) should interview the victim as soon as possible. This is not to say that patrol officers should not get the vital information that they need to dispatch to the other officers on the streets (such as an offender description, direction of travel, weapons used), but that the detailed interview should be conducted by a task-force investigator.

There is no need for a supervisor of any rank to interview the victim. From time to time supervisors, sometimes of high rank, try to get involved in an investigation by interviewing the victim. Most have good intentions, but all are misdirected. This is an example of micro-management at its worst.

If a victim complains about a specific investigator, then it would be prudent for the supervisor to interview the victim about that complaint. But that is not what we are talking about here. We are talking about supervisors who get in the way at the scene by attempting to interview victims. The worst part is that many of these supervisors have not had much experience doing detailed interviews of victims. The bottom line is that a good supervisor does what they are supposed to do – supervise.

Investigators who are dealing with living victims have many responsibilities. A wise investigator once said that a victim is like a glass of water; every time you show photos, conduct lineups, re-interview, or utilize them in some manner, you take a drop of water out of that glass. A good investigator will temper his use of the victim so the glass will not end up empty at the time of trial.

One or two investigators – preferably the lead investigator(s) – should be assigned as a contact person for the victim. The same investigator should contact the victim, when the need arises. Victims tend to react negatively when a barrage of different investigators contacts them. Imagine how you or one of your loved ones would feel if you were contacted by a different investigator every time the police needed your assistance. A strange voice (and face) can be disturbing to a victim who was violently assaulted – even if it is a police investigator. The same goes for a deceased victim's family, or a witness.

Victims should be notified, when possible, of all planned media events surrounding the case. Victims can feel "left out" of the investigation when they are not updated and have to rely on the media for information.

Investigators should schedule contacts with the victim or victims. A task force is a team, and the living victim is the most important part of that team. It is imperative that victims be kept updated as to the progress of the investigation. This can be done weekly at the start of the investigation and then extended to monthly or longer if the investigation becomes very lengthy. The investigators should confer with the victim and ascertain how often they would like to be contacted. This contact plan does not imply that investigators must divulge every detail to the victim. Obviously, there are details that the victim cannot know about for legal purposes (i.e. taint identification, trial testimony, etc.) and if the investigator has any questions about this they should contact the District Attorney's office representative assigned to prosecute the case.

THE BEHAVIORAL-ORIENTED INTERVIEW

A task force responsible for investigating a sexual assault case should assure that every victim is asked the 14 questions contained in the *behavioral-oriented interview*. Retired FBI Supervisory Special Agent Roy Hazelwood developed these questions as a means to ascertain the offender's motivations and thereby make it easier to accurately profile the offender. They also assist in linking cases through behavior. The answers to these questions can be invaluable to an investigation and will assist in the preparation of both a criminal and a geographic profile. It is recommended that the behavioral-oriented interview be mandatory for all stranger sexual assault cases whether part of a major case or not.

Victim interviews conducted by police officers and investigators can range from the highly detailed account to the one paragraph narrative that says nothing. The behavioral-oriented interview gives structure to an interview, and allows the victim to answer some very important questions. If the victim has not been asked the behavioral-oriented questions it might be a good idea to give them a written copy so they can answer them at their own pace in private.

All sex-crime investigators are urged to incorporate the behavioral-oriented questions in their victim interviews. This way when cases are linked and a task force is formed, investigators will not have to go back and ask these questions at a time when the victim's memories may have faded.

UTILIZING PSYCHOLOGICAL AND GEOGRAPHIC PROFILES

Psychological and geographic profiles may be a very useful tool for a task force when utilized properly.

Prior to employing any type of profiler, investigators should ask these important questions:

- Is the profiler familiar with or does he have experience with the type of case being investigated?

- What is the exact method he uses to come to his conclusions?

- What case materials are required?

- Will he visit the crime scene or scenes (if a crime scene exists)?

- Will investigative suggestions be included in the profile?

Be very wary of any profiler who:

- Is disinterested or unfamiliar with the importance of using physical evidence to establish offender behavior (who will just take the task force's word for it, or who offers a complete profile based upon things read in the newspaper).

- Who shows no interest in visiting the crime scenes.

- Whose profile seems to be taken directly from organized/disorganized, or one of the typologies.

- Who refuses to write their profile down.

- Whose profile is less than two pages long.

- Whose geographical profile is not based upon a sound psychological profile prepared by a competent psychological profiler (many geo-profilers will attempt, inappropriately, to construct one themselves).

- Whose sole purpose in soliciting a profile appears to be for profit, or personal gain and recognition.

In any case, it is imperative that the profile, whether psychological or geographical, be prepared as a written report that can be perused by task-force members – "Casual, verbal advice appears to make little impact and to be easily forgotten." (Det. Chief Inspector Gary Copson, London Metropolitan Police, 1995.)

Another important component of any profile is investigative suggestions. A good profile will include investigative suggestions for the task force to follow up on. This may include areas to re-canvass, persons to re-interview, types of crimes to focus on, as well as many others suggestions. The important thing to remember here is that these suggestions should be followed up and investigated to the fullest.

When a profile is prepared, the task force should be prepared to meet with the profiler. At this meeting any and all questions and concerns of the detectives can be addressed. It is common for detectives to have many questions about psychological and geographic profiling and if these questions go unanswered it could pose the danger of hindering an investigation – thus the meeting with the profiler. Investigators should never be hesitant about questioning a profile itself, or a profiler regarding their methods or conclusions.

The results of a psychological and geographic profile should be treated as a tool that the task force can use to develop investigative strategies to solve the crime. They are not written in stone, and suspects should not be eliminated, or accused for that matter, based on a psychological or geographic profile alone. In the same respect, suspects and tips can be prioritized based on the profile. Prioritization can be very useful when tips are inundating the task force.

PROFESSIONALIZING CRIMINAL PROFILING

Brent E. Turvey, M.S.

In the preface of this book, we discussed how any profession is defined by its ability to regularize, to criticize, to restrain vagaries, to set a standard of workmanship, and to compel others to conform to it. We further explained how this definition assumes uniform terms, definitions, ethics, standards, practices, and methodology.

This textbook is a first attempt by the author to establish terms, definitions, ethics, standards, practices, and methodology for deductive criminal profilers who wish to use behavioral evidence analysis in their work. Though certainly not complete, it is a start with a solid foundation; a jumping-off point for those currently involved in casework. What remains now is to establish some standards for training and education, and a frank discussion about peer review.

PEER REVIEW

Peer review is the process of putting one's work product forward for examination, review, and critical analysis by one's professional community. The purpose of peer review is to encourage professional competency by allowing an open dialogue about the veracity of research, theories, and methodology, and to further give one the opportunity to gain valuable feedback from one's colleagues in order to refine, rethink and, when necessary, rebuild. It is an invaluable, integral part of professionalization. Any method, group, or individual that considers itself above (or actively evades) the peer-review process cannot be considered professional, or even trustworthy. This, by the way, extends to those who espouse ideas whose basic premises are so vague as to be intellectually intangible (falling under the category of a *vagary*).

Although this is a very fundamental and necessary part of the professionalization process, there is much evasion of, and resistance to, peer review in the criminal-profiling community. Now, do not misunderstand. Some in the criminal-profiling community do publish their theories and "research." But few in the community have the conviction to make a critical analysis of that published work, for fear of political sanction by a particular group, organization, or individual. In such an environment, putting one's work forward in a professional journal hardly constitutes participation in the peer-review process.

Students and colleagues are therefore not only encouraged to openly review and critically analyze the ideas and theories at work in this text, but should do so to all theories and ideas in the published literature on criminal profiling.

It is the only way we will learn from each other, and the only way we can begin to encourage and expect competency from each other.

But remember, while this author encourages students and colleagues to ask the question "Why?" until they are blue in the face, until they have achieved satisfaction or disenchantment, others in the community are not quite so used to having their ideas and notions questioned. Be prepared for the sting of political reprisal. After all, no good deed goes unpunished.

EDUCATION AND TRAINING

> I get calls from students who say "I'm about to get my masters in psychology and I want to get into profiling – where do I sign up?" I tell them to go be a cop for 20 years.

> (Mike Prodan, Graduate of the FBI Fellowship Program, former profiler for the California Department of Justice, from Haddock, V. (1997) "Manhunter," *San Francisco Examiner Magazine*, July 20.

Being in law enforcement can be an excellent way to get exposure to cases, and gain investigative experience. However, law enforcement experience does not give anyone a blank check to call oneself a criminal profiler. The experience that one gains is commensurate to the types of cases one works, and the duties one performs as a part of that work. For example, a law-enforcement officer who works fraud cases for 20 years has no business working homicide. A law-enforcement officer who works vice for 20 years has no business putting themselves forward as an expert in the area of sex crimes. And a crime analyst, who does not visit crime scenes as a part of their regular duties, has no business putting himself or herself forward as an expert in crime reconstruction, or wound pattern analysis.

To many, the above may seem obvious. Unfortunately many individuals, especially former law enforcement officers with non-sex-crime and non-homicide backgrounds, put themselves forward as experts on all forms of investigation – under the guise of having *x* number of years law enforcement experience. This is wholly inappropriate, and cannot be tolerated when people's lives or liberty are at stake.

As we have learned in this text, the deductive method of criminal profiling demands advanced training in the forensic sciences, a strong background in psychology, extensive knowledge regarding medico-legal death investigation, and the appropriate investigative experience. It is truly a multi-disciplinary approach.

Specific recommendations for education and training include:

- Undergraduate degrees in a behavioral science (psychology, sociology, anthropology).
- Graduate degree programs in forensic science, psychology, psychiatry, or sociology.
- Internships with sex-offender treatment programs, with law-enforcement crime-scene units, homicide units, sex-crimes units, or with Medical Examiner/Coroner's offices, etc.

The important thing is to get the education and experience that is commensurate with the types of analysis that one desires to perform, and never opine outside of one's particular area of formal education or experience.

Being in law enforcement is fine, as long as it does not rob one of crucial critical-thinking skills, but it is no substitute for a liberal arts education and an advanced degree. Keep in mind that the value of a liberal arts education is not in the information that one learns, necessarily. It is in the broad exposure of one's mind to many perspectives, ideas, and ways of thinking. And ultimately it is intended to hone one's critical thinking and organizational skills. Both are invaluable to the criminal profiler.

Ultimately, this author views the future of criminal profiling as the work of forensic generalists, with dual cores of psychological knowledge and investigative experience. Criminal profiling is not a black box – it is an investigative and analytical philosophy. This author therefore sees the future of criminal profiling as a partnered task, shared by forensic scientists, the mental-health community, and the investigative community. We have begun to achieve something of that partnership here with this text. It is the hope of each contributor of this work that students and professionals alike will realize something useful from our efforts.

Abrasions: An excoriation, or circumscribed removal of the superficial layers of skin, indicates an abraded wound.

Accelerant: Any fuel (solid, liquid, or gas) that is used to initiate or increase the intensity or speed of the spread of fire.

AFIS: Automated Fingerprint Identification System.

Alienist: A psychiatrist that specializes in the legal aspects of mental illness.

Amoral: Unconcerned about conventional interpretations of right or wrong, and giving those issues no weight in decisions.

Anger Excitation (AKA Sadistic) Behaviors: These include behaviors that evidence offender sexual gratification from victim pain and suffering. The primary motivation for the behavior is sexual, however the sexual expression for the offender is manifested in physical aggression, or torture behavior, toward the victim.

Anger-Retaliatory (AKA Anger or Displaced) Behaviors: These include offender behaviors that are expressions of rage, either towards a specific person, group, institution, or a symbol of either. The primary motivation for the behavior is the perception that one has been wronged or injured somehow.

Ante-mortem: Refers to wounds that occur during the period before death. They tend to be associated with injuries that result in a lot of bleeding either internally or externally.

A-priori Investigative Bias: A phenomenon that occurs when investigators, detectives, crime-scene personnel, or others somehow involved with an investigation come up with theories uninformed by the facts. These theories, which are most often based on subjective life experience, cultural bias, and prejudice, can influence whether or not investigators recognize and collect certain kinds of physical evidence at the scene, and can misinform the development of investigative strategy.

Arranged Crime Scene: A disposal site where an offender has arranged the body and the items within the scene in such a manner as to serve ritual or fantasy purposes. This can be found when victim's bodies are displayed post-mortem in a very public location, when victims are placed in humiliating sexual positions after death, and when the position of the body serves the purposes of a particular offender ritual.

Arson: The term arson is a penal classification; it is used to refer to the intentional setting of a fire with the intent to damage or defraud.

Behavioral Evidence: Any type of forensic evidence that is representative or suggestive of behavior.

Behavioral Evidence Analysis: The process of examining forensic evidence, victimology, and crime-scene characteristics for behavioral convergences before rendering a deductive criminal profile.

Behavior-Motivational Typology: A motivational typology that infers the motivation (i.e. Anger-retaliatory, Assertive, Reassurance, Sadistic, Profit, and Precautionary) of behavior from the convergence of other concurrent behaviors. Single behaviors can be described by more than one motivational category, as they are by no means exclusive of each other.

Behavioral-Oriented Interview: A set of questions designed to elicit the behavioral aspects of the victim–offender interaction from the victims of sex crimes. This interview strategy assists not only in corroborating the facts of a case, but it can give the criminal profiler the information needed for case linkage, motive assessment, and the development of investigatively relevant strategy.

Blitz Attack: The delivery of violent, overpowering force by an offender.

Blunt Force Trauma: These are divided into categories of Abrasions, Contusions, Lacerations, and Fractures.

Bomb: An explosive that is detonated by impact, proximity, timing, or other predetermined means.

Broad Targeting: Any fire or an explosive that is designed to inflict damage in a wide-reaching fashion. In cases involving broad targeting, there may be an intended target near the point of origin, but it may also be designed to reach beyond that primary target for other victims in the environment.

Case Assessment: Any process that involves sorting through case material in order to understand the nature of what is there, for the purposes of informing how those involved may or may not be able to proceed.

Case Linkage: The process of demonstrating discrete connections between two or more previously unrelated cases.

Case-Linkage System: Refers generally to any database of cases or case-related information that is designed to assist in the process of case linkage.

Chop Wound: This injury is the result of a heavy instrument with a sharp edge. It goes deep into the tissue, can be associated with bone fractures, and can have a combination of incised and lacerated characteristics.

CODIS: The Combined DNA Index System.

Cold Case: An unsolved case that has seen a period of relative inactivity.

Collateral Victims: Those victims that an offender causes to suffer loss, harm, injury, or death (usually by virtue of proximity), in the pursuit of another victim.

Common Sense: Non-transferable native good judgement, referring to knowledge accumulated by an individual that is useful for, but specific to, making decisions in the areas and locations that they frequent.

Computer Crackers: Computer crackers, sometimes mistakenly called hackers, are individuals who use computer networks to commit a range of crimes including intrusion, data theft, vandalism, harassment, and extortion.

Con Approach: The con approach is characterized by an offender who gets close to a victim by use of a deception or a ruse.

Control-Oriented Force: A term that should be used to describe physically aggressive offender behavior that is intended to manipulate, regulate, restrain, and subdue victim behavior of any kind. It is often found in combination with corrective force.

Contusions: These are injuries (often caused by a blow of some kind) in which blood vessels are broken, but the skin is not. They can be patterned (imprinted, not directional) and non-patterned.

Convenience Aspect: This refers to anything that an offender chooses by virtue of being available or less difficult to choose than something else. Often present when an offender is constrained by time, unprepared, or seeks to avoid detection.

Coroner: Coroners are most often elected or appointed officials, and may not be required to be licensed physicians. In some jurisdictions, they need only meet an age requirement and reside in the district.

Corpus Delicti: Literally interpreted as meaning the "body of the crime," – refers to those essential facts that show a crime has taken place.

Corrective Force: A term that should be used to describe physically aggressive offender behavior that is intended to admonish a victim for noncompliance or poor compliance to commands, and subsequently encourage their future compliance.

Crime Reconstruction: The determination of the actions surrounding the commission of a crime. This may be done by using the statements of witnesses, the confession of the suspect, the statement of the living victim, or by the examination and interpretation of the physical evidence. Some refer to this process as crime-scene reconstruction, however the scene is not being put back together in a rebuilding process, it is only the actions that are being reconstructed.

Crime Scene: A location where a criminal act has taken place.

Crime-Scene Characteristics: The discrete physical and behavioral features of a crime scene.

Crime-Scene Staging: A term that refers to any conscious action taken by an offender to misdirect an investigation by altering the physical evidence at a crime scene. This term does not extend to families attempting to preserve the dignity of their loved ones.

Crime-Scene Type: The nature of the relationship between offender behavior and the crime scene in the context of an entire criminal event (i.e. point of contact, primary scene, secondary scene, intermediate scene, or disposal site).

Criminal Profile: A court-worthy document that accounts for the physical and behavioral evidence relating to the known victimology and crime-scene characteristics of a particular case, or a series of related cases, in order to infer investigatively relevant characteristics of the offender responsible.

Criminal Profiling or Offender Profiling: A general term that describes any process of inferring distinctive personality characteristics of individuals responsible for committing criminal acts.

Criminologist: A professional who studies crime, criminals, and criminal behavior. They are involved in the documentation of factual information about criminality and the development of theories to help explain those facts.

Cybercrime: Any offense where the *modus operandi* or signature involves the use of a computer network in any way.

Cyberspace: William Gibson coined this term in his 1984 novel *Neuromancer*. It refers to the connections and conceptual locations created using computer networks. It has become synonymous with the Internet in everyday usage.

Cyberstalking: The use of computer networks for stalking and harassment behaviors. Many offenders combine their online activities with more traditional forms of stalking and harassment such as telephoning the victim and going to the victim's home.

Cybertrail: Any convergence of digital evidence that is left behind by a victim or an offender. Used to infer behavioral patterns.

Deductive Criminal Profile: A set of offender characteristics that are reasoned from the convergence of physical and behavioral evidence patterns within a crime or a series of related crimes. Pertinent physical evidence suggestive of behavior, victimology, and crime-scene characteristics are included to support any arguments regarding offender characteristics.

Deductive Criminal Profiling: A method that describes, and bases its inferences on, the behavioral evidence in a particular case, or a series of related cases.

Deductive Reasoning: An argument where if the premises are true, then the conclusions must also be true. In a deductive argument the conclusions flow directly from the premises given.

Defensive Force: A term that should be used to describe physically aggressive behavior that is intended to protect the individual administering it from attack, danger, or injury. The application of this term to a behavior does not imply, by its nature, that the behavior was legally or morally justified. Rather it is meant to describe behavioral intent.

Diagnostic Wound: An injury inflicted by any emergency or medical personnel during treatment. These can include needle marks, various incisions and puncture marks, and even bruising caused by rough handling or transport.

Dichotomy: A term that refers to a division into two polarized or contradictory parts or opinions.

Digital Evidence: Any and all information stored on or transmitted by a computer (or other electronic device) that can be used to establish that a crime has been committed, and/or provide a link between a crime and its victim, or between a crime and its perpetrator.

Disposal Site/Dump Site: This term is used to refer to the place where a body is found. A primary scene may be used as a disposal site, or the offender may move the body to another location.

Empathy: The identification with and understanding of another's situation, feelings, and motives.

Environmental Wound Patterns: Injuries received from items in the environment, unrelated to a criminal attack.

Equivocal: Anything that can be interpreted in more than one way or anything where the interpretation is questioned.

Equivocal Forensic Analysis: A review of the entire body of physical evidence in a given case that questions all related assumptions and conclusions. The purpose of the equivocal forensic analysis is to maximize the exploitation of physical evidence to accurately inform the reconstruction of specific crime-scene behaviors.

Equivocal Wound Patterns: Injuries whose source is disputed, or where there is more than one potential source, may be referred to as "equivocal wound patterns."

E-mail, or Email: A service that enables people to send electronic messages to each other.

Ethics: Refers to values, rules, or standards that have been established to govern the conduct of the members of a profession.

Experience: The accumulation of applied knowledge through lived events.

Experimental Force: A term that should be used to describe behaviors involving force that fulfill non-aggressive, curiosity driven, or psychological and fantasy-oriented needs.

Explosive: Any material that can undergo a sudden conversion of a physical form to a gas with a release of energy. Explosives are used to create *explosions*, which are defined generally as the sudden conversion of potential energy (chemical or mechanical) into kinetic energy with the production of heat, gases, and mechanical pressure.

Fire Setting: The intentional ignition of combustible material. This is a neutral term that can be used to describe behavior, instead of the penal classification of *arson*.

Forensic Pathology: The branch of medicine that applies the principles and knowledge of the medical sciences to problems in the field of law. It is the charge of the forensic pathologist to document and understand the nature of the interaction between the victim and their environment in such a manner as it caused their death.

Forensic Psychiatrist: A forensic psychiatrist is a psychiatrist who specializes in the legal aspects of mental illness. The psychiatrist is trained to elicit information specific to mental disorders through face-to-face clinical interviews, a thorough examination of individual history, and the use of tested and validated personality measures.

Geographic Profiling: The inference of offender characteristics through the analysis of location selection and the relationships between crime scenes.

Handwriting Analysis, or Graphology: The inference of a person's personality characteristics based solely on the style and manner in which they write. This is not to be confused with *handwriting identification*.

Handwriting Identification: A sub-discipline of *questioned document examination* (QDE), Handwriting Identification is the process of establishing the authorship of a document by observing its distinguishing, individual features of the handwriting.

Hard Characteristics: Those offender attributes that are a matter of verifiable, uninterpreted fact. They are evident by virtue of demonstrable, unequivocal existence in the form of some kind of permanent, unalterable documentation.

High-Risk Victim: An individual whose personal, professional, and social life continuously exposes them to the danger of suffering harm or loss.

Immoral: Contrary to accepted morality.

Incident Risk: The risk present at the moment an offender initially acquires a victim by virtue of their state of mind and hazards of the immediate environment.

Incise (cut): This injury is the result of a sharp instrument being drawn across the surface of the skin, even into the tissue, and is longer than it is deep.

Incomplete Offense: An offense that does not contain enough MO behaviors to complete the offense. An incomplete event might include the following: The victim, instead of being easy prey, turns around and kicks the offender in the groin. The offender may be stunned and limp away or the victim may create an opportunity to flee the scene. Or during the attack on his victim, the offender might be unwittingly witnessed by a passerby and flee the scene. Either way, the event would not have included the full potential range of offender MO behaviors, and would therefore be incomplete.

Indoor Crime Scene: A crime scene that is inside of a structure, with some form of cover from the elements of nature. Includes houses, apartments, buildings, sheds, garages, warehouses, cabins, tents, caves, and so on.

Inductive Criminal Profile: A criminal profile that refers to the characteristics of typical offenders derived from broad generalizations, statistical analysis, or intuition and experience.

Inductive Criminal Profiling: Any method that describes, or bases its inferences on, the characteristics of a typical offender type. This includes the employment of broad generalizations, statistical analysis, or intuition and experience.

Inductive Reasoning: Inductive reasoning involves broad generalizations or statistical reasoning, where it is possible for the premises to be true while the subsequent conclusion is false.

Intended Victim: A person, group, or institution that was meant to suffer loss, harm, injury, or death as the result of an attack. The intended victim and the *target* may be one and the same. There may also be more than one intended victim.

Intermediate Scene: Any crime scene between the primary scene and the disposal site, where there may be evidence transfer. Examples include vehicles used for transporting victims, and locations used to store victim remains before removal to a final disposal site.

Intent: The planned or expected results or purpose of an offender's actions.

Internet: A global computer network linking smaller computer networks, that enable information sharing via common communication protocols. Information may be shared using electronic mail, newsgroups, the WWW, and synchronous chat. The Internet is not controlled or owned by a single country, group, organization, or individual. Many privately owned networks are not a part of the Internet.

Internet Service Provider, or ISP: Any company or organization that provides individuals with access to, or data storage on, the Internet.

Interrupted/Incomplete Offense: An offense that does not contain enough MO behaviors to satisfy the offender's motive.

Intimacy: Intimacy can be defined as pertaining to or indicative of one's deepest, most essential nature. For those who have been socialized, this tends to refer to healthy, shared expression of emotions, needs, and feelings.

Intuition: Knowing or believing without the use of reason, or rational, articulable processes. If one has a belief or something that one "just knows," and is unable to articulate the reasoning behind it, it is likely that intuition or "gut instinct" is the culprit.

Investigative phase: The investigative phase of criminal profiling generally involves behavioral evidence analysis of the patterns of unknown offenders for known crimes.

Items Taken – Evidentiary: Items that the offender believes may link them to the victim and/or the crime.

Items Taken – Personal: Items taken from the victim or the crime scene that have sentimental value to the offender.

Items Taken – Valuables: Items taken from the crime scene that the offender believes may have financial value.

Laceration: A torn or jagged wound, which tends to have abraded and contused edges. Lacerations can be differentiated from sharp force injuries by the recognition of tissue bridging from one side of the laceration to the other (indicating shearing or crushing force).

Lethal Force: A term that should be used to describe physically aggressive behavior that is primarily intended to result in death. By itself, it is distinguishable from punishment oriented force in that it involves only the amount of force necessary to cause death. It does not however, have to involve overkill.

Lifestyle Risk: Lifestyle risk is a term that refers to the overall risk present by virtue of a individual's personality, and their personal, professional, and social environments. The belief is that certain circumstances, habits, or activities tend to increase the likelihood that an individual will suffer harm or loss. Furthermore, it is also affected by the personality traits possessed by the victim. Lifestyle risk, then, is a function of who the victim is and how they relate to the hazards that their common environments contain.

Linkage Blindness: The failure to recognize a pattern that links one crime with another crime in a series of related cases.

Locard's Exchange Principal: The theory that anyone, or anything, entering a crime scene both takes something of the scene with them, and leaves something of themselves behind when they leave.

Location Type: The type of environment that a crime scene exists within. The four general types are indoor, vehicles, outdoor, and underwater.

Love Map: A love map describes an idealized scene, person, and/or program of activities that satisfy the particular emotional and psychological needs of an offender.

Low-Risk Victim: An individual whose personal, professional, and social life does not normally expose them to a possibility of suffering harm or loss.

Medical Examiner: A medical examiner may have state, district, or county jurisdiction, and are appointed. They must be licensed physicians and may even be Board Certified Forensic Pathologists.

Medium-Risk Victim: An individual whose personal, professional, and social life can expose them to a possibility of suffering harm or loss.

Method of Approach: A term that refers to the offender's strategy for getting close to a victim.

Method of Attack: A term that refers to the offender's mechanism for initially overpowering a victim once they have made their approach. It is appropriate to describe a method of attack in terms of the weapon, and the nature of the force involved.

Method of Control: Those means used by an offender to manipulate, regulate, restrain, and subdue victim behavior of any kind throughout the duration of an offense.

Modus Operandi: *Modus operandi* (MO) is a Latin term that means, "a method of operating." It refers to the behaviors that are committed by an offender for the purpose of successfully completing an offense. An offender's *modus operandi* reflects how an offender committed their crimes. It is separate from the offender's motives, or signature aspects.

Motive: The emotional, psychological, or material need that impels, and is satisfied by, a behavior.

Motivational Typology: Any classification system based on the general emotional, psychological, or material need that is satisfied by an offense or act.

Narrow Targeting: Any fire or explosive that is designed to inflict specific, focused, calculated amounts of damage to a specific target.

Negative Documentation: The recording of what was not present, or what did not happen, such as a lack of injury.

Newsgroups: The online equivalent of public bulletin boards, enabling asynchronous communication that often resembles a discussion.

Offender Characteristics: An offender's discrete physical, personality, lifestyle, and behavioral features.

Offender Profiling: *See* Criminal Profiling.

Offender Skill Level: An offender's proficiency or expertise in the execution of their offense behavior.

Offense Gone Wrong: An offense that contains unintentional, unplanned MO behavior, which increases the offender's risk or criminal status. An example would be an offender who accidentally kills a victim during a robbery, increasing their criminal status to that of a murderer.

Opportunistic: Any unplanned element or item that is seized upon by the offender for inclusion in an offense. It can refer to an opportunistic victim, an opportunistic offense, an opportunistic weapon, or an opportunistic location.

Outdoor Crime Scene: A crime scene that is exposed to the elements of nature. Examples include fields, forests, ravines, canyons, ditches, roadsides, deserts, and so on.

Peer Review: The process of putting one's work product forward for examination, review, and critical analysis by one's professional community. The purpose of peer review is to encourage professional competency by allowing an open dialogue about the veracity of research, theories, and methodology, and to further give one the opportunity to gain valuable feedback from one's colleagues in order to refine, rethink, and, when necessary, rebuild.

Peri-mortem: An imprecise term that refers to injuries inflicted in the time interval just before or just after death.

Petechiae: Minute points of bleeding caused by trauma that results in an increase in venous pressure and an increase in capillary pressure that then causes damage to the inner walls of those capillaries. They are not to be confused with *Tardieu Spots*.

Point of Contact: The location where the offender first approaches or acquires a victim.

Point of Origin: The specific location at which a fire is ignited, or the specific location where a device is placed and subsequently detonated.

Polygraph, or "Lie Detector": A machine that simultaneously measures breathing, blood pressure, pulse rate, upper body movement, and galvanic skin response (the amount of moisture secreted by the skin). It is used during suspect interrogation and is based on the theory that when a person is being deceptive their body will respond or react (out of the fear of detection).

Post-mortem: Refers to wounds that occurred during the period of time after death. They tend to be associated with injuries that did not result in bleeding or hemorrhaging.

Power Assertive (AKA Entitlement) Behaviors: These include offender behaviors that are intended to restore the offender's self-confidence or self worth through the use of moderate to high aggression means. These behaviors suggest an underlying lack of confidence and a sense of personal inadequacy, that are expressed through control, mastery, and humiliation of the victim, while demonstrating the offender's sense of authority.

Power Reassurance (AKA Compensatory) Behaviors: These include offender behaviors that are intended to restore the offender's self-confidence or self worth through the use of low aggression or even passive and self-deprecating means. These behaviors suggest an underlying lack of confidence and a sense of personal inadequacy.

Precautionary Acts: Precautionary acts are behaviors committed by an offender before, during, or after an offense that are consciously intended to confuse, hamper, or defeat investigative or forensic efforts for the purposes of concealing their identity, their connection to the crime, or the crime itself.

Precautionary Force: A term that should be used to describe physically aggressive offender behavior that results in wound patterns which are intended to hamper or prevent the recognition and collection of physical evidence, and thwart investigative efforts.

Preselected Crime Scene: This refers to a disposal site that an offender chooses prior to actually committing an offense, by virtue of it being particularly suitable for the activities that they wish to engage the victim with. In outdoor cases, it may be a small clearing just out of sight and earshot from a well-trodden path, or an indoor location that the offender must transport the victim to.

Primary Scene: The location where the offender engaged in the majority of their attack or assault upon their victim or victims.

Profit-Oriented Behaviors: Behaviors that evidence an offender motivation oriented towards material or personal gain. These can be found in all types of homicides, robberies, burglaries, muggings, arsons, bombings, kidnappings, and most forms of white-collar crime, just to name a few.

Psychiatry: The branch of medicine that deals with the diagnosis and treatment of mental disorders.

Psychological Autopsy: A term that refers to the process that death investigators and mental health experts use, in collaboration with each other, to determine the state of mind of a person before they died.

Psychopath: An individual capable of what most would consider horrible, heinous acts, and recognizing the harmful consequences of their acts to others, but incapable of feeling remorse, and subsequently unwilling to stop.

Psychopathy: A personality disorder defined by a distinctive cluster of behaviors and inferred personality traits, most of which society views as pejorative. Defined by a demonstration of the personality traits in *Hare's Revised Psychopathy Checklist* (PCL-R).

Punishment-Oriented Force: Brutal and short-lived levels of force that are reflected in extensive, severe wound patterns. In cases where brutal force is used, it is not uncommon for the victim to require hospitalization, or to die, as a result of the injuries inflicted. It must be made clear that homicide is not necessarily the desired result in such cases.

Remorse Aspect: This refers to a disposal site where there is evidence that the offender felt some regret over the victim's death. This can be seen in behaviors that attempt to "undo" the homicide, including washing the blood off a victim, dressing them in clean clothes, and placing them in a natural state such as sleeping, sitting in a chair, or in the seat of a vehicle.

Restraint: Any item found in the crime scene, or brought to the crime scene, which is used to physically control, limit, contain, or restrict a victim.

Sadistic Behavior: Actions that are oriented towards the intentional infliction of victim pain, in order to induce suffering, which sexually arouses the offender.

Scientification: The bolstering of any method or theory, by a group or individual, via technological affect or professional affect, for the purposes of making that method or theory appear more credible.

Search Engine: A database of Internet resources that can be explored using key words and phrases. Search results provide direct links to information.

Secondary Scene: Any location where there may be evidence of criminal activity outside the primary scene.

Serial Arson: Two or more related cases involving fire-setting behavior.

Serial Bombing: Two or more related cases involving the use of explosives.

Serial Killer: A term first coined by Robert K. Ressler to described offenders that are obsessed with fantasies that go unfulfilled; pressing them onward to the next offense.

Serial Homicide/Murder: Two or more related cases involving homicide behavior.

Serial Rape: Two or more related cases involving rape or a sexual assault behavior.

Sexual Fatality: Any investigation into a death that occurs in association with sexual activity (consensual and non-consensual).

Sexually Oriented Force: A term that should be used to describe physically aggressive offender behavior that is intended to satisfy sexual needs. The best way to determine whether this is true for any particular behavior is to note whether it occurs in concert with traditional sexual behavior, with clearly eroticized behavior, in association with sexual materials, or in a sexual context. Though these things by themselves are by no means conclusive indicators.

Sharp Force Injury: These are divided into the categories of: *stab* wounds, *incise* wounds (cuts) and *chop* wounds. Examples include injuries inflicted by axes, hatchets, machetes, swords, and meat cleavers.

Signature Aspects: The emotional or psychological themes or needs that an offender satisfies when they commit offense behaviors.

Signature Behaviors: Signature behaviors are those acts committed by an offender that are not necessary to complete the offense. Their convergence can be used to suggest an offender's psychological or emotional needs (signature aspect). They are best understood as a reflection of the underlying personality, lifestyle, and developmental experiences of an offender.

Sociopath: This term is used to describe the same behavior manifestations and inferred personality traits as are evident in a psychopath. The explicit exception is that sociopaths have a syndrome forged entirely by social forces and early experiences.

Soft Characteristics: Those offender attributes that are matter of opinion. They require some kind of interpretation in order to be defined. They also include things that are subject to natural or intentional change with the passage of time without any kind of permanent, verifiable record.

Souvenir: A souvenir is a personal item taken from a victim or a crime scene by an offender that serves as a reminder or token of remembrance, representing a pleasant experience. Taking souvenirs is associated with reassurance-oriented behavior and needs.

Stab Wound: An injury that is the result of being pierced with a pointed instrument. The depth of the injury into the tissue is usually greater than its width in the skin.

Staged Crime Scene: This refers to a disposal site that an offender has contrived for the purposes of purposefully misleading the investigation. This may be in the form of a murderer placing a gun in the hand of a shooting victim, or in the form of making a ligature strangulation appear as a suicide by hanging.

Statement Analysis: A method for examining written words independent of case facts, exclusively for the purposes of detecting deception.

Surprise Approach: An offender who gets close to a victim by lying in wait for a moment of vulnerability to exploit.

Symbol: Any item, person, or group that represents something else such as an idea, a belief, a group, or even another person.

Sympathy: A relationship or affinity between persons or things, in which whatever affects one, correspondingly affects the other.

Synchronous Chat Networks: By connecting to a synchronous chat network via the Internet, individuals can interact in real-time using text, audio, video and more. Most synchronous chat networks comprise chat rooms, sometimes called channels, where people with similar interests gather.

Syndrome: A cluster of related symptoms that collectively suggest or characterize a grouping of individuals. The clinical diagnosis of any syndrome involves comparing an individual's behavior and symptoms with the behaviors and symptoms of others in similar circumstances that have been studied in the past.

Tardieu Spots: Tardieu spots are seen in hanging cases as, with time, punctuate hemorrhages occur due to hydrostatic rupture of the vessels from blood pooling in the forearms, hands, and legs. They are not to be confused with *petechiae*.

Target: The object of an attack from the offender's point of view.

Task Force: A team of individuals assembled for the purposes of investigative information gathering, information organization, and information sharing in a major case or series of related cases. The primary goals of a task force include the streamlined development of investigative leads and strategy, the coordination of investigative efforts and resources, and the identification and investigation of suspects.

Threshold Assessment (TA): An investigative tool that reviews the *initial* physical evidence of behavior, victimology, and crime-scene characteristics for a particular case, or a series of related cases, in order to provide immediate direction. A TA is not to be confused with, or used as, a criminal profile.

Trial Phase: The trial phase of criminal profiling involves behavioral-evidence analysis of known crimes for which there is a suspect or a defendant (sometimes a convicted defendant). This takes place in the preparation for both hearings and trials (criminal, penalty, and/or appeal phases of the trial are all appropriate times to use profiling techniques).

Trophy: A personal item taken from a victim or crime scene by an offender that is a symbol of victory, achievement, or conquest. Often associated with assertive-oriented behavior.

Typology: Any systematic grouping of offenders, crime scenes, victims, or behaviors by virtue of one or more shared characteristics.

Underwater Crime Scene: Refers to crime scenes that are beneath the surface of any body of water. Examples include lakes, ponds, creeks, rivers, oceans, and reservoirs.

Undoing Behavior: The symbolic reversal of a crime. This can include washing or bathing the victim, placing a pillow under the victim's head, covering the victim with a blanket, sitting the victim upright in a vehicle, or otherwise returning the victim to a natural looking state.

Vehicle Crime Scene: Refers to crime scenes that are mobile. Examples include cars, trucks, boats, ships, trains, airplanes, motorcycles, blimps, and so on.

Verbal Script: The language used by an offender during an offense, as well as the language that they command the victim to use. Scripting is used to direct the victim verbally and behaviorally.

Verbal Resistance: This term refers to when a victim defies an offender with words. This can include a victim who shouts for help, screams when attacked, pleads for mercy, verbally refuses to follow commands, or who tries to negotiate or bargain.

ViCAP (Violent Criminal Apprehension Program): The FBI's nationwide data information center, specifically designed for collecting, sorting, and analyzing information regarding solved, unsolved, and attempted homicides, unidentified bodies, and missing persons cases where there is a strong possibility of foul play.

ViCLAS (Violent Crime Linkage Analysis System): Canada's nationwide crime data information system. It is specifically designed for collecting, sorting, and analyzing information regarding all solved, unsolved, and attempted homicides, solved and unsolved sexual assaults, missing persons (where there is a strong possibility of foul play and the victim is still missing), unidentified bodies (where the manner of death is known or suspected to be homicide), and all non-parental abductions and attempted abductions.

Victim Selection: The process or criteria by which an offender chooses or targets a victim.

Victimology: A thorough study of all available victim information. This includes items such as sex, age, height, weight, family, friends, acquaintances, education, employment, residence, and neighborhood. This also includes background information on the lifestyle of the victim such as personal habits, hobbies, and medical histories.

Voyeur: One who receives sexual gratification from viewing erotic scenes and behavior.

Weapon: Any item found in the crime scene (available materials), or brought to the crime scene by the victim or the offender, that is used for the purposes of administering force.

World Wide Web (WWW): A service on the Internet providing individual users with access to a broad range of resources, including email, newsgroups, and multimedia (images, text, sound, etc.).

Wound Pattern Analysis: The recognition, preservation, documentation, examination and reconstruction of the nature, origin, motivation and intent of physical injuries.

X-Factor: Any unknown or unplanned influence that can affect crime-scene behavior during an offense.